THE QUEST FOR PROUST

THE QUEST
FOR PROUST

by

ANDRÉ MAUROIS

Translated from the French by
GERARD HOPKINS

CONSTABLE · LONDON

Published in Great Britain 1984
by Constable and Company Limited
10 Orange Street, London WC2H 7EG
Copyright André Maurois
Translation copyright Gerard Hopkins
First published 1950 by Jonathan Cape
ISBN 0 09 466000 X
Printed in Great Britain by
St Edmundsbury Press
Bury St Edmunds, Suffolk

CONTENTS

ILLUSTRATIONS

TRANSLATOR'S NOTE

ALL major quotations from Proust's novel have here been given in the late C. K. Scott Moncrieff's version, published by Chatto & Windus in twelve volumes (the last of these translated by Stephen Hudson), between the years 1922 and 1931. A reference has, in every case, been given in a footnote. For the rendering of shorter passages, not so acknowledged, I take full responsibility.

No attempt has been made to reproduce Monsieur Maurois's title. That, in view of Mr. Scott Moncrieff's choice (*Remembrance of Things Past*), would have been impossible. Monsieur Maurois has called his book *A la recherche de Marcel Proust*, and our English name for the series of volumes that make up the novel permits of no such adaptation.

Translation is, to a very large extent, a matter of what Professor Toynbee would call 'Challenge and Response'. Very few, if any, general rules can be laid down for its practitioners. I shall not, therefore, apologize for having left, here and there, in the quotations from the *Notebooks*, a few words in the original French. This I have done very seldom, but it has seemed better to me, where the jottings referred to expressions and locutions set down by Proust for future use by the characters of his story, not to attempt translation. I shrank, not unnaturally, from searching the 3000-odd pages of the English edition for the accepted rendering of the final form assumed by these happy thoughts, nor could any translation, however brilliant, have conveyed the exquisite rightness of these inspired scraps.

GERARD HOPKINS

1949

AUTHOR'S PREFACE

AT the end of this book the reader will find a list of the works I have consulted, but I wish here to acknowledge a number of more personal debts. Madame Gérard Mante-Proust, who watches over her uncle's papers with intelligence and devotion, has been good enough to let me consult and quote from the unpublished *Memoranda* and *Notebooks* of Marcel Proust, as well as from numerous letters to and from his parents. But for her kindness and generosity my book would never have had such novelty and completeness as it may now claim to possess. I owe much to Léon Pierre-Quint's critical study — which must ever be the main source for those embarking on Proustian exegesis; to books by Ramon Fernandez, Pierre Abraham, Henri Massis, Georges Cattaui and Anne-Marie Cochet, as well as to two more recent works, one by Henri Bonnet, the other by Noël Martin-Deslias. Whatever comment is necessary on the subject of Proust's style has been made already by Jean Pommier and by Jean Mouton. In the sections dealing with matters of biography, the recollections of men and women who knew Proust personally have been of the greatest value to me. I have been able to discuss him with Jacques-Emile Blanche, Daniel Halévy, Georges de Lauris, Jean-Louis Vaudoyer, Edmond Jaloux, Henri Bardac and Jean de Gaigneron. I have been in touch with Céleste Albaret. At Illiers, Monsieur P.-L. Larcher showed me the various scenes which served as models for Combray. I am deeply grateful, too, to my friend and fellow author, Professor Henri Mondor, for permission to consult the dissertation which he wrote on Proust during his student years, and to Monsieur Alfred Dupont for allowing me to look at a number of unpublished letters. I have read with attention books by Elisabeth de Grammont, Princess Bibesco, Marie Scheikevitch, Robert Dreyfus, Fernand Gregh, as well as the many volumes of the *Correspondance*. Monsieur Jacques Suffel has, with his customary courtesy, made smooth my work of research at the Bibliothèque Nationale, and my wife, not for the first time, has shown herself to be the best informed of all possible collaborators.

A. M.

P.S. The Copyright in all the unpublished manuscripts, *Memoranda*, *Notebooks* and family letters, which Madame Gérard Mante-Proust has allowed me to consult, belongs to her. They may be reproduced and translated only with her permission.

CHAPTER I

CHILDHOOD AND VOCATION

*What a man is at twelve years old, so will he be all through his life.
His tricks of sitting down, of reaching a hand, of turning his head, of
executing a bow, have by that time taken their final form and will
persist to the end.*   ALAIN

THE story of Marcel Proust, as it is presented to us in the
pages of his book, was that of a man who was devotedly
attached to the magic world of his childhood: of a man who
felt, very early on, the need to make some permanent record of
that world and of the beauty which he had discovered in certain
moments of experience; of a man who, knowing his own weakness,
long hoped that he would not be called upon to leave the paradise
of family life, and that it might be possible for him, instead of
struggling with his fellow men, to win them by the sweetness of
his nature; of a man who, having suffered the hard blows of life
and felt the biting lash of many passions, himself became sometimes harsh and sometimes cruel; of a man who, after his mother's
death, was driven from his refuge, but managed, thanks to illness,
to lead a sheltered existence, and, in a condition of semi-monastic
seclusion, dedicated the remaining years of his life to the task of re-
creating his lost childhood and subsequent disenchantment; of a
man who, in the end, successfully made of Time thus Regained the
subject matter of one of the greatest works of imagination of all
time.

I

MIXED STRAINS

It was Illiers, in the beginning — a small township not far from
Chartres, on the confines of La Beauce and Perche — that formed
the temporary, the highly personal, setting for the Earthly Paradise. The *Prousts* had been settled there for several centuries, a
good old local family, solidly rooted in the soil. For a child who

spent his holidays at Illiers it was possible to get to know a typical French country town, an ancient church topped by a hooded bell-tower, the rich brogue of the district, a mysterious code of provincial manners and those virtues of 'The French folk of Saint-André des Champs' whose faces, carved in the Middle Ages on porch and capitals, were still to be seen, unchanged, in the doorways of shops, in the Square on market-days and in the fields.

The Prousts of Illiers had, in the course of centuries, known much change of fortune. One of them, in 1633, became Collector of Dues to the Lord of the Manor. For this office he had to pay yearly to the Marquis d'Illiers the sum of five hundred *livres* in the currency of Tours, and undertake to 'supply a candle to the church of Notre-Dame de Chartres at the annual feast of Our Lady of Candlemas'. His descendants numbered both merchants and farmers, but the family always maintained its connection with the Church and, at the beginning of the nineteenth century, we find a Proust, the novelist's grandfather, carrying on the trade of candle- and taper-maker at Illiers. The doorway of the house in which Marcel Proust's father was born can still be seen in the Rue du Cheval Blanche. The dwelling is rough and rustic in appearance, and is approached by an arched flight of sandstone steps, looking 'as though it had been scooped by a maker of gothic images from the very stone he might have used for his cribs and calvaries'.

In it were born two children: a son, Adrien, and a daughter who later married Jules Amiot, owner of the largest business in Illiers, a drapery establishment standing in the 'Place' 'where, when one visited it before Mass, one was greeted by the delicious smell of unbleached calico'. Aunt Amiot was destined, after many and prolonged incantations, to be ultimately transformed, for her nephew and for the world at large, into Aunt Léonie. Her very unpretentious house in the Rue du Saint-Esprit had, as the novel describes, two entrances: a front door which Françoise used whenever she paid a visit to Camus's grocery store, facing the home of Madame Goupil who got 'properly soaked' as she went to Vespers in her silk dress; and the back gate of the tiny garden where, seated of an evening under the great chestnut that grew in front of the house, the Prousts and the Amiots could hear the low metallic screech of rusty iron announcing the arrival of those intimates who 'came in without ringing', or the double tinkle, timid, rounded, golden-toned, of the little bell that heralded a stranger.

Adrien Proust, our Proust's father, was the first of his line to leave La Beauce. His father, the chandler, had intended him for the priesthood. He went with a scholarship to the Collège de Chartres, but very soon abandoned all idea of proceeding to a Seminary and, though his faith remained unshaken, decided to study medicine. This he did in Paris, where he acted as house physician in a number of hospitals and later became head of a clinic. He was a handsome man with a noble appearance and a kind heart. In 1870 he met a young girl with delicate features and velvety eyes, Jeanne Weil by name, fell in love, and married her.

Jeanne Weil was the daughter of a rich Jewish family hailing originally from Lorraine. Her father, Nathée Weil, was a stock-broker. Her uncle, Louis Weil, an old bachelor, was the owner of what in those days ranked as a suburban villa, a large house standing in its own garden in the Rue La Fontaine at Auteuil. There, on July 10th, 1871, his niece gave birth to her eldest son, Marcel. Madame Proust's pregnancy, which took place during the siege of Paris and the Commune, was difficult. For that reason she went for safety to her uncle's house in the 'village of Auteuil'. Marcel Proust remained all through his life in close contact with his mother's family. Each year, until the state of his health made such an expedition impossible, he visited the grave of his Weil ancestor. 'No longer does anyone' — he wrote sadly, towards the end of his life — 'not even I, since I cannot leave my bed, make a pilgrimage along the Way of Rest that leads to the Jewish ceme-tery, where my grandfather, in fulfilment of a rite which he never understood, used, each year, to lay a pebble on his own parents' grave. . . .'

Through the medium of his mother's family, Marcel Proust learned to know, in their main features, the manners and charac-ter of the Jewish section of the French middle class. Later, he was to paint its portrait in a fashion that varied between the ruthless and the affectionate. Did he, himself, inherit any of its physical marks or moral traits? Many of his intimates, when describing him, spoke of an oriental atmosphere. Paul Desjardins saw him as 'a young Prince of Persia with the eyes of a gazelle'. Madame de Grammont said that his face 'looked definitely Assyrian when he let his beard grow'. 'Proust!' — remarked Barrès, 'an Arab story-teller in a gate-keeper's lodge. No matter on what varied canvases he stitched his arabesques, they all of them resembled the flowers and fruits upon a box of Turkish Delight.' Denis Saurat finds in his style echoes of the Talmud: 'long, complicated sentences, heavily charged with relative clauses', while Edmund Wilson, the American critic, discovers in his work 'that apocalyptic gift of moral indignation which marks the utterances of the Hebrew prophets'.

Proust was at pains to encourage this view, for he attached great importance to heredity. His Jewish characters, no matter how worldly, no matter how refined, have about them something of the Hebrew Prophet whenever he brings them upon the scene, and describes, say, Bloch entering the drawing-room of Madame de Villeparisis — 'as though he were emerging from the heart of the desert, his neck thrust obliquely forward, as strange and highly-flavoured a figure, in spite of his European costume, as one of Descamp's Jews'.

But to reconstruct a writer's temperament on the evidence of a few over-simplified traits is always an arbitrary performance. So multiple a personality is an artist that the critic can always find in him what he wants to find. Had Barrès known nothing of Proust's semi-Jewish origins, would he have guessed them from the mere reading of his books? If there was something of the Arab story-teller about Proust (which is debatable) may not the perfectly simple reason be that he had frequently read, and much admired, the *Arabian Nights*? — and was not Barrès himself, that prince of Lorraine, reproached by Gide for exhibiting an excessive orientalism?

That Proust's place is in the true tradition of French, of Western, culture it is impossible to deny. Bred on the French classics, the language that he wrote and spoke was theirs, rejuvenated and strengthened though it might be by an admixture of such linguistic usages as were current among the peasants of

La Beauce. Madame de Sévigné and Françoise did more to form his style than ever did the Talmud — which he had not read. But Thibaudet does no more than indulge in fair comment when he establishes a connection between Proust and Montaigne — who also had a Jewish mother. Both writers were gifted with a 'universal curiosity', with a taste for rambling reflection, with a love of images expressive of movement. In the plastic element, the outer rind, of things, they saw only an appearance beneath which they had to penetrate if they were to find that interior movement which the visible merely expresses and stills to a momentary immobility. A Montaigne, a Proust, a Bergson, have managed to root firmly in our rich and complex literature what may be called the Franco-Semitic element.

That the mixed strain happens to be Franco-Semitic is unimportant: what matters is that it is a mixed strain. In literature, as in heredity, 'cross-breeding' of this kind is a source of health. The mind thus presented with standards of comparison is strengthened. The novelist who has on one side a Jewish, on the other a Catholic, family, is in a position to know the features of each much better than would otherwise be the case. To Proust, the man of the world, it was given — 'thanks to the facts of racial inheritance, to see clearly a truth of which most men of the world are ignorant'. Gide has noted that the 'best critics and the best artists are usually to be found among those who have inherited a mixed strain. In them opposing stresses coexist, grow to maturity, and neutralize one another'. Those whom every impulse drives forward down the *same* road become men of fixed views. Those who, on the other hand, carry within them a conflict of tendencies, are endowed with an intellectual life which is, to an unusual degree, rich and fluctuating.

Such duality of origin frequently produces, in early years, a natural agnosticism. Though Marcel Proust was brought up in the Catholic religion, and though all his work may be defined as a prolonged attempt to attain to a highly personal form of mysticism, there is no evidence that he was ever a 'believer'. One of the rare passages in which he gives expression to some degree of belief in the soul's immortality is that in which he describes the death of Bergotte. But it ends on a question rather than an affirmation.

19

He would have liked to believe. 'Would it not be sweet to find again those whom we have left, or will leave, beneath another sky, in a land vainly promised and uselessly awaited?' But, 'because something is desirable, it does not follow that we can believe in it. Alas! the contrary is too often the case . . .' There is an entry in the *Memoranda* that runs as follows:

> It is with much regret that I find myself here at odds with a distinguished philosopher, the great Bergson. Among the points on which I join issue with him, let me mention this. Monsieur Bergson claims that consciousness overflows the body and extends beyond it. Where memory or philosophic thought is concerned, that is obviously true. But such is not Monsieur Bergson's meaning. According to him, the spiritual element, because it is not confined within the physical brain, can, and must, survive it. But the fact is that consciousness deteriorates as the result of any cerebral shock. Merely to faint is to annihilate it. How, then, is it possible to believe that the spirit survives the death of the body?. . .[1]

Proust, from his earliest years, had an acute sense of the beauty of churches, of the poetry of religious ceremonies, even if he was not one of those who, in the words of Mauriac, know that awareness of this sort is an expression of 'the truth'. In company with his brother Robert, he would carry hawthorn branches to the church at Illiers and lay them on the altar of the Virgin. From such expeditions was born his great love of 'that most catholic and delicious of blossoms'. Never, in later life, could he see the hedges starred with these charming flowers of piety without feeling about him 'the atmosphere of vanished Mays, of Sunday afternoons, of faith, of sins absolved . . .' His mother had refused to become a convert. She clung all her life long with a proud obstinacy, if not to the Jewish religion, at least to the traditions of her race. But his father was a practising Catholic, and Marcel never ceased to be conscious of the virtues of Christianity. If he found much to blame in the anti-Semitism of certain priestly readers of *La Libre Parole*, his detestation of anti-clericalism was

[1] Unpublished.

no less strongly marked. He was indignant when the curé was no longer invited to attend prize-giving at the secular school of Illiers:

> Children at school are being brought up in the belief that people who are on terms of intimacy with the priest are people to be avoided, and in that, as in other ways, France is being split into two conflicting nations. But I remember this small village, huddled against the niggardly earth which is the mother of all avarice, where the only note of aspiration towards the sky (often dappled with clouds, but no less often an expanse of divine blue miraculously transfigured by each evening's sunset over La Beauce) is the charming steeple of our church. I remember the curé who taught me Latin and the names of the flowers in his garden. Above all, I knew the mentality of my father's brother-in-law — the deputy-mayor and a violent anti-clerical — who refused, after the passing of the Decrees, to raise his hat to the curé and was a constant reader of L'Intransigeant, — though, as a result of the Affair, he added to it La Libre Parole. Yet I cannot help thinking it regrettable that our old curé should not be invited to attend Prizegiving. He represented something harder to define than the Social Order as symbolized by the chemist, the retired tobacconist and the optician, and was, in himself a thoroughly respectable citizen. He should have been invited if only for the sake of the intelligence expressed by that charming steeple. It points with such spiritual significance into the setting sun and melts so lovingly into the pink clouds, and, to the stranger arriving in our village for the first time, has a finer, a nobler, a more disinterested and meaningful look, and speaks more eloquently of love, than any of the surrounding buildings no matter to what degree they may be sponsored by our most recent enactments.

In 1904, at the time of the separation of Church and State, he wrote a number of fine articles on the subject of this 'Massacre of Churches' — articles of which his mother thoroughly approved.

The family life in which he grew up showed no sign of stress or conflict. It offered him, rather, the spectacle of that perfect union, that perfect goodness of heart, which made him so peculiarly vulnerable all through his life. It may, perhaps, be not altogether healthy for a young boy to live in an over-sweet and emotional climate, because its constant presence prevents the heart from growing a protective skin. Marcel Proust suffered from the impossibility under which he laboured, of finding anywhere else so loving a shelter as that provided by his mother and his grandmother. Coming to maturity, as he did, in a small society where the least shade of feeling was carefully recorded, he grew up in habits of politeness, gentleness and exquisite sensibility, but acquired also a strongly marked tendency to suffer should the vigilant affection be withdrawn, and also to dread wounding or causing pain to others. This in the battles of life, was to show as weakness.

Both his grandmother and his mother were highly educated women and unwearying readers of the classic authors. Quotations from Racine and Madame de Sévigné adorned and enriched their conversation. There is still in existence a notebook in which Madame Adrien Proust was in the habit of copying out, in a thin, sloping hand, the passages that most pleased her in the books she read. A natural modesty led her to keep this private anthology secret. 'It was a sort of egotistical consideration for her own people that made mamma conceal her quotations from the works of others', said Proust more than once. Again, in a letter to Montesquiou: 'You do not know Mamma. Her extreme modesty hides from almost everybody her extreme superiority . . . In the presence of persons whom she admires — and her admiration for you is boundless — this excessive reserve becomes complete dissimulation of merits which I and a few of my friends know to be incomparable. As to the ceaseless self-sacrifice which is the story of her life, it would be hard to find anything, anywhere, more deeply moving. . . .'

The nature of the passages thus preserved by Madame Proust give evidence of a taste for generalizations, of mental subtlety and also of a certain melancholic resignation. Those that deal with the pain occasioned by absence and separation are numerous. Her letters prove that she wrote with elegance. It is clear that the germ of many of Marcel's characteristics, and of almost all those ascribed to the 'Narrator's' mother, are to be found in her. Lucien Daudet has noted the points of resemblance between mother and son: 'The same long, full face, the same silent laughter when anything amused her, the same attention given to every word one uttered, that kind of attention which, in the case of Marcel Proust, some people took for absent-mindedness because he looked as though his thoughts were elsewhere, though, actually, it was marked by a high degree of concentration.'

'What would you like for a New Year's present?' his mother once asked Marcel.

'Your affection,' was his reply.

'But you'll always have *that*, you little silly! — I meant what *thing*. . . .'

How fond he was of hearing her call him 'My little scrap of guinea-gold, my little canary', and, in her letters, 'My little wolf'!

His maternal grandmother, who became his constant companion and assumed the responsibility of taking him to the seaside, we have learned to know well in the pages of the novel — a charming, eager creature, liking to walk bare-headed through the rain, striding round the garden, loving nature, the belfry of Saint-Hilaire and all works of genius, because they had in common that absence of vulgarity, of pretentiousness, of meanness, which she valued above all things. People at Illiers were inclined to laugh at her, though always with affection; to think of her as being a little 'touched in the head', because she was so different from everybody else. Not that their attitude ever gave her a moment's concern. 'She was humble of heart, and of so sweet a nature that her tenderness for others, her refusal to parade her own concerns and her own sufferings, combined to produce a smile which, while it expressed irony in all that related to herself, was for the members of her family in the nature of a caress, since she could never look at those she loved without seeming to lavish on them with her eyes a sort of passionate endearment. . . .'

The circle, then, in which Proust lived as a child, was essentially 'civilized'. To say that he belonged to the lower middle class on his Illiers side, and to the upper as a result of his parents' success in life, is of little importance, for a similar combination may often produce results of a devastating vulgarity. Rather was the atmosphere in which he grew up one that was diffused by a 'sort of natural aristocracy, knowing nothing of titles . . . an aristocracy in which every social ambition was legitimate because life was governed by the dictates of the finest of fine traditions'. The contribution made by Dr. Adrien Proust was a high seriousness, a scientific approach to life which Marcel was to inherit. To this his mother added a love of letters and a delicious sense of humour. She it was who first shaped her son's taste and mental outlook:

> About the confection of certain dishes, the right way of playing Beethoven Sonatas, the duties of a hostess, she was convinced that she knew best, and could gauge precisely the degree in which others came up to, or fell short of, her standards. Her idea of perfection in each of these three activities was almost the same, and consisted in something that might be called simplicity of means, soberness and charm. She recoiled in horror from the idea of using spices, except when they were absolutely necessary, from any affectation in piano-playing and the abuse of the pedal, from unnatural behaviour or over-much speaking of oneself when one was giving a party. She had but to take a single mouthful, had but to hear one note, had but to look at a card of invitation, to claim at once that she could tell whether she had to do with a good cook, a genuine musician or a well-brought-up woman. 'She may have more fingers than I have, but she shows a lack of taste in playing that simple *andante* with so much emphasis' — 'She may be very brilliant and have many good qualities, but to talk of herself like that displays a lack of tact' — 'I have no doubt she knows a great deal about cooking, but she can't manage beef-steak and potatoes. . . .'[1]

Such, precisely, were Proust's views on style.

It is important to stress the fact that the family was tenderly united, and that the validity of traditional morality was never called in question by its members. The tragedy that resulted for Marcel from his discovery of the great world and of himself, is to

---

[1] *Marcel Proust: A Selection from His Miscellaneous Writings.* Translated by Gerard Hopkins (Allan Wingate, 1948).

be explained in terms of the brutal contrast between a reality that was harsh and not seldom base, and the life he had known in the midst of his own people where he had been sheltered by the goodness of his mother and his grandmother, by their nobility of mind and by their moral principles. These two women seem to have adored and spoiled the delicate child whose temperament so much resembled their own. The answers that he made at the age of thirteen to certain questions contained in the birthday-book belonging to Antoinette Félix-Faure (later, Madame Berge), show very clearly the bent of his thoughts and feelings during the early period of his life. Because, hitherto, they have been curiously mutilated and distorted, I reproduce the original text:

What do you regard as the lowest depth of misery?
   To be separated from Mamma.

Where would you like to live?
   In the country of the Ideal — or, rather, of my ideal.

What is your idea of earthly happiness?
   To live in close contact with those I love, with the beauties of nature, with a quantity of books and music, and to have, within easy distance, a French theatre.

To what faults do you feel most indulgent?
   To a life deprived of the works of genius.

Who are your favourite heroes of fiction?
   Those of romance and poetry, those who are the expression of an ideal rather than an imitation of the real.

Who is your favourite character in history?
   A mixture of Socrates, Pericles, Mahomet, Musset, Pliny the Younger and Augustin Thierry.

Who are your favourite heroines in real life?
   A woman of genius leading an ordinary life.

25

Who are your heroines of fiction?
> Those who are more than women without ceasing to be womanly: everything that is tender, poetic, pure and in every way beautiful.

Your favourite painter?
> Meissonier.

Your favourite musician?
> Mozart.

The quality you most admire in a man?
> Intelligence, moral sense.

The quality you most admire in a woman?
> Gentleness, naturalness, intelligence.

Your favourite virtue?
> All virtues that are not limited to a sect: the universal virtues.

Your favourite occupation?
> Reading, dreaming and writing verse.

Who would you have liked to be?
> Since the question does not arise, I prefer not to answer it. All the same, I should very much have liked to be Pliny the Younger.

Dr. (later Professor) Adrien Proust shared his wife's feelings in the matter of family obligations, but lived more in the world than she did. During the last years of the nineteenth century he climbed the ladder of success with dignified speed, became Inspector of French Public Health Services and a great authority on 'preventive measures' at times when epidemics were rife, represented France at numerous international conferences, and put forward his name as a candidate for the Institute, an episode to which we owe the marvellous conversations with Monsieur de Norpois. He would have liked to see Marcel subjected to a more rigorous discipline in preparation for life, but soon discovered that, if his second son, Robert, was vigorous and high-spirited, his eldest boy suffered so much from exacerbated nerves that any form of punishment, any hint of reproach, inevitably produced a dangerous crisis. There is, in *Swann*, a scene which certainly belongs to Marcel's childhood. It is concerned with an evening on which his mother, because she had friends coming to dinner, failed to go to his room for their customary good-night kiss. Profoundly miserable 'as a lover who feels that she whom he loves is detained in some place of entertainment where he cannot join her', he could not overcome his longing to embrace his mother, cost what it might, on her way up to bed. This act of disobedience provoked a show of anger on the part of his parents, but the boy seemed so miserable, and sobbed so desperately, that his father took pity on him even before his mother did, and said: 'I don't see that it is going to help matters much to make him really ill. There are two beds in his room. Perhaps you had better spend the night with him . . .' This incident, as Proust himself tells us, marked a turning-point in his life because from it dates his familiarity with the agonies of love, and also because it was on that night that his mother finally abandoned any attempt to strengthen his will-power. The defeatist attitude of a nervous subject, which was to cause him gradually to withdraw from the life of society, and was to make him both a seriously sick man and a great artist, began on that evening at Combray.

II

THE SETTINGS OF CHILDHOOD

Proust's childhood was passed in four different 'settings', all of which, transposed and transfigured by his art, have become familiar to us. There was, first of all, Paris, where he lived with his parents in a solid, middle-class house at 9 Boulevard Malesherbes. He was taken every afternoon to the Champs-Elysées, where, beside the wooden horses and the laurel shrubbery, across 'the frontier guarded at regular intervals by the little bastions of the barley-sugar women', he played with a group of small girls of whom Gilberte became the composite portrait. They were Marie and Nelly de Benadaky, Gabrielle Schwartz and Jeanne Pouquet (to become, much later, Princesse Radziwill, the Comtesse de Contades, Madame L. L. Klotz and Madame Gaston de Caillavet).

The second 'setting' was Illiers, where the family spent the holidays at Aunt Amiot's house, No. 4 Rue du Saint-Esprit. What joy, as soon as he got out of the train, to run down to the Loir, and to see again, according to the season, hawthorns and buttercups at Easter, poppies in summer in the fields of wheat, and always the old church, its tile-hung belfry dotted with crows — a shepherd guarding a flock of houses. How pleased he was to be back in the room where tall white curtains hid the bed with its flowered counterpane and embroidered coverlet. He loved to find, unaltered since he had left them last, the trinity beside his bed, consisting of a blue-patterned glass, a sugar-bowl, a water jug. On the mantelpiece stood the glass bell within which the clock still chattered and, hanging on the wall, a picture of Our Lord above a sprig of consecrated box. But what he most enjoyed were the long days of reading spent at the 'Pré-Catalan', a diminutive park so called by Uncle Amiot who owned it, a garden lying on the far bank of the Loir, enclosed by a most beautiful hedge of hawthorn, at the far end of which Marcel, seated in a rustic arbour which stands there still, could enjoy the deep silence of the countryside broken only by the golden sound of church bells. There he read George Sand, Victor Hugo, Charles Dickens, George Eliot and Balzac. 'No days, perhaps, of all our childhood are ever so fully lived as those we had regarded as not being lived at all: the days spent wholly with a favourite book.'

The two final 'settings' were secondary. There was Uncle Weil's house at Auteuil where the 'Parisians' took refuge in hot weather, and from which some of the elements used to compose the picture of the Combray garden were afterwards taken. Louis Weil was an old bachelor whose impenitent 'adventures' shocked Marcel's rather strait-laced family. There, sometimes, they would meet certain 'lovely ladies' who took pleasure in fondling the child — Laure Hayman, for instance, the elegant demi-mondaine who was descended from an English painter, Gainsborough's master, and who 'sat' for the preliminary sketch of Odette de Crécy.

Finally there was the Channel coast, to one of the resorts of which, Trouville, Dieppe, and at a later date Cabourg, Marcel Proust was packed off for part of each summer. Out of these places Balbec was born. There is an entry in Madame Adrien Proust's diary: *Letter from Marcel: Cabourg, 9th September, 1891*: 'How different from those summers by the sea when Grandmamma and I, fused together, used to struggle against the wind, talking all the while . . .' Fused together . . . never was boy so *fused* with an adored family.

> As the result of a miracle of tenderness which had imprisoned my thought in each one of her ideas, of her intentions, of her words, of her smiles and glances, there seemed to exist between us a peculiar, a pre-established harmony, which made of me — her grandson — so much her own possession, and of her — my grandmother — so much mine, that had it been suggested that either of us should have been replaced, she by some woman of superlative genius, I by some man of the noblest sanctity ever known since the world began, we should have smiled, knowing full well that each would have preferred the worst fault of the other to all the virtues to be found in the rest of humanity. . . .

There is much pleasure to be enjoyed in making pilgrimages to places which served as the setting, or as the raw material for the setting, to works of great art: in seeking in Saumur or Guérande the sights that Balzac saw, at Combourg those melancholy twilights in the home that Chateaubriand has painted for us, at Illiers the May-Day hawthorns and the reeds by the Vivonne. But, because they cannot bring to life the pictures so marvellously limned by the writer's magic, such comparisons serve but to make evident the vast distance that separates the model from the finished work. 'If we had any need of proof that there exists not *one* universe, but as many universes as there are living individuals, what could better provide it than the fact that, when we see in some collection of pictures a barn, a church, a farm or a tree, we say to ourselves — "Ah! an Elstir!", thus recognizing them as so many fragments of the world that Elstir, and none but Elstir, saw . . .' In just such a way did Proust see 'Prousts' in all the landscapes of his childhood. As Renoir touched all flesh with the rainbow of his palette, so did Marcel hang his garlands of rare adjectives upon the trees of La Beauce and of the Champs-Elysées. But this beauty remains his own peculiar gift, and those who see in nature only what nature gives will be bitterly disappointed if they try to find in those places the lovely iridescence and the velvety texture of his epithets.

He himself has spoken of the disenchantment that lies in wait for those who go to see the places that seem so delicious to readers of Maeterlinck or of Anna de Noailles: 'We should like to see that field which Millet (for we can learn from the painters no less than from the poets) shows us in his *Spring*. We should like to go with Monsieur Claude Monet to Giverny on the Seine, to that bend of the river which he half reveals to us through morning mists. The truth of the matter is that it was the mere chance of going to stay with friends or relations that led Madame de Noailles, Maeterlinck, Millet or Claude Monet to paint one particular garden, one particular field, one particular bend of the river, rather than another . . .' The enchanted park described by Proust, where he used to sit reading beneath a rustic arbour, within sight of the white gate which marked 'the limits of the park' and of the fields beyond, starred with poppies and blue corn-flowers, we shall never find. That garden is more than the 'Pré-Catalan' at Illiers. To each one of us it once was known, by each one of us it has been lost. For only by reason of our childhood did it have existence in the world of our imagination.

III

SICKNESS AND GENIUS

Marcel Proust was nine years old when there occurred in his young life an incident of capital, of, as he later said himself, of the *most capital*, importance. He suffered an attack of breathlessness (asthma or hay-fever) so violent that ever afterwards he had, during the spring season, to avoid all contact with nature. From then on he was destined to lead the life of an invalid, never free from the threat of a recurrent attack. It is generally agreed today that asthma and hay-fever are often no more than nervous afflictions closely allied to a morbid craving for tenderness. Many asthma cases have suffered in their youth from an excess, or a lack, of maternal affection, with the result that they have been sometimes led into a state of utter dependence on their mother, or cling desperately to other props — to a husband, a wife, a relation, a friend, a doctor. Their attacks of breathlessness are, in reality, a species of appeal. Of this theory Marcel Proust would seem to have been a living proof. We know what torments he endured whenever his mother was absent. All through his life he remained a man who felt that he was dependent on others. To be loved, praised, desired, was the prime need of his being. He never felt safe unless he could call upon more than the normal amount of affection.

Certain of his characteristics derived directly from this state of mind. He was always anxious to please, always thoughtful of the needs and desires of others. He overwhelmed his friends with gifts. He wanted to be true to the idea that they had formed of him, and was filled with remorse whenever he failed to be so. Up to the time of his parents' death, Proust suffered from the knowledge that he had been a disappointment to them and, from then on, worked so hard that ultimately he killed himself. He never had that indifference to the sufferings and the opinions of his familiars which makes the cynic. He was a trifle too suave, too complimentary and, because his habit of flattery was, in fact, a form of defence mechanism, found compensation in moods of pitiless criticism which he confided to the secret pages of his *Memoranda* and his *Notebooks*. So much was this so that an excess of tenderness could with him, by a curious transmutation, be changed into cruelty. In order to conciliate those terrible beasts of prey that all human beings with the exception of his mother and grandmother, seemed to him to be, he made a point of showing modesty, of being too modest, so modest that he habitually denigrated everything he wrote. He quite sincerely believed that

31

he could achieve nothing unaided. He would complain, would announce, that he was ill or ruined, would exploit his sufferings and take pleasure in his own jeremiads, simply because he regarded an excess of wretchedness as the surest means of opening for himself a credit-account of sympathy. He could not do the simplest thing without asking the advice of his friends — give a dinner, sell a piece of furniture, send a present of flowers. His usual attitude was: 'Help me because I am weak and tactless.' Love and friendship were always to him matters of prime importance, because in early life he could face life only if he felt himself to be beloved. Whenever he feared that he was not a favourite he became suspicious, a prey to the most torturing refinements of emotional analysis.

This neurosis (no other word can describe a state of mind so definitely morbid) contributed to his formation as a minute and subtle analyst of the passions. He could register finer shades of feeling than Constant or than Stendhal, because he was more sensitive than either. He was well aware of the power that this weakness gave him. 'Only suffering can sharpen observation and teach us about life, can make it possible for us to take to pieces a machine about which, otherwise, we should know nothing. A man who falls into bed like a log, and lies there as though dead until he wakes in the morning when it is time to get up, can never expect to make — I won't say discoveries of major importance, but even a few comments, on the nature of sleep. He scarcely knows that he is asleep. A dose of insomnia is of no little value to those who would appreciate the gift of sleep, who would seek to cast even the feeblest ray into that mysterious darkness. A faultless memory is not the best of instruments with which to probe the phenomenon of memory . . .' A completely normal lover gets on with his loving and does not embark upon a dissertation about love. 'It is among those who belong to the magnificent, the lamentable, family of neurotics that we find the salt of the earth. They it is, and not others, who have founded religions and achieved masterpieces. The world will never know how much it owes to them, nor yet what they have suffered in the act of giving . . .' And again: 'There is in sickness a Grace which brings us close to the realities which lie on the further side of death.'

MARCEL PROUST'S FATHER

MARCEL PROUST'S MOTHER

But it is not enough merely to be a sick man in order to become an analyst of genius. Sickness, however, is one of the wheels of that piece of mental mechanism which increases the power of analysis. 'One can almost say that the mind of the creative man is like an artesian well. The deeper the level to which his sufferings can sink, the higher the level to which its productions will rise . . .' Sickness, by compelling Proust to live a cloistered existence for most of his life, by making it possible for him at a later period to see his friends only at night, or by compelling him not to see them at all, by forcing him to look at fruit trees in blossom through the closed windows of a sick-room or a carriage, freed him, on the one hand, from the exigencies of society, thus leaving him the leisure in which to meditate and read and patiently pattern out his words, and, on the other, gave enhanced value to the beauties of nature which he had known in the days of his happy childhood when, on the banks of the Vivonne, he had gazed enraptured at the white and purple clusters of lilac in Swann's garden, the fall of sunlight on an old bridge, or the buttercups of Combray.

It is certain that, ever since the days of his childhood, he had been obsessed by a desire to write, and in particular to grasp a beauty which he felt to be imprisoned beneath the surface appearances of things. In a vague, confused way he knew that his task was to liberate an imprisoned truth by giving it expression: 'The tiled roof . . . dappled the pond with pink in a way that I had till then never noticed. Seeing on the surface of the water, and on the wall, the pale hint of a smile that repeated the gaiety of the high heavens, I waved my umbrella and shouted in my enthusiasm — "Zut! zut! zut!" But even while I was doing so, I realized that what I ought to have been concerned with, instead of resting satisfied with the opacity of that inexpressive word, was making an effort to see more clearly into the nature of my delight . . .' We should do well to remember those words . . . *ought . . . making an effort to see more clearly . . . liberate an imprisoned truth*, for in them, already, lies the whole of Proust.

To write: that was his secret ambition. But he believed that he had no talent, because, as soon as he attempted to find the subject for a novel similar to any of those which brought him so

33

much enchanted pleasure, he was conscious at once of impotence. The forms, the colours and the scents which he brought back with him from his walks, preserved by a protective screen of images, like fish in an angler's basket covered with grass to conserve their freshness, did not seem to him to be suitable material for a literary work. They were too simple, too special. Nevertheless, when one day Dr. Percepied had taken him driving, and he had found a seemingly inexplicable pleasure in watching three belfries in the plain, and had noticed how, as a result of the movement of the carriage and the winding of the road, they seemed constantly to alter their relations one to another in space, he had been made aware, once again, that what he most wanted to do was to formulate his mysterious sense of delight in words and phrases. He asked the doctor for a pencil, and at once composed a fragment which he later inserted, almost unchanged, in the text of *Swann*. 'I never gave what I had written a second thought, but when, sitting in the corner of the carriage where the coachman regularly put the basket containing the fowls which his master had bought in Martinville market, I had finished setting down my thoughts, I felt so happy, so sure that I had satisfactorily disposed of those belfries and of the truth concealed in them, that, just as though I had been myself a fowl and laid an egg, I started to crow at the top of my voice.'

On that day our Marcel Proust was born: a writer, capable of understanding that the duty of the poet is to plunge to the heart of his impressions: that the humblest of objects can deliver up the secrets of the universe, if only he can see them with the 'eyes of the spirit'. Marcel was still a child. Not yet could he attain to the truths hidden beneath the scrub, the orchards and the daylight of La Beauce. But even then he could feel something of their presence.

CHAPTER II

SCHOOL, THE GREAT WORLD AND THE ARMY

Pleasure is a sign of the true functioning of our powers.
ARISTOTLE

I

THE LYCÉE CONDORCET

IN spite of his bad health and his attacks of asthma, Marcel Proust had a normal, in fact a more than usually successful, career as a schoolboy at the Lycée Condorcet where literature was held in honour, not in the erudite and traditional fashion then in favour at Louis-le-Grand and Henri IV, but in a way that was precious, decadent and modern. At that time there existed in the Lycée Condorcet, a small group composed of boys drawn from two or three different 'years', all of them middle class in origin, and all of them stuffed to bursting with a passion for 'letters' — Daniel Halévy, Fernand Gregh, Jacques Bizet, Robert de Flers, Jacques Baignères, Robert Dreyfus, Louis de la Salle, Marcel Boulanger and Gabriel Trarieux. Round about 1888 the school had become a sort of club with a power of attraction so great that a number of pupils, Proust among them, would arrive early and engage in long discussions 'under the scanty shadow of the trees that adorned the Cour du Havre, until the rolling of the drum advised, rather than compelled, them to go to their form-rooms'.

What did they read? Everything that could at that time be regarded as modern — Barrès, France, Lemaître, Maeterlinck. In their opinion Léon Dierx and Leconte de Lisle were 'difficult' poets, whose work was a closed book to members of an earlier generation. Marcel Proust shared these tastes and was long faithful to them. A failure to admire Maeterlinck was one of the Duchesse de Guermantes's more absurd characteristics. Thanks to his mother, Marcel had long been on familiar terms with the classics and was particularly fond of Saint-Simon, Baudelaire,

La Bruyère, Madame de Sévigné, Musset and George Sand. He was a great reader of the *Arabian Nights* and, in translation, of Dickens, Thomas Hardy, Stevenson and George Eliot. 'Two pages of *The Mill on the Floss* are enough to start me crying.' It is surprising that no one has yet pointed out the close resemblance between the opening pages of *Swann* and those of *The Mill on the Floss*, for it is startling. 'I have been pressing my elbows on the arm of my chair, and dreaming that I was standing on the bridge in front of Dorlcote Mill as it looked one February afternoon many years ago . . .' — at which point the reader is transported into the past. Substitute the Vivonne for the Floss, and the two mental landscapes become interchangeable.

Marcel Proust grew up under the influence of Leconte de Lisle and of his study of the classics. During his schooldays, round about 1886, he suffered to some extent from that grandiloquent pedantry which he was later to ascribe to Bloch. On one occasion a young woman who was one of his mother's friends promised to sing him some Gounod and some Massenet, on condition that he should compose her literary portrait. *Marcel Proust to his grandmother:* 'I am sorely embarrassed. Madame Catusse is bound to see this portrait, and, though it is I who make it, I swear by Artemis the white goddess, and by Pluto of the burning eyes, that I feel, even if she does not, a certain shyness at the idea of saying baldly that I find her charming . . . I bless the immortal gods for bringing here a woman so astonishingly well informed, one who has learned so much, and who spreads about her so surprising an aura of delight. *Mens pulcher in corpore pulchro.* My curse upon those spirits that wage war on human peace of mind, and have compelled me to utter such stale compliments in the hearing of one who so holds my affections, who has been so kind to me, and is so utterly adorable.'[1]

Pluto . . . Artemis . . . the immortal gods . . . the spirits that wage war on human peace of mind . . . It was this dead and vanished self that the author of *Swann* was later to ridicule in the character of Bloch.

Even at this early age he astonished his young friends by his precocity. The most intelligent among them felt confusedly that

[1] From Alfred Dupont's collection.

they were in the presence of a fantastic but undeniable genius. When they started, a *Revue Verte* consisting of a single manuscript copy passed round among a group of subscribers, or a multi-graphed *Revue Lilas*, it was to Proust that they turned for contributions. But his uneasy, his excessive and neurotic affection never ceased to amaze them. 'His boyhood friendships', says Jacques Émile-Blanche, 'were the occasion for him of much disenchantment. A man who played with him as a child has described how terrified he felt when Marcel one day came up to him, took him by the hand, and declared that what he craved was an affection that should be tyrannical and total. Even in those days he pretended to find in those about him all the sublimer virtues, though, in the secrecy of his heart, he judged all individuals at their true worth. People like Proust are fated to be lonely. . . .'[1]

His odd humility (product of a desire to please) shocked his friends. 'I could never be so presumptuous as to compare myself to you' — he wrote to Robert Dreyfus, his junior by one year. 'This tone', remarks the latter, 'irritated and bewildered his best friends. Nor were they less surprised by his touchiness . . .' 'Why', asked Marcel, 'should Daniel Halévy, after behaving in what amounted to an extremely friendly fashion, suddenly decide to have nothing more to do with me, let me see it only too clearly, and then, four weeks later when we were no longer on speaking terms, go out of his way to say "good morning"? Then there's that Bizet cousin of his. Why should *he* utter the friendliest sentiments, only, from then on, to have even less to do with me? What are they after? Do they want to wash their hands of me, mystify me — or what? I had thought they were so charming. . . .'

This theme of 'charm' had the effect of irritating the young critics who set out to pass judgment on him. Being themselves a great deal more aggressive than he was, they thought his sensibility affected. When he used words like 'tenderness', which quite genuinely evoked in his mind the sweet and distinguished atmosphere in which he had spent his childhood, he merely aroused feelings of suspicion and exasperation among his schoolfellows. To judge from the way he spoke, he was prepared to make sacri-

[1] JACQUES ÉMILE-BLANCHE, *Souvenirs sur Marcel Proust* (Revue Hebdomadaire, July 21st, 1928).

fices of a kind that no one dreamed of asking of him, sacrifices that nothing but love between the sexes could possibly justify. They felt all at sea. 'Most human beings are put out of countenance by those monsters of our species whom the world knows as artists . . .' adds Blanche: 'Very few of the Condorcet youngsters can have found much to please them in the compliments lavished on them by young Proust, or in the subjects which he liked to discuss.'

Those of his friends, like the Halévys, who could appreciate the beauty of the language that he used habitually, and 'the resources of a memory which never failed him and had been nourished on reading of a kind that most of us no longer indulged in', were disconcerted by the pomposity of his manners, by the way in which he kissed their mothers' hands, by the gifts of flowers and chocolates with which this stripling overwhelmed 'nice, simple women who were unaccustomed to being treated in that way'. Enemies of frivolity in any form, they were surprised to find that the 'World' attracted him, that he was avid for details about some member of the Jockey-Club met in the house of Laure Hayman, his great-uncle's mistress with whom he sometimes went about. Already he 'was pondering in a mood of feverish excitement the problem of making an entry into aristocratic society and taking it by storm'. Much later his critics accused him of being a snob, which was unfair, because the Proust of *A la Recherche du temps perdu* had got far beyond that stage, and viewed the great world only in the light of an admirable museum in which historical and zoological specimens are preserved. Certainly in the days of his youth the aesthetes of the Lycée Condorcet were thoroughly disconcerted by his 'weakness for a title'.

His school work, however, did not suffer from such dissipation as he was guilty of. When reading literature, he had two different teachers, and their influence upon him was complementary. Monsieur Cucheval was a 'typical schoolmaster' — unpolished, crude, sharp-tongued, talkative and highly flavoured. 'Don't think a boy's a fool because he goes out of his way to talk "stupid", and is impervious to exquisite patternings of words and rhythms. In every other way he may be a thoroughly sound fellow, and a blessed relief from all the other fools who are for ever turning fine phrases. A chap like that is a pure delight' (sound Combray common sense). The other, Maxime Gaucher, literary critic of *La Revue Blanche*, was a liberal-minded man of great charm, who at once became devoted to Proust, let him show up compositions which had nothing whatever to do with the subject set, and actually made him read them aloud to the class which expressed its opinion of them with boos and cheers. 'The result of all this was that at the end of two months a dozen young asses were writing decadent prose, that Cucheval was convinced of my deleterious influence, that I had produced a state of civil-war in the class-rooms, and that a great many of the boys regarded me as a *poseur*. Fortunately, this condition of affairs lasted only for those two months, though even four weeks later Cucheval was saying: "*He'll* get through all right, because with him it was all my eye. But he'll be responsible for fifteen others being ploughed . . . ." '

One day, when a school inspection was taking place, Gaucher asked Proust to read one of his essays to Eugène Manuel. That mediocre poet was much incensed and said:

'Isn't there some boy at the bottom of the class who can write in a more limpid and correct style?'

'Sir,' replied Gaucher, 'none of my boys writes copy-book French.'[1]

As a matter of fact, Proust was already a critic of no inconsiderable talent.

Here is one of his 'Essays'. Gaucher had set his pupils to comment on a passage in Sainte-Beuve:

> *To be a passionate lover of Corneille one must be no enemy to a certain amount of 'bravura'. To feel passionate love for Racine is to run the risk of having, to excess, what we, in France, call 'taste', a quality that may, at times, be highly distasteful.*

The creations of poetry and of literature are never the outcome of pure thought. They are, in addition, the expression of a personality which differs with each artist, and takes on something of his individuality. So long as the writer is influenced, though not carried away, by temperament, so long as he submits to the highest dictates of his art (sometimes

[1] Quoted by ROBERT DREYFUS in his *Souvenirs sur Marcel Proust* (Grasset, Paris, 1926).

called 'rules'), while, at the same time, imparting to them his own peculiar force of mind — that novelty of approach which is his alone — he may be said to be at the summit of his powers. He writes *le Cid*, he writes *Andromaque*, and, by giving expression to the highest that is in him, seems to be the spokesman of the very spirit of mankind. But sometimes at the beginning, sometimes at the end, of his career, before he knows, or when he has forgotten, how to discipline his individual tendencies, it is them, and them only, that he voices. Instead of sensitive, he is elegantly precious. The heroic, over-stressed, shows as extravagance. Prior to *Andromaque* he can write only *Les Frères Ennemis*, and, later, incapable of producing a second *Cid*, declines from *Agésilas* to *Attila*. The very quality which once gave charm, life and *newness* to his work, is seen, when unduly magnified, as the error of his genius, the cause of his decadence. But is he not most himself at that precise moment when, not yet assured of perfection, he has failed to fuse what is most original in his gift with the beauties of the art he practises? Do not those whose love is greater than their power of detached admiration, who praise Corneille and Racine, not so much as great writers, but because one of them discovered a new subtlety of the exquisite, the other a new aspect of the sublime, find a peculiar pleasure in those works of a given poet which display most clearly both his qualities and his defects, in which he no longer softens, no longer (modifies), no longer keeps them subordinate, no longer fuses them with the totality of his art? When that happens, is not the image of the adored author then imprinted upon the charmed sensibility of the disciple, at once more accurate, narrower, more personal? Does not *his* Corneille show as rather *too* proud, *his* Racine as *too* subtle? It is, no doubt, in the light of such exaggerated deference that Sainte-Beuve's statement is to be understood. I do not believe for a moment that what he meant was that the Tragedies of Corneille exhibit too much bravura, or the Tragedies of Racine 'too much sensibility'. He can scarcely have meant that those qualities are to be regarded as being the characteristic defects of their less successful compositions. It is more probable that, when he committed himself to that judgment, he was thinking in particular of those fervent admirers of both poets who are more 'cornelian' than Corneille, more fascinated by Quinault than by Racine, and inclined to value, to *over*-value, the blemishes of both. But if the works in which personality is seen in so extreme a form that it becomes a *caricature of sensibility or of the heroic* in Corneille, in Racine, or in both, or, perhaps we should say, if the extreme expression of themselves which devoted admirers have drawn from their artistic practice, produces an appearance of *bravura* or of preciosity, is it not because these things are *potentially present* even in their masterpieces, are, as it were, foreshadowed as an end to which the natural bent of their minds will ultimately lead them? When Climène tests Rodrigue so highly, we are left in no doubt, it is true, about the genuineness of her moral scruples — scruples which are not, perhaps, always sufficiently present in Corneille's later work — but do we not feel that she produces rather too many of them, that, to use an Army phrase, she 'trots them out on parade' rather too much? Why does she draw back quite so violently when she is about to be reunited with her lover, if not because she is inspired by what one might call the coquetry of renunciation, or because she wants to lead him on to make display of a superfluous amount of heroism and constancy? What strong, what noble souls are theirs — but don't they know it! How skilled they are at setting their heroism in the brightest possible light, at playing the changes on, at widening the field of, their noble temperaments. True, we are being bidden by Corneille to watch a high drama of scruple, but what superb variations he performs on the sentiments, what magnificence of *style* he introduces! It is as though he were taking peculiar delight in unrolling before us, with all the glitter of pomp and circumstance, a 'Pageant of Love and Duty'. And if of Racine we may say that, even when his situations are most daring, he never fails by his superb use of language to keep the action within the 'tight discipline of propriety', can we be blamed for thinking that he takes rather too much pleasure in doing so, that he shows rather too much ingenuity in the handling of his theme, that he sometimes identifies his art to excess with the *over*-formal, the *over*-subtle? If our contemporary critics insist so loudly on directing our attention to the harsh realism that lies behind the Tragedies of Racine, are we entitled to object? Is not the fact that we have made this discovery so late in the day merely a proof of the loving care with which he smoothed and fused the form of his drama? To fail to say at once what he has to say, or, rather, to say it with a refinement of manner which spreads a veil of elegance (of almost sensual delight) over the underlying horror; to turn his back on a more direct method knowing nothing of complicated half-tones — all this may not be habitual with Racine (unless we wish to regard it as his habitual defect), but the fact remains that, in other writers, it is the source of a peculiar grace which we have grown accustomed to describe — not wholly without justifica-tion — as being 'racinian'. But one can love a great man without necessarily excusing, still less adoring, his faults, and that kind of love is not the least good nor the least elevated. It consists in eschewing the dilettante approach to a great writer, in *not* passing over his faults, as we might pass over the faults of a child or an actor:

> Et ce n'est pas, ma sœur, imiter notre mère
> Que de tousser et de cracher comme elle[1]

in not so much identifying his originality with his defects, as in seeing in his good qualities the true direction of his genius and the law of his development. If we understand love in this sense, we can, indeed, love passionately — and to love Racine passionately means, in that case, to love the deepest, the tenderest, the most painful and the most sincere of those intuitions which he brought to the understanding of so many charming and martyred existences, just as to love

[1] The actual quotation from *Les Femmes Savantes* (Act I, scene 1) is:
    Et ce n'est point du tout la prendre pour modèle
    Ma sœur, que de tousser et de cracher comme elle.
Marcel was quoting from memory, and, therefore, inaccurately. It was a habit that he never lost. See, for instance, in *Chroniques*, where he misquotes Hugo (pp. 212 and 213); Vigny (p. 215); Baudelaire (p. 217); and Sully Prudhomme (p. 231).

Corneille means to love, in the integrity of its beauty and in the unbending quality of its pride, the highest possible realization of an heroic ideal.[1]

Here we have a true foretaste of Proust the writer. In all these four large foolscap pages, he never once breaks off to start a new paragraph. Such 'running on' is not, with him, an affectation. It is his way of expressing the unbroken flow of his thought. The 'cutting up into lengths' imposed by educational tradition, may be useful, but it is artificial, and he will have none of it. Maxime Gauchet was right in thinking that this critical fragment gave evidence of an astonishing maturity of mind. This impression is confirmed by the 'Sketches' which Proust contributed to the school magazine, the *Revue Lilas*: 'What horror can reside in familiar things as one lies awake before the night is old, with, overheard, someone playing waltzes, and in the next room the nerve-racking clatter of crockery . . . Thin pencils of moonlight strike through scarce-perceptible gaps in the red curtains and turn the room-walls blue . . . I open the window to take one last look at the sweet, wild, round-cheeked face of my darling moon. Then I close it. I go to bed. The lamp, set on a small table close beside my pillow, in a litter of glasses and bottles, of cool drinks and slim books in precious bindings, of letters that tell of friendship and of love, casts a dim light into the corners of my library. Hour of all hours divine! Not mine the power to overcome nature or familiar things, but at least I can consecrate them. I have draped them in the garment of my spirit, turning them to emblems of something that is secret and superb. . . .'

It is rare to find so much mystical impressionism in a schoolboy of fifteen. No less remarkable is the following letter, written to Robert Dreyfus during the summer holidays of 1888:

I am quite sure that what we take to be the interpretation by ourselves of this or that character is, actually, nothing but the effect of associated ideas . . . Suppose, for instance, that in real life, or in some work of literature, you are shown the spectacle of a man shedding tears over the misfortune of another. Now, just because, whenever you have seen anybody

[1] Unpublished text in the possession of Professor Henri Mondor.

43

crying from sheer pity, it so happens that the person in question has been good, gentle and sensitive, your natural deduction is that *this* man, too, is sensitive, good, etc. For our interpretation of a character is based only on certain leading features of which we have knowledge, and we assume that these features *imply* others. But such interpretation is, in fact, pure guesswork. For this reason it is that Coquelin, faced by the fact of Alceste's avoidance of his fellow-men, jumps to the conclusion that the reason for such avoidance is that he is actuated by an ill-humour which is both crabbed and comic, whereas Worms sees in the same character a noble contempt of base passions. Similarly, in real life. Halévy completely boycotts me, and goes out of his way to make me realize that he is doing so on purpose; then, a month later, comes up to me and says 'good-morning'. Now, among the many different persons of whom I am composed, one is an excessively romantic gentleman who, though rarely vocal, remarks on this occasion. 'He's doing it to tease you, to amuse himself, to put you to the test, and then, later, regrets his behaviour because he does not want to be estranged from you altogether.' This 'me' represents Halévy in the light of a whimsical friend who wants to know me. But another, and more aggressive 'me' — whom I like very much better — points out that the truth is really simpler; that Halévy finds me insufferable, that the warmth of my responses appears to his own, much more level-headed, nature, at first absurd and ultimately boring; that he wants me to realize how 'clinging' he finds me, and how anxious he is to be quit of me. Only when he is quite sure that I shall not force my presence on him, does he venture to address me. The 'me' in question does not know whether this trivial action is inspired by pity, indifference, or a spirit of moderation. What he *does* know is that it is completely unimportant and not worth worrying about.

Reading this, we are filled with admiration for the subtlety of the analysis, and with amazement that so young a boy should be so complex.

His 'Philosophy' year (1888-89) was the period of his greatest intellectual enrichment. About this time a form of 'immanent immaterialism' was taking the place of the materialism preached by Taine and Berthelot. Alain was finding Lagneau's lectures on Plato and Spinoza as refreshingly definite as black ink on white paper. Lachelier, Fouillée and Boutroux were clearing the ground for the coming of Bergson. Proust had the good fortune to sit under Darlu ('a good brain' said Anatole France of him, and the words might have the air of damning with faint praise, were it not for the fact that Darlu had said precisely the same of France). This man from the south, warm-blooded, sarcastic and with a gift for pricking his pupils' minds awake, performed the remarkable conjuring-trick — according to Fernand Gregh — of producing philosophy from the top hat which stood on his desk and always served him by way of an example whenever he needed some material object for purposes of demonstration. 'Product of a diseased brain — Sganarelle philosophy' was Darlu's comment on an essay once shown up by the top boy of his class. But his influence on Proust was deep and lasting. In his course of lectures on the reality of the external world, he treated his subject so poetically that Proust was able, later, to 'incorporate in his novel a whole world of thought, and even a style, which, till then, had been the special preserve and method of the philosophers . . . '[1] Proust, when he was older, read Renouvier, Boutroux and Bergson, but he never ceased to regard Darlu as his master, and it was Darlu who set in motion that long-drawn-out meditation on the unreality of the sensible world, on memory and on the problem of time, which is known to us as '*A la Recherche du temps perdu*'.

There is still in existence a letter written by Madame Adrien Proust to her son who, presumably, had left school before the ceremony of prize-giving took place. '*Le pauvre loup* has not got much to show in the way of school rewards. He failed to win any prizes, except a second in maths, but got an honourable mention for general excellence, another honourable mention for philosophy, and a third for physics. Fortunately, he is taking it all very calmly. I met the Head-Master, Monsieur Jallu, and he said: "Your son can rest assured that his Professor thinks very

[1] Albert Thibaudet.

highly of him. I had a long talk about him with Darlu, who spoke glowingly of his abilities!" . . .' Madame Proust must have been ill-informed, because the prize-list of the Lycée Condorcet for the year in question shows that Marcel won the Prize of Honour for Philosophy.

She was, just then, staying with her uncle at Auteuil. Marcel was at Fontainebleau with a friend. The letters of both mother and son are full of references to what they have been reading. 'I have just sent you a parcel containing *Curé de Campagne, Chouans, Julius Caesar* — all of them lib. cop' (*which was their way of referring to Library Copies*). 'Be sure to bring them all back. I send you a thousand kisses, the accumulated love of a whole week. Look after yourself, dear boy . . .' She herself was reading Loti, Sévigné, Musset (*Fantasio, Les Caprices de Marianne*), and George Sand's *Mauprat*. Marcel shared his mother's enthusiasm for Sand's prose — 'which breathes the very essence of goodness and moral distinction' — and for Tolstoy's novels. About other authors they did not see eye to eye: 'I am not going to say anything about what I am reading, my dear, because I am deep in Madame du Deffand, and I know that you have a poor opinion of the eighteenth century. . . .'

She brooded over him from a distance. *Madame Adrien Proust to her son:* 'Have you been doing any work? What time do you get up? . . . and go to bed? . . . *Pauvre loup*, I have no liking for arid natures, yet am reduced to wishing yours to be such rather than to see you in the grip of an excessive melancholy. "Can you not, sir, reduce it to silence?" — not your melancholy, for that is only too eloquent, but yourself. What you most need is to grow a protective skin over your heart, that it may not be too easily hurt, too sensitive . . .' *Marcel Proust to his mother:* 'My sweet, darling mother: I got up early this morning and went into the woods with Loti. Darling, what a fool I was not to do that before; I shall certainly do it a lot in future. As soon as I got under the trees it was lovely, all cool and sunlit, and I laughed aloud from sheer happiness, though there was no one with me; it was a pleasure just to breathe, to feel, to move my limbs. I felt as I used to feel at Tréport, or at Illiers that year when I was busy with Augustin Thierry — much, much happier than when I used to

46

go walking with Robert. *Le Mariage de Loti* increased my sense of well-being — gave me the same sort of feeling I have when I have been drinking tea. I read it lying in the grass by the small lake which was violet in the shadows, with gleams of sunshine here and there which set a sparkle on the trees and water. *Dans l'étincellement et le charme de l'heure.* I understood, or, rather, felt, what a wealth of sensations is expressed by that delightful line of Leconte de Lisle. You see, I always come back to him. . . .'[1]

II

FROM SCHOOLBOY TO DANDY

Strong though the intimacy was between mother and son, their ways of life quickly diverged. Madame Adrien found no pleasure in the great world, and knew it scarcely at all. The Prousts of Illiers had done no more than graft a country family on to her own Hebrew stock. Dr. Proust, who was well on the way to becoming one of the high priests of official medicine, dreamed of one day offering his candidature to the Académie des Sciences Morales, and did his best to maintain such contacts as might be useful to him. But his wife very often let him go to parties without her, and when important dinners were in the wind his sons used to watch with admiring eyes while he adjusted the red ribbon of a Commander of the Legion under his white tie.

Ever since his boyhood Marcel had shown a liking for Society, a liking that ultimately became one of the necessities of his being. Some of his school friends, Jacques Baignères and Gaston de Caillavet, for instance, had young mothers who did much entertaining. In their houses he had made the acquaintance of Madeleine Lemaire whose studio, at that time, was the meeting-place of a 'salon'. His friend, Jacques Bizet, introduced him to his mother who, before her marriage, had been Geneviève Halévy, the daughter of Fromenthal Halévy, the composer of *La Juive*. She was the widow of the composer of *Carmen*, and had taken as her second husband a rich lawyer called Émile Straus. Madame Straus at forty-three was still beautiful, with her warm, brown

[1] Unpublished letters: by courtesy of Madame Gérard Mante-Proust.

gipsy eyes, and a gracefulness that 'had about it something primitive, oriental and melancholy'. Though she was not a woman of any great culture, she appealed to Proust by reason of her charm, her waywardness, her 'wit', and of her letters which he rather daringly compared to those of Madame de Sévigné. 'Above all, she was deliciously feminine. Her mind, which Proust immortalized by borrowing it for Madame de Guermantes, was a mixture of common sense and of a sort of flickering and surprised gaiety which made it possible for her to say the most impossible things with an air of complete innocence. She had a whimsical fancy, and, in that, resembled her cousin, Ludovic Halévy. Her mockery was unforced and kindly, her logic quite unpredictable . . . Nobody admired her more than did Monsieur Straus who, to that extent, and to that extent only, served as a model for the Duc de Guermantes.'[1] To Madame Straus the schoolboy Marcel Proust paid a respectful and symbolic homage. He smothered her with flowers, actual as well as figurative, and begged her not to think that his love for her had grown less just because, for some days, he was unable to send her chrysanthemums. 'The fact is, as Mademoiselle Lemaire can tell you, that I walk every morning with Laure Hayman, and frequently take her out to luncheon — which costs so much that I have nothing left over for flowers. Indeed, except for a sixpenny bunch of poppies for Madame Lemaire, I don't think I have sent any to anyone since my last gift to you.' He long continued to overwhelm her with fantastic offers of service. 'If, Madame, I could do anything to oblige you — deliver a letter in Stockholm or in Naples, or do whatever you might like to ask of me — I should be the happiest of mortals . . .' Sincere though his pretty compliments were, he never deceived himself. The devoted 'page' might pretend to be in love, but he knew that his 'lady' and protectress attached no more importance to his play-acting than he did himself. On one occasion he wrote her a very shrewd letter to which he referred as '*The Truth about Madame Straus*':

I thought at first that you cared only for beautiful objects, and had a deep understanding of them, — only to realize

[1] FERNAND GREGH, *L'Âge d'Or* (Grasset, Paris, 1947).

MARCEL PROUST WITH ROBERT DE FLERS (left) AND LUCIEN DAUDET (right)

MARCEL PROUST IN HIS EARLY TWENTIES

later that they mean nothing to you. Then I thought that you cared for 'people', only to realize that *they* mean nothing to you. I think now that you care only for a certain way of living which serves to set off, not so much your intelligence as your temperament, not so much your temperament as your tact, not so much your tact as your clothes. You are, in fact, a person who cares for this way of living more than for anything else — and who knows how to charm. And, because you know how to charm, you mustn't laugh at me and think that I love you the less. To prove that the very reverse is the case . . . I shall send you still lovelier flowers. You will be annoyed, Madame, because you do not smile upon those sentiments which lead me to sign myself in ecstatic pain,

> De Votre Indifférence Souveraine
> Le plus respectueux serviteur. . . .

But he remained the humble slave of his Dear Lady Disdain, and made use of many of the traits of the kindly egotist when he came to create the Duchesse de Guermantes. Oriane's red slippers had their origin (as is proved by a dedicatory inscription which he wrote in one of the volumes) in an incident of which Madame Straus was the heroine.

Laure Hayman, 'that strange courtesan coloured with preciosity', doted on the young Proust, took him with her everywhere, and called him 'Mon petit Marcel' or 'Mon petit Saxe psychologique'. When Paul Bourget made her the heroine of his novel *Gladys Harvey*, she gave Marcel a copy, bound in the flowered silk from one of her own petticoats. He asked her to tell Bourget how much he admired the book, and Bourget replied as follows:

> This young Marcel of yours — this Saxe psychologique, as you call him — must be a really delightful creature, if I can judge of him from the letter which you so very graciously sent me. His comment on the passage in *Gladys* referring to Jacques Molon, proves that he has a mind which is capable of thinking about what he reads, and his enthusiasm warms my heart. Please tell him that I look forward to having the great pleasure of meeting him as soon as I have finished the piece of work to which I am at present harnessed. His father gave

him three pieces of advice, and you a fourth. To these I am going to add a fifth: never to let his love for letters die. A time will come when he will no longer love my books, because, at present, he loves them to excess. Claude Larcher knows only too well that when one loves too much, one is on the point of ceasing to love at all. But let him never cease from loving that beauty of art at which he guesses, and for which he seeks through the medium of my unworthy self. And though this advice, coming to him from the mouth of a Delilah, will sound somewhat ironic, tell him to work hard and develop what his charming intelligence already bears within it. . . . [1]

What a very strange young man he must have been at that time! Like the Narrator of his own novel, he seems to have been of no specific age. Are we to think of him as a child or as an adolescent? Impossible to tell. 'There was a great deal more in him of the schoolboy he had so recently ceased to be than of the dandy he wished to become. During his years at the Condorcet he was very much the "young gentleman", with his butterfly collars and a flower in his buttonhole. At a later period he went in for pale green ties, loosely knotted, baggy trousers and a frock-coat with voluminous skirts. He carried a malacca cane which he had a way of twirling whenever he stooped to pick up a dropped glove (his gloves were pearl-grey with black stitching, and were always crumpled and dirty), or was engaged in putting on or taking off its fellow. He was for ever leaving odd gloves about, and would implore their return by post in return for a new pair or for half a dozen new pairs, which he liked to present as a thank-offering to anyone who would be kind enough to find his strays for him. The same thing was constantly happening to his umbrellas, which would get themselves left in cabs or in the halls of his friends' houses. No matter how dilapidated they might be, he continued to use them when his appeal for their return was answered, though he invariably bought the friend in question a new one at Verdier's. His top-hats very soon took on the appearance of hedgehogs or skye-terriers, as a result of being brushed the

---

[1] From a letter in the possession of Daniel Halévy.

wrong way, or rubbed against the skirts or furs of his driving-companions. Most of them came from Binder's. . . .'[1]

In the portrait which Blanche painted of him he appears as a young man with rather too large a head and wonderful eyes, 'a liquid eye, brown in colour with golden lights . . . One's attention was riveted by its expression, in which a melancholy bred of his contemplation of the world, seemed to swim in a medium of lively malice. The blank stare of complete indifference which he could suddenly assume at will, would show the golden flicker of a fervour which came from brooding on infinite perspectives'. His hair was black, thick and always unruly. His ties were rather too light in colour, and he sported an orchid in his buttonhole. There was, in his appearance, a mixture of the dandified and the limp which reminded one, for a brief moment, of Oscar Wilde. 'A Neapolitan prince in a novel by Bourget', was Gregh's description of him.

> He was fully aware of his own beauty. On summer evenings, on his way out to dine, he would derive an exquisite pleasure from sauntering along the streets, a light, unbuttoned overcoat revealing his starched shirt-front, and a flower in his button-hole — the 'smart' flower in those days was always a white camellia. It gave him intense delight to see in the eyes of those he passed a gleam of admiration for his adolescent grace. In this self-satisfaction there was something of a young man's fatuous conceit, and a tiny pinch of that 'sense of evil' which even at eighteen he already possessed, and from which, later, he was to draw much inspiration. Sometimes he would exaggerate his natural grace by an assumed affectation. But his mannerisms were never crude, just as the flatteries of which he was so lavish, and the exaggerated expressions of friendship which were typical of him, never lacked intelligence. We, his familiars, went so far as to invent a verb — *to proustify* — which we used when we wanted to describe an attitude of rather too self-conscious concern for others, which found expression in an interminable and delicious parade of what would, popularly, have been known as 'chichi'. . . .[2]

[1] JACQUES ÉMILE-BLANCHE, *Souvenirs sur Marcel Proust* (Revue Hebdomadaire, July 21st, 1928).
[2] FERNAND GREGH, *L'Age d'Or*, p. 161.

Even those whom he very often irritated enjoyed meeting him, because he was so far more intelligent and amusing than most people.

Though he played the part of *cavaliere servente*, cajoling and talkative, to many women, though he was a Cherubino who found pleasure in the frou-frou of silk skirts and was passionately curious about everything that had to do with feminine *toilettes*, he was later to confess to Gide that he had 'never had any but a platonic feeling for women, and had known the meaning of love only with other men'. Tied to his mother's apron-strings as he was, and modest to excess, it must have meant agony to him when first he discovered his possession of those instincts which he, no less than other people, regarded as abnormal and criminal. I give below the rough draft of a passage from his unpublished *Notebooks*, which he was to use later, much revised, and in a slightly different form, for his novel. It describes how a taste for senti-mental inversion can take root in a pure heart:

One who, for a long time, has failed to realize that his desire is not for women, leaning with a friend over some book of poetry or some collection of bawdy pictures, will press closely to him, convinced that this craving for physical contact is bred of a shared desire for women. Men of this kind, fully conscious of what they feel in the presence of those various delineations of love which they find alike in literature, in art, in history and in religion, fail to see that the bodily shapes in which they incarnate their emotions are quite different from those imagined by their friends. They interpret their feelings in their own special way, and, because of this con-fusion of mind, derive nourishment for their vice from the romanticism of Sir Walter Scott, the subtleties of Baudelaire, the idea of Honour preached by medieval Chivalry, the melancholy of mysticism, the purity of form achieved by the sculptors of Greece and the painters of Italy, so that they await the coming of Rob Roy with all the excitement of Diana Vernon, and persuade themselves that they are like everybody else, because they find an echo of their melancholy, their scruples and their disenchantment in Sully Prudhomme and in Musset. Nevertheless, some instinct warns them to keep silent about their sufferings, so that they are like the kleptomaniac who is as yet unaware of his unfortunate tendency, and hides his weakness — the better to exploit it. . . .'[1]

Throughout the years of his youth he pretended that he was strongly attracted by women, and actually may have been. But he has himself pointed out that inverts, the better to protect themselves against those who are hostile to their manner of life, and from motives, too, of prudence, habitually wear a mask. 'The walls and mirrors of their rooms are hidden beneath a display of pictured actresses. They write verses — "I dote on Chloe in despair — She is divine as she is fair — I love none other anywhere . . ." Who knows but what those photographs of women are not the beginnings of hypocrisy?'

Elsewhere in the *Notebooks* he puts forward, as a sorry excuse, the theory that what others call aberration may, after all, be perfectly natural — 'especially among young people, because of certain female characteristics which may sometimes persist until a relatively late age, like those embryonic organs which disappear with the coming of maturity, or like that indetermination of feeling that finds expression in mere vague ecstasies of affection, which is fixated on a beloved object before the effects of sublimation or of functional specialization have made themselves felt'. He illustrates his meaning with a reference to the 'ridiculous fact that there are times when one commits an act which is directly at odds with those of which one is habitually capable'. He was already speaking with pity of that unhappy race of men 'who have to deny themselves, as something foul, what, in fact, is the innocent source of all their happiness. They are sons without mothers, because to their mothers they must lie their whole life long, even at the last moment when they close their eyes in death . . .' There can be little doubt that a conflict between filial affection and the claims of inverted love filled his mind with confusion during the years of his young manhood.

Massis is fully justified in thinking that Proust, at this time, was

[1] Unpublished.

filled with a pathetic desire 'to make himself a better man, to prove his worth, to achieve something praiseworthy', and that his heart, which was naturally susceptible to feelings of pity and gentleness, was not always averse to ideas of moral duty. I would go further and say that it never was. 'It may be', wrote Proust, 'that only genuinely vicious persons are capable of feeling the moral problem in its full intensity. To this problem the artist finds a solution, not in terms of his individual life, but in those of a more generalized and literary kind. Just as the great doctors of the Church often began their careers — though with no loss to their essential goodness — by making acquaintance with the sins of their fellow men, and, from the knowledge thus acquired, achieved their own personal sanctity, so does it often happen that great artists, even when their natures are essentially evil, may learn from their very vices to recognize the existence of a general moral law . . .' The forbidden passions portrayed in Proust's books are redolent of remorse and shame. What a profound change must have come over him when he was about twenty, can be seen if we read the answers he then made to the same questionnaire as that presented to him at the age of thirteen. This second version reveals, as yet, not hardness or bitterness, but spiritual anguish, latent remorse, an insatiable craving for tenderness and a desire to be swept off his feet by the strength of his instincts.

Your most marked characteristic?
> A craving to be loved, or, to be more precise, to be caressed and spoiled rather than to be admired.

The quality you most like in a man?
> Feminine charm.

The quality you most like in a woman?
> A man's virtues, and frankness in friendship.

What do you most value in your friends?
> Tenderness — provided they possess a physical charm which makes their tenderness worth having.

What is your principal defect?
    Lack of understanding; weakness of will.

What is your favourite occupation?
    Loving.

What is your dream of happiness?
    Not, I fear, a very elevated one. I really haven't the courage
    to say what it is, and, if I did, I should probably destroy it
    by the mere fact of putting it into words.

What, to your mind, would be the greatest of misfortunes?
    Never to have known my mother or my grandmother.

What would you like to be?
    Myself — as those whom I admire would like me to be.

In what country would you like to live?
    One where certain things that I want would be realized — and
    where feelings of tenderness would always be reciprocated.
    [Proust has underlined the last half of this sentence.]

What is your favourite colour?
    Beauty lies not in colours but in their harmony.

What is your favourite flower?
    Hers — but, apart from that, — all.

What is your favourite bird?
    The swallow.

Who are your favourite prose writers?
    At the moment, Anatole France and Pierre Loti.

Who are your favourite poets?
    Baudelaire and Alfred de Vigny.

Who is your favourite hero of fiction?
    Hamlet.

Who are your favourite heroines of fiction?
Phèdre [crossed out by Proust] Bérénice.

Who are your favourite composers?
Beethoven, Wagner, Shuhmann [*sic*].

Who are your favourite painters?
Leonardo da Vinci, Rembrandt.

Who are your heroes in real life?
Monsieur Darlu, Monsieur Boutroux.

Who are your favourite heroines of history?
Cleopatra.

What are your favourite names?
I have only one at a time.

What is it that you most dislike?
My own worst qualities.

What historical characters do you most despise?
I am not sufficiently educated to say.

What event in military history do you most admire?
My own enlistment as a volunteer!

What reform do you most admire?
[Marcel Proust has left this question unanswered.]

What natural gift would you most like to possess?
Will-power and irresistible charm.

How would you like to die?
A better man than I am, and much beloved.

What is your present state of mind?
Annoyance at having had to think about myself in order to
answer these questions.

Le principal trait de mon caractère.
La qualité que je désire chez un homme.
La qualité que je préfère chez une femme.
Ce que j'apprécie le plus chez mes amis . . .
Mon principal défaut. . . . .
Mon occupation préférée . . . .
Mon rêve de bonheur . . . .
Quel serait mon plus grand malheur. . . . .
Ce que je voudrais être . . . .
Le pays où je désirerais vivre . . . . .
La couleur que je préfère . . . .
La fleur que j'aime . . . .
L'oiseau que je préfère . . . .
Mes auteurs favoris en prose . . . . .
Mes poètes préférés . . . .
Mes héros dans la fiction . . . .
Mes héroïnes favorites dans la fiction. . .
Mes compositeurs préférés . . . .
Mes peintres favoris . . . .
Mes héros dans la vie réelle . . . . . .
Mes héroïnes dans l'histoire. . . . . . .
Mes noms favoris. . . . .
Ce que je déteste par-dessus tout. . . .
Caractères historiques que je méprise le plus.
Le fait militaire que j'admire le plus . .
La réforme que j'estime le plus . . . .
Le don de la nature que je voudrais avoir .
Comment j'aimerais mourir. . . . . . .
État présent de mon esprit. . . . . . .
Fautes qui m'inspirent le plus d'indulgence.
Ma devise . . . .

THE QUESTIONNAIRE

To what faults do you feel most indulgent?
Those that I *understand* [the word is underlined by Proust].

What is your motto?
I prefer not to say — for fear it might bring me ill-luck.[1]

III

THE AWKWARD WARRIOR

He entered the army in 1889, before he was due for service, so as to profit from the 'Voluntary System' (abolished the following year) under which he would have to do only one year with the colours. He was posted to the 76th Regiment of Infantry, stationed at Orléans where, thanks to the fact that he was blessed with a colonel who was 'intelligent', or, in other words, susceptible to civilian influences and not unaffected by letters of introduction, he did not suffer unduly from the difference between life at home and life in barracks. There exists a rather pathetic photograph in which he is depicted as a slovenly 'footslogger', wearing an overcoat several sizes too large for him, and a peaked 'képi' perched like a flower-pot above his 'Persian prince' eyes. To Robert de Billy, the future ambassador, at that time doing his military service with the artillery at Orléans, Proust's bearing and speech seemed far from military. 'He had large, questioning eyes, and his manner of talking was both subtle and engaging. He used to speak to me about Monsieur Darlu, who had taught him philosophy at the Condorcet, and the noble sentiments that seemed to have been bandied about within the precincts of that Right-Bank academy, struck me — the ex-modern-side student of poor old Louis-le-Grand — as probably worthy of scorn, though possibly sublime. . . .'

In the instructional platoon, Proust was seventy-third out of seventy-four. The precocious schoolboy was not exactly a brilliant soldier.

[1] *Les Confidences de Salon*, published by Lesueur-Damby, 19 Rue de Bourgogne, Paris. This copy is the property of Mr. Edward Waterman.

Still he did not complain, and expressed himself as feeling some surprise at finding how well, on the whole, he stood the life.

Marcel Proust to his father [September 23rd, 1889]: '. . . I am far from unwell (stomach apart) and not even a prey to that general mood of gloom of which my absence from home this year might, so easily, be regarded as — if not the cause, at least the occasion, and, therefore, the excuse . . . But I do find great difficulty in concentrating my mind, in reading, in learning by heart and remembering what I have read. I have no time for a proper letter. This is just a note to say that I constantly think of you with affection. No more at present, dear Papa. Remember me to the poet, your neighbour, whose recollection of me would be peculiarly precious, and tell Madame Cazalis that I am at her feet. You may be interested to hear that a number of servant-girls from Cabourg seeing in me the traditional "soldier-boy", have sent me, much to the scandal of the Derbaunes, a thousand kisses. I, however, proved false, though the servant-girls have had their revenge, and I am punished, if Monsieur Cazalis will allow me to quote a line from one of the loveliest of his poems — *"Pour avoir dédaigné les fleurs de leurs seins nus."* Your son, with a big hug,

MARCEL PROUST'[1]

Madame Adrien Proust to Marcel: 'One month's already gone, darling. There are only eleven slices of the cake left for you to eat, and of these, one or two will be consumed on leave. I have thought of a way in which you may make the time seem shorter. Put aside eleven slabs of chocolate (you know how fond you are of chocolate), and make up your mind to eat one on the last day of every month. You will be surprised to find how quickly they vanish — and, with them, the months of your exile. . . .'

He spent his Sunday leaves in Paris, happy to have this opportunity of seeing his friends. He would often on these occasions go to the house of Madame Arman de Caillavet, that dominating hostess, and Anatole France's Egeria, whose son, Gaston, had

---

[1] Unpublished: in the possession of Madame Mante-Proust.

become one of his best friends, and who carried his 'charming ways' to the point of seeing him off each Sunday evening by the Orléans train. *Marcel Proust to Jeanne Pouquet:* 'When you remember that, in those days, there were no such things as taxis, you will, I think, be really astounded when I tell you that he invariably drove me to the station on Sunday evenings to catch the 7.40 train . . . On one occasion he actually went all the way with me to Orléans! . . . My feeling of friendship for Gaston was terrific . . . He was my sole subject of conversation in the barrack-room, and my batman, the corporal, etc., came to think of him as a sort of God, so much so, indeed, that one New Year's day they sent him an address conveying their respect!'

It was at Madame de Caillavet's house that he met Anatole France, whose style he much admired, and from whom he borrowed more than one characteristic when he came to create Bergotte. He had always thought of France as a 'gentle, white-haired bard'. When he found himself in the presence of a man with a nose 'like a snail's shell', a black chin-tuft and a slight stammer, he was disappointed. France, whom he had 'built up, drop by drop, like a stalactite, from the limpid beauties of his books', failed to fit his preconceived notion of him as soon as it was necessary to 'find a place for the snail-shell nose and the black chin-tuft'. Nose and chin-tuft forced him to start again from the beginning. It was disheartening to find that 'after believing for so long that I had been clinging to the tail of a balloon, I found myself hanging on to a man with a chin-tuft', and to feel not at all sure that he would be able to soar into the air.

'You, who are so fond of the things of the intelligence . . .' France said to him.

'I am not at all fond of things of the intelligence, but only of life and of movement', Proust replied.

In this he was sincere. Intelligence was so natural to him that he attached very little value to its activities. What he really envied and admired was the grace of those who live instinctively.

FIRST STEPS IN THE GREAT WORLD

He would have liked, when he left the army, to go on with his studies. Even as a child he had realized that his true vocation was writing, and had ever envisaged the discipline of letters as something that was both exigent and exclusive. But he adored his parents and would not willingly go against their wishes. Dr. Proust was anxious that he should go into diplomacy.

Marcel Proust to his father: Dearest father, my hope is that, ultimately, I shall be able to return to my literary and philosophical studies, for which I believe myself to be fitted. But, realizing as I do, that with each passing year I am becoming subjected to forms of discipline that are more and more practical, I think it a good thing to choose, here and now, one of the definite careers you offer. I am prepared to work seriously for the Foreign Office examination or for the École des Chartes — whichever you prefer ... As to the Law, I should like it far less than a stockbroker's office: I know I shouldn't stick it for more than three days! It isn't that I am not still convinced that any other occupation, other, I mean, than literature and philosophy, will be so much *time lost.* But there are degrees of unpleasantness. Never, in my gloomiest moments, have I thought that anything could be more hideous than to practise as a barrister. In so far as life in the embassies may save me from *that,* I regard it, if not as my vocation, at least as a remedy.'[1]

It is interesting to note that, at this period of his life, he regards everything other than literature and philosophy as so much *time lost.* But, since filial respect condemned him to lose his time, and since the highway to the embassies lay through the École des Sciences Politiques, he proceeded to enter that establishment. There he found Robert de Billy and Gabriel Trarieux. In their company he attended the lectures of Albert Sorel, Albert Vandal

[1] Unpublished letter in the possession of Madame Mante-Proust.

and Leroy-Beaulieu. He listened attentively, took no notes and scribbled on the virgin page of his exercise-book:

> Vandal exquis, repand son sel,
> Mais qui s'en fout, c'est Gabriel,
> Robert, Jean et même Marcel,
> Pourtant si grave d'habitude[1]

Gravity? — no doubt, but frivolity too. To say that is not to be guilty of a contradiction in terms. 'Frivolity is a state of mind marked by vehemence.' He enjoyed going to tennis-parties with Gaston de Caillavet and his friends at the house on the Boulevard Bineau at Neuilly. Delicate health would not allow him to play, but his conversational gifts soon formed a circle about him, under the trees, of young girls and their not yet middle-aged mothers. 'The refreshments were his department, and he always arrived with an enormous box of sweets. When it was hot, he was sent off to a near-by Bar for beer and lemonade. These drinks he would carry back, with much groaning, in an awful old basket borrowed from the proprietor. Sometimes a ball would drop bang in the middle of the cakes, making girls and glasses jump. Marcel always maintained that the players did it "out of mischief, and for no good reason. ..." '[2]

But there may, for all that, have been a perfectly 'good reason', of which the guilty parties were themselves unconscious — Marcel's charm. Very often his sensibility and his animation got on his friends' nerves. They were faintly jealous of him and, though they intended no harm, had in fact no precise intention of any kind, were not averse to bringing discord into the 'Court of Love' — as they called the 'gossip circle' when they were in poetic vein. The game finished, the players would take their relaxation 'within the budding grove', and there savour, with the ladies, Marcel's prattling. Many years later, referring to a book on which he was then working, he wrote to Jeanne Pouquet (who

---

[1] The elegancies of old Vandal's wit
  Appeal to Gabriel and Robert not a bit,
  Nor yet to Jean, and even fail to fit
  The usual gravity of Marcel's mood.
[2] JEANNE MAURICE-POUQUET, *Quelques lettres de Marcel Proust* (Hachette, 1929).

had since become the wife of Gaston de Caillavet) recalling those days to her mind. 'You will find in the text something of the emotion that I used to feel when I was in the habit of asking whether you were going to be one of the tennis-party. But why remind you of things which, with an absurd and rather spiteful obstinacy, you now pretend that you never noticed? . . .'

Indeed, the young girl, already as good as engaged, had never taken very seriously a courtship that was barely noticeable. Nevertheless he did, on one occasion, after a rehearsal of a *Revue* in which Jeanne Pouquet played the part of Cleopatra and Marcel, with conspicuous lack of success, officiated as prompter, send her the following verses — which he himself dismissed as beneath contempt:

On a young lady who tonight assumed the role of Queen Cleopatra, to the undoing and future damnation of a certain young man who happened to be present: and on the metaphysical essence, doubly distilled, of the said Lady.

Peut-être autant que vous Cléopatre était belle,
Mais elle était sans âme: elle était le tableau,
Inconscient gardien d'une grace immortelle
Qui, sans l'avoir compris, réalise le Beau.
Tel est le ciel en sa grise harmonie,
Il nous ferait pleurer tant il est triste et las,
Il exprime le doute et la mélancolie
   Et ne les ressent pas!

Vous avez detroné la reine égyptienne:
Vous êtes à la fois l'artiste et l'œuvre d'art.
Votre esprit est profond comme votre regard,
Pourtant nulle beauté lors n'égalait la sienne.
Ses cheveux sentaient bon comme les fleurs des champs.
J'eusse aimé voir briller, sur ses chairs tant aimées,
Le long déroulement des tresses embaumées.
Sa parole était lente et douce comme un chant;
Ses yeux brillaient dans un fond de nacres humides;
Elle arrêtait son corps en des poses languides . . .

Vous avez détrôné la reine de Cydnus.
Vous êtes une fleur et vous êtes une âme.
Nul penser n'habitait son front ceint de lotus.
Ce n'est pas si gracieux pour une femme.[1]

It was a very indirect and prudent declaration, which never emerged from the realm of fiction.

Far more serious for him was the question of a career. Professor Proust and his wife were too indulgent to bring continuous pressure to bear on him. When Marcel failed in the second part of his Law examination, they felt 'all adrift'.

Marcel Proust to Robert de Billy: '. . . I am just about as puzzled as I well could be, because I've *got* to decide on a career if I'm not to disappoint papa. I feel more and more drawn to the Public Audit Office. This is how I argue the matter. If I don't want to make my career abroad, and am content to settle down in the Foreign Office here, I shall be as bored as I should be in the Public Audit. Probably I should find the latter rather more difficult to get into, but that is compensated by the fact that the probationary period would not absorb my mind to the exclusion of all other interests. I should

[1] Perchance Queen Cleopatra was as fair
As you, but had no soul: was but the sign,
Knowing it not, of something there
That held in guard immortal grace to shrine
Fair Beauty's self. So does a lowering sky
In a great weariness send down the rain,
Sad messenger of doubt and melancholy —
Yet feels no pain.

You have dethroned great Egypt's Queen:
You are at once the artist and his art.
Fathomless as your eyes, your spirit broods apart:
Yet beauty like to hers since has there never been.
Her hair was fragrant as the flowered land.
Fain had I seen upon her lovely brow
The glittering pageant of her scented flow
Of tresses. Gentle her voice that ever fanned
The air to singing: limpid her changing eyes,
And yielding all her body's mobile ecstasies.
The Queen of Cydnus have you indeed cast down:
You are a flower, yet, no less, a soul.
Her lotus-twined brow knew not the frown
Of thought. As far from woman was she as we from the pole.

have plenty of time for other things ... Never have I felt
so much in need of your advice, and I do so wish you were
here ... What is there left for me if I am not to become a
barrister, a doctor, a priest, or. . . ?'

At long last he obtained his parents' consent to his doing what
he had always wanted to do — attend lectures at the Sorbonne
without having any definite end in view. It was at this period that
he came under the influence of Henri Bergson who, as a result of
his marriage with Mademoiselle Neuburger in 1891, had become
his cousin, and who, like Darlu, believed that poetry and philosophy must go hand in hand. 'I am so glad', wrote Proust to one of
his friends,[1] 'that you have read Bergson and feel drawn to him ...
It is as though we were standing together on a high hill ... I think
I have told you how much I admire him, and how good he has
always been to me ...' The two men, however, did not really
see eye to eye, and Bergson, towards the end of his life, said to
Floris Delattre that no work of art can truly be called great that does
not exalt and brace the spirit and this *A la Recherche du temps perdu*
most certainly, in his opinion, does not do. I hope to show later
that it is perfectly possible to take a different view.

Superficially considered, the four or five years that followed
the period of Marcel's military service, were lost years. The
truth, however, is that he was busy storing his honey and filling
the pigeon-holes of his mind with characters and impressions. All
about him, the worlds of literature and politics were producing
new schools and new parties. The strife between Naturalism and
Symbolism was setting the young men of the rising generation
at odds. Marcel Proust was not greatly interested in general
theories. As at Illiers he had garnered a harvest of natural
images, so in Paris he tried to analyse the achievements of art and
to make himself familiar with them. From some of his friends he
learned about painting, and would spend long hours at the Louvre:
from others about music. All agreed in condemning as excessive
his interest in the Faubourg Saint-Germain. It was, says Gregh,
due in part to the fact that he regarded the Faubourg as a kingdom

[1] Georges de Lauris, *A un Ami: Correspondance inédite de Marcel Proust, 1903-1922*
(Amiot-Dumont, Paris, 1948), p. 205.

Peut'être autant que vous Cléopâ-
                    tre était belle.
Mais elle était sans âme : elle était
                    le tableau
Inconscient gardien d'une grâce
                    immortelle
Qui sans l'avoir compris réalise
                    le Beau.
Tel encor est ce ciel en sa grise
                    harmonie
Il nous ferait pleurer tant il est triste
                    et las
Il exprime le doute et la mélan-
                    colie

POEM WRITTEN BY MARCEL PROUST
TO JEANNE POUQUET IN 1892

Et ne les ressent pas !

Mais

Vous avez détrôné la reine égyptienne.

Vous êtes à la fois l'artiste et l'œuvre
d'art.

Vôtre esprit est profond comme vôtre
regard

Pourtant nulle beauté lors n'égalait la
sienne.

Ses cheveux sentaient bon comme
les fleurs
des champs

J'eusse aimé voir briller sur ses
chairs tant aimées

Le long déroulement des tresses embaumées

La parole était lente et douce
   comme un
      Chant
Ses yeux brillaient dans un fond
      de nacès humide
Elle arrêtait son corps en des poses
               languides

~~Pourtant vous~~

Vous avez détrôné la reine ~~royale beauté~~
         vaincue
Vous êtes une fleur et vous êtes une âme

~~Nul penser~~
   ~~elle était faite~~
Nul penser ~~ne trouble~~ n'habitait son
      front ceint de lo.
            tus
Ce n'est déjà pas si gracieux pour une
               femme

À Mlle Pouquet, cette petite ~~comédie~~

Sur une Demoiselle — *salut* — *qui* *respects*
plus profonds
représenta cette nuit la reine
que la pièce
Cléopâtre + pour le plus grand
trouble et la future damnation des yeux d'un jeune
homme qui était là

    Et sur la double essen-
ce métaphysique de la dite
demoiselle.

        Marcel Proust

which he would never succeed in entering. Why is it that he later took such delight in the dazzling social success of a man like Swann? The reason should be obvious: it bore so close a resemblance to his own. In himself, as in Swann, the prestige gained by taste and intelligence managed to overcome a host of hostile prejudices. He did, to be sure, once write to Paul Souday, pointing out what an effort it had needed to put himself in the position of a Narrator who knew no Duchesses, and longed to know them, because he himself had always lived in the great world. That was one of the rare occasions on which he was guilty, consciously or not, of inexactitude. His conquest of Society did, it is true, begin early, but it *was* a conquest, and he had had to fight for it.

His progress upwards began in the houses of those hostesses whom he had known in his youth: Madame Straus, Madame Henri Baignères, her sister-in-law Madame Arthur Baignères (the 'Undefended Tower'), Madame Arman de Caillavet and also Madeleine Lemaire, the water-colourist 'who has created more roses than anybody after God', and in whose salon Proust made the acquaintance of the Princesse Mathilde, and met, for the first time, the Comtesse Greffulhe and Madame Chevigné, both of whom were to serve him as models later on. It was there that he became intimate with the musician, Reynaldo Hahn, 'who had every merit to excess and a genius of charm'. Three years younger than Marcel, born in Venezuela but deeply imbued with French culture, Reynaldo had a precocious talent, exquisite taste and an oddly universal intelligence. Whether playing and singing at the piano, or talking of books and people, he could improvise in a manner that was delicate, mercurial and quite inimitable. 'I love the way you sing', Pauline Viardot once said to him: 'it is so simple and so true.' His friends felt the same about his conversation.

Marcel Proust and Reynaldo were born to be friends. They had the same deeply critical love of culture, the same horror of over-emphasis, and in their assumed frivolity there was something of the same painful solemnity. It was to Reynaldo that Proust owed his understanding of music, and that collection of scattered fragments which gave birth to the 'little phrase' of

Vinteuil. They were devoted to one another. Together they read the great masterpieces of literature, Marcus Aurelius, and *Les Mémoires d'Outre-Tombe*, and were at one in admiring the nobility which radiates from those works. Marcel valued very highly Reynaldo's innate feeling for the beauties of literary achievement and Reynaldo praised Marcel for feeling that the musical passage which, in Duparc's *Invitation au Voyage*, stresses the words *Mon enfant, ma sœur* has an effect of redundancy. They both loved nature; they both indulged in moods of melancholy pessimism. 'One must grow resigned to the feeling of sadness which inevitably becomes the daily bread of all persons of intelligence', wrote Reynaldo in his diary, 'and direct one's gaze upwards, if one is not, as Madame de Sévigné says, to fall a prey to impatience.' Marcel Proust's philosophy was scarcely different. Upon a perfect community of tastes they built a friendship which kept them, for many years, inseparable.

In 1893, at Madeleine Lemaire's, Proust met Comte Robert de Montesquiou, a 'gentleman-poet' (then about thirty-eight), 'whose general airs and carriage were copied by a crowd of disciples . . . a man whose very arrogance had a seductive charm'.[1] An aesthete 'at once absurd and fascinating, half musketeer, half prelate'[2] he was said to have been the original of Huysmans' Des Esseintes. In his verse, and in his collection of rare 'pieces', he revelled in the complexites of the *fin de siècle*. 'His hands, impeccably gloved, performed a variety of elegant gestures with much smooth flexing of the wrists . . . Occasionally he would remove one glove and point heavenwards an exquisite, exclamatory hand of which the sole adornment was a single but exotic ring. And, as the hand went up, so would the intonation of his voice rise to a pitch of stridency like the sudden blare of brass in an orchestral ensemble, or drop with a plaintive hint of tears, while his eyebrows drew together into the semblance of a circumflex accent . . . '[3] Some there were who accused him of effeminacy. To this charge he made arrogant reply:

[1] FRANÇOIS MAURIAC, *Du côté de chez Proust*, pp. 50-1 (La Table Ronde, Paris, 1947).
[2] J. DE RICAUMONT, *Lettres de Robert Montesquiou au Prince Sévastos* (Revue de Paris, July 1947).
[3] E. DE CLERMONT-TONNERRE, *Robert de Montesquiou et Marcel Proust* (Flammarion, Paris, 1925) *passim*.

L'efféminé souvent dompte la femme et l'homme
Sans être dominé.
Voulez-vous bien me dire où gît le faible, en somme
Et la faiblesse, alors, de cet efféminé?[1]
His self-conceit was insolent beyond belief, yet he could talk
brilliantly, and comment with great originality on men and
pictures, poets and artists. He played the pontiff in the salons
of Paris, where he started a fashion for Whistler and Gustave
Moreau. He could, he boasted, open all doors to those whom he
chose to take under his wing. But, at heart, he was an unhappy
man, the victim of a 'strange, maladjusted temperament which he
was incapable of changing, from which he could never escape'.
His harshness was the fruit of this unhappiness, his arrogance the
expression of a desire to give evidence of a virility which many
thought he did not possess.

At their very first meeting, Proust saw at once how valuable
such a man might be to him in his two rôles of social aspirant and
writer. His earliest letters to him he signs — 'Your humble,
ardent and wholly fascinated Marcel Proust.' He was aware of
Montesquiou's thirst for admiration, and set himself to quench it.
'You are something very much more than the exquisite decadent
of popular imagination . . . the one really superior man of your
world . . . the greatest critic of the arts that there has been for
a very long while . . . at once Cornelian and Hermetic . . .
Your mind is a garden filled with rare blooms . . .' If he submitted
one of his Essays to Montesquiou, it was only, he wrote, 'after
first having to overcome the sense of my ridiculous presumption
in daring to exchange a poor earthworm against a starry firmament'. He praised his patron's flashing glance, the persuasive
thunder of his voice. 'I am for ever, my dear sir, seeing you with
fresh eyes. My knowledge of you, my sense of your bigness,
continually grows. I feel like a man climbing a mountain and
awed by the ever expanding view before his gaze. Yesterday, I
turned one more corner, and the vista then opened to me was the
finest I have yet encountered. But have I, even now, reached the

---

[1] Not seldom the effeminate to either sex will play
The master, yet never bow the knee.
How then can he be weak? — I bid you say:
Where, in such a one, can we true weakness see?

summit? . . .'[1] But there is another of his letters in which a note of ambiguity sounds in the symphony of adulation: 'Are you soon returning to that Versailles whose pensive Marie Antoinette you are, and self-willed Louis XVI? I salute Your Grace and Your Majesty. . . .'

For all this unprecedented praise he sought a return. 'Would you, I wonder, introduce me to some of those ladies who are never tired of talking about you; the Comtesse Greffulhe, the Princesse de Léon? . . .' The Comtesse Greffulhe who, before her marriage had been a Caraman-Chimay, excited Marcel's curiosity to an unusual degree. Montesquiou invited him to a party where he saw her as the future Princesse de Guermantes. 'She was wearing a headdress of Polynesian elegance, with a fall of purple orchids to the neck, the effect being that of one of those "flowered hats" of which Monsieur Renan speaks. It is difficult to judge of her, because judgment involves comparison, and there is about her something that one could find in no one else, or, indeed, any-where *at all*. But the secret of her beauty lies in its brilliance, and especially in the enigmatic quality of her eyes. I have never seen so lovely a woman. . . .'

Gradually, Proust became one of Montesquiou's intimates. He grew familiar with his 'moods of affability and sulkiness, his reticences and bursts of frankness, his timidities, his moments of rash imprudence'.[2] Storms gathered. Mutual friends told the poet that Proust was in the habit of indulging in cruel mimicry, that he had caught to the life his voice, his laugh, his style, and would, like him, stamp his foot and throw out his chest, 'with just his glint of laughter in the eyes, and his way of nervously gesturing with his fingers'. Jupiter thundered: the mortal trembled. 'Who can feel anger at the thunderbolt that strikes him, since it comes from Heaven?' As to the 'imitations', what were they but the product of excessive admiration? 'If the charge goes further, if anyone has used in your hearing the word "cari-cature", I have only to quote your own remark that "*When what someone else has said is repeated, it is never true.*"' Finally, Proust

---

[1] *Correspondance générale de Marcel Proust: Tome I; Lettres à Robert de Montesquiou* (Plon, Paris, 1930), pp. 40, 53, 67, etc.
[2] J. DE RICAUMONT, op. cit.

gave his solemn word that he would refrain from such 'monkey-tricks', and Montesquiou continued to initiate him into the 'poetry of snobbery'.

For, if one was to believe in the Great World, it was essential to live in the intimacy of a man 'who never entertained a single doubt of its reality'. There was nothing base in Proust's liking for Society. What amused him was not so much the fact of his being invited as the opportunity it gave him to examine the social machine, to probe 'into the relations of human beings to one another in the world of fashion and the realm of love'. He was filled with curiosity about 'smart people', but so he was about people of all kinds. 'I have drawn no distinction between working people, members of the middle class, and aristocrats, and would choose my friends indifferently from all those varying levels, with perhaps, a preference for the workers, and, after them, for the aristocrats, not so much on grounds of taste' but because they are 'ready to be polite to anyone who comes their way, and behave like those pretty women who are only too pleased to distribute their smiles when they know what happiness they give to their recipients.'

The great world counted for him, says Lucien Daudet, 'much as flowers count for the botanist, and not at all as they count for the gentleman who buys a bouquet'. Had he been confined within the limits of the *literary* world, he would have produced a very poor crop. To a woman friend he said one day: 'Madame de Chevigné is for ever at me to meet Porto-Riche. But I *am* Porto-Riche. I had much rather get to know Mademoiselle d'Hinnisdal.' He realized, as Racine and Balzac had done before him, that a world whose members are not compelled to work for their living, a world, that is, in which there was freedom for every sort of development, was the ideal seeding-ground for human passions, and the backcloth against which they could be shown to the best advantage. His power of judgment was always marked by a fine lucidity. 'The artist must serve only the truth, and must have no respect for rank. In so far as he takes any note of it at all in composing his pictures, it can only be as of one among many principles of differentiation, on the same level as, say, nationality, race and environment. There is something of interest to be found at every social level, and it is a matter of equal concern to the artist whether he portray the manners of a queen or the habits of a seamstress . . . ' In cultivating Montesquiou, he was preparing the ground for Charlus. 'Proust is much to be admired for having ventured into the monster's jaws in his determination to paint an accurate picture of what he might find there: for having allowed himself to be inoculated with the virus of snobbery, and so made it possible to gain a truer knowledge of it.'[1]

The word 'snob' is not really applicable to Proust except during one short period of juvenile intoxication. The true snob likes a person, or accepts an idea, not because the person is likeable, or because the idea seems to him to be true, but because both happen to be fashionable, and familiarity with them gives him a sense of self-satisfaction. But that could never have been said of Proust. He was always genuinely interested in his monsters. 'To take pleasure in somebody's company merely because one of his ancestors went on the Crusades, is a matter of vanity: intelligence has nothing whatever to do with it. But to take pleasure in somebody's company because his grandfather's name is frequently mentioned in Alfred de Vigny or in Chateaubriand, or (and I don't mind admitting that I find this particular seduction quite irresistible) because her family arms appear in the great Rose-Window at Amiens . . . that is where intellectual sin really begins. . . .'[2]

A sin may be intellectual, but it remains a sin. It is not snobbery in its pure essence. Proust loved to study, in Paris no less than at Illiers, the historical formation of various social environments, and the way in which they grow old and worm-eaten, until at last they break down altogether. Montesquiou was a superb specimen, and life within the confines of his 'Court' provided an ideal post of observation. He demanded adulation, and Marcel, the better to observe him, paid the price he asked. 'Our excessive compliments are like Notes of Hand. Sooner or later they will have to be settled, and the threat of them hangs over our heads all our life long . . .' Because he had spoiled Montes-

---

[1] FRANÇOIS MAURIAC, *Du côté de chez Proust* (La Table Ronde, Paris, 1947).
[2] *Pastiches et Mélanges: Journées de Lecture.* Translated by Gerard Hopkins in *Marcel Proust: A Selection from His Miscellaneous Writings* (Allan Wingate, London, 1948).

quiou by the very extremity of his praise, Proust found himself condemned to increase the dose each time it had to be administered. But he did not regard flattery as a very heinous crime. 'Flattery is sometimes no more than the overflow of tenderness, frankness the slobber of ill-humour.' He has been accused of being obsequious, but his most effusive friendships were for people who gave him nothing in return but the pleasure of their company. One such friend was Reynaldo Hahn, another was the young Englishman, Willie Heath, dead at twenty-two, to whose memory he dedicated his first published volume: '*To my friend Willie Heath, who died in Paris on the 3rd October, 1893....*'

> Often, of a morning, I would meet you in the Bois where, having seen me from afar, you would await my coming, standing at ease beneath the great branches like one of those young lords painted by Van Dyck, whose pensive elegance you shared. Their elegance, like yours, is less a matter of clothes than of bodies, and even their bodies seem to have derived it — to be forever deriving it afresh, from the spirit that inhabits them. It is a moral elegance. Everything on those occasions combined to heighten that melancholy resemblance, even to the background of leafy shadow against which Van Dyck so often immobilized a King taking his daily saunter. Like so many of his models, you, too, were fated to die young, and in your eyes, as in theirs, one could see in alternation the darkness of presentiment and the sweet light of a resigned awareness. But if your proud race belonged of right to the brush of a Van Dyck, it was of Da Vinci that one was reminded by the intensity of your spiritual life. Often, with finger raised, and with smiling, inscrutable eyes, held silent by the ultimate riddle of the Universe, you would bring to my mind a recollection of Leonardo's *John the Baptist*. It was our dream, in those days almost our plan, to spend more and more of our lives with one another in a circle of men and women chosen for their great-heartedness, and sufficiently far removed from foolishness and vice and malice to give us a feeling that we were proof against the arrows of men's spite....'

Swann loved Odette because he fancied that he saw in her Zephora, the daughter of Jethro, as she is depicted in one of the frescoes of the Sistine Chapel. Similarly, Proust loved Willie Heath because, for him, he was Da Vinci's John the Baptist. There is great beauty in that dedication. It tells of the delicate sentiment that animated friendships at which the evil-minded shot their poisoned arrows, and also of the desperate melancholy deep in the heart of the charming youth who set out in evening dress with a flower in his buttonhole, to discover the great world. There are passages in the *Notebooks* that bring vividly to mind those days of affection, anguish and purity:

> . . . Sometimes they have a friend of their own age, or younger, for whom they feel an ardent love, and then they dread, worse even than death, the thought that he should ever know the sin, the vice that fills them with a sense of shame and remorse . . . Fortunately, they think him incapable of such knowledge, and then is added to their love something of veneration and respect, such as an old lecher may feel for a pure young girl, so that they are ready, for his sake, to make great sacrifices . . . If, at some moment of mourning, they pluck up courage to touch his forehead with their lips, the joy that comes to them is of a kind to warm them all their lives . . .

Only a very hard, or a very foolish, man would laugh at that passage. Proust, when it was written, had engaged in a struggle with himself. He introduced one of his earliest short stories with this quotation from the *Imitation of Christ*: 'The desires of the flesh drive us hither and thither; but, the deed once done, what is left? — only remorse of conscience and an expense of spirit. We set forth in joy and often return in sadness, and the pleasures of the night often make our morning gloomy. Thus do the joys of the flesh at first bring delusive happiness, but, in the end, wound and slay . . .' He would gladly, in all sincerity, have kept his affections on the Platonic level. But love, no matter how perverted, is love still, and suffers from love's storms. In vain does it strive to resemble the constancy and quiet of friendship.

CHAPTER III

EARLY WORKS

An amateur is one whose search for beauty has never become a profession, and the word is never used in a complimentary sense. ALAIN

I

LE BANQUET

THE desire to write gave him no rest. On those evenings when he occupied the 'bottom of the table' in the houses where he was invited because he was such good company, he would listen to 'the Brichots, the Saniettes and the Norpois, holding forth in front of the gilt-bronze fenders', at Madame Straus's and at Madame de Caillavet's. The stars of the 'dinner firmament' at that time, were Bourget, France, Brochard, Vogüé, Maupassant, Porto-Riche, Hervieu, Hermant, Vanderem. Marcel Proust burned incense at their shrines — and took their measure. They, for their part, struck by his penetrating intelligence, deplored the fact that he did scarcely any work.

'How do you manage, Monsieur France' — asked Proust — 'how do you manage to know so much?'

'The answer is quite simple, my dear Marcel. When I was your age, I was not, like you, good looking. Nobody, in fact, much cared for me. Consequently, I was never asked out, but stayed at home reading, reading endlessly.'

Already his former school friends were trying their wings in many different directions. Jacques Bizet was a dresser at one of the hospitals. Fernand Gregh had published his first volume of verse, and was reading for his Master of Arts degree in Literature. Henri Rabaud, one of Massenet's pupils, had great hopes of winning the Prix de Rome. Marcel was still uncertain of his future, and his friends never ceased to wonder at his life of studious idleness. What could he not have done if only he had turned his mind to something? In 1892, Fernand Gregh wrote a 'pen portrait' of Marcel:

73

Fabrice craves the affection of others, and has it. He attracts women, and a certain kind of man, by his beauty . . . He has, too, what is sufficient to gain him the friendship of the average man, — charm, an all-enveloping charm, which, despite its seeming passivity, is really very active. He produces the impression that he is giving — though all the while he is taking . . . Everyone who has known him has been, in turn, his friend. But because he loves, not so much his friends as his own image in them, he quickly tires, and can terminate a friendship with an ease which is equalled only by the pains he formerly took to begin it. In this matter, the dexterity of his performance is beyond all praise. Let me add that he is peculiarly skilled in the art of flattery, and can always lay his finger on the vulnerable spot in each man's vanity. Better still he knows when not to flatter those who dislike flattery, and that, in itself, is one way of giving pleasure. He is quite capable of waiting for an hour in the rain or the snow to meet a friend whom, a fortnight later, he will quietly drop overboard, and whose name, in two years' time, he will have to hear repeated several times before he can fit a face to it. But all this gives a very poor idea of his ability to charm . . . It is not just that he has good looks, grace, wit and intelligence. All these things he has at once, and such a concurrence of qualities makes him even more engaging than does the ingenuity of his flattery. . . .

It was the great period of 'Symbolism'. New magazines were flourishing, numerous as hawthorn buds in May. The Condorcet group, consisting of Gregh, Proust, Bizet, Louis de la Salle, Daniel Halévy, Robert Dreyfus, Robert de Flers, with the later addition of Léon Blum, Gabriel Trarieux, Gaston Arman de Caillavet and Henri Barbusse, decided to start one. Each of the founder-members was to contribute ten francs a month, and this would produce a sum sufficient to launch a monthly journal limited to four hundred copies. The choice of a title gave rise to much passionate controversy. Robert Dreyfus suggested *Le Chaos*: other proposals were: *Les Divergences, Opinions et Variétés, l'Anarchie Littéraire, Varia, Revue Timide, Revue des Opinions, l'Indépendance, Le Toupet périodique, Revue des Futurs et Conditionnels, Aperçus littéraires et artistiques, Chemins dans la Brume, Les Tâtonnements, Vers la Clairière, Les Guitares,* etc. . . . . The Minutes, drafted by Jacques Bizet, state:

> We have decided definitely to take as our title *Le Banquet*. It was necessary to bring some pressure to bear on Messrs Fernand Gregh and Robert Dreyfus before this choice could be ratified.
> N.B. Some minutes later Monsieur Gregh rallied enthusiastically to our title, and, after two hours had elapsed, Monsieur Dreyfus, who had been hunting for me everywhere, ran into me in the street and declared that he thought our title a 'very good one' — praise which, in his mouth, is far less lukewarm than it sounds . . . A reading committee, consisting of Messrs Daniel Halévy, Robert Dreyfus and Marcel Proust has been appointed. Its verdict, though always open to discussion, will determine the acceptance or rejection of contributions. . . .

In practice, the Reading Committee failed to function, and the proposed oligarchy became a dictatorship — that of Fernand Gregh, the editor and instigator of *Le Banquet*. The life of the magazine carried it through only eight numbers, but almost all the members of the editorial committee were destined to achieve fame or, at least, notoriety. Young though they were, many of them contributed articles on Nietzsche, Swinburne and Schopenhauer. They were surprised and faintly shocked when Marcel Proust proposed to write for *Le Banquet* a series of portraits of female leaders of fashion and of celebrated courtesans, written in a *fin de siècle* style smelling strongly of France, Maeterlinck and Montesquiou. They indulged his whim, however, because they loved his wit and the sound of his voice — 'that voice, with its undercurrents of laughter, hesitating and self-conscious, which Proust adopted when he told a story. He told it tormentedly, organizing his narrative into a system of locks and vestibules, interspersing it with exhausted drops, pauses and elaborate courtesies, and all the while fanning out his moustache, with white-gloved fingers. . . . '[1]

[1] JEAN COCTEAU, 'La Voix de Marcel Proust' (*Nouvelle Revue Française*, January 1st, 1923).

His friends reproached him for the number of articles he wrote to please others, to be '*nice*' — a word which, whenever he spoke of himself, he always enclosed, ironically, in inverted commas. In the very first number (March 1892) he wrote a highly eulogistic review of a very indifferent 'Christmas Story' which had been published in the *Revue des Deux Mondes*. Its author was Louis Ganderax, a member of the staff of the École Normale Supérieure. Like so many professors of the day, Lemaître, Desjardins, Doumic, Brunetière, he regarded the teaching trade as a high road to literature. He was so morbidly scrupulous an editor that he would draw attention to the repetition of some word or phrase at an interval of several pages and, as France said, would 'track down a hiatus' into the very interstices of a word. He was a close friend of Madame Straus, and that fact alone, in Proust's eyes, was sufficient justification for an article. But what the editors of *Le Banquet* did not, and could not, see was that Marcel Proust was using the shoddy little story as an excuse for trying out his method.

Perhaps the most fragrant of all those flowers of literature which a little thought so quickly serves to wither, is what I may, perhaps, be allowed to call, our mystic hope in the future. The unhappy lover who, rejected today as he was yesterday, hopes that tomorrow she whom he loves but who loves not him, will have a sudden change of heart; the man whose powers are unequal to the duty laid upon him, who says to himself 'tomorrow I shall find that, by some miracle, the determination now so lacking, is mine at last'; — all those who, with eyes fixed upon the East await a sudden gleam (believing in such) which will fill the sullen sadness of their sky with radiance — these, one and all, indulge a hope of the future which is mystic in the sense that it springs wholly from their own desires, and can find justification in no rational anticipation. Alas! a day always comes when we no longer feel that at any moment a passionate letter may reach us from the fair one who, till then, has shown herself so utterly indifferent when at last we realize that men's characters do not change with dramatic suddenness, that our desires cannot control the wills of others, dominated as they are by irresistible forces —

yes, a day comes when we understand that tomorrow will be no different from today since of today will it be made. . . .

He praised Ganderax for giving his story a worldly setting:

Art sends its roots so deep into our social life that, in the particular fiction that serves to clothe a general truth of sentiment, the manners and tastes of a period or a class may often play a large part, and may, in a very definite fashion, add greatly to the pleasure it can give us. Was it not to some extent because his audience consisted of ladies of the Court who revelled in the torments of human passion that Racine, when he wished, in those dramas all compact of guilt and loveliness, to show the consummation of tragic destinies, chose most frequently to summon back to life the ghosts of dead princesses and of kings? . . .

In *Le Banquet* we may read, too, the portrait of the Comtesse Adhéaume de Chevigné, whom Proust admired, and thought, though never very seriously, that he loved, and who drove him to despair when, after he had pursued her into the shade of the trees of the Avenue Gabriel, she would give him no answer, but repeated parrot-wise a single phrase: 'Fitz-James is waiting for me': a portrait in which we can already see a foreshadowing of the whole race of Guermantes — 'doubtless engendered by a Goddess and a bird'.

Often at the theatre she is to be seen leaning on the edge of her box, her white-gloved arm thrusting straight upward with the pride of a flower's stem, to where her chin rests on the garnered splendour of her hand. Her superb body fills to perfection the white, habitual gauziness of clothes that hang about her now like folded wings. The thought comes to one of some dreaming bird perched on an elegant and fragile leg. Charming it is, too, to see her feathered fan fluttering beside her, beating at her with its white wing . . . She is a woman lost in dreams, an animal filled with delicate energy, a peacock with wings of snow, a hawk with precious stones for eyes; she moves in a mist of fable, and thrills us with a sense of beauty. . . .

This is genuine Proust, though not, perhaps, Proust at his best. We miss the long swell of the extended rhythms, the suavity of the lovely phrase. Much over-painting will be necessary before that portrait can boast the finish of a Vermeer. But already the essential images are present which, later, will be built up into the solid presentation of Oriane.

If, in 1892, Proust's love of truth risked being smothered by his desire to please, he was fully conscious of the danger. At the head of the two chapters which compose a story of his entitled *Violante ou la Mondanité*, he inscribed the following quotations from the *Imitation*: 'Have little to do with young people, or with those who dwell in the great world . . . Eschew desire to make a grand display before those who wield power': and, 'Lean not upon a reed that sways in the wind, nor put your confidence in it; for all things are as grass and their glory passes like the flowers of the field. . . .'

The story lacks life, and its characters have the same sort of discarnate unreality which we find in Maeterlinck. The very names of his heroes, at this time, are without material substance and the scene of their existence is 'of the stuff of dreams'. But in that tale the life that its author was living already stands condemned. Well might he have said, making a gloss on Flaubert, 'Violante — *I* am Violante.' The woman who gives her name to the story had been corrupted by a friend, having learned from her 'shameful things of which, till then, she had been ignorant. In them she had found a source of sweet delight, but, with it, shame . . . The strong swell of charity which would have cleansed her like a sea-tide, and levelled all the inequalities that clutter up a worldling's heart, was checked by innumerable dams set up by egotism, coquetry, ambition . . .' Augustin, who loves Violante, hopes that disgust may save her: 'But he had counted without a force which, if it draws its nourishment from vanity, can overcome disgust, contempt and even boredom, namely, the force of habit . . .' The autobiographical element in these passages is as crude as it is obvious. Youth's love of playing with abstractions drains the story of all life. Nevertheless, the essential facts of the author's own drama — natural nobility — accidental soiling — shame, and finally habit — all are there. But *Le Banquet* soon died, having lived, like all such magazines, only so long as the initial enthusiasm lasted: and Marcel Proust's existence showed once again as frivolous, brilliant, sorrowful and empty.

II

DOMESTICITIES

From 1892 to 1900 Proust's manner of life was modified by illness, but the change was progressive and slow. His attacks of asthma increased in number and intensity. There were, however, long intervals between them, during which he could lead a more or less normal existence — going to parties, staying at Auteuil with his great-uncle, at Trouville with Madame Straus or Hugo Finlay, the Banker, and at Evian-les-Bains. He even undertook trips into the French countryside, and later went both to Holland and to Italy. But because his attacks were always more violent in the day-time than at night, especially in summer, he got gradually into the habit of working and seeing his friends at times which nobody else would have dreamed of devoting to those purposes.

He was living with his parents at No. 9 Boulevard Malesherbes:

> . . . It was a large, handsome house, with those spacious, comfortable rooms which we associate with the prosperous middle-class families of the period between 1890 and 1900. The impression it has left with me (I can see it all again quite clearly if I shut my eyes) is that of a somewhat dark interior crammed with heavy furniture, swaddled in hangings, choked with carpets — the prevailing colours being red and black — the sort of interior that was typical of its age, and was not so far removed as we are inclined to think, from the world of sombre bric-à-brac that we find in Balzac.[1]

Doctor Proust, though age had thickened his features, had, with his grey beard and still black moustache, that air of high

[1] FERNAND GREGH, *L'Age d'Or*, p. 154.

nobility which we find in Holbein's portraits of great merchant-princes. His second son, Robert, was like him in appearance, and was making good progress with his surgical studies. Marcel was so bound up with his mother that he remained as much dependent on her as he had been when a small child. Dr. Proust was a critical and distressed observer of their constant embraces, their excessively emotional relations. The supreme concern of Madame Adrien Proust and of Marcel had always been to 'pacify' papa, and they lived in a perpetual conspiracy directed to achieving this purpose. Whenever Marcel found it impossible to sleep, he would write letters to his mother, and leave them in the hall, so that she might find them there in the morning when, at last, he had managed to drop off.

> Darling Mamma: — I can't sleep, so I am writing this note just to say that I am thinking of you. I should so very much like — and have made up my mind that I soon shall be able — to get up at the same time as you, so that the two of us could take our morning coffee together. To feel that we fill the same period of time with our sleeping and our waking, would — will — be for me a dear delight. I went to bed at half-past-one with the intention of doing so . . . and I am planning to change the order of my nights, so as to bring them more into accordance with your wishes, and shall feel, physically, much closer to you when our lives are arranged to the same time-table, in the knowledge that we have about us the same rooms, that we breathe air of the same temperature, observe the same rules, and mutually approve of one another, even if — at the moment, alas! — that satisfaction is withheld from us. I am sorry that I left the smoking-room desk in so untidy a state, but I was working very hard up to the last moment. This excessively handsome envelope is the only one that I could find. Don't let Marie-Antoine talk too much, and please shut the kitchen door so that I shan't have to hear her voice.
> . . . My attack was so violent that it kept me from writing, and I am afraid that this note is not at all what I meant it to be. You won't be at all pleased with it . . . and I would so much rather please you, even if it meant having an attack,

than displease you and be spared one . . . So I will just send you a kiss and leave it at that, because I am on the point of dropping off. I've not taken any Trional, so *please* no noise, and no windows. By the time this reaches you I shall already be asleep. . . .

. . . An attack of asthma of *quite incredible violence and tenacity* — that is the sad schedule of a night which I had to spend upright on my feet, but in spite of it I got up early. God knows what sort of a day I shall have! At this moment (about seven o'clock) I am drinking hot coffee and milk. *Please* don't let them open so much as a crack before half-past 9 or 10, because the results would be terrible. There is an odd sort of dust in my room, and a smell which was left, I think, by the barber. They probably had a good deal to do with this frightful attack, and they'll start it up again the moment I go back to my room. I occupied the time by reading an extremely interesting article by Lenotre in *Le Temps*. A thousand fond kisses. . . .[1]

This morbid affection, like all excessive feelings, was productive of occasional friction. The mother, responsible for the running of her house, could not but side with the servants when they complained of being disturbed at the most unearthly hours in order to prepare fumigations. Blamed by her husband for being too indulgent, she would, for short periods, assume a mask of severity. Marcel, accustomed to an endless routine of spoiling, took such changes ill. One harsh word would set him sobbing the whole night long. If, on the other hand, he showed signs of becoming restive, and strove to free himself from her control, she was miserable at the thought that her influence over him was waning. 'So long as my little boy was content to be led by me, all went well. But as soon as children grow up they think they know better than their mothers, and want to have their own way . . .' She knew that he was generous to recklessness and, when he was on his travels, kept as tight a hold on his expenses as she would have done had he been a boy of fifteen.

[1] Unpublished letters, in the possession of Madame Mante-Proust.

Marcel Proust to his mother: 'Two mornings ago you sent me 300 francs. That day I spent nothing. Yesterday my return-ticket to Thonon cost me 2 francs, 10, and the carriage which I had to take when I went to the Brancovans in the evening, 7 francs, including tip. Out of the 300 francs I have spent (1) 167 francs in settlement of a bill: (2) forty francs more on a bill for medicines, cotton wool, etc., which I had ordered on account, though as a rule I pay cash, for reasons that I will explain: (3) 10 francs (Monsieur Cottin said that was the amount I ought to give) to the waiter who brings up my morning coffee from the kitchen: (4) 10 francs to the lift-boy who has done all sorts of odd jobs for me — which was what young Galand said I ought to tip him. I am writing this in a hurry, and may have overlooked some item. But the total of the above comes, if I am not wrong, to 167 + 40 + 10 + 10 = 263.10, which leaves me only 300 − 263.10, or (if I have done the sum correctly) 63.90 . . . So much for business. Chat and affection follow tomorrow. A thousand kisses.'[1]

His circle of friends was growing gradually wider. Not only was he making progress in high society but, slowly though surely, was advancing into the world of letters. It was the period of 'that pleasing, simple-minded, massenet-ic and dumasfils-ist renaissance'[2] which, starting with Sarcey and Gounod, pressed onwards to Daudet, Maupassant and, later, to Bourget and Loti. Proust who, as a child, had delighted in Alphonse Daudet, whom he regarded as the French Dickens, made his acquaintance in the flesh at the house of Madame Arthur Baignères. With Reynaldo Hahn he became a regular visitor at the 'Thursdays' in the Rue de Bellechasse. The novelist's sons had developed a friendship for him, Lucien the youngest, in particular, who had something of Marcel's humour and keen sensibility, and shared his horror of ready-made phrases which 'give one the toothache and set one squinting' — 'Squinneries' they called them — '*The vast expanse of blue*', '*La Côte d'Azur*' — for the Mediterranean, '*Albion*' — for England, '*The Emerald Isle*' — for Ireland, '*Our Boys in Blue*' — for

---

[1] From an unpublished letter in the possession of Madame Mante-Proust.
[2] Leon-Paul Fargue.

the French army, '*The Rocky Isle of Guernsey*' — for exile, the whole
of the song which is called *Paimpolaise*, etc. It was a 'Squinnery',
too, for anyone who didn't know English to throw off a phrase
like 'Bye, bye'. Any 'Squinnery' would set them off giggling un-
controllably (though Marcel concealed his merriment behind his
hand), and these fits of mirth, when indulged at the expense
of persons liable to take offence, could be very embarrassing.
Doubled up with laughter, and quite beyond the power of
speech, Lucien Daudet and Marcel Proust had, on one occasion,
to take refuge in flight when Montesquiou turned on them his
disapproving and suspicous eye. He never forgave them.

Lucien Daudet was well aware of his friend's eccentricities, of
the detailed, though mad and nebulous, theories which he held
on the subject of dress ('You must be careful of your appearance',
wrote Madame Adrien Proust; 'and *please* no more Frankish-king
haircuts'), and was not slow to contradict the exaggerations of
those who did not know Proust well, and described him as being
always a glutton for social tit-bits, *always* dressed in a way that
outraged accepted fashions, with scraps of cotton wool showing
above the collar of his coat, which he kept turned up for fear of
draughts, *always* prodigal of hyperbolic flattery, *always* scattering
ridiculous tips.[1] It *was* true, of course, that a scrap of cotton wool
might *occasionally* show above his collar, and that his friends would
push it out of sight with a smile and a murmured 'Really, Marcel!'
It *was* true that one evening he had borrowed a hundred francs
from the Hall Porter at the Ritz, and then added with a kindly
smile, 'Keep them, I meant them for you . . .' But those who
loved him paid little attention to such harmless oddities. What
they admired in him was 'an almost childlike gentleness, a charming simplicity, an air of distinction that was at all times visible, a
natural nobility of feeling', a code of good manners which was
as strongly stressed in his dealings with the humble as with the
mighty (he would, for example, address a letter to Monsieur le
Concierge de Monsieur le Duc de Guiche), a generosity which
would involve him in an endless search, whenever he wanted to
give a present, before he could find something that he thought

[1] Lucien Daudet, *Autour de soixante lettres de Marcel Proust* (Gallimard, Paris, 1929),
pp. 13, 16, 18-19, 25, 27, etc.

really pretty, something that he hoped the recipient might like, something from a really good shop. 'Fruit and flowers for a woman always had to come from Lemaître or Charton: jellies intended for a sick friend would be ordered at Tanrade's. If he happened to borrow a handkerchief when he had forgotten his own, it was always returned to its owner folded between two sachets of Houbigant. The smallest wedding-present necessitated days of discussion and hesitation: he *must* find something that would precisely harmonize with the personalities of the two people concerned, something that would not just do for anybody ...' As to those excessive tips of his — a negligible facet of his generosity — his assumed ignorance of the value of money was, says Lucien Daudet, a deliberate pretence indulged in for the express purpose of making people believe that, if he was good to those who served him, it was never 'on purpose', but, as it were, as the result of a mistake. His large-scale charities were kept carefully concealed, but all through his life, he could never hear misfortune mentioned without wanting, at once, to contribute to its alleviation.

These qualities, added to his personal charm, brought him many friends, and kept them loyal. To be one of them was not easy, because 'he was always filled with mistrust, and had a certain contempt for humanity even in those early years, a contempt which work and the relative solitude of his life greatly increased, so that he was sometimes unable to distinguish between those who were capable of meanness and those who were not ...' But when he did become intimate with anybody there was something touching in his almost childlike gaiety, in the deep nobility of his nature which on those occasions found expression. Those of his familiars whom Lucien Daudet used most often to meet at the Boulevard Malesherbes were Reynaldo Hahn, Robert de Billy, Frédéric de Madrazo, the painter ('Coco Madrazo') and Robert de Flers. The two brothers Proust, Marcel and Robert, were fast friends. In spite of their differences of character, in spite, too, of the fact that, in the normal disagreements of every day, Robert usually sided with his father while Marcel had the support of his mother, 'their affection for one another gave real meaning to the phrase: *brotherly love*'.

In 1895, in order to satisfy Professor Proust who had so long wished to see him embarked upon a profession, Marcel agreed to sit for an examination which would qualify him as 'honorary attaché' at the Bibliothèque Mazarine. He was the most detached of attachés, and his life became one long series of 'leaves'. Still, there were periods when he was on duty, and Lucien Daudet would fetch him from the Institut and take him off to spend a few hours at the Louvre, or to a matinee of classical drama at the Comédie Française. Marcel, carrying a vaporizer filled with some sort of antiseptic, would hold forth in front of the pictures, explaining to Daudet the beauty of Fra Angelico's colours which he described as 'creamy and edible', or the difference between Rembrandt's two *Philosophers*. 'He was a wonderful critic of art. Most people at that time were ignoramuses where painting was concerned. Whatever he found in a canvas, whether of pictorial significance or intellectual meaning, was marvellous and communicable. It was never just an arbitrary, personal impression, but something unforgettably true that belonged, objectively, to the picture he was considering. . . .'

> . . . He would come to a halt in front of the man with the red nose and the red dress, smiling down at a child, and exclaim: 'It's the living image of Monsieur de Lau! It's quite unbelievably like him! . . . How nice it would be if it really was he! Ah, my dear' — he would go on, with that curious puckering of the nose which was so typical of him, and that display of animal spirits which he would sometimes produce, as though there were some overplus of energy in himself from gallopings and frolics in the open air — 'what fun it is to look at pictures! . . .'[1]

He was still assiduous in his haunting of the great world, but he saw something, too, of what the younger Dumas called the 'half world'. With this he came in contact at the house of Laure Hayman, that 'lovely, sweet and firm friend' whom he observed with all the meticulous concentration of a collector of human types, and whom he loaded with flowers, both actual and episto-

[1] Lucien Daudet, op. cit., p. 18.

lary. *Proust to Laure Hayman:* 'Dear friend and dear delight — here are fifteen chrysanthemums . . . I hope that the stalks are excessively long, as I ordered them to be, and that the flowers, proud and sad as you are, proud because they are beautiful, sad because of life's foolishness, will bring you pleasure...' Laure Hayman prided herself on her knowledge of French and English, and had a way of trying out upon her friends the products of an ill-informed pedantry. One on occasion she reproached Proust for having written *comme qui dirait*:

> Anatole France — Proust replied — with whom I am sitting at this moment, assures me, and gives me leave to tell you, that the particular locution to which you take exception is irreproachable and not at all vulgar. Need I tell you that I sacrifice it on your altar with all my heart, and would rather be wrong with you than right with all the Académie at my back. In this France thoroughly agrees with me . . . I kneel before you for absolution, and embrace you fondly — if absent-mindedly. . . .

Very absent-mindedly — of that there could be no doubt. But in 1896 he told her, 'in the kindest possible way', of the death of 'poor old Uncle Louis Weil', at whose house he had first met the Lady in Pink. *Proust to Laure Hayman:* 'Knowing, as I do, how fond you were of him, I did not want you to learn of the event from the newspapers . . . I have an idea that it will make you feel a little sad, but it is kinder, isn't it, to tell you like this? . . .' And next day: 'I have just received your little note. Thank you for saying what you do about my uncle. His religion makes no provision for funeral services. There will be a small gathering at his house, 102 Boulevard Haussmann, at half past three, and we shall go straight from there to Père Lachaise (but I am afraid that it may prove too tiring for you, and there will be very few women in the party). But what a ridiculous idea that is of yours that you could possibly shock anybody by your presence! They would all be deeply touched. . .' Laure Hayman did not go to the funeral, but she sent a 'cyclist messenger' to the cemetery with a wreath — the only one, for there were no flowers at the ceremony. 'When

86

mamma was told, she gave instructions that the wreath should be buried with my uncle, and this was done. It might well be said of you, as it was said of a certain lady in the seventeenth century, that "goodness of heart and generosity were not the least of her elegancies. ..."'

The one lasting sorrow of this period was the death of his grandmother. Proust and his mother had been at one in their admiration of this superb old lady who had been more Sévigné than Madame de Sévigné herself. *Madame Adrien Proust to Marcel:* 'I, too, occasionally come across, in Madame de Sévigné, thoughts and savings, that please me much. She says of one of her friends, speaking of her relation with her son, "I, too, know a mother who counts for little in herself, having been wholly made over into her children." Is that not true of your grandmother? — only — she would never have said it. ...'

The death of her mother produced in Madame Adrien Proust a sudden and touching transformation. 'It is not too much to say that she had lost all her gaiety. She seemed to have become melted and fixed into a sort of image of supplication, to be afraid lest, by raising her voice, she might offend the mournful presence that never quitted her . . .' She had taken on, suddenly, the semblance of the departed, whether because her great sorrow had hastened a metamorphosis and brought to the surface someone who already existed within her, or because regret had acted on her with a power of suggestion and imprinted upon her features a resemblance that had always been potential. Now that her mother was dead, she seemed to have a scruple about being other than the woman whom she had so truly admired. She went to Cabourg and sat on the beach where her mother had sat, reading the *Letters* of Madame de Sévigné from the copy that the dead woman had always carried with her. Swathed in crêpe, she walked, a figure all in black, with timid, pious steps, on the self-same sands that those loved feet had trodden before her, and seemed to be looking for one, dead and gone, whom the waves would bring back ... But, deep though the mourning was that she observed, she never imposed it on her family. She asked only that they should be true to what they genuinely felt.

Madame Adrien Proust to Marcel: 'Why should you not have written to me, *"because you spent your days in weeping, and because I am sad"*? Your writing to me then, my dear, would not have increased my sadness. Your letter would have brought to me the echo of what you were feeling, and, for that reason alone, would have given me pleasure. The knowledge that you are thinking of your grandmother never makes me sad; on the contrary, it is a source of happiness to me. It is happiness for me to follow you in our letters — as I might follow you here — and to know that you express yourself fully in them. Don't, darling, discipline yourself *not* to write for fear of making me sad, because that is the reverse of what your letters do. Think of her, my dearest, — join with me in keeping her memory warm — but don't spend long days in tears, for they will only weaken you, and she would not have wished it. On the contrary, the more you think of her, the more you ought to be as she would have wanted you to be, the more you ought to behave as she would have wished you to behave. . . .'[1]

III

LES PLAISIRS ET LES JOURS

But, alas, he still felt unable to work or to behave as that exigent and desolate ghost would have wished. Most of his friends were beginning to despair of young Marcel, to doubt the quality, and even the existence, of his productions. And then, in 1896, he announced the forthcoming appearance of his first book. It was to be called *Les Plaisirs et les Jours*, a title imitated from Hesiod, with the substitution, in a mood of rather naive cynicism, of *Pleasures* for *Works*. Doubting his own true value, and feeling the need of a supporting arm, he had asked Madame de Caillavet to persuade Anatole France to provide a Preface (that she might run no risk of a refusal, Egeria had in part written it herself). Madeleine Lemaire contributed a number of water-colours, and Reynaldo Hahn some pages of music. The resultant volume was

[1] Unpublished letter in the possession of Madame Mante-Proust.

too elaborately adorned, too richly escorted, and too expensive (thirteen francs fifty was a scandalous price at a time when the normal sum asked for a book was three francs). Its 'silken pages' were bound to prejudice against it the minds of the austerer critics.

Indeed, not even the most clear-sighted of critics could have guessed, from *Les Plaisirs et les Jours*, that its author would one day be a great literary 'discoverer' and renovator. It was like many other books of its period. Both in its good qualities and its bad, it was reminiscent of the *Revue Blanche*, Jean de Tinan and Oscar Wilde, with, here and there, a few echoes from the classics, quotations from the *Imitation*, from Plato, Theocritus and Horace, and parodies of Flaubert and la Bruyère. Anatole France, in his brief but enthusiastic Preface, said: 'My young friend's book is rich in weary smiles and tired attitudes, which are lacking neither in beauty nor nobility', and spoke of his 'mobile, penetrating, and genuinely subtle intelligence . . . The poet in him has struck straight to the heart of men's secret thoughts and veiled desires . . . A hot-house atmosphere . . . orchids of sophisticated knowledge . . . a strange and sickly beauty . . . What we breathe in his pages is the *fin de siècle* climate of decadence. . . .'

But for us who know the true Proust in the period of his finished and achieved success, it is not difficult to recognize in this collection of fragments hurriedly put together by a young man hungry for publication, traces of the genuine Proustian essence. This, for example, from the Prefatory Note:

> When I was a child I thought that no character in Holy Writ had ever been afflicted with a more miserable fate than Noah, because of that imprisonment of forty days within the Ark, imposed upon him by the Flood. Later on, I was often ill, and, for many long days was confined within an ark of my own. Then it was I understood that Noah could never have had so clear a view of the world as when he gazed upon it from within his ark, sealed though it was, and when darkness was over all the earth. . . .

'Is not absence, for those who love, the most certain, the most effective, the deepest-rooted, the least destructible of presences?' . . .

89

In that sentence we have a foretaste of *Albertine Disparue*. '... The time that lies ahead of us will, in an hour, have become the present, and as such stripped of its charms, though, provided our spirit is capable even in a small degree of taking the long view, of focusing well ordered distances, when it is left behind, it will find them again upon the path of memory...' And this praise of illness: 'Ecstasy of life suspended, that real Truce of God, which breaks the slavery of labour, the dominance of sinful lusts ... We long for death ... but, though it may loosen the bonds that hold us to life, it cannot loosen those that bind us to ourselves, nor from that most restrictive of them all — the will to live that we may achieve merit and amass it. ...'

This last sentence brings to life once again the moral side of Proust's nature. No matter what he might *do* he never succeeded in freeing himself from the virtues which he had learned in the bosom of his family. It was impossible for him to transfer to any of his masculine heroes the powerful, the agonizing love which he felt for his mother. The nature of this love he does, to some extent, describe when, in speaking of a young girl in one of his stories, he depicts her as suffering atrociously because she can imagine the pain which the discovery of her ill-doing will bring to her mother. This obsession is present in all that Proust ever wrote. In *La Confession d'une Jeune Fille*, the heroine's mother dies, as the result of having seen her, through a window, in her lover's arms. Much later we are offered a similar theme in the episode of Vinteuil's daughter, and later still in a description of the Narrator's own feelings. Insensibly, remorse becomes degraded to sadism.

Henri Massis makes much of the evidential value of this same *Confession*, and, indeed, so many details of the story recall what we know of its author's youth that we can scarcely avoid giving it a wider reference. It is difficult for us not to recognize the mother who says good night to the heroine after she is in bed, and then leaves off doing so in order to brace and tranquillize a morbid sensibility. We know that 'abdication of the Will' was the central feature of Marcel's personal drama, and in *Les Plaisirs et les Jours* it is shown as that of a young girl's. 'What really displeased my mother was my lack of will. Whatever I did, I did on the impulse of the moment. So long as my life was under the influence of heart and spirit, it could not be wholly bad . . .' But, deprived of will-power, the heroine is incapable of resisting the 'evil thoughts' which the corrupt influence of another has sown in her mind. 'Love might be dead, but habit had taken its place, and there was no lack of immoral young people to exploit it . . . At first, I was tormented by terrible moods of remorse, and made admissions that were not understood . . .' A very slight transposition reveals the inner truth of this passage (the interpretation is conjectural only, but the evidence is too strong to be ignored). What we are being shown is the spectacle of a young boy of fifteen, who has learned from depraved companions the secret of pleasure which brings him a confused emotion of horror and delight, making confession to a mother so innocent that she scarcely understands the purport of his words. 'Many were the tears I shed when I spoke to her of these terrible things which only the ignorance of youth had allowed me to put into words. She listened with the sweetness of an angel, though without really understanding anything of what I said, and, in the goodness of her heart, made light of it, and so helped to lift the burden that lay upon my conscience. . . .'

It is not difficult for us to imagine the long and painful struggles from which he always emerged defeated; the efforts he made to subdue those cravings of the senses which, as soon as the crisis was past, left him with nothing but 'feelings of remorse and the consciousness of a waste of spirit'; the lapses from grace; the lengthening tale of failures. There could be no greater error than to think of Proust as amoral. Immoral, perhaps, but suffering atrociously on account of his immorality. 'Wherever I have dealt with immorality, the subjects of it have always been people afflicted with a delicate conscience, people too weak to will the good, yet too noble to revel in evil, people aware only of the suffering caused them by the terrible dilemma of their situation. The pity with which I feel compelled to speak of such victims purifies all my efforts to paint their portraits. . . .'

The style of this early book is still very far from that of *A la Recherche du temps perdu.* It is not a bad style — far from it, but the phrasing is still in the classic tradition, and there is something artificial about the polished coldness of the tone. Not yet does the rhythm follow the complex undulation of the author's sensibility. Still, here and there the reader's expectations are rewarded:

> Ambition intoxicates more surely than does fame; desire puts forth blossoms which possession withers. It is better to dream one's life than to live it. Indeed, to live it is to dream, though with less of mystery, less of clarity. The dream becomes vague and heavy like those dispersed and errant visitations of the night that haunt the embryonic consciousness of ruminant beasts. The plays of Shakespeare are more beautiful when read in the study than when seen upon the stage. The poets who have created imperishable lovers have had, more often than not, experience only of squalid serving-maids, and the voluptuaries whom we envy are quite incapable of visualizing the lives which they lead, or, rather, which lead them. . . .

We find, in *Les Plaisirs et les Jours*, pictures of sea and country-side which give promise of the master yet to be. That is obvious, but it is obvious only because we know what was to come later. We are in the position of those writers of our own day who can see with certainty the premonitions of the Reformation, of the Revolution, in signs and portents which were unintelligible to those living at the time. In 1896 this perfunctory, over-orna-mented, inexpert and charming volume served but to confirm the distressed diagnosis of the small Condorcet group, their feel-ing that its author was a gifted and intelligent worldling for whom no future could be prophesied. 'When Marcel Proust was about twenty-five,' writes the faithful Robert Dreyfus, 'we were shocked and infuriated by his faults.' In the course of a *Revue*, staged at the house of Jacques Bizet, his friends made gentle fun of him, Léon Yeatman providing an imitation of his voice:

Proust (to Ernest, Spirit of Youth)
  'Have you read my book?'

Youth
  No, sir, it is too expensive.

Proust
> Alas! that is what everybody tells me! Have *you* read it, Gregh?

Gregh
> I have just cut the pages, in order to review it.

Proust
> And do you find it too expensive?

Gregh
> Certainly not, it is good money's worth.

Proust
> It is, isn't it? — A Preface by Monsieur France — four francs ... Pictures by Madame Lemaire — four francs ... Music by Reynaldo Hahn — four francs ... *My* prose — one franc ... a few of my poems — fifty centimes — total, thirteen francs, fifty ... not excessive, I think.

Youth
> But, sir, there is a great deal more than that in the *Almanach Hachette*, which costs only twenty-five sous!

Proust (with a guffaw of laughter)
> That *is* a good joke ... I shall laugh myself sick!

But his laughter must have been rather painful. The publication of *Les Plaisirs et les Jours* had failed to establish Marcel as a writer in the eyes of his generation. Montesquiou, in one of his volumes, gave it a few patronizing lines. Marguerite Moreno recited the *Portraits of Painters* at *La Bodinière*. Not one of the serious critics so much as mentioned Proust's name. 'They regarded him', says Valéry Larbaud, 'as the author of a book with a quaint title ... the book of a worldly amateur, the kind of thing that might have been issued by a country-town printer, a book about which they could find nothing to say. He had contributed to the *Figaro*, written a few parodies, achieved a "literary

93

exercise" . . .' Marcel himself was conscious of failure, and wrote to Robert Dreyfus: 'You are the only one of us who has *done* anything — *exegisti monumentum.*' How, at that time, should he have thought it possible that he had it in him to build his epoch's monument?

IV

DELAYED MANHOOD

How did he spend his time? First and foremost, in writing letters, 'mad, magical' letters, overbearing, cajoling, 'questioning, breathless', ingenious, witty letters that played up to the vanity of their recipients, embarrassing them with ironic hyperbole, tormenting them with contemptuous comment, wooing them with a charm of tone. But they must have been more charmed than irritated, for, one and all, they kept them — though it was a good twenty years before he was to achieve fame. After his death, these treasures, carefully stowed in all the drawers of Paris, emerged into the light of day.

Very often they conveyed reproaches. 'Marcel Proust is the very devil', said Alphonse Daudet on one occasion, referring to his disturbing and superhuman power of seeing into other people's motives. He was a difficult friend. 'One sometimes wounded him without meaning to,' said Lauris: 'the real truth about him was that he had no belief in his fellow-men, and was forever detecting non-existent reserves and coldnesses. Heaven knows what he read between the lines! . . .' Reproaches would arrive in writing. One might have parted from him at two o'clock in the morning and, on waking, find beside one's plate at breakfast, a thick envelope, delivered by hand, containing a letter in which he analysed with pitiless lucidity everything one had said — and left unsaid. The invalidish life which he led, his 'interminable nights of sleeplessness', gave him every opportunity to apply his powers of imagination to disentangling the motives of his own behaviour, as well as those of his friends and intimates; and this bred in him that 'genius for suspicion' to which all who knew him have drawn attention.

In the Great World he continued to exercise his gifts as the 'genealogist and entomologist' of French Society. New intimates had been added to his earlier group of friends. The young Duc de Guiche, a man who might have stepped straight out of the eighteenth century in its hey-day, and was far more interested in optics and hydrostatics than in gossip, had known him when he was an 'obscure young man asked in at the last moment to make up the numbers at Madame Straus's table'. Another target for his adulation was the Comtesse de Noailles, a great poet, a brilliant and vivacious beauty, a woman of mordant and unconventional wit, who immediately came under the spell of his 'superb intelligence, his suave and nervous sweetness, his unexampled gifts'. No one knew better than he how to find each new collection of her verse better than the one before, or could justify his enthusiasm with such an array of subtle arguments. No one knew better than he how to praise the woman in the same breath as the poet.

> *Marcel Proust to Madame de Noailles:* 'You are too endearing. I understand so well how it was that men, in the ages of Faith, loved the Holy Virgin, for she turned her face from none, and all — the lame, the blind, the lepers, the paralytics and the unhappy, could touch the hem of her robe. But you are greater still, and at each new revelation of your inexhaustible heart I understand a little more certainly how firmly set your genius is in the foundations of eternity. And if to be told that you are greater even than the Holy Virgin may anger you a little, let me compare you to that Carthaginian goddess who inspired in all men the stirrings of desire, and in some the instincts of piety. . . .'

At about the same time he made the acquaintance of Antoine Bibesco, a Roumanian Prince, whom Marcel described as 'the most intelligent of Frenchmen', and of his brother, Emmanuel. Their friendship was intimate and jealous, with something about it of a secret society. They had a private language of their own, in which the Bibescos were the *Ocsebib*, Marcel, *Lecram*, Bertrand de Fénelon, *Nonelef*. A secret was '*a tomb*', and '*to play the hyena*' meant to violate a tomb. The bringing in of friends who were outside the group was described as *'operating a conjunction'*. At a later stage, the Bibescos operated a conjunction between their cousin Marthe, a young woman as brilliant as she was beautiful, and Marcel. It was she who noted that the Bibescos, together with Reynaldo Hahn, were for him — kept prisoner by his ailments — the purveyors of dreams, the bearers of images.[1]

There was something symbolical in the fact that he was still living in the room that he had occupied as a child, that, as in the old days, he was regularly working on the dining-room table. His father, being a very busy man, left the house early. This meant that Marcel could lie late in bed, secure in the knowledge that his mother would not give him a 'blowing up'. Only after he had had his breakfast did he finish dressing and buttoning his boots (a peculiarly difficult achievement for one who, like him, was asthmatic). In the evenings, if he happened to be feeling ill and did not go out, he would be found in the dining-room, sitting by a roaring fire at the big table with its red serge cloth, busy writing in a school exercise-book, by the light of a Carcel lamp, because he liked its soft radiance. Madame Proust would sit dozing beside him in an armchair. There was an element of infantilism in his way of life at this time. But to remain a child is to become a poet.

When he was feeling well, he dined out. He was much sought after because of his wit. His imitations made him very popular in the drawing-rooms of Paris. 'He took off Montesquiou's laugh, and expressed great admiration for Madame Greffulhe's, which, like the carillon of Bruges, dropped notes upon the listening air in the most unexpected fashion. He would play a little scene in which he represented Madeleine Lemaire seeing her guests off: "You sang like an angel this evening, Madame de Maupeou! That Brandès woman is quite amazing — never a year over twenty . . . *such* an *artissste* [referring to Madrazo] . . . Good night, Montesquiou, you dear, great, sublime poet . . . Take care not to catch cold, Ochoa . . ." and then, "come along, Suzette." And on her way upstairs she would tell her dogs what she really thought about all the people she had been entertaining.'

[1] *See* PRINCESS BIBESCO, *Au Bal avec Marcel Proust* (Gallimard, Paris, 1929), and the same author's *Le Voyageur Voilé* (Editions de la Palatine, Geneva, 1947).

But what Marcel liked above all else was to give rather solemn dinner-parties in his parents' house, where he would gather 'round the azaleas and the white lilac' the numerous prototypes of Saint-Loup, Bloch and Oriane, with a sprinkling of people like Bourget, Hervieu, Madame de Noailles, Anatole France and Calmette. 'Marcel, in full evening dress, his shirt-front looking rather battered, his hair untidy, breathing with difficulty, his magnificent eyes glittering in the dark-shadowed rings left by long nights of sleeplessness, would play the charming child, exerting himself to bring his oddly assorted guests — some of them merely condescending, others lavish in adulation, but all of them comparative strangers to one another, and, therefore, on their guard — into a happy relationship . . . Often, when he felt anxious (or curious) about the effect they might produce on one another, he would move his own plate in the course of a meal, and sit by each in turn, taking his soup with one, his fish (or scrap of fish) with another, and so on, until dinner was over. By the time the dessert appeared, he had, presumably, made the round of the table. This manœuvre was evidence of his good-nature, of his wish that they should all enjoy themselves, for he would have felt miserable had he supposed that anyone there might feel ignored or slighted. But this succession of moves had a double motive — the desire to pay an unusual compliment, and the wish to make sure, through the medium of his natural per-spicacity, that the aura projected by each was favourable. The results were invariably excellent, and no one at his parties was ever bored. . . .'

It would be untrue, as well as unlikely, that his parents approved this mode of existence, or yielded without remonstrance to the exigencies of their spoiled son. Madame Adrien Proust often felt herself torn as between husband and child. Even at the most successful of these dinners, friends did, occasionally, 'put their foot in it'.

Marcel Proust to his mother: 'The party was, as you say, delightful, thanks to the sweet way in which you planned it all, and to your talent for organization. But I did have a good cry after dinner, not so much because I felt upset by that ridiculous remark of Bibesco's — and Papa's most unfair rejoinder — as because I realized that one can rely on *no one*, and that people one had thought one's best friends are capable of such fantastic lapses that, all things considered, they are really more trouble than they are worth. I have told Bibesco over and over again how the false interpretation you *will* put on the way I choose to arrange my life, poisons my whole existence, and now that I have resigned myself to the fact that I cannot prove you wrong, I feel that, in all this, I have a right to be worried about you, whereas you have really no right at all to be worried about me. To make doubly sure, I took him aside before dinner, and said: "No jokes about tipping, *please*, and none of those absurd questions to Papa, like 'don't you think, sir, that perhaps if Marcel wrapped up less . . .' etc." Whatever the pleasure I may derive from having my friends to dinner, and seeing them so brilliantly, so charmingly, received by you, I would rather do without it altogether, if these gatherings of intimates, which ought to be so cordial, are to degenerate into squabbles which leave a deep scar in Papa's mind, and strengthen prejudices which no amount of evidence will ever eradicate.'[1]

Sometimes an argument would flare up between Marcel and his parents on the subject of the guests he had invited.

Marcel Proust to his mother: '. . . About that dinner which you insist on calling, with such delicate tact, my *"party of tarts"*, I have not yet fixed on a day, though I think that the 30th March, or, perhaps, the 25th, will be the most probable, because I can't put it off, and because it is more important for me to arrange it before Easter than to bother about the bankruptcy in which it looks like landing me. I must give it at a restaurant since you refuse to have it here . . . Calmette and Hervieu, to say nothing of the others, are as useful to me as Lyon-Caen is for Papa, or Robert's "bosses" for him. You give dinners for *them* all right without complaining that the house is going to be turned upside down. No matter

[1] Unpublished letter, in the possession of Madame Mante-Proust.

how ill I may be feeling when the day comes, I shall be there. I find it very hard to believe, unless you're just acting out of spite, that what is possible in *their* case, is impossible in *mine*. . . .'[1]

For, even in his relations with his mother, there occurred those 'brief but inevitable moments when a man hates those he loves'. She irritated him by the reproaches which she levelled at him for leading a life of fashion and worldliness, by her insistence that he should begin to do some work and, above all, because (and this is one of the hardest things in life to endure) she loved him. So jealous is love, whether of wife or mother, that it is often easier for it to come to terms with the invalidism of the loved one than with his perfect freedom of movement. Marcel constantly felt that he was a prisoner:

Marcel Proust to Madame Adrien Proust: '. . . The truth is that when I feel well, the sort of life that keeps me so exasperates you to the point of demolishing it, until I fall ill again. This is not the first time. I caught a cold the other evening. If it turns to asthma — and, as things are now, it probably will — I have no doubt that you will again be perfectly sweet to me as soon as I am in the same state I was in twelve months ago, at about the same time of the year. It really is miserable not to be able to enjoy both health and affection simultaneously. . . .'

. . . Moved by the perverse prescience that afflicts all mothers you could not have chosen a more unfortunate moment to write as you do, and so to bring to nothing the triple improvement that *could* have come about the morning after I dined with the Pierrebourgs (last Thursday). . . .

. . . I told you, about the 1st December, when you were complaining about my intellectual inactivity, that you really were impossible. For seeing how genuinely restored to life I was, instead of approving, and delighting in, what had made the change in me possible, nothing would satisfy you but that I should start working again immediately. . . .

[1] Unpublished letter, in the possession of Madame Mante-Proust.

... The way I always behave ought to please you. I cannot say as much for *your* conduct. I can't imagine myself — if I were in your place — refusing to give, not one dinner, but a hundred! But I don't bear you any grudge, and I only ask that you should not write letters to me which call for a reply, because I am completely exhausted. ...

Then his asthma returned and, with it, affection.

... The outing did not make the breathlessness worse, but I was foolish enough to walk back, and, by the time I got home, was chilled to the marrow. But I thought of you with so much affection that, but for my fear of waking you, I should have gone to your room. Is it to the return of asthma and hay-fever — my natural physical state — that I owe this burgeoning of what is my natural moral one? I don't know. But it is a long time since the thought of you has so flooded me with emotion. I am terribly tired just now, and can scarcely hold my pen, with the result that I am putting what I want to say to you (I fear) very badly — namely, that ill-humour makes me selfish and won't let me be kind, and, in particular, that, for some years now, the disappointment that certain words of yours have caused me to feel, words which, though not very frequent, have, nevertheless, had a great effect on me because of their contemptuous irony and harshness (paradoxical though that may sound), has kept me from cultivating an attitude of kindliness which, I felt, you did not understand. ....[1]

V

THE 'AFFAIR'

That was what Marcel Proust was like round about 1898. The umbilical cord had not been cut, and he found life possible only if he could be fed with the emotional nourishment supplied by a daily course of maternal affection. While, however, there was

[1] Fragments of several unpublished letters in the possession of Madame Mante-Proust.

much of the child about him so long as he remained in the bosom of his family, he could, if called upon to show courage, behave in an extremely virile fashion. 'I had inherited from my grand-mother' — wrote the 'Narrator' — identifying himself, in this passage, with the author — 'a lack of personal pride so extreme that it could only too easily issue in the form of lack of dignity . . . But at last, experience of life did manage to teach me that it is a bad thing to smile affectionately when somebody mocks one, instead of feeling resentful . . . Such anger and wish to wound as I did know, came my way quite differently, in sudden accesses of fury.' By dint of realizing that the friends he most respected would not endure being treated with lack of consideration, he came at last to show in words and actions that there was another side to his nature, in which pride was a dominant element. A word or a gesture in a restaurant was enough to set him on his high horse, and there were occasions when such incidents actually led to a duel.

> I remember the silence that fell on our table at Larue's one evening when, quite calmly, and with not so much as a quiver of his white hand as it lay upon the table-cloth, he refused, with calculated and controlled insolence, to shake hands with someone whom he suspected of having spoken ill of him. . . .[1]

In 1897 he considered that he had been insulted by something that Jean Lorrain had written about *Les Plaisirs et les Jours* in the public press, and sent two friends to call upon the offending journalist. These friends were Jean Béraud, the painter, and Gustave Borda — known as 'Sword-thrust Borda' — a marvellous duellist, a man of delightful and ornate wit, and an incomparable second. The duel was fought with pistols, and was inconclusive. Béraud never forgot the rainy winter morning at the Tour de Villebon, and the pluck shown by Marcel Proust for all his weakness of physique.

The Dreyfus Affair provided him with fresh opportunities for a display of courage. A wave of anti-Semitism broke over France.

[1] GEORGES DE LAURIS: *A un Ami* (Amoti-Dumont, Paris, 1948), p. 25.

Proust was too much devoted to his mother (and also, was too fair-minded) not to react, even when, as in the case of Robert de Montesquiou, it meant standing up to somebody whose anger he dreaded. *Proust to Montesquiou:* 'I did not reply yesterday to the questions you put to me about the Jews, and for this very simple reason. If, like my father and my brother, I am a Catholic, I have a Jewish mother. That, you will understand, is sufficient reason why I should refuse to take part in such a discussion. . . .'

On the matter of tolerance, he was completely at one with his friend, Madame Straus, who had been brought up 'in the tradition of the Halévy family, where, for many years, all religions had mingled and rubbed shoulders'. She herself had never been converted. 'I have too little religion', she said, 'to change what I have got.' She showed, however, the greatest respect for the convictions of others. Still, when the Affair made it necessary to take a definite stand, she never hesitated, in spite of her liking for several of the 'stars in the opposition camp' (Jules Lemaître, Maurice Barrès), and made no effort to retain on her visiting-list such fanatics as felt themselves estranged by her pro-Dreyfus sentiments. Proust who, with France and Madame de Caillavet, had become a militant 'pro', urged her on:

Proust to Madame Straus: 'Monsieur France, at the request of Monsieur Labori, wants to get a number of prominent persons to sign an address to Picquart. Monsieur Labori thinks that it might impress the judges. We are anxious to get a lot of fresh names, and I promised Monsieur France that I would ask whether you feel you could approach Monsieur d'Haussonville. There is no objection to your telling him that the suggestion comes from France. The text of the address will, of deliberate intent, be so moderately worded that none of the signatories need feel in any way committed so far as the Dreyfus Affair in general is concerned. I think it scarcely likely that a kind and high-minded man like Monsieur d'Haussonville will refuse you. Monsieur France, like everybody else, is of the opinion that his name, which is from every point of view, incomparable would have the most tremendous consequences on the future — not of the Affair, but of

Picquart, who appears to be in a very gloomy state of mind.
I say "his future" and not "him", because he is displaying a
serenity of temper which has moved France — that most
detached of men — to speak of him in extremely affectionate
terms. . . .'

It was Louis de Robert who, one evening at a party given by
Charpentier, the publisher, had introduced Proust to Colonel
Picquart, the hero of the occasion. When the latter was imprisoned in the fort of Mont Valérien, Proust managed, not without difficulty, to send him a copy of *Les Plaisirs et les Jours*. He
had become a passionate advocate of Dreyfus, and his attitude
was all the more courageous because it meant his breaking with
a great many Society people whose friendship he had always
seemed to value very highly. His sense of justice was considerably
stronger than his snobbery, but he was far too intelligent ever
to become a fanatical and foolish partisan. His moment of triumph
came when the whole business began to assume the appearance
of a tragedy. *Proust to Madame Straus:* 'I have not seen you since
the Affair, which began like a Balzac novel (Bertulus, the
magistrate in *Splendeurs et Misères des Courtisanes*; Christian Ester-
hazy, the country nephew in *Illusions Perdues*; du Paty de Clam,
Rastignac and his secret meetings with Vautrin in outlying
suburbs) has turned Shakespearean in its development of headlong
events. . . .'

The common front presented by Proust and Anatole France
had brought the two men very close together. 'There are no
friendships now but political friendships', Marcel had said,
writing to France to approve his attitude. Never had he so much
admired him as now, when the older writer was showing a new
side of himself as champion of the innocent:

Dear Master: I send you all fond wishes for the New Year,
and for your own good health. The year just past was,
indeed, your finest hour. 'It was then that the name of
Great was given to Alexander' . . . No one has shown a
higher courage than you — who have so nobly hymned that
virtue, nor have you grounds for envy of the tragic Greek
because he achieved victories elsewhere than in the field of

letters. Indeed you have stepped down into the arena of public life in a way not hitherto seen in this century, not as Chateaubriand, not as Barrès, for the purpose of winning yourself a name, but determined to make the great name that is already yours weigh in the scales of Justice. Not that I needed any such excuse to admire you as a just, good and honest man. I have loved you, and have, therefore, known your qualities. But your action has served to show to others things they did not know, things that they admire no less than the prose of *Thais*, because they have the same nobility, the same beauty, the same perfection of harmony. . . .[1]

But his one never-failing confidante in all that concerned the Affair was his mother, who strongly shared his feelings and his faith. Mother and son observed the attitude of their friends, and of any strangers they happened to meet, trying, like Bloch in the novel, to read in their reticences the true nature of their opinions. When Marcel Proust was at Evian in 1899, he learned that the Comte and Comtesse d'Eu were to be his fellow guests at the Splendid Hotel. In his letters home, he spoke of them, always in the light of the Affair, depicting them with the pen of a novelist:

Proust to Madame Adrien Proust: 'The Eus seems to be good, simple souls, but I remain very stiff, very hat-on-the-head in their presence. "All communication broken off since Rennes." Finding myself the other day with the old gentleman in front of a door through which two persons could not go abreast, I stood back to let him pass, and this he did, but not before he had swept his hat off with a great gesture, not condescendingly, not in the d'Haussonville manner, but like a nice, polite old thing. It was the kind of attention I never have from any of the people for whom I "stand aside", people who, being "unpretentious middle-class folk", are more unbending than princes. . . .'

Young Galand introduced me to two gentlemen of the name of Langlois, very ugly, and so much alike that one could not

[1] Unpublished letter in the possession of Monsieur Alfred Dupont.

tell them apart, and who, determined not to talk of the Affair let all sorts of things bubble to the surface of their speech from what must have been a very muddy bottom: things like — 'Forain did some wonderful drawings in the *Ps-s-s-t* . . . Félix Faure, now he *was* a patriot, if only he were living now! . . . Don't talk to me of shorthand. You should have seen what use the *Figaro* made of it this summer — a lie in every line. . . .'[1]

But, at a time when the pro-Dreyfus elements allowed the Affair to colour all their judgments, and to make them wholly in capable of fairness or even of pity, Marcel Proust never lost his sense of proportion. He refused to quarrel with the Daudet family. He was delighted when the accused man was rehabilitated in 1901, to find that there was to be a 'happy ending' for Dreyfus and for Picquart, 'such as one gets in fairy-tales or novelettes', but viewed with distaste the spectacle of General Mercier being insulted by Barthou, 'whose Dreyfus sentiments were only a few weeks old'.

Proust to the Comtesse de Noailles: 'The whole story would be incredibly comic were it not for the fact that the paper speaks of General Mercier being "very pale" — "General Mercier looking paler than ever". It is horrible to read these things, because, even in the wickedest of men, there is a poor, innocent old horse whose heart, liver and arteries, guiltless though they be, suffer abominably from overstrain. The moment of victory is ruined for me by the thought that there's always somebody who's got to be downed. . . .'

Though, in the course of the Affair, he had come up against the active hostility, not of the Church, but of certain congregations, he wrote an article for the *Figaro* in which, with great skill and a fine passion, he defended the churches which Briand's project threatened to strip of their proper functions. To friends of his, who hotly supported the scheme for undenominational schools, because they believed that the scheme would further French

[1] Unpublished letters in the possession of Madame Mante-Proust.

unity, and because they wished to guard against any recurrence
of the sort of injustice typified by the Affair, he wrote that if he
thought that undenominational schools would lessen the ferment
of hatred he would support them, but that he was convinced,
on the contrary, that if the flame of Catholicism were to be extinguished (should such a thing be possible), a generation of
infidel clericals would arise that would be far more violently anti-
Semite, anti-Liberal and a hundred times worse altogether. He
concluded on a firm note:

> ... The century of Carlyle, Ruskin and Tolstoy, even though
> it be, too, the century of Hugo, even though it be, too, the
> century of Renan (to say nothing of its having been the
> century of Lamartine and Chateaubriand), is not an anti-
> religious century. Even Baudelaire clung to the Church, at
> lease in a sacrilegious sense. But all this has nothing to do
> with the question of Christian schools, in the first place,
> because one does not kill the spirit of Christianity by closing
> a lot of Christian schools, and because if the Christian spirit
> is to die, it will die just as surely under a theocracy: secondly,
> because the spirit of Christendom, and even Catholic dogma,
> has nothing in common with that fanaticism of party which
> we are out to destroy, though, in fact, what we are actually
> doing is to copy it. . . .[1]

It is clear from this passage that, even then, Proust had
already achieved an astonishing mastery of both thought and
style, taken though it is from a letter to a friend, written on
the spur of the moment, merely because he wanted to unburden
himself.

The Affair had helped him to move, in his judgments on the
world, from an attitude of easy good-nature to one of courage.[2]
In his studious obscurity, he had become (though scarcely anybody realized it), by dint of reading, working and developing
his own inborn gift of taste, one of the best of French prose-

---

[1] GEORGES DE LAURIS, *A un Ami: Correspondance inédite de Marcel Proust, 1903-1922*
(Amiot-Dumont, Paris, 1948), pp. 69-70.
[2] PIERRE ABRAHAM, *Proust, Recherches sur la création Intellectuelle* (Rieder, Paris, 1930).

technicians. Such was his skill in taking to pieces the mechanism
of the supreme 'styles', that he could parody them with a skill
which led Jules Lemaître to say: 'It makes one afraid to write.
It is more than extraordinary, it is terrifying.' Everything went
to show that he was among the best-read men of his time. It
looked as though his urge to write would prove irresistible. But
he was close on thirty, and so far he had failed to make his mark,
had not even seriously tried to do so. Why was he still content
to remain on the fringes of life?

The answer to that question is — that he would not face facts.
'The first condition of being a writer is to accept oneself.'[1] How is it
possible to release the hidden waters, if one will not dig down to
the level at which they are to be found? Even now, Proust refused
to face self-knowledge. His frivolity was deliberately assumed
with the object of avoiding self-expression. Between his 'good-
child' attitude of family worship, and his own secret life, the gap
was too large to leap. Truths about passion, character and conduct crowded in upon him. But he had come by them in the
course of shoddy, detestable intrigues, and their suspect origin pre-
vented him from speaking of them. Before he could write a great
book he would have to learn that the materials from which it must
be built were precisely those trivial delights, those shameful
agonies, which the ordinary man suppresses, but which the artist
hoards as unconsciously as the seed secretes those elements within
itself from which the growing plant will draw its nourishment.

As in the old Illiers days, he still held communion with nature,
art and life. He experienced moments of deep reverie, during
which his whole being was 'as might be, in a state of trance'.
Reynaldo Hahn was once a witness of one of them, and felt that
his friend's intelligence and sensibility were 'driving straight to the
root of things'. They had been walking together in a garden, and
had just passed a bed of Bengal rose trees when, all of a sudden
Marcel, with childlike simplicity, and speaking with a trace of
sadness, said: 'Do you mind if I stay behind for a moment? I
want to have another look at those rose trees . . .' Reynaldo left
him, walked round the house, and returned to find Marcel
precisely where he had left him, staring fixedly at the roses:

[1] BERNARD GRASSET.

His head was bent, and there was an intent look on his face. He was screwing up his eyes and frowning, as though in passionate concentration. With his left hand he kept on pushing the end of his small, black moustache between his lips and nibbling it. I had a feeling that he had heard me, that he saw me, but that he wanted neither to move nor speak. I passed him in silence. A moment later, I heard his voice calling to me. I turned and he ran to meet me. As soon as we were together again, he asked whether I felt 'annoyed'. I laughingly reassured him, and we resumed our conversation where we had left it off. I did not ask him about the rose episode. I said nothing whatever about it, and made no attempt to pull his leg. In an obscure sort of a way I felt that I mustn't. . . .[1]

He may have been tearing from the roses their secrets as he could tear those of human beings from their minds. But, if so, he alone knew it.

[1] REYNALDO HAHN, *Hommage à Marcel Proust*: Volume I of *Les Cahiers Marcel Proust* (Gallimard, 1927), pp. 33-4.

CHAPTER IV

THE END OF CHILDHOOD

*I had held intelligence in thrall to comfort. When I loosed the chains, I
thought but to free a slave, only to find that I had given myself a master.
I lacked the physical strength to satisfy him, and knew that he would be
the death of me if I did not resist.* MARCEL PROUST

I

RUE DE COURCELLES

IN 1900, Dr. Proust and his wife moved to a house — 45 Rue
de Courcelles — standing at the corner of the Rue Monceau,
'a great echoing place with a wide staircase'. The rooms
were vast and sumptuously furnished. Marcel used to spend his
evenings working in the big dining-room, the walls of which were
austerely panelled in mahogany. The table held books, papers,
and an oil lamp 'the mild golden illumination of which he
particularly liked'. There, when the electric lights had been
switched off and the house was asleep, he would sit reading
Saint-Simon, Chateaubriand, Sainte-Beuve and Emile Mâle. He
never kept his door shut against familiar friends — Antoine
Bibesco, Georges de Lauris, Louis d'Albuféra, and Bertrand de
Fénelon whose bright eyes and flying coat-tails were later to
take their place among the list of elements that went to make up
Saint-Loup's charm. Pretty Louisa de Mornand would sometimes
look in, after the theatre, to say good night. It is worth remarking
that all these people, actress, diplomat scholar, poet and horseman,
considered it a privilege to be counted a friend of this obscure
invalid who seemed to be using them as a means by which he
might explore the world. 'To us he was like some foreign noble-
man wrapped about in the mystery of a land which existed only
in his mind and memory.'

Sometimes Dr. Proust would make a brief appearance, and tell
a story bearing on medicine or politics. Madame Proust, always
fragile, always shy, would say something nice to her son's friends,
and then withdraw with an air of melancholy discretion, though

not before she had sounded a note of warning: 'Darling, if you go out tonight, do wrap up well ... it's very cold ... You will look after him, won't you, Monsieur? ... He had one of his attacks of breathlessness earlier this evening.' His asthma was growing worse, and quite often, though his dress shirt was laid out ready for him in front of the wood fire which was always burning in the dining-room, even in summer (he had a horror of cold linen, saying that it was damp), he would, at the last moment, give up any idea of leaving the house. When that happened, he would dine off a cup of steaming coffee, and offer his friends cider — a memory of La Beauce — 'with bubbles misting the glass, and beautifying with a myriad points of light, its pink-flushed sides'.

Sometimes he dined at Larue's or Weber's, wearing a great overcoat even in spring, his face looking deathly white beneath its crown of black hair. There were evenings, too, when he entertained at the Rue de Courcelles, where his parents allowed him to play the host. It gave him great pleasure to bring together men who, when not his guests, were at daggers drawn as a result of the Affair, Léon Daudet, for instance, and Anatole France. Madame de Noailles, then at the peak of her youthful brilliance, was one of the ornaments of these dinners. Occasionally Montesquiou would come, and then, what endless care was necessary in choosing those who were to meet him! *Proust to Montesquiou:* 'I shall invite the ones you mention, and nobody else ... You didn't tell me whether you would allow me to include Madame Cahen. I have made a careful note of the enemies who must be deleted from the list. ...'

When he was feeling comparatively well, he would take trips with the object of looking at trees, pictures and beautiful churches. He went to Holland with Bertrand de Fénelon, to Burgundy with Louis d'Albuféra, to Venice with his mother. Those were, for him, occasions of high adventure.

> *Marcel Proust to Madame Adrien Proust:* 'I shall sleep tonight at Amsterdam, and be back in Paris either Sunday or Monday, eager to kiss my darling Mamma and my dear Papa after so long an absence. I should probably never have

had the courage to face so extended a separation if I had decided on it all at once. But I lengthened my trip almost from day to day. More than once I have fully expected to be seeing you within the next twenty-four hours, and never dreamed that I could be a whole fortnight without embracing you . . . I hate the idea of returning to Paris, even though it's to see Bibesco (if he hasn't already gone away), Reynaldo and the rest. It means such a change of atmosphere. But at least it is a place that I know well . . . Illiers would be hateful, and anywhere else, in my present mood. Fénelon has been kindness itself. You wrote him a charming letter addressed to Monsieur de Fénélon with an acute accent, and you spelt Bibes*k*o with a K . . . But it doesn't matter a bit. . . .'[1]

It was some considerable time before he himself learned that it was incorrect in French to say *De* Guiche, *De* Fénelon . . . 'Would you,' he asked, 'say Dyck and not Van Dyck?' As late as 1903, he could still write — 'I have got to get off my daily letter to de Flers and to de Billy.'

In summer, when he could count on a respite from his breathlessness, he would pay surprise visits to Léon Daudet at Fontainebleau, to Madame Alphonse Daudet in Touraine, to the Finlays or to Madame Straus in Normandy. Gaston Gallimard, his future publisher, saw him for the first time at Bénerville, where he was staying with Louisa de Mornand. He had walked over from Cabourg.

I can still remember him as he burst upon my vision, in an ill-fitting black suit with the coat buttoned up crooked, a long velvet-lined cloak, a high, starched collar, and a shabby straw-hat, too small for him, which he wore tilted over his forehead. He was high-shouldered, and had thick straight hair. His patent-leather dress-shoes were covered with dust. A man dressed like that on a bright, sunny day, should, by rights, have looked ridiculous, but the effect he produced was somehow one of pathetic charm. One was conscious of a kind of elegance, but, at the same time, of a supreme indifference to all elegance. There was nothing very extraordinary about his

[1] Unpublished letter in the possession of Madame Mante-Proust.

having undertaken the long journey on foot. At that time there was no other way of covering the seventeen kilomètres which separated Cabourg from Bénerville. All the same, the considerable effort involved, which had left marks of exhaustion on his face, was evidence of his goodness of heart. His account of the walk was delightfully dry, but it never seemed to occur to him that such an expedition on a hot day was a remarkable proof of friendship. He had stopped several times on the way, at various Inns, in order to recruit his strength with coffee. He described it all so simply that I was at once won over. . . .[1]

'It was at this time,' says Georges de Lauris, 'that several of us made trips with him to see the churches and monuments that he loved. There was never any fear that he would not be ready, no matter how early the start, because on those occasions he did not go to bed at all. The only refreshment he took on the road was *café au lait*, for which he always paid generously. We went, I remember, to Laon and to Coucy. In spite of his exhaustion and shortness of breath, he insisted on climbing to the top of the great tower, which the Germans later destroyed. It comes back to me that he made the ascent leaning on the arm of Bertrand de Fénelon, who kept up his spirits by humming the *Good Friday* music. As a matter of fact it *was* Good Friday, and the fruit trees were blossoming in the Spring sunshine. I can see him, too, in front of the church at Senlis, all attention while Prince Emmanuel Bibesco explained, with an air of modesty as though he were not in any way imparting information, the characteristics of the bell-towers of the Île-de-France. . . .'

II

RUSKIN, OR THE INTERCESSOR

His mother kept on begging him to 'undertake some piece of serious work'. She had an unquestioning belief in her 'little

[1] GASTON GALLIMARD, *Première Rencontre*. See *Hommage à Marcel Proust:* Volume I of *Les Cahiers Marcel Proust* (Gallimard, Paris, 1927), pp. 56-7.

precious', sincerely admired his immense erudition, was quite sure that he was far more talented than anybody else. 'It makes me *furious*', she wrote, 'that you should have the *face* to say that I don't read your letters. I *do* read them, over and over again, sucking them dry, and then, in the evening, returning to them in case there may be some tit-bit that I have missed . . .' He was perfectly well aware that he was talented, but had a presentiment that once he really undertook the only kind of work for which he was suited, he would devote his life to it. Instinctively, he recoiled from the prospect of the sacrifice involved:

> *Marcel Proust to Madame Adrien Proust:* 'I do believe that if only I could be relieved of my various troubles . . . I know what you will say to that. You will say that there are people who have just as many as I have, but who work all the same "to keep a roof over their families' heads". I know. But worries like mine, and even worse than mine, much worse, do not necessarily produce in everyone the same degree of suffering. Don't you see, you have got to consider two entirely different things: the material *fact* which is the cause of the suffering, and the individual's *capacity* for suffering, which depends upon his temperament. Still, I am sure that there are many people who suffer as much as, and more than, I do, and yet manage to work. But don't forget that many who are in some sort ill, are told that they *mustn't* work — usually too late. I would so much rather stop too soon. And I know I'm right. There is work *and* work. Literary work constantly forces one to exploit the very feelings that are most closely connected with suffering ("*Quand, par tant d'autres nœuds, tu tiens à la douleur*"). It is like a man who starts moving an injured limb which he ought to be keeping still. What I really need is frivolity and distraction. . . .'[1]

But Madame Proust would not be put off. He had spoken about a novel. Was he getting on with it?

> *Marcel to Madame Adrien Proust:* '. . . If I can't say that I have done any work, as yet, on my novel, in the sense of being

---

[1] Unpublished letter in the possession of Madame Mante-Proust.

absorbed by it, of having the whole thing mapped out, I can assure you that the notebook I bought (and which does not represent by any means all I have done, because I was previously working on loose sheets) — is filled — and it has one hundred and ten large-size pages. . . .'[1]

What did that notebook contain? Memories — some of which were presented in the form of a conversation with his mother. 'Do you remember, mamma, how you used to read me *La Petite Fadette* and *François le Champi* when I was ill? You had called in the doctor, and he had given me something to reduce the fever and make it possible for me to take some food. You said nothing: but I knew from your silence that you were listening, but only out of politeness, and that you had already decided in your own mind that you wouldn't give me any of the things he had prescribed, and that you wouldn't let me eat so long as the fever was on me. You kept me on a diet of milk until you were convinced, from your knowledge of such things, that my skin was moist and my pulse strong. You had no confidence in the doctor. Your listening to him was pure hypocrisy . . .' Moral reflections: '. . . With reference to the above, I must show that when I am being worldly, I attach too much importance to the danger of worldliness, and, when my memory is weak, too much importance to the act of automatic recollection. People in the grip of an ideal always think that what is most difficult is best. This is an instinctive moral reaction which serves to counterbalance our vices and weaknesses.' Natural descriptions: '. . . Other things, also seen at the seaside. The sun had gone down. My window, like a ship's porthole, was entirely filled by the sea from which the darkness had begun to drain its splendour, though giving it life, so that it surrounded me, infinite yet familar, a sea such as a sailor would have liked to spend the night with in mute communion . . . The sun, setting on the sea, was a golden disk in which the gulls looked motionless and yellow like large water-flowers [name of the yellow water lily] . . .' There were even one or two more finished sentences and sketches of characters, though the whole thing, as yet, was fragmentary and confused.

[1] Unpublished letter in the possession of Madame Mante-Proust.

But why, if he still hesitated to embark on his novel, should he not undertake some work of scholarship? For some years he had been reading, and admiring, Ruskin, whom Robert de la Sizeraine and Jacques Bardoux had recently revealed to a French public. A publisher had already asked him to do some translations, but had then gone bankrupt. Why should he not take them up again? The curious thing is that Proust knew scarcely any English, and that when he tried to write it he committed one mistake after another. But a cousin of Reynaldo Hahn's, Marie Nordlinger, helped him. Robert d'Humières, the translator of Kipling, was frequently consulted. Madame Adrien Proust made a 'word for word' version which Marcel then proceeded to polish, copying it, in his fine handwriting, into school exercise-books. Reynaldo Hahn has given us a description of Proust lying at full length, his great shining eyes fixed on Ruskin's text — 'on those pages which he could not construe, though nothing of their sense escaped him'. *Marcel Proust to his mother:* '... Don't bother about the translation — I have done it myself. Unravel for me, if you like (orally) the Preface to *Sesame* ... I have been working so frantically that these few words are all I can send you.'

It is clear that there was something of an elective affinity between Proust and Ruskin. Proust came of a rich, cultivated, middle-class family: like Ruskin, he had been 'coddled' in childhood by over-fond parents, and had spent long days in a garden, observing, with meticulous curiosity, birds, flowers and clouds. Both men had begun their careers as prosperous amateurs, had known, that is, an existence which is not without its dangers, because it keeps the child, or the young man, from all contact with real life, though, on the other hand, by equipping him with an unusual degree of sensitive awareness, and making it possible for him to indulge in prolonged meditation, it creates in him a feeling for fine shades, which is a rare and very special gift. 'There is, somewhere in Ruskin,' Proust wrote to Lauris, 'a magnificent passage of which we should never lose sight. He says that God's two great commandments are: *"Work while you still have the light"*, and *"Be merciful while you still have mercy"*.' There lay the true Proust: there it was that he had found himself. 'The real force of genius is to make us love a thought which we feel to be more real than we are ourselves.' By devoting five or six years to the study of Ruskin, Proust submitted to a spiritual discipline which made his full development possible. 'I want this translation of mine to be alive', he said. 'It will at least be faithful, faithful as love and pity are faithful.'

Most certainly it is alive, but to call it a translation is not enough because the translator has enriched the original work by the addition of a Preface and Notes which break new ground. Proust, in a very real sense, adopted and assimilated Ruskin's thought. That is to say, he transformed it into the stuff of his own mind. 'There is no better way of attaining complete awareness of one's feelings, than to try to recreate in one's mind the feelings of a master . . . The attempt strikes deep into the consciousness, with the result that not only one's own thoughts, but his as well, emerge into the light of day . . .' Ever since Proust had made the acquaintance of Ruskin's books, he had felt that they would reveal one whole aspect of the world till then unknown to him, that they would enrich that universe of cities, monuments and pictures which, so far, he had failed to penetrate deeply or to possess. And that is precisely what did happen.

> I suddenly saw the universe as something of infinite value. My admiration for Ruskin gave such high importance to the objects he had made me love, that they seemed as though charged with greater richness even than life itself. It was a time when I believed, quite literally, that my days were numbered. I went to Venice that I might, before I died, approach, touch, and see incarnate in Palaces, crumbling yet still standing and flushed with pink, Ruskin's ideas on the domestic architecture of the Middle Ages. . . .[1]

Ruskin was, for Proust, one of those Spirits of Intercession of whom we all of us have need when we are young, and some of us throughout our lives, if we are to make contact with reality. Ruskin taught him how to look at things and, more especially, how to describe what he saw. A natural taste for the infinitely small

[1] MARCEL PROUST, 'John Ruskin', in *Pastiches et Mélanges*. Translated by Gerard Hopkins in *Marcel Proust: A Selection from His Miscellaneous Writings* (Allan Wingate, 1948).

variations of fine shades, a gift for registering the 'slow-motion' notation of the emotions, and what amounted to a *greed* in savouring all colours and all forms — these were common to both men.

They agree in giving to science an important part to play in the composition of a work of art. Ruskin says that every class of rock, every variety of soil, every cloud formation, must be studied and rendered with geological and meteorological exactitude. Proust sets himself the task of describing human feelings with the precision of a doctor. Ruskin felt the need to sacrifice every duty, every pleasure, even life itself to what was, for him, the only possible way of making contact with reality. Proust, too, held that an artist's most pressing concern is to arrive at the closest communion with a reality which, in the last analysis, is the reality of himself. 'This Beauty' — he wrote of Ruskin — 'to which he thus found himself dedicated, was conceived by him, not as an object of delight existing to give him pleasure, but as a reality infinitely more important than life itself, for which he would have given his own. That, you will discover, was the starting-point of all Ruskin's aesthetic philosophy . . .'[1] It was to a large extent, too, the starting point of Proust's own aesthetic and moral doctrine.

From his grandmother and his mother he had inherited a love for, and an understanding of, the French seventeenth century. Without Ruskin, however, he would have been without 'any understanding of the Middle Ages, a sense of history, and the feeling of a sort of natural sympathy for all things that have grown dim with age, and an awareness of their continuing presence'. It was as a result of his love for Ruskin that he discovered the treasures of our Cathedrals, that he studied and consulted Émile Mâle, that he made a trip to Rouen accompanied by Albuféra and Louisa de Mornand for the express purpose of looking for one tiny figure among the carvings of the Library Door described by Ruskin, that he visited Vézelay and Sens.

Proust to Georges de Lauris: 'One morning I was seized with a mad desire to violate the little sleeping cities (please note

[1] MARCEL PROUST, 'John Ruskin' (*Pastiches et Mélanges*). Translated by Gerard Hopkins in *Marcel Proust: A Selection from His Miscellaneous Writings* (Allan Wingate 1948).

that I say *cities* and not sleeping *pretties*),[1] lying, some to the West in the radiance of a waning moon, some to the East in the splendour of a rising sun, but I resisted it and stayed in the train. I reached Avallon about eleven, had a look at it, took a carriage, and got to Vézelay after a three hours' drive, and in a fantastic state of mind. Vézelay is quite prodigious. It is set in a sort of Swiss frame, and stands in complete isolation on a mountain which dominates its neighbours and is visible for many miles in all directions. The peacefulness of the whole scene has to be seen to be believed. The church is huge, and reminds one more of a Turkish Bath than of Notre Dame, for it is built in alternating stones of black and white — a delicious Christian mosque ... I returned the same evening to Avallon with such a bout of fever that I couldn't take my clothes off, and spent the whole night walking about the place. At five in the morning I learned that there was a train due to leave at six. I took it. I saw a lovely little medieval town called Semur, and at ten o'clock got to Dijon, where I saw many lovely things, including the great tombs of the Dukes of Burgundy, of which no plaster cast can give you any real idea, because they are in polychrome. By eleven o'clock that evening I was back in Evian. . . .'

But it was in the matter of style that Ruskin's influence on Proust was decisive. 'Ruskin, though invisible, permeates all Proust's aesthetic.' Read any description by Ruskin of a wave, of a precious stone, of a tree, of a flower-species. If it be well translated it might be thought to come straight out of Proust. 'Ruskin', writes Gabriel Mourey, 'in *Stones of Venice*, describing the façade of Saint-Mark's, speaks of "the gleaming of the golden ground through the leaves behind them, interrupted and dim, like the morning light as it faded back among the branches of Eden, when first its gates were angel-guarded long ago": and of "the confusion of delight, amidst which the breasts of the Greek horses are seen blazing in their breadth of golden strength, and

---

[1] This is the nearest that one can get in English to Proust's play on the words *villes* and *filles*. The French text runs 'lisez bien *villes* et non des petites *filles* endormies'.

Translator

the Saint-Mark's lion, lifted on a blue field covered with stars, until at last, as if in ecstasy, the crests of the arches break into a marble foam, and toss themselves far into the blue sky in flashes and wreaths of sculptured spray, as if the breakers on the Lido shore had been frost-bound before they fell, and the sea-nymphs had inlaid them with coral and amethyst" . . . Is not that pure Proust?'

In the Preface to *Sesame and Lilies*, called *Journées de Lecture*, we come on a rich vein of that same ore which was later worked into *La Recherche du temps perdu*. By the time he wrote his novel, Proust had learned many essential truths. He knew, thanks to Ruskin, that the *matter* of a book is of little importance, that he could write a masterpiece merely by confining himself to describing the garden of his childhood, his room, his village, his family: 'For one of the effects of the love that the poets waken in us, is that it makes us attach a literal importance to matters which, for them, are expressive of emotions personal to themselves.' The landscapes and the people described do not matter: 'What makes them seem to us more beautiful than all the rest of the world, is that they give us, like some wavering reflection, the effect that they once produced on genius. . . .'[1]

He understood, too, what, in *Swann*, was to be given as his grandmother's gospel — that perfection is achieved by simplicity of means, by sobriety and charm, and that second-rate writers may be divided into two main types, 'those who write badly, and those who write too well'. All the notes on style with which he adorned his Preface to *Sesame and Lilies*, are marked by an unerring and meticulous precision. 'Racine's most famous lines have become celebrated because they can produce the sense of delight by reason of a familiar piece of linguistic daring which stands like a dangerous bridge between two gently-rounded banks. "*Je t'aimais inconstant, qu'aurais-je-fait fidèle?*" What pleasure we derive from encountering such expressions, the almost flat simplicity of which give to the sense, as to certain faces in Mantegna's pictures, a sweet completeness, a marvellous touch of colour!

---

[1] These two quotations are from *Days of Reading, I*, printed in *Pastiches et Mélanges*, and translated by Gerard Hopkins, in *Marcel Proust: A Selection from His Miscellaneous Writings* (Allan Wingate, 1948).

Et dans un fol amour ma jeunesse *embarquée*
Réunissons trois cœurs qui n'ont pu *s'accorder.* . . .'[1]

He, too, was to take pleasure, from now on, in introducing into some long, resplendent passage, a quite ordinary word which has the effect of throwing it into relief, of deepening its human significance: or, on the contrary, at the end of some piece of description having to do with a quite prosaic event where it sounds a chord of abstract solemnity. For example, recounting how, as a child, he would snuggle down in bed and pull the sheets over his face, he evokes in a memorable phrase 'the church that rings out for all the town the sleepless hours of men and lovers'.[2]

When the Prefaces and Notes to the *Bible of Amiens* and *Sesame and Lilies* were published, he still remained almost completely ignored. Only a very few among the critics, and among his friends, could see in them the promise of the future. Still, some there were who did. André Beaunier wrote an enthusiastic article in *La Renaissance,* and Louis de Robert, at that time enjoying a high reputation as a novelist, sent a letter of generous praise to Proust whom he did not yet know. *Marcel Proust to Georges de Lauris:* 'I am amazed to learn from Madame de Noailles and the members of her set that I have produced a piece of sublime and admirable writing. I don't believe a word of it, unfortunately! But I can't tell you how sweet these unexpected tributes are to me. . . .'

But such shrewd estimates were few and far between. Anatole France, to whom he sent a copy of the *Bible of Amiens* — 'as an expression of my infinite admiration, of my respectful affection, and of a sense of obligation which I can never forget' — attached no importance to it. But the fact remains that in 1904, thanks to Ruskin the Intercessor, Proust succeeded in penetrating into those hidden regions of the self where the true life of the spirit has its source. He had ceased to live on the surface in that state of mental passivity which had made of him a toy of the world's pleasures and the world's desires. He had found his true genius, and it was now

---

[1] *Days of Reading, I,* in *Marcel Proust: A Selection from His Miscellaneous Writings,* translated by Gerard Hopkins (Allan Wingate, 1948).
[2] *Days of Reading, I,* op. cit.

to spurt and gush with a power all the more torrential for having been hitherto untapped. 'I am going full speed ahead. There are so many things I have to say.'

He had already got beyond Ruskin. 'My love for Ruskin remains unshaken — only, I do sometimes find that the reading of his books somewhat chills it . . .' He was already seeking in his private memories the true subject of his book. For years, while his friends had condemned his laziness, he had been gathering his materials. We have his *Notebooks* — those strange volumes ('modern-style' Odette would have called them) decorated in the manner of 1900, and probably the gift of some lady of his acquaintance. They are filled with precious jottings. They prove that, from this point on, he was planning a long novel which should express his sense of disenchantment when forced to contemplate reality, his happiness when paying court to memory, the rare moments of illumination when he grasped eternity. 'If ever I manage to write the great work which I have in mind, you will see . . .' In order to write that great work, all he now needed was will-power, solitude and, most important of all, emancipation.

III

DEATH OF HIS PARENTS

Neither his Ruskin studies, nor the occasional articles which he continued to contribute to the *Figaro* (signing them sometimes *Dominique*, sometimes *Horatio*) constituted work of sufficient importance to set at rest Proust's uneasy awareness that he was neither giving a fair field to his gifts as a writer, nor justifying the confidence which his parents had in him. He knew that he was destined to be a man of one great book, and already he had a confused idea of the shape that such a book would assume. But he was frightened of it, because what he had to say seemed to him to be shocking, painful and intensely intimate. In spite of his strict and orthodox upbringing, he had been led by his temperament into the world of sexual inversion. There were attachments from which he could not break free. A number of squalid individuals, wholly unworthy of his affection, raged like wild beasts in the mud of that one region of the heart into which his true friends never penetrated. Many of these latter never even guessed at the existence of Proust's secret life. But he knew only too well that, if ever he was to produce a masterpiece, it would be only by dint of grasping the ugly truth, by rubbing at a sore which was never wholly healed. *Sodome et Gomorrhe* was his first choice of title for the novel he was planning to produce.

For a long time he took refuge in finesse. How could he possibly talk to a father whose attitude to life was serious and severe, to a mother whose nature was one of extreme modesty, about things that neither of them would understand? How could he write of them, knowing that his parents would be among his earliest readers? Occasionally, in his letters, he did make veiled reference to sorrows and crises of the heart, but only at once to cover up his tracks. He was at pains to keep in circulation the legend of his hopeless passion for Jeanne Pouquet. He set himself to assume the rôle of rejected and inconsolable lover, and made so public a show of himself in the part that Gaston de Caillavet took offence. His young wife was very naturally surprised when she was asked, suddenly, to 'see less' of Marcel, and, in particular, never again to ask him to the house.

> *Marcel Proust to Jeanne de Caillavet:* 'If I had known that Gaston has been ill and is now taking a rest, I would never have written to you . . . you know that I love him — I can say, taking in its literal sense an expression which universal insincerity has cheapened — *with all my heart.* I am deeply attached to both of you, feeling for one a friendship that was once almost morbid in its intensity, and for the other a hopeless passion. Both emotions have become more moderate with the passage of time, but they are still strong. I hope that this period of rest will soon restore him to complete health, and am heartbroken at the thought that I may have done anything to disturb it. . . .'[1]

The poems that Louisa de Mornand received from Proust breathed gallantry, but his letters were full of virtue. 'I would

---

[1] Unpublished letter.

rather die than lift my eyes to the woman whom a friend loves . . .'
On another occasion he wrote to her, recalling the memory of
Marie Radziwill (Benardaky before her marriage): 'A woman
who was the great love of my boyhood, when she was fifteen years
old. At that time I would willingly have died for her . . .' With
his mother he kept up the pretence that he might, quite possibly,
marry. *Marcel Proust to Madame Adrien Proust:* 'Be very careful
what you say about wanting me to marry. I gather that France
thinks I might do for his daughter. But, since this is something
I would never consider, you must move cautiously . . .' He was,
he said, much relieved when, in December 1901, the 'France girl'
married Captain Mollin, General André's A.D.C. Even his
friends were long deceived by these illusory schemes.

> *Proust to Georges de Lauris:* 'As for me, I feel love only for young
> girls (at the moment I love nothing, as you may well suppose),
> as though life were not complicated enough as it is. You will
> tell me that marriage was invented to deal with just such
> eventualities. But young girls don't remain young girls when
> they are married. One can have a young girl only once. I
> do so understand Blue Beard: he was a man with a weakness
> for young girls. . . .'

And, later:

> I may have some news for you soon, Georges, or, rather, I
> want to ask your advice. Don't you think it would be criminal
> on my part to ask a young girl to share my horrible life, even
> if she weren't afraid of the prospect? . . .

He continued to assume an attitude of adoration towards such
women as were out of his reach, the mistresses of his friends, or
irreproachable matrons. To the engaging Louisa de Mornand he
sent a copy of the *Bible of Amiens* with a somewhat outspoken
inscription:

> *To Louisa de Mornand*
> > *Ring'd by flames of her adorer's eyes*
> (Mornand is certainly not the present participle of the verb
> *morner*, for this archaic verb had a meaning the nature of

which I have forgotten, though I do know that it is highly improper, and God knows! . . .) Alas! those who have failed with you — in other words, the whole race of men — can no longer take delight in other women. Hence this couplet:

A qui ne peut avoir Louisa de Mornand
Il ne peut rester que le péché d'Onan. . . .

and one of *Sesame and Lilies* with these words: *You I could have loved, as you know full well.* But the real objects of his passion, moving him to feelings of delight and horror, were the various anonymous young men whom, with a wave of his magician's wand, he was one day to metamorphose into Albertine.

All his friends were settling down. In 1903 his brother, Robert, married Marthe Dubois-Amiot, and left the Rue de Courcelles for the Boulevard Saint-Germain. In 1904, the Duc de Guiche married Elaine Greffulhe, the only daughter of that Comtesse Greffulhe whom Proust had so much admired, and whose photograph he had tried in vain to get Montesquiou to give him. *Proust to the Duc de Guiche:* 'I told Madame Greffulhe that one of the reasons for your marriage (though only one) was that it might make it possible for you to have her photograph. She laughed so charmingly, that I should like to tell her the same thing ten times over. I wish I could think that my being a friend of yours would get me a similar privilege. . . .'

All his life long Proust set extraordinary store by the possession of photographs. He had a regular collection of them in his bed-room, which he would show to his friends. He would study the depicted face with the same concentration that he had devoted to roses and hawthorn trees, as though in an effort to free the imprisoned soul or to draw from the cardboard a mute avowal.

Ten years later he wrote to Simone de Caillavet, Jeanne Pouquet's daughter: 'If you would send me your photograph, it would give me enormous pleasure . . . I shall think of you, photograph or no photograph, but my memory, stupefied by drugs, has such lapses that photographs have become very precious to me. I keep them handy, as a sort of moral support, and am careful not to look at them too often for fear of exhausting their virtue . . .

In the days when I was in love with your mamma, I did the most extraordinary things in order to get hers, but all without success. I still get New Year's cards from a number of people in Périgord with whom I once struck up a friendship for the sole purpose of getting that self-same picture. . . .'

He gave his friend Guiche a very unusual wedding present, a revolver in a case adorned by Frédéric Madrazo who, with a series of little scenes in gouache, had transformed the 'case of a lethal weapon' into a kind of magic box, bearing, on each of its sides, a reproduction of the floral games in which the poetical young lady whom he had just married had taken part.[1] Proust was full of envy of the honeymoon spent at the Château de la Rivière, on the outskirts of the Forest of Fontainebleau. 'What is so lovely about the happiness of others', he said one day to Antoine Bibesco, 'is that one believes in it.'

What little happy home life he himself had was rapidly breaking down. At the end of the year 1903 his father had a stroke, while he was at his work, and died. Marcel dedicated his translation of the *Bible of Amiens* to him: 'To the Memory of my Father, struck down at his work, 24th November, 1903, died 26th November, this translation is affectionately dedicated.' Madame Proust had been a devoted wife, and she never really recovered from the shock of his death. The rest of her life was given up to his memory, which she cultivated with an astonishing multiplication of anniversaries and mortifications. One day in each month, in each week, even, was kept sacred to him, and on those occasions even the tiniest pleasure was forbidden. Marcel played his part in this *culte* with exemplary loyalty.

Marcel Proust to Madame Adrien Proust: '24 September, 1904: I believe that I am thinking of you with even more affection than usual — if such a thing were possible (which it isn't), on this 24 September. Whenever this day comes round — though all the thoughts, hourly accumulated, that have come to us since the first moment ought to make the lapse of time

---

[1] PRINCESSE DE BIBESCO, *Le Voyageur Voilé* (Editions de la Palatine, Geneva, 1947), p. 30. 'Floral games' is the name given to the literary competitions held yearly in Toulouse.

seem long, though, as a matter of fact our habit of keeping
it in constant remembrance, our lively sense of how happy
we once were, our habit of thinking that all that has happened
since is only a bad dream — makes it, on the contrary, seem
like yesterday, I find that I have to go through a process of
calculation before I can bring myself to realize that already
ten months have passed,[1] that one could have been unhappy
for so long, that there are still many long years of unhappiness
ahead, and that for ten months now, poor, dear Papa has been
beyond enjoying anything, has been cut off from all the
sweetness of life. . . .'[2]

On these recurrent 24ths he refused all invitations. *Proust to
Montesquiou*: 'I know that Mamma would be terribly upset if I
should choose that day to enjoy myself... especially since the
more intellectual the pleasure the keener it would be ... So, I
am afraid I must say — no ...' As far as possible during the
years 1904 and 1905 he lived with and for his mother. In August
1905 he took her to Evian, and there she became seriously ill
with a kidney complaint. 'She is back in Paris now,' he wrote to
Montesquiou, 'and the state of her health is such that I am in
perpetual anguish and misery . . .' It seems probable that those
exquisite pages of *Le Côté de Guermantes*, in which he describes the
grandmother's death, were inspired by what he witnessed at this
time.

The Sister who acted as nurse to the dying woman has told us
that in Madame Proust's eyes 'her son Marcel was still a small
boy of four'. In that same son's *Notebooks* we find the following
paragraph tucked away in the corner of a page. 'Mamma was at
times very unhappy, though I did not realize it, because she never
cried except in moods of tenderness or at moments of spiritual
contemplation. She died quoting Molière and Labiche to me.
The nurse had left the room for a moment, and she said: *Son
départ ne pouvait plus à propos se faire* — "The little boy mustn't be
frightened: his mother will not leave him." *Il ferait beau voir que
je sois à Étampes et mon orthographe à Arpajon* . . . That was the last

[1] Proust wrote 'six', but this is so obviously a mistake for 'dix' that I have ventured
to correct it. – Translator.

[2] From an unpublished letter in the possession of Madame Mante-Proust.

thing she said clearly. Only, at the end, when she noticed that I was trying to keep back my tears, she smiled with a queer little pucker of the lips, and I could just make out these words — for her speech had by now become very confused: *Si vous n'êtes Romain, soyez digne de l'être.*'

For a few days her condition seemed to be improving. *Proust to Montesquiou:* 'Whatever hope this slight improvement may bring (and I can't tell you how delicious that word *hope* is to me, for it seems to make it possible for me to go on living), that we may yet emerge from the depths in which we have been plunged till now, the journey back will be so long that each day's progress, if God so will that it continue, cannot but be almost imperceptible. Since you are so kind as to take an interest in my sorrow, I will write again should anything decisive, and of an encouraging nature, occur to put an end to our anguish. But don't, please, take the trouble to send for news. I can't tell you what my sufferings have been . . . She knows how incapable I am of living without her, how unarmed I am in the battle of life, and if — as I am terrified and tormented to think may have been the case — she realizes that perhaps she has got to leave me for ever, she must have been torn by the most terrible anxiety. Merely to think about that is sheer agony for me. . . .'

She died, and Marcel's despair moved his friends to feelings of intense pity. From *Reynaldo Hahn's Journal:* 'I have been thinking a great deal about Marcel, and his loneliness. I still have the vision of him crying by Madame Proust's deathbed, and smiling down at the body through his tears . . .' To Laure Hayman Proust wrote: 'Now my heart is empty, empty as my room and my life . . .' *To Montesquiou:* 'I have lost her. I witnessed her suffering, and I think she knew that she was going to leave me, that she could not give me any last words of advice, that it was agony for her to endure that enforced silence. I feel, too, that my ill-health filled her life with pain and anxiety.'

His mother had been the one person whose love had never, for long, disappointed him. She understood all and forgave all. Who would there be now to treat him as the child that he still was? Who was there now to call him 'Little silly' and 'My precious'?

Proust to Madame Straus: 'It isn't going out, no matter how ill I may be, that I mind, but coming home. My first words as I entered the front-door always used to be — "Is my mother in?" — and even before the answer came I would see her, standing there, afraid to enter my room lest her presence might lead me to say something when my breathing was troublesome, waiting anxiously to see whether I was over-tired. Alas! this constant worrying about me added to her grief, and the knowledge that that was so gnaws at me, fills me with remorse, and makes it impossible for me to find even a moment's happiness in the memory of our times together. It is not enough to say that those memories are with me all the time. It is in them that I live and breathe: they alone are the realities of my days. When the feeling of anxiety, which is all mixed up with them, becomes too obsessive and threatens to send me mad, I try to control and modify it. For the last few days I have been a little less wakeful, but when I am asleep my intelligence is in abeyance, so that I cannot repress that terrible urgency of recollection, cannot minister to my pain and soften it with happier thoughts. In that state I am defenceless against the attack of every agonizing impression. There are moments when I seem to be growing used to misery, when I feel that the joy of living will come back, and then I am filled with self-reproach, so that suddenly new waves of pain break over me. For this sort of misery is not a single experience. At every moment regret takes on a new shape, stimulated by some impression that recalls things like it in the past. When that happens my wretchedness takes on a hateful novelty, and the anguish that then I feel is like something I have never known before, as violent and as searing as when I first began to suffer. . . .'

Proust has described the alternations of despair and forgetful-ness, the moments of respite and relapse, the Intermissions of the Heart. But for a long time the memory of his mother never left him. Léon-Pierre Quint has told us how, ten years later, Marcel would say to one of his friends in a voice that was like a muted groan: 'Let me show you Mamma's picture' — uttering the word

THE TENNIS PARTY

Mamma's in soft, die-away tones. But there was nothing of the actor about him, and in the interval he had taken up his life again. 'He would talk and laugh, but behind the words and behind the laughter one could sometimes hear the voice of Madame Proust, the voice whose sound was always in his ears from morning until night . . .'[1] His sadness was increased by feelings of remorse when he remembered how deeply he had disappointed his parents. Both of them had been so proud of his intellectual gifts: both of them had died before he had produced any considerable body of work. 'But,' he would say, 'the thought that Mamma retained to the end her illusions about my future is a source of great happiness to me. . . .'

It has been said truly that in remorse, and in the desire never to give the lie to those illusions of his mother's, he found strength to embark upon his work, and the strength of mind to carry it through to successful completion. That is no doubt so, but it should be remembered that by 1905 he had already amassed innumerable notes designed to aid him in his great design. The worlds that he was later to create had not yet taken on their final form, but were hovering in the secret places of his mind, still nebulous and colourless. Nevertheless, the matter of which they were to be compacted already existed, and the genius that was to give them their final solidity.

The Preface to *Sesame and Lilies* had, in fact, contained potentially the whole first section of the novel. The feeling was even then with Proust that nothing awaiting him in the future could possibly produce more delicious emotions than those he had enjoyed in the days when he was discovering not only the world but himself. 'It is because I believed in both things and people as I roamed them [the roads of Combray], that the things and people I got to know through them make up the sum of what alone I now take seriously, of what alone can bring me pleasure. Whether it be that the creative faith has withered in me, whether it be that reality is only given its true form in memory, the fact remains that when to-day I am shown new flowers for the first time, there is about them something unreal. The way to Méséglise with its lilacs, its hawthorns, its cornflowers, its poppies and

---

[1] Lucien Daudet, *Autour de soixante lettres de Marcel Proust*, pp. 46-7.

its apple-blossom: the Guermantes way with its tadpole-haunted 'river, its water lilies and its buttercups, have remained for me and ever will remain the very image of that country in which I should like to live, where all that matters is that one can go fishing, can idle in a punt, can see the ruins of Gothic keeps, can find adrift among the fields some huge and massive church, similar in all respects to Saint-André des Champs, a mass of honey-coloured stone as native to the countryside as any mill: and the cornflowers, the hawthorns, the apple-blossom which even today I see upon my journeys at once lay hold upon my heart because their true home is in that deep layer of myself which is the past. . . .'

The only true Paradise is Paradise Lost. The promise of those full and lovely hours of childhood can never come again, save in the brief moments of love which temporarily give back to us the simple enthusiasms of our earliest years. But, in order to discover that magic world of the past, to paint its picture, to transform it into the material of fiction, we must be able to get outside it, and that was precisely what Proust so long as his parents were alive had never been able to do. 'Quite recently I have begun again to hear distinctly, if I take the trouble to listen, the sobs which I struggled to repress when my father was present, in which I was free to indulge only when I was alone with Mamma. The truth is they have never ceased, and it is only because now a great silence rings me round, that I can catch the sound of them again, like those Convent bells which, all day long, are so far submerged beneath the noises of the streets that they seem to have stopped, but in the silence of the evening hours are once more audible. . . .'

His mother's death had exiled him from the paradise of child-hood. The moment had come at last when he could recreate it. For this act he was marvellously well equipped. He had inherited from his scientific father a gift of accurate diagnosis, and from his mother the gifts of intuition and taste. He possessed a style, great culture, a knowledge of painting, music and architecture. He had acquired a rich and precise vocabulary. His intelligence was 'unsusceptible to consolation', and had been rendered by solitude sensitive even to excess. Most important of all, he had developed a prodigious memory peopled with scenes and conversations. He had not frittered away the harvest of his childhood and his adolescence, as so many do, in reading bad 'boys' books'. He had reached the age of great undertakings with his granaries filled to bursting. Finally, to his parents he owed that sense of duty without which nobody, be he artist or man of action, can achieve anything outstanding. But with him the sense of moral obligation took that special form of artistic responsibility which consists in painting with absolute truth and complete courage what is *seen*. Such courage is infinitely rare. Most writers, whether consciously or not, either embellish life or distort it; some, because they dare not display the vanity of what all men, including themselves, hold most dear; others, because their own grievances conceal whatever in the world there may be of greatness and of poetry; almost all of them, because they lack the power to go beyond appearances and release the imprisoned spirit of beauty. It is not enough to observe. The artist must penetrate beyond the object, beyond the creatures of flesh and blood, to the mysterious truths concealed in them. Beauty is like those fairy-tale princesses who have been shut up in a castle by some mighty magician. We may, after much striving, open a thousand doors and yet not find them, and most men, urged forward by the active enthusiasms of youth, tire of the search and soon abandon it. But a Proust will sacrifice everything in order to reach imprisoned loveliness, and a day of revelation comes at last, of illumination and of certainty, when he finds his glittering and concealed reward. 'One knocks', he says, 'on many doors that open on to nothingness. Against the only one that leads into reality, for which one might seek in vain a hundred years, one bumps by accident, and it swings back of its own accord.'

CHAPTER V

ENTRY INTO LITERATURE: 1905-12

He had the appearance of a man who lives no longer in the daylight and the open air; the appearance of a hermit who has not left his forest depths for many years, with something in his face that told of anguish, the mark, as it were, of a pain which is beginning to grow less. About himself he spread an aura of bitter kindliness.   LÉON-PAUL FARGUE

I

A STRANGE BEING

'WHAT have you done to me! What have you done to me! If we let ourselves think for a few moments we shall, I believe, agree that there is probably no devoted mother who could not, when her last day dawns, address the same reproach to her son. The truth is that, as we grow older, we kill the heart that loves us by reason of the cares we lay on it, by reason of the uneasy tenderness that we inspire and that keeps it for ever stretched upon a rack. . . .'[1]

These words are quoted from a short piece of narrative contributed by Proust to the *Figaro* a few months after his mother's death. It concerns a sensitive and kindly man who went suddenly mad and became a parricide. It is difficult to believe that when he wrote them he was not thinking of his own mother. Not that he had struck her down with dagger-thrusts: far from it, for he had cherished her with a love born of despair, and if, now and again, in scribbled notes, he had played the spoiled child and rounded on her, his periods of ill-temper had been always short, and had never in any way lessened the adoration in which he held her. Nevertheless, he did feel that he was responsible for 'the slow work of destruction which is wrought in a much loved body by a painful and disappointed tenderness'. The scene in

[1] 'Sentiments Filiaux d'un Parricide' (*Pastiches et Mélanges*) Translated by Gerard Hopkins as 'Filial Sentiments of a Parricide', in *Marcel Proust: A Selection from His Miscellaneous Writings* (Allan Wingate, 1948).

which Mademoiselle Vinteuil and her friend profane the portrait of the old musician was, in his book, to stand for 'a symbol of his conscience, bred of remorse',[1] and perhaps of the shameful pleasure to be derived from the very act of profanation.

He knew now that never again, in real life, would he be in contact with that world 'founded on goodness, on scruple and on sacrifice', the existence of which he had refused to deny as long as she, in whom its ideal seemed to be incarnate, still lived. What happiness was there still for him to seek? Worldly successes? — he had had them all and seen their vanity. Passion? — he was the follower of a 'gloomy heresy' which made it impossible for him to know the joys of a tranquil heart. Faith in God? — he would have liked to believe, but could not. All that remained for him was escape into the unreal. Marcel Proust was to enter literature as others enter religion. His retreat would have to be accomplished by stages because, for a long time to come, the claims of his work would make it necessary for him to maintain diplomatic relations with the world. Until the very end of his life, a ghost, padded with cotton wool, topped by a pale face whose shaven cheeks looked blue, so black he was,[2] would continue to haunt on the stroke of midnight certain houses in Paris, certain hotel vestibules. The real Marcel was henceforth to live in the past.

'The Ark had been closed, and it was night upon the earth . . . The world on which Noah gazed in that diluvian darkness was a world that existed only in his own mind. . . .'[3]

Between 1905 and 1911, at some date not exactly known, Proust began to put his novel into shape. 'We knew', said Lucien Daudet, 'that he was busy on a work about which he only occasionally spoke, and then apologetically.' Here and there in his letters one gets a hint of what was going on. Fragments of the book appeared in the *Figaro* in the form of essays: *Au Seuil de Printemps: Épines Blanches, Épines Roses — Rayon de Soleil sur le Balcon — L'Église de Village.* In 1909, Marcel read the first two hundred pages to Reynaldo Hahn, and was heartened by the warmth of his friend's response. In the same year he consulted Georges

[1] MARIE-ANNE COCHET, *L'Âme Proustienne* (Imprimerie des Établissements Collignon. Brussels, 1929).
[2] RAMON FERNANDEZ, *Proust* (Editions de la Nouvelle Critique, Paris, 1943).
[3] ROBERT BRASILLACH, *Portraits* (Plon, Paris, 1935).

de Lauris about the name *Guermantes*, and asked his opinion on the desirability of dividing the work into volumes. Behind a thick curtain of sickness and mystery, Proust silently set his stage and rehearsed his cast. Not until 1905 had he found sufficient strength in himself to sacrifice the present to the remembered past. 'The poet is to be pitied who, with no Virgil to guide him, has to cross the circles of Hell, all burning sulphur and flaming pitch, casting himself into the fire that rains from Heaven that he may bring back with him a few of the denizens of Sodom...' The death of his parents, the maturing of his ideas and, almost certainly, an experience of sudden illumination, contributed to set him working. He felt very ill. Would he live long enough to complete his book? He knew that his brain was a 'rich seam containing a vast expanse of mineral deposits, all precious and all various...' But would he be granted sufficient time in which to exploit it?

The novel which he had to write would be long. 'He would need many nights; perhaps a hundred, perhaps a thousand...' It would be as long as the *Arabian Nights*, but quite different. To bring his writing to completion he would have to have determination and an infinity of courage. 'I had lived a life of idleness and dissipation, of sickness, invalidism and eccentricity. I was embarking on my work when already near to death, and I knew nothing of my trade...' He has said, somewhere, that laziness had preserved him from facile accomplishment, and sickness from laziness. That is true. But for his early period of dissipation he might have started to write too early, might have produced facile works which had been simmering for too short a time. But for his illness which, as it grew worse, forced him to stay at home and made it possible for him to prevail upon his friends to accept his strange way of life, he could never have contrived those long periods of solitude without which no great work can ever be born.

For fifteen months he stayed on in the Rue de Courcelles, in the flat where his parents had died, 'so as to see the lease out'. Then at the end of 1906 he moved to 102 Boulevard Haussmann, a house that belonged to the widow of his uncle, Georges Weil, the magistrate. *Marcel Proust to Madame Catusse:* 'I could not reconcile myself to the idea of moving straight away into a house that Mamma had never known, and so have taken a sub-lease, for one year, of a flat that formerly belonged to my uncle, at 102 Boulevard Haussmann, in a house where I sometimes used to dine with Mamma, and where I was present at my uncle's death in the very room that I am to inhabit. But for these memories, its gilded cornices and flesh-coloured walls, the dust of the neighbourhood, the incessant noise, and even the trees that press against the windows, make it the kind of place that I should not willingly have chosen. . . .'

In this new room Marcel insisted that his bed and the little table which he called his 'pinnace', loaded with books, papers, fountain-pens and the materials needed for his fumigations, close beside it, should be placed in exactly the same position as they had occupied in the Boulevard Malesherbes and the Rue de Courcelles, in such a way that he could get an 'oblique view of all who entered, with the daylight coming from the left — when, by chance, the daylight was admitted — and, also on the left, the warmth of the fire which, as he complained, was always too fierce or too mild. . . .'[1]

The volumes piled upon the 'pinnace' had almost all been borrowed from friends. When the old home had been broken up, the family library had been buried beneath a litter of furniture, chandeliers and tapestries too numerous to fit into more congested quarters, with the result that Marcel could get at none of his own books. From time to time he would lend Georges de Lauris a Sainte-Beuve or a Merimée which he had just bought, saying: 'Keep it. If I want it I will ask you for it. It would be lost in my flat. . . .'

The move had meant for Marcel exile and tragedy. He had, in his usual way, called all his closest friends into consultation. One evening Madame de Noailles was rung up on the telephone by the wine-waiter at the Hôtel des Réservoirs at Versailles, who had asked with conscientious simplicity, whether she 'advised Monsieur Proust to take the flat in the Boulevard Haussmann'. Madame Catusse had received numerous letters. 'Do you think that the furniture from Mamma's room (the blue room) would

[1] Lucien Daudet, op. cit., p. 51.

collect too much dust, or that it would do for me? Do you think it is pretty? Would you advise it for the small drawing-room, or do you think that the furniture from Papa's study in the Rue de Courcelles would be better? . . .' And if Madame Catusse's charming eyes expressed disapproval of the wash-basins, how, he asked, could they be improved? Could she buy him a Persian rug for the large drawing-room? The tapestries were too big for his new walls. Ought he to have them cut, or merely folded?

But, above all, she *must* do something to save him from noise. If the other tenants had jobs to be done, was it not their duty to get the workmen to come at night, seeing that he, Marcel, always slept in the day? Madame Catusse found the mission difficult, and it was Madame Straus's turn to be mobilized. Didn't she know the Monsieur Katz whose mother set all those infernal hammers going? Couldn't she ask him not to let the men start working before midday? 'I will pay him any indemnity he likes to ask . . . I have persuaded one of the other tenants to have his work done between eight o'clock [in the evening] and midnight . . .' But it would be better still if Madame Katz could be prevailed upon not to have any workmen in the place at all: 'because, no matter how often one begs them to work on the other side, and to make as little noise as possible, no matter how much one tips them — and the concierge as well — the first thing they do is to waken the neighbour and invite him to share their merry-making: *Frappez marteaux et tenailles* — an injunction that they carry out with a sort of religious fervour. . . .'

Madame Straus, all irony and devotion, asked Monsieur Katz to luncheon, but his mother continued with the task of building — 'though Heaven knows what! for after all these months, twelve workmen a day all frenziedly tapping could, by this time, have erected something as monumental as the Pyramid of Cheops, something that passers-by would see with astonishment rearing its head between the *Printemps* Store and Saint-Augustin . . .' No sooner was the Pyramid of Katz completed, than it was the turn of Monsieur Sauphar: 'Monsieur Straus has told me that "Sauphar" is the name of the kind of loud trumpet that used to be sounded in the Synagogue to wake the dead for Judgment. There is not much difference between those Sauphars of old and the

Sauphars of today . . .' The concierge of the building was called upon to intervene: 'Madame Antoine, I should be much obliged if you could find out what is happening in Dr. Gagey's flat, where the hammering is continuous . . . At four o'clock someone was driving nails into, and boring through, the wall etc just over my head. Who was it? — the workmen, the chauffeur or the man-servant? . . . Do try to find out and drop me a line, either this evening or tomorrow, if it wouldn't be too much trouble. . . .'[1]

Finally, he discovered a remedy, which was to have his room entirely lined with cork. Thus, it was between four walls padded with this material, and proof against all noise from outside, that he wrote his great work. Round him were ranged his *Notebooks*, school exercise-books bound in black American cloth, from which he cut selected passages for inclusion in the finished manuscript. The room was filled with the yellow eddies of his fumigations, and reeked of their pungent smell. Through this cloud the visitor would catch sight of Marcel, looking pale and rather puffy, his eyes shining in the enveloping fog, dressed in a nightshirt over which he wore numerous woollen pullovers, all of them a mass of burns, and coming unravelled. Ramon Fernandez has described one of his nocturnal visits to the Boulevard Haussmann, and the sound of Proust's voice, 'that miraculous voice, discreet, absent-minded, abstracted, discontinuous, muffled — which seemed to be producing sounds from somewhere behind his teeth, be-hind his lips, behind his throat, from somewhere situated in the region of his intelligence . . . His wonderful eyes seemed to adhere *physically* to the furniture, the fabrics, the various odds and ends in the room. It was as though he were breathing in through all the pores of his skin the reality contained in that room, in that moment, in me — and the ecstasy apparent on his face was that of a medium in the act of receiving invisible messages from material objects. He was prodigal of admiring exclamations, which I did not take for flatteries, since, wherever his eyes came to rest, there he would leave the imprint of a masterpiece . . .' It was on this occasion that he asked Fernandez, who knew Italian, to repeat several times the words *senza rigore*. Proust listened with his eyes shut, and, much later, Fernandez came on the passage

[1] *Quatre lettres de Marcel Proust à ses concierges* (Albert Skira, Geneva, 1945).

in the *Jeunes filles en fleurs* where that *senza rigore* is mentioned as 'evoking the feeling of harsh thunder combined with tender spirituality'. This incident serves to show how every phrase in his book was an experience, a memory, and also to what extent this seeker after sensations practised the art of 'integral intuition'.

Every visit took on the semblance of a consultation. He put his questions with passion, precision, incredulity, and if his interlocutor showed signs of wandering always brought him back to the subject in hand. Or, reversing the process, he would himself diverge with the object of surprising an avowal or awakening a memory. Quite often he made his inquiries by letter: *Proust to Lucien Daudet:* 'When you were quite a child you saw the Princesse Mathilde. It ought to be easy for you to build up (describe to me) one of her *toilettes*, the kind of things she would have worn on a spring afternoon, one of those sort of mauve crinolinish affairs that she affected, perhaps a hat with streamers and trimmed with violets, something, anyhow, that you almost certainly must have seen . . .' He wrote to Madame Straus asking her to advise him on the subject of fox-furs which he wanted to buy for a young woman. The furs were fictional, and the young woman was the Albertine of the novel. Sometimes he would send off a messenger at night, because when he was suddenly visited by a desire to know something he had to know it at once. Already, in the days when he was translating Ruskin, his friends the Yeatmans had described how one evening there had been a ring at their door-bell. It was Proust's manservant who said in the most natural way in the world, 'Monsieur has sent me to ask Monsieur and Madame what became of Shelley's heart'.

Each specialist was consulted on his own subject. Reynaldo Hahn on music, Jean-Louis Vaudoyer on painting, the Daudet family on flowers. In all such matters he insisted on having the correct technical term, 'so that a musician, a gardener, a painter or a doctor would think, as he read, that Proust had devoted years to the study of music, horticulture, painting or medicine'. 'We did our best', says Lucien Daudet, 'to give him the information required — not always knowing exactly why he asked — on the subject of the kind of cake one would have been likely to find in the confectioner's shop on Sunday after Mass in some country

town, or what shrubs would be in bloom at the same time as hawthorns and lilacs, and what the name of the flower was that wasn't
a Hyacinth, but that looked like a Hyacinth and was used in the
same way, etc.' From women he would ask for information on
the subjects of which they had special knowledge. *Proust to Madame
Gaston de Caillavet:* 'I wonder whether you can give me, for the
book I am just finishing, a few dressmaking points? (Please don't
think that was why I rang you up the other day: it was just that I
wanted to see you . . .)' There follows a number of searching
questions about the dress worn by Madame Greffulhe at the
Italian play in the theatre at Monte Carlo 'when she was sitting
in a very dark front box, about two months ago' (the answers were
to be used in describing what the Princess de Guermantes was
wearing at the Opera). He would have liked to see the dresses
and the hats worn by the ladies of his acquaintance twenty years
earlier, and expressed indignation on hearing that they had not
kept them. 'My dear Marcel, it's twenty years since I wore that
hat! I've no longer got it.' — 'That, Madame, I find it hard to
believe. No, the truth is, you don't *want* to show it me. It's there,
but you have made up your mind to provoke me. That makes
me very unhappy. . . .'[1]

One evening, at half-past eleven, he turned up at the Caillavets
— old friends whom he had not seen for a long time. 'Are Madame
and Monsieur still up? Could they possibly make it convenient
to see me? . . .' Of course they would see him!

'I am wondering, Madame, whether you would give me a very
great pleasure? It is many years since I saw your daughter. I
may never come to this house again . . . and it is extremely unlikely that you will ever bring her to mine. By the time she is of
an age for dancing, I shall no longer be going out. I am an
extremely sick man. Consequently, Madame, what I ask of you
now is that I should be permitted to see Mademoiselle Simone
tonight.'

'But, Marcel, she has been in bed for ages!'

'I implore you, Madame, to go upstairs and to see whether she
is asleep, and, if she is not, to explain matters to her. . . .'

Simone came down and was introduced to the strange visitor.

[1] Léon Pierre-Quint, *Marcel Proust, sa vie, son œuvre* (Éditions de Sagittaire, 1936).

What was it that he hoped to find in her? — the impressions he needed in order to paint the portrait of Mademoiselle de Saint-Loup, the daughter of the woman whom the Narrator had once loved.

It was in pursuit of pictures of the past that, whenever he happened to be well enough, he still travelled. 'I do manage to get out, but only occasionally, and then by a stroke of good luck. As a rule, it is to go and look at hawthorns or at the finery of three apple trees in their gala dresses under a grey sky.' When his attacks became too frequent he dared not even so much as look at the chestnuts of the Avenue through closed windows, and a whole autumn passed without his once seeing the colours of the outside world. When 'holiday-time' came round he made 'a frightening and platonic meal off time-tables, and planned in his mind endless circular tours' — which he enjoyed in imagination, stretched on his sofa.

On such occasions, however, as he did feel slightly better, he would risk an outing. 'Exceptions to the rule are the magic of existence', he said. The Duchesse de Clermont-Tonnerre entertained him one evening at Glissolles when he was touring Normandy in a hired car, looking at the flowers through closed windows. 'The headlights were focused on the long vistas of rose trees. The blossoms looked like beautiful women just awakened from sleep . . .' He revisited, 'under the overcast indifference of a rainy sky, from which they had succeeded in filching a few precious scraps of light (the result of a miracle which might have been commemorated in the Cathedral along with others far less interesting), the windows of Évreux'. That he might endure the fatigue of these journeys, he lived exclusively on *café au lait*, and thanked his hostess for having 'steered him upstairs when tottering from an excess of cafeine'.[1] In 1910 he played with the idea of staying for a while at Pontigny: 'Do you know Paul Desjardins' lay Abbey of Pontigny? If I were well enough to put up with its discomforts, I should be sorely tempted. . . .'

But it was to Cabourg, above all, that he went whenever he could manage it, there to body forth the ghosts of Balbec and

[1] E. DE CLERMONT-TONNERRE, *Robert de Montesquiou et Marcel Proust* (Flammarion, Paris, 1925), p. 104.

'l'ombre des jeunes filles en fleurs'. *Proust to Madame Gaston de Caillavet:* 'I have been thinking a great deal about your daughter. What a shame it is that she is not going to Cabourg! Not that I have made up my mind to go there myself this year, but if I knew that she was to be there, I should not hesitate. . . .'

Whenever he stayed in an hotel, he always booked three rooms (so as to run no risk of having noisy neighbours). One of these would be occupied by Félicie. 'Do you think it would be *very* foolish of me to take my old cook to the hotel?' The suite had to be cheerful, comfortable and so placed that he *would not hear anybody walking about over his head.* At a pinch, he would reserve the corresponding room on the floor above. He remained shut up all day, working and questioning the hotel servants who gave him much precious information about the visitors and the staff. When the sun went down, and his enemy, the daylight, was finally vanquished, he would go downstairs armed with a parasol and stand for a moment or two at the front entrance like some night-bird which, when darkness falls, emerges from its shadowy retreat — first of all assuring himself that the dulled radiance was not due merely to a passing cloud, and that the sun would not return to the attack. Later, seated at a large table in the dining-room, he would entertain — a quiet, chilly, charming host — and offer champagne to all who came to speak with him.

In Paris he still frequented certain houses, hot on the tracks of his characters, but usually arrived so late that the other guests, seeing him, would exclaim: 'Marcel! — why, it's struck two!' — and take to their heels. Such was the behaviour of Anatole France at Madame Arman de Caillavet's Wednesdays. He was very little interested in Proust, notwithstanding the fact that, whenever he published a new book, the latter wrote him a letter of enthusiastic praise:

> . . . What happy evenings there are in store for me with Crainquebille, le Doyen Malorey, General Decuire, Putois and Riquet, now brought together freshly born from the marvellous sea-spume of your genius, august though they already had become because of the empire they have succeeded in exercising over men's minds in the time that has

elapsed since those days when they changed the face of the world so profoundly that they seem to bear upon their shoulders the majesty of all the centuries . . . The *Manœuvres de Montil* contains, if I am not mistaken, that wonderful scene in which the General loses his Brigade and runs about looking for it — a version of the Battle of Waterloo episode in the *Chartreuse* written with irony and genius. The dialogue, too, — equalled only in Balzac, but far more beautiful — when the General is looking at Van Orley's tapestries. 'You have a very large place here' — 'You could have brought your Brigade with you, sir. I should have been happy to receive it.' Those three sentences are firmly fixed in my memory as constituting the finest comic triptych ever painted by a master hand, quite perfect in their kind, startling one by the genius of their invention, and so utterly convincing in their unexpected and quite flabbergasting truth. I seem to remember, too, a request from an editor for an article 'redolent of the aristocracy'. The only piece I have had time, as yet, to read — the book reached me only ten minutes ago — is the *Christ de l'Océan*, which moved me deeply. What, perhaps, I love best — where I love so much — is *Putois*. And then, you see, I know the story of it, for I had it from your lips in those happy days when I was able to see the little flower, then still living, which had suggested the sculptured form that you have introduced into your sublime cathedral. Thank you, again, dear Master, for not forgetting a poor invalid whose continued existence you alone remember. The greatest men are always the Salt of the Earth. . . .'[1]

When Proust entertained on his own account, it was no longer, as in the days of his parents, at his own house, but in some restaurant — preferably the Ritz — whose *maître d'hôtel*, Olivier Dabescat, with his air of discreet distinction, simple dignity and knowledge of how such things ought to be done, enchanted him. The giving of a dinner for Calmette, the Editor of the *Figaro*, always so friendly and so ready to extend hospitality to his articles, became for Proust an event necessitating long letters to Madame

[1] Unpublished letter in the possession of Professor Mondor.

Straus, and telephone calls (which he never made himself) to each of the guests — to Gabriel Fauré, who was to play — because Reynaldo Hahn was in London singing before King Edward VII and Queen Alexandra . . . and then, could Monsieur Joseph Reinach be asked if the Duc de Clermont-Tonnerre was to be present — and what was the order of precedence as between Fauré, 'who is no longer young, Calmette, in whose honour the dinner is being given, Béraud, who is very touchy, and Monsieur de Clermont-Tonnerre, who is younger but traces his descent from Charlemagne? — and what about the foreigners? . . .'

At long last the dinner actually took place, in a private room at the Ritz panelled in cerise brocade and filled with gilded furniture. Considerable surprise was caused by the presence, in this scheme of decoration, of 'two furred and padded Lapps' who turned out to be Proust and Madame de Noailles. Risler, engaged at the last moment, played Wagnerian overtures. Dinner done, the tips had to be distributed. Marcel wanted to give Olivier three hundred francs, but the guests flung themselves upon him in an effort to modify his generosity. He promptly gave more.

But Cabourg, the Ritz and his various nocturnal visits were, all of them, in the nature of sudden attacks planned to bring him information about the enemy, in other words, the outside world. His real life, during those years of work, centred round his bed where he lay writing, surrounded by what Félicie, whom he had inherited from Madame Proust (she is the Françoise of the novel), called 'them bits of paper', meaning his *Memoranda*, his *Notebooks* and his innumerable photographs. As a result of all the snippets being stuck one on top of the other (collectively, they were to build up the most wonderful book in the world), they became badly torn. 'All moth-eaten' — said Françoise. "'Tis a crying shame; why, the bottom of that there page isn't no more than a bit of lace' — then, scrutinizing it as a tailor might examine a piece of material — 'Don't think as how I can furbish *that* up, 'tis too far gone . . .' But nothing was lost, and slowly, like one of Françoise's beef dishes, the work to which Marcel Proust was, literally, to give his life, took shape.

OUT OF THE MAIN STREAM

In that Ark of his, padded with cork, he saw less and less company. Women were scarcely ever admitted to the Boulevard Haussmann. He disliked the idea of their seeing him in a clutter of medicaments, in a mist of fetid vapours. When he felt the need of them he went to their houses or entertained them in a restaurant. Servants played a large part in his life. Two of them, Félicie and Antoine, had been with his parents and stayed on with him. He studied their language, wondered at their devotion, submitted to their despotism. As a sick and eccentric man he came to rely on them. It was necessary, therefore, that he should get to know them well and anticipate their reactions.

Similarly with his men of business. Although since the death of his parents he was in enjoyment of a considerable fortune, he believed, and asserted, that he was ruined. The necessity of making a tax-return, no matter how unimportant, terrified him, and he delegated this duty to certain obscure cousins who happened to be specialists in the subject. On the question of investments he asked advice of all and sundry, approaching the problem with a great air of mystery and reluctance. 'I should very much like to know whether Monsieur Straus holds any shares in Australian gold-mines . . . and when I say "whether he holds", I don't want you to think that I am being vulgarly inquisitive, but only whether he has been persuaded to buy, whether anybody has given him a tip. Somebody, the other day, was speaking to me about Australian mines, but I can't remember which. . . .'

He was susceptible to the poetry of the Stock Exchange, to its charm, to the romantic appeal of the rather old-fashioned engravings that adorned his share certificates, but he complicated even the most modest of his deals by his fears, his suspicions, his second-thoughts and his hesitations. Young Albert Nahmias, who acted as his broker, used to receive astonishing letters from him, which were rendered almost unintelligible by the multiplicity of their detail:

A PAGE FROM ONE OF PROUST'S NOTEBOOKS

Dear Albert: My health is so bad just now that I don't know how I am to explain my present devilishly complicated situation. Put briefly, the position is this. I shall have, at most, about a hundred thousand francs to invest. But I gather from the Crédit Industriel that, in this matter of selling out, the 4th March is settling day, which means that they won't have the money before the 3rd. But I shall have to draw a cheque for 100,000 francs, dated the 3rd, and this they will honour as soon as the sale has been completed (that is to say, as I understand it, either the 4th March or the 3rd). It won't, in any case, be later than the 4th. I needn't tell you that the transaction is as safe as houses. I guarantee that there will be enough funds in my account to meet the cheque.

If this arrangement seems all right to you (the Crédit Industriel assure me that it is all in order and that I need fear no delay, which is as good as to say that all will be well, because they are extremely reliable people), all you need do — with your knowledge of how my account stands — is to reckon how many shares I ought to take up. I don't want to spend more than, roughly, a hundred thousand, which, I suppose, represents something like 270 Rand and 275 Crown, though perhaps not all paid up (the brokerage charges to be included in that sum, or exceeding it by only a very little. I mean, I don't want to find, after I have paid the hundred thousand, that there is still something owing.) Like Aranyi, I keep on saying the same thing over and over again, but I am so anxious that there shouldn't be any mistake. (I don't want anything to be carried over: I shall take up part of the shares and sell the rest.)

If, however, for some reason or other, Léon dislikes the idea, and if he should say to you 'it's a bit late in the day to take up the shares now', etc., then (but I must know for certain by tomorrow, the 29th) I won't take up any, and, instead of drawing a cheque for a hundred thousand, shall just settle up the debit balance. But in that case, I still hold to it that nothing must be carried over, and shall get rid of the lot. But I see no reason why my first suggestion should cause any difficulties, and I rather think it is the one Léon will prefer. Let me have a line tomorrow. If all is well, I shall immediately send you a cheque for a hundred-thousand (but post-dated 3rd March). I should like Léon to send the certificates in my name to the Crédit Industriel, whenever it suits him to do so. I have no idea how this part of the business is dealt with, because I am concerned only with the bit that concerns me, and that is more than enough! You may well imagine that I am calling down silent curses on the head of the individual who, by causing all this delay, without considering *my* convenience in the slightest (it *would* happen just when I'm going through one of my bad spells) thought he was being mighty clever by waiting until settling day before paying the money in to my account! The Crédit Industriel sees nothing out of the ordinary in all this, but *I* find it nerve-racking! Let me repeat. If Léon would rather I didn't take up any of the shares but sold the lot, he has only to say so. But I must know what he thinks by tomorrow. In any case, I don't want anything to be carried over. If I *do* take up the shares, it is essential that I buy the *same* quantity of *Rand* and *Crown*, that is to say, 270 *Crown* and 270 *Rand*, or 260 *Crown* and 260 *Rand* (according to what money is available after settling up my account, the whole sum not to exceed a hundred thousand francs). But if it is a question of five more *Rand* than *Crown*, or five more *Crown* than *Rand* (or even ten or twenty), I don't very much mind.

If you telephone, please be very careful not to mention anything about all this *here* — nothing about shares, etc.

Do you know whether cheques for such large amounts are made out in the same way as cheques for a hundred francs?

Affectionately   MARCEL[1]

He confided some of the *Notebooks* bearing on the novel to this same Albert Nahmias, for him to get the contents typed.

Dear Albert: do you still want to rival Oedipus and struggle with the Sphinx-like mysteries of my handwriting? If you do,

[1] Unpublished letter.

146

I can send you some notebooks which surpass in obscurity anything you have ever seen. But only if you *want me to*. Don't do it just to please me, because I can manage. . . .
. . . Forgive me for asking you rather an odd question. The fact is, something rather unexpected has happened which would make your answer to it very welcome. Have you ever had occasion, for any reason, to have somebody shadowed? If so, have you kept the address of the Private-Detective Agency which you employed, and are you still in touch with it? . . .[1]

This wish to have somebody shadowed was connected with his squalid love-affairs. In the early part of his life he had formed attachments for certain beautiful youths, like Willie Heath, and, technically 'pure' though these friendships doubtless were, there was something suspect about them. At a somewhat later date, however, he had met a throughly diabolical character (like someone in a Balzac novel) called Albert Le Cuziat. Our knowledge of this individual is derived, for the most part, from what Maurice Sachs has written about him.[2] 'He was born in Brittany. Eager to see the capital, he got his local Curé to give him a letter of introduction to a priest in Paris who enjoyed the intimacy of Prince O. . . . The Prince took him on as an under-footman. At that time Albert was very good-looking, tall, slim and fair-haired. No doubt he was, by nature, both obedient and affectionate. Prince R. . . ., one of his master's friends, took a liking to him, asked to be allowed to have him, and promoted him to be butler in his own household. . . .'[3]
Albert loved obeying orders as much as others love giving them. 'He developed a passion for the aristocracy, members of which it was his duty to admit each evening to the house.' Very soon no one could surpass him in knowledge of the origins, the intermarriages and the quarterings of all the great families.
Proust formed an attachment for him. 'This has led certain people to believe that Albert was Albertine. But to hold that

---

[1] Unpublished letter in possession of Alfred Dupont.
[2] See *Nouvelle Revue Française*, July 1st, 1938.
[3] MAURICE SACHS, *Le Sabbat* (Editions Corrêa, Paris, 1946), pp. 279-86.

view', wrote Maurice Sachs, 'is to have a very imperfect idea of Proust's method of composition. The sex of Proust's heroine is never, admittedly, very clearly defined. She remains little more than a generalized embodiment of love, and the reader is free to give her what face he pleases. The most one can say is, that in the matter of names, there certainly are a number of coincidences scattered throughout the book. It is, for instance, true that Albert had an adventure with a soldier called André. Albert himself never claimed to have had any relations with Proust other than those of "confessor" and procurer. There is, however, one character in the book whom he came to resemble more and more closely with each year that passed, and that is Jupien.'

Like Jupien, Cuziat opened a 'curious' establishment . . . a place of abominations, where Albert-Jupien presided in the rôle of Prince Serenissimo of Hell, and for which Proust, like the Narrator in the novel, gave him several pieces of the family furniture which had been stored in a coach-house in the Boulevard Haussmann when they were crowded out of the flat. Albert, at fifty, was 'a bald man, going grey at the temples, with very thin lips, very blue eyes and a very sharp profile. He used to sit enthroned at the receipt of custom, rigid, motionless, and, as often as not, reading a volume of history or some pamphlet that had to do with genealogy'. He was almost the only person who was familiar with the seamy side of Proust's life. There was something frightening about him, because he found compensation for his unpleasing masochism in occasional sadistic indulgencies.

These 'shameful relationships of the world and the flesh' were, for Marcel, responsible for a number of unfortunate mistakes and of constant anxiety. His every movement, even when he had nothing to hide, had to be wrapped in mystery. *Madame Arman de Caillavet to her son:* 'Two years ago I used frequently to run into Marcel at Prouté's, my print-dealer. His explanation was that he happened to be on his way to the Passage des Beaux-Arts where he was working on a novel in the flat of a friend who remained nameless . . . Now, the Passage des Beaux-Arts was where Oscar Wilde died under an assumed name. It is all very mysterious . . .' Was Proust in the habit of going secretly to visit Wilde, who was then living in exile? Quite possibly. But why should he be so secretive about what was, after all, no more than an act of charity?

More than once there was a 'prisoner' in the Boulevard Haussmann flat. Those of Proust's friends who went there early in the evening never saw the mysterious guest. They spent their time listening to the dazzling monologue which came to them, through clouds of smoke, from the bed. It took the form of a glittering series of imitations, parodies and mocking comments. When they were finished, Proust would give a start, and rub his face with both hands, framing his nose between two fingers. His mockery was sometimes, though not always, kindly. Although he wrote, and genuinely believed, 'that the man of talent must, essentially, be good-hearted', he could, on occasion, be cruel. There were two distinct persons in him — the 'sugar-daddy', to use Fernandez's phrase, who was capable of great generosity, not so much because he was kind, as because, in the world of social contacts, he was eager to conciliate those with whom he had nothing in common — and the 'saint' who acted in response to genuinely humane impulses, as when, for instance, one evening he rescued a young servant-girl freshly arrived from the country, whom he found almost dead with fear at the bottom of the stairs because she was terrified of the dark. There was nothing 'bogus' about the 'saint' — for Proust was far too imaginative not to understand other people's miseries. 'Now that she has been left all alone in the world', he said, speaking of some woman he knew, 'I feel under certain obligations to her': and, again, writing to Jean-Louis Vaudoyer — 'I can feel the sufferings of my friends: it is a sort of gift I have, which life has developed to excess.' Nor was it only the sufferings of his friends that he felt. Strangers in trouble could always rely on him for sympathy.

Marcel Proust to Madame Gaston de Caillavet: 'I want to ask a favour of Gaston, but, because I know how busy he is, I am writing to you in the hope that you may be able to find out whether or no he is likely to be able to do what I want. There is a poor singer called Père, in whom I take a certain amount of interest because his wife is consumptive and has had to give up the stage. They have one little girl. He used to sing

Mireille at the Opéra Comique (he must be about thirty-eight
— I have never actually met him), but he is running to fat
and is now suitable only for comedy parts. He is very anxious
to have an audition at the Apollo. Before asking Gaston
whether he could arrange this for him, I thought I had
better find out whether his singing was tolerable (as a matter
of fact, this was before the idea of Gaston occurred to me).
I sent him along, therefore, to Reynaldo, who assures me that
his voice is quite good enough to get him a job, and that he
could probably arrange to have him taken on at the Trianon-
Lyrique. But the poor fellow has got a mania about this
audition at the Apollo (Reynaldo thinks he stands much less
chance there: still, the Apollo is what he wants), and I gather
that Gaston is the person most likely to be able to do something in that line. If, for one reason or another (strained
relations with Franck, or anything else) Gaston should find
it embarrassing to ask this sort of favour, please be perfectly
open with me. I should hate to think that I had made myself
a nuisance to him, especially on behalf of someone who is
personally unknown to me, and who interests me more by
reason of the difficult situation in which he finds himself
than because of his talents, which are no more than mediocre
(I'm not, you see, trying to deceive you about his artistic
gifts). He really is in a very bad way, and would, I should
imagine, jump at any sort of job, no matter how small, at the
Apollo. He once ran a cinematograph company, or something
of that sort. . . .[1]

In his view of the world, every human being is a mixture of
good and bad. Monsieur Verdurin is capable of generosity
though, at bottom, he is a throughly unpleasant creature, and
under all his sarcasms, Monsieur de Charlus hides real goodness
of heart. Proust himself knew that, like his heroes, he had goodness and badness in his own nature. The Great World had caused
him much suffering as a young man, and he revenged himself
upon it ruthlessly in the pages of his book, and in his conversation.
Even his friends were haled before the 'bed of justice' and summed

[1] Unpublished letter.

up with Godlike impartiality. Many of his intimates were terrified of his pitiless lucidity, and might well have repeated on their own account what Alphonse Daudet had once said — 'Marcel Proust's the very devil!' Every 'scrap of gossip had to be teased out'. 'Lying there propped up in his bed, leaning slightly forward, his hands clasped in front of him, or else with a pencil between his fingers, he would absorb the gist of what was told him and give it form.'[1] Then would come the questions — insistent, repeated again and again, pitiless. Marcel would be hoarding his honey. A little later Reynaldo would turn up, Reynaldo to whom his friend's work owed much, both because of the scenes he described so inimitably, and because it was from him that Marcel had learned to love music.

At midnight the 'prisoner' would appear, a kind of secretary, and stand listening silently to the talk going on round the bed. These Adonises (for the post was held by several young men in succession) were, like Albertine, kept in complete isolation. If, as a great favour, they were allowed to go out, they had to account for every moment of their time. If they played truant, and so caused intense suffering to their employer, he drew from the experience those emotional torments which he needed for his Narrator. To a friend who once complained of being crossed in love, he said: 'What, do you mean that you are emotionally unhappy? — then, all I can say is, you're very lucky!'

To those of his friends who were quite normally submissive, he never mentioned the subject of inversion. Even in his book, he attributed sexual aberration to Charlus, to Nissim Bernard, to Monsieur de Vaugoubert and to a hundred others, but never to the Narrator. Much later, at about the time that *Si le grain ne meurt* was published, he gave Gide this piece of advice: 'You can tell everything, but only on condition that you never say "*I*" . . .' In Gide's *Journal* there is a passage of capital importance, because it explains the transposition of Albert and Albertine. 'Again this evening, we talked almost the whole time about Uranian love. He said that he bitterly regretted the "irresolution" which had led him — in the hope of bolstering up the heterosexual part of his

[1] JACQUES POREL, *L'Imagination dans l'amitié* (*Nouvelle Revue Française*, January 1st, 1923).

book — to transpose into "*l'Ombre des jeunes filles en fleur*" every
gracious, tender, and delightful emotion which he had experienced
in homosexual relationships, with the result that it was only the
grotesque and abject aspects that were left for *Sodome*. He seemed
very upset when I said that he had apparently wished to pillory
Uranian love. He protested loudly, and it dawned on me finally
that what we find squalid, laughable or repulsive, did not seem
so to him. . . .'[1]

He could so easily have won the affection of men of the noblest
character. Why then did he make life so difficult for himself?
It would seem that his dream of perfect happiness took the form
of an almost animal sensuality enjoyed in the company of young
persons. Suffering as he did from an excess of intelligence,
scrupulosity and analytical acuteness, he craved a complementary
balance of the flesh, and sought for it in vain. Brasillach tells us
that he had a great admiration for Colette, and would cry whenever he read her stories of young women who could find simple-
minded and instinctive happiness. 'Over-sensitive, intelligent and
unhappy, he indulged in dreams that differed very little from those
of the kind of writers who build up an imaginary paradise in
Tahiti on the strength of a few pictures by Gauguin. What he
wanted above all things was that life should be simple, and that
was why he turned back to his childhood. . . .' The ditch that
separated the poetry of his work from the compromises of real life,
grew ever wider. Speaking, in his *Notebooks*, of Bergotte, he
develops a justification for this hiatus:

> His work was much more moral, much more preoccupied with
> the good, than is the case with pure art, much more concerned
> with sin and with scruples, so that he was forever finding
> sadness in the simplest things, always catching a vision of
> unplumbed depths beneath the surface of every day.

> When it came to his own life, he was much more immoral,
> far more tightly held in thrall to sin and evil, than is the
> ordinary run of humanity, less worried by, or far more easily

[1] ANDRÉ GIDE, *Journal*, *1889-1939* (Gallimard, Paris, 1939; Bibliothèque de la
Pléiade) pp. 692-4.

152

fighting free of, the scruples that control other men, with the result that he could do things from which less sensitive natures would abstain. Those who, like Legrandin, loved his books and knew about his life, found something comic — which they held to be highly typical of the times — in contrasting some of his wonderful sayings which were so austere, so sensitively scrupulous, that, by comparison, high-minded men of an earlier age would have seemed coarse and utterly careless of moral standards, with certain notorious actions that he had committed, certain scandalous occurrences of his own career. And, maybe, it *is* typical of the age that its artists should be more conscious of the anguish of sin, yet more hopelessly enslaved to sin, than were those of an earlier time, denying their lives to the world at large, clinging to the old standards of honour, to the moral landmarks of a period now dead, from motives of self-love, and because they honestly regard their own conduct as scandalous. Contrariwise, in the matter of private conduct, their idea of the good is, in some sort, a painful consciousness of evil, which they must be for ever analysing, for it consists more in self-laceration than in abstinence. Perhaps it is that just as certain morbid symptoms may be produced by two entirely different diseases, so, too, there may be cases of gross wickedness which are due not to lack, but to excess, of sensibility. Consequently the astonishment which many feel at being confronted with refined and subtle work produced by men who, they think, belong to the first of these two classes, may be in part dissipated if, probing beneath the surface, they find that their authors are, in fact, members of the second. . . .[1]

III

THE WORK

The Ark was still moored to the bank by a few ropes — here a friendship, there a passion — but already Proust's real life was in his book. *Marcel Proust to Georges de Lauris:* 'Work is the only thing.

[1] Unpublished extract, in the possession of Madame Mante-Proust.

Life may bring disappointments, but in work is consolation. One's real life is elsewhere, not in life so-called, nor yet in what we think of as the after-life, but in some dimension *outside* life, if a word that draws its meaning from the conceptions imposed on us by space can be said to have any meaning in a world freed from spatial disciplines . . .' He knew perfectly well what he meant to do. He meant to write a novel of two thousand pages which would have in it something of the *Arabian Nights*, something of George Eliot, something of Thomas Hardy, something of Saint-Simon and yet would be different from all of them, a novel of which the principal character would be Time, a novel in which, after first exploring the Paradise of childhood, he would debouch into the Hell of Sodom. The shape of this novel was clearly visible to his inward eye, and he had already written its opening and its closing passages.

During these same years, 1906-12, he had other minor enter-prises on hand. It was his intention to collect his occasional pieces into a volume, to publish his parodies — things so perfect that they really constituted criticism of a new and original kind, and to write a Study of Sainte-Beuve. He frequently spoke to Georges de Lauris of 'the *Sainte-Beuve* which is already completely written in my mind . . .' 'May I ask your advice? I am going to write something on Sainte-Beuve, and already have two articles (of magazine length) worked out in my mind. One of them is con-ceived on classic lines — something like Taine's Essay, but less good. The other would open with a morning scene — Mamma coming to me while I am still in bed, and I telling her about the article I mean to write about Sainte-Beuve, and developing it in conversation. Which of these do you think would be the better?' From the same friend he borrowed the seven volumes of *Port-Royal*. 'No, I haven't begun *Sainte-Beuve* yet, and don't feel at all sure that I can begin it. But you can take my word that it won't be at all bad, and I hope you will read it . . .' Then, in 1909: 'I am so exhausted, Georges, as a result of starting on *Sainte-Beuve* (I am hard at work on it, and hate the whole business), that I don't know what I am saying to you. . . .'

The *Sainte-Beuve* was never finished. There is nothing in the *Notebooks* but a rough sketch of *Sainte-Beuve et Baudelaire* which seems to be a fragment of the Essay he had planned. It is addressed to Madame Proust, and begins as follows:

A poet who writes in prose (except, of course, when he deliberately writes 'poetically', like Baudelaire in his minor poems, and Musset in his plays). Musset in his stories, his critical essays, his Academy discourses, is a man who has turned his back on his genius, who has ceased to draw from his inner consciousness the forms that he finds in a super-natural world which is his own exclusive experience. But he still has a lingering recollection of these things, and the power to prevent us from forgetting them. At some turn in the writing we find ourselves thinking of certain celebrated 'lines'. They are invisible, they are not there at all, but in some vague way they seem to show behind phrases which anyone might produce, and to give them a sort of grace, a kind of moving and allusive majesty. The poet has with-drawn, but the diffused light of his genius still hovers behind the clouds. Nothing of it remains in the social figure, the diner-out, the ambitious climber, yet it is in that aspect of the man that Sainte-Beuve thinks he can discover the essential truth of the absent poet. *I realize that your love of Baudelaire is only partial. You have found in his letters, as in Stendhal's, cruel references to his family.* Cruel he is, in his poetry, with a cruelty that is linked with an infinite degree of sensibility. His hardness is all the more astonishing because one gets the impression that he, too, has felt the sufferings that he de-scribes and presents in so unmoved a fashion, that he has felt them in the very fibres of his being. Certain it is that in his wonderful poem, *Les Petites Vieilles*, there is not a single one of those old women's pains that has escaped him. . . .[1]

Proust used part of this Essay in *A propos de Baudelaire*, which was published in *Chroniques*, and part in the Preface that he wrote for *Tendres Stocks*.[2] The above passage, which has never been

[1] Unpublished fragment, in the possession of Madame Mante-Proust.
[2] See *Marcel Proust: A Selection from His Miscellaneous Writings*, translated by Gerard Hopkins (Allan Wingate, 1948), *About Baudelaire* and *Preface to Tendres Stocks*.

published, is interesting, not only for its intrinsic quality, but for what it reveals: 'cruel with a cruelty that is linked with an infinite degree of sensibility' is true no less of Proust than of Baudelaire.

But *Sainte-Beuve* and *Pastiches* were interludes only. His real work at this time, the work which filled the years and absorbed his powers, was the novel. What were the elements of personal experience on which he drew in writing it? Every novelist when he lays the foundations of a book, has at his disposition a reserve of material which he has stored up in the course of his life. This he can complete later by research, by talk with friends; but a point of departure he must have. Balzac could manœuvre in a large field. He could call at will on his knowledge of business, on what Madame de Berny had told him, on what he had learned from other women and, especially, on his own memories as a lawyer's clerk. What was it that Proust knew really well?

Illiers: a narrow world which contained his father, his grandmother, his mother and his aunts. Paris: its doctors, the Champs-Elysées, a few women of the type of Laure Hayman, and later of Madame Straus and Madame de Chevigné, the 'salons' of Madame Greffulhe, Madame de Beaulaincourt, Madame Arman de Caillavet — a world, in short, of high Society. Through his Weil uncles at Auteuil he had made contact with a Jewish environment. At Cabourg and at the tennis-parties in the Boulevard Bineau he had met a number of young girls. Of the 'people' he knew only so much as came to him by way of Félicie, Antoine and Jean Blanc (Professor Proust's servants) and, later, of Céleste and Odilon Albaret, and of a few lift-boys and hotel porters. Then there were his memories of life in the Army, his recollections of a few Combray tradespeople. All in all, a very small cross-section of French life. But the smallness did not matter. He set about exploring his vein, not in extent but in depth. In art, the subject-matter is nothing. Cézanne could compose masterpieces from three apples and a plate.

Deny it though he might, Proust had accumulated a whole collection of notes on this limited universe. For a long time, perhaps ever since the time of *Les Plaisirs et les Jours*, he had been playing with the idea of a large-scale work, though only in a very vague way. He had a rough idea of the general background, and of one or two of his characters. He filled notebook after notebook. Nothing is more interesting than to watch the novelist at work. In those jottings one finds hints, comments, memories of things said, turns of phrase peculiar to this or that person, occasionally a general idea, sometimes marked '*Capital*' or '*Most Capital*'.

MEMORANDA

Most Capital for the last notebook: certain pleasing impressions of great heat, of cool weather, of travelling, come back to me. But where had I had those peculiar experiences? The names of the places were buried in obscurity. I clearly remembered being with Albertine. Would her memory have been better? Our past vanishes into the shadows. That blazing day when she sat sketching in a sunken lane, because it was cooler — it wasn't *Incarville*, though the name was something like that. . . . Incar . . . Inc . . . No . . . however fondly I woo those obscure memories, it doesn't seem likely that the name will come back.

&

ref Tansonville — ask Monsieur Mâle whether the monks wore golden vestments at Christmas and Easter. Litanies.

&

Capital — for the hotel scenes — what was the word that the hall-porters use instead of *livery*? — *staff* instead of *servants*

&

For Monsieur de Guermantes — 'Je vais distiller ce régale'
For Françoise: 'A cause que . . . En *errière*
Make Bloch use the words 'bouquin' and 'bouquiner'

&

Monsieur de Norpois: 'Inutile d'annoncer *urbi et orbi*'
Monsieur de Norpois: 'Il faudrait savoir se decider rapidement, ce qui ne veut pas dire à la legère, ni à l'aveuglette

&

See on back of last page something *most capital* for the death of Bergotte. Rendezvous with death. It comes. Bush in the sky. Must remember to dictate something for inclusion in my will. No one must be forgotten.

&

Whenever Françoise wanted to get information from anybody she never put a direct question, but, with a smiling, timid, interrogative and mischievous expression, would say 'I suppose your uncle has his villa at Nice? . . . I suppose he was a landed proprietor? . . . in such a way that one was compelled to answer 'Yes' or 'No', because if one had just said '*perhaps*' — which wouldn't have been true — one would have given the impression that one was lying.

&

When Étienne de Beaumont or Lucien [Daudet] — but especially the former — records the words of some fashionable woman-relation or close friend — in speaking of something that has happened, they report her as repeatedly saying — 'You see, Étienne *dear*' . . . 'It's quite simple, Lucien *darling*. . . .'

&

Music: that hand-to-hand struggle to the death of two motifs — one constantly emerging from the other.

&

Balzac: Meeting of Vautrin and de Rubempré by the Charente. Vautrin's talk — like Montesquiou's — 'What it's like to live alone, etc. . . .' Physiological significance of these words . . . Vautrin stopping in order to visit Rastignac's house; *Tristesse d'Olympio* of paederasty.

&

Phrase emerging from a piece of music, like a stage 'extra' till then unnoticed.

&

The whole is a laborious piece of fiction, because I lack imagination, but it is filled with feelings that I have carried in my consciousness for a very long, too long a, time; because my mind has forgotten, my heart has gone cold, and I have fashioned for it with difficulty the clumsy circumstances that lie upon it like a weight, though from them each of these feelings emerge.

&

Add — Paris, posters, theatres, illusions. (2) Throw-back to first meeting with the 'jeunes filles'. (3) after the death of my grandmother, ghosts. Insert somewhere the bit about Félicie not knowing what's the matter with me.
(Félicie + a certain Marie + another old servant of the Illiers days = Françoise).[1]

These jottings, some of which still contain the names of actual people, were later incorporated in the 'fragments' which make up Proust's *Notebooks*. There we find whole scenes, rewritten two, three or four times, and improved at each re-writing. By working through these we can reconstitute the original draft of the finished book. It seems certain, as I have pointed out, that he first intended to write a novel about Swann, in the third person. *Un Amour de Swann* is a fragment rescued from this earlier version. That was why Proust always smiled when he found himself labelled as a 'subjective' novelist. Had he carried out his original plan,' he said, the critics would all have called him 'objective'. There are, for instance, in the *Notebooks* a number of scenes that give us a foretaste of *Jeunes filles en fleurs*, but in which Charles Swann plays the part of the hero, and the young girls are called, not Albertine and Andrée, but Maria, Solange, Septimie, Anna.

Anna — Of all these girls, Maria and Solange were the ones he liked the least. When he was on the point of leaving for Querqueville, he did not trouble to find out whether they

[1] The unpublished *Memoranda* of Marcel Proust from which these extracts are taken are now in the possession of Madame Mante-Proust.

were going there too, and learned that they would probably not be there, only on the day before he left: when he discovered that they *were* there, he made no effort to see them, and did not go to any of the places they frequented, though, by force of circumstance, he frequently ran into them. And because all the members of the group were young and pleasing, there were certain days on which Septimie and Anna were his centre of attraction, and the same thing would occur on the day following. But there were other times when Arabella or Renée was the favourite. The 'weakness' that he had had for Anna, and, later, for Septimie, had, as a matter of fact, become frozen as the result of absence, or because of some thoughtless action of theirs, or because ill-health had dulled their good looks: but sentiments are like seeds, they can remain frozen for a long time, and yet, 'come up' again. . . .

&

. . . Then she gave him her word that it was false. He put the idea out of his mind and thought no more about it. This one revelation made the idea of Anna horrible to him; he was furious with her; he treated her abominably, spoke ill of her and tried to do her harm, showing himself, the while, increasingly affectionate towards Septimie. One day he brought things to such a pitch with Anna, that they had to have an explanation. Anna was miserable under this persecution, and the knowledge that she was so touched him. So, he said to her: — 'Will you swear to me to give a true answer to the question I am about to ask?' — 'Yes, I swear' — 'I am in love with Septimie, and word has reached me that there are relations of a certain kind between you. Is that true?' Anna was indignant: 'I swear it isn't!' For a moment, his mind was set at rest, but the slightest thing was enough to reawaken his suspicions. He was forever crushing Anna beneath a weight of sarcasm. 'It's very odd,' people began to say; 'last year Swann was very fond of Anna, this year he seems to hate her.' To Septimie, on the other hand, he was charming, and seemed to take a positive delight in letting Anna see his

JETHRO'S DAUGHTER BY BOTTICELLI

From the Sistine Chapel

preference for Septimie, and Septimie's kindness to him. Then, his jealous suspicions abated. He began to feel a great liking for Juliette. . . .'[1]

In the course of the successive versions, the names of the characters became altered. Odette de Crecy was originally called Françoise, then Carmen. The scene in which Swann hunts for her in all the restaurants of the Boulevard, and which, in the novel, terminates with the incident of the orchids, is foreshadowed in this similar, but less finished, one.

Carmen — Swann had just visited, in despair, the last of all the restaurants that might have occurred to her, and was walking, obsessed by his thoughts and seeing nothing, when he all but collided with her as she was getting into a carriage in front of Durand's. She uttered a faint, startled cry, and he took his seat beside her. It was some moments before she could collect herself. She seemed almost speechless with terror. Meanwhile, the carriage moved off. Suddenly the horse, taking fright at a tram, pulled up short. Once again she uttered a cry. 'It's nothing', he said, and, supporting her with his arm, repeated — 'Nothing's happened' — then, 'Don't talk, don't say anything to me, just answer my questions by signs. In that way you won't get out of breath. You don't mind my keeping my arm like this, do you? It will give you support in case the horse gets restive. . . .'

He put his arm about her shoulders, and she, not used to such behaviour, said — 'It doesn't worry me at all' — '*Please* don't talk, or you'll get breathless again: just make a sign, like this. Are you sure my arm doesn't inconvenience you?' He laid his hand against her neck, and, as delicately as though he were touching a flower, began to stroke her cheek, which was like a large over-blown red rose. His other hand was on her knee. He said: '*Sure* I'm not inconveniencing you?' Very faintly she shrugged her shoulders, as if to say 'You're crazy!' and, above her slim neck, in her small, scented, sullen face

[1] Unpublished fragment in the possession of Madame Mante-Proust.

with its look of a big, pink blossom, her bright eyes shone like two tears. He hesitated a moment, his head bent forward, looking at her. He stared as though he were seeing her for the last time, as though he would never look at her again. The slim neck leaned towards him, seemingly forced down by its own weight, and the small face, as though over-ripe and responding to some force of attraction in him, drooped slowly to his lips. . . .'[1]

In the earlier *Notebooks* the Duchesse de Guermantes is a Comtesse, and the Narrator, her lover, embraces her — an occurrence which, in the finished novel, would have been in the highest degree improbable.

The other evening, when I had taken the Comtesse back from a party to the house where she was still living, but where I myself had for some years ceased to live, and just as I was about to kiss her, I suddenly held her face away from mine in an effort to see her at a distance, as though she were a picture, wanting to recapture what I had felt in the days when I used to see her stopping in the street to speak to the dairy-woman. I longed to experience once again the harmonious effect of the blue eyes, the delicate nose, the disdainful lips, the long waist, the sad expression, and, keeping focused before my eyes the past that I had thus found again, to lean forward and to kiss what, in those days, I had always wanted to kiss. But, alas! the faces we kiss, the places we live in, the dead we bury, no longer have whatever it was that we wanted to love, whatever it was that made us so eager to live in that particular place, whatever it was that set us trembling at the thought of losing a particular person. When art, which claims to hold the mirror up to nature, suppresses the precious truth of imaginative impressions, it suppresses all that is really precious in life. If, on the other hand, it manages to recover such fancies, it at once gives value to every kind of vulgarity — to snobbery, among others; if, instead of depicting Society as it really is, that is to say, nothing at all — as is true,

1 Unpublished fragment in the possession of Madame Mante-Proust.

too, of love, of travel, of pain, when we have possessed the desired objects etc, — it seeks to find its image in those unreal colours (though that unreality is the only true reality) which the yearning of young snobs sets upon the Comtesse with the violet eyes driving out in her Victoria on summer Sunday afternoons. . . .'[1]

In this scene we have a curious mingling of the Duchesse de Guermantes and the Albertine of the kiss episode.

But it is worth noting a still more curious fact. In the *Notebooks*, Monsieur de Norpois and Monsieur de Charlus are, for quite a while, one and the same person who (on his first appearance) advises the Narrator to enter the Diplomatic Service, makes, like the Baron in the novel as we have it, violent advances to him, and ends, as in *Le Côté de Guermantes*, by getting into a cab driven by a young and drunken coachman. This composite individual who, by a process of fission, was to give birth to two of the most remarkable monsters in the whole of French literature (Charlus and Norpois), is called, first, Monsieur de Guray, and, later, Monsieur de Quercy. In the *Notebooks* Monsieur de Quercy has a conversation with the Narrator which is too photographic a rendering of the actual, too little transposed, and seems to have been inspired by talks which Marcel had had with Montesquiou, and also with Nisard, the Ambassador, who had given rather lukewarm support to Dr. Proust's candidature for election to the Académie des Sciences Morales et Politiques.

'I can't,' said I, 'give you an answer at once, sir. Your proposal makes me very happy. The conditions which you impose, as, for instance, my not leading a social life, would involve no sacrifice for me. But there is one thing I think I ought to tell you' — looking into my heart, I tried to give verbal expression to feelings that, for some considerable time, had been vaguely stirring there. 'You see, sir, you want me to give all my attention to the study of history: you urge me to go in for a life of diplomacy, politics and action. I have

[1] Published in the magazine *Soleil* (Paris, 1947). The original is in the possession of Madame Mante-Proust.

many faults, sir; my character is not a particularly good one. I am young, I am frivolous-minded, and these drawbacks, which I am doing my best to disperse, have so far stood in the way of my doing what I really want to do, which is, to write. But I shouldn't feel at all satisfied if, at the very moment when I thought I might succeed in getting the better of myself, and so be able to devote my energies to what I regard as my true destiny, a profession, an employment, and a number of obligations which, if imposed by you, I should take very seriously, were, from solid reasons of duty and virtue, to stand in the way of my doing what, till now, I have not been able to do because of my faults.'

'But why should it keep you from writing? You could give much time to producing historical works. Did not Monsieur Guizot write every bit as well as you could ever hope to write?'

'What I want to go in for' — said I nervously — 'is pure literature, fiction, poetry, I am not yet sure which. . . .'

By this time we had reached my door. 'Ah! my poor young man,' exclaimed Monsieur de G. . . . in a wheezing voice, and on a note of disdainful irony, 'you live in times when the world is being changed for the better by the discoveries of science, for the worse by the triumph of democracy in other lands, in other, perhaps you will allow me to say, races, and by the increase of armaments, so that one never knows, when one goes to bed, whether one will wake the next morning to the sound of Prussian guns, of rioting mobs, or to the news of a Japanese invasion: you live in times that have given us the telephone and the telegraph, but have made it impossible for us so much as to write a letter, and yet you think that people have nothing better to do than read your books; you believe that you can have no more interesting employment than to record your trivial impressions and all the unimportant things that happen to you! My poor young man, how very French the French are! — or rather, how Byzantine, how

Chinese, how like those denizens of China who are incapable of beating the Japanese — although they outnumber them — for the simple reason that they are ruled by the "literate". If there are many Frenchmen like you, the name of France will soon be wiped from the map of the world. You say that you love literature — fiction, in other words what is a more or less flat counterfeit of life, a body of conjectures, all more or less inexact, instead of a reality about which only the few have any accurate knowledge. I have offered to be your guide in the discovery of that real world, to make it possible for you to set your shoulder to the wheel of great matters, to give you right of entry into the schemes of nations and the secrets of Kings — and you choose, rather, to spend your life sitting at a desk and dipping your pen into an ink-well! And in order to say what, may I ask? What do you know of life? The kind of literature of which you speak, poetry and fiction, is of value only if, as in the case of Monsieur Deroulède, for example, it can stimulate generous passions, can rouse feelings of patriotism in the human breast. That was the rôle assigned to poetry in the Ancient World, that was the only poetry which Plato was willing to admit into his Republic. Therein lies the sole value of poetry, and, in fiction, the only novels worth considering are those that reveal certain great human truths. Insofar as the novel can do *that* I am prepared to lift, in favour of Balzac, or, at least, of some of his books, the embargo that I lay on literature in general. There can be no doubt that a work like *Splendeurs et Misères des courtisanes*, for example, does reveal the underlying reality of a great truth, and I, for one, can never read certain passages in that book without feelings of admiration. But I defy you, and with you three quarters of its readers, to guess what that truth is. I am prepared to show you the treasures of life instead of the scraps and parcels of truth which are to be found in novels. A stuffed humming-bird may be beautifully coloured, but, in my opinion, it is not nearly so interesting to look at him as to go hunting the living creature through primeval forests. . . .'

'Sir,' I replied, 'you have every appearance of being in the

165

right, yet I know, too, that I am not wrong. Besides, you are speaking only of realistic fiction. You completely ignore the poetry of nature.'

'But, my dear sir,' went on Monsieur de Quercy angrily, '*you* have no monopoly of the poetry of nature! I am just as susceptible to it as you are. The poets describe sunsets, and sunrises, too, which they have never seen, whereas I can witness things a hundred times more beautiful every time I motor or cycle through a forest on my way to a shoot, or tramping the countryside. Oh, my young friend' — and here a softness crept into his voice — 'what times we might have together, you and I, if only you were not so foolish. You would soon realize that the experiences I have described put all your poets into the shade.'

'But that is not at all the same thing, sir. I may not be quite clear about *what* I feel, though I know that I feel it very strongly. I am quite sure that our disagreement comes from mutual misunderstanding, and that, where poetry and fiction are concerned, you have an eye only for the content of the work, its subject, which may, indeed, be identical with what you see when you are walking, or when you are caught up in a life of passions and colours.'

He stopped me. 'Oh! let us have no sensibility, I beg of you! What a muddled mind you have — though that is not your fault. You are a product of our splendid system of Higher Education, and were taught metaphysics, a science, that is to say, which is the modern counterpart of astrology and alchemy. But you have got to earn your living, and living becomes every day more expensive. Let us assume, for the sake of argument, that you do succeed in forcing your way into literature — I am, you see, taking the rosiest view — let us assume that you will one day become one of our leading authors, not only a great writer but a successful one, — well, do you realize that Monsieur Bourget, whom I sometimes meet at the house of the Princesse de Parme — and excellent company he is — do you realize that Monsieur Bourget has to work a great deal harder than any ambassador in order to make a very much smaller income, and that, speaking generally, his life is a great deal less pleasant than it would be in one of the Embassies? At his age, and with his intelligence, he would by this time, if he had gone in for diplomacy, have had an embassy of his own. He knows a great many very nice people, but he would have got to know still more, and would occupy a position in Society far better than he can hope for now, unless, of course, he manages to get elected to the Académie. He is at an age when one appreciates precedence at the dinner table. I am pretty sure that, taking all in all, he would be much happier as an Ambassador.'

'I am afraid, sir,' I said, 'that I cannot have expressed my meaning very clearly. If it is our outer life, the size of an establishment, a secure position in Society, and an old age crowned with honours, that we regard as the true reality, and literature or diplomacy merely as the means by which we may attain to it, then you are overwhelmingly right. But true reality is something quite different. It exists *within* us, and the fact that our life is a tool — something in itself without importance, though indispensable as a means of expression — which we use in order to earn an income of a thousand francs as an Ambassador, or to make a living by our work of writing books, is as nothing by comparison with it. . . .'

These passages do contain an element of the essential Proust, but they suffer from a lack of integration, of the master's finish. More serious still, the central theme of the novel (the unreality of the external world as compared with the reality of the world of the spirit) is stated too explicitly. In the book as Proust ultimately wrote it, this theme is suggested by the employment of symbols. It shows as a watermark in paper shows: it is concealed in the massive sonority of the whole. These early attempts give the measure of the vast amount of labour that was demanded of the author. The beauty of Proust's style was the result of no happy accident, no natural gift, but of constant efforts made by a man of great culture, exquisite taste and acute poetic sensibility. On every page of the *Notebooks* we find him thinking aloud, weighing alternatives, hammering away at problems.

167

It might be better to put the diplomat, the financier, the Club etc in the part where Charlus goes to see Jupien. He asks for news about the war. That'll be better.

&

Consider making Monsieur de Charlus say, in the course of the war: 'Do you realize that there are no more footmen, now, no more Café waiters? The moulded splendour of the masculine form has altogether vanished! That implies a vandalism far greater than the destruction of the Angels of Rheims. Just think of it, I got a telegram the other day, and it was delivered by . . . a woman!'

&

Before getting to this point, I must make a little adjustment, roughly as follows:
'*Do you know the Verdurins?*' — and then almost precisely as in the rough draft, down to the page there marked . . . [here there is a blank in the manuscript] . . . then, on the same page, at the sentence — '*How could one refuse anything to so charming a little lady?*' lead on with, perhaps, *The Verdurins' salon was not* . . . after which insert all the bit about the salon. Then —

The first impression produced by Swann on the Verdurins was excellent. All that the charming little lady had said about the circle in which he moved, had led Madame Verdurin to fear that he might be a bore. But he was nothing of the sort.[1]

It thus becomes clear that Proust constructed his work by bringing the material to a high temperature, and then 'running' the various fragments into the molten mass, or, let us say, by bringing these fragments into juxtaposition so as to form a mosaic in accordance with a pre-established design. In adopting this method he resembled many of the great artists whom he admired. Of this he was fully conscious:

[1] Unpublished fragments in the possession of Madame Mante-Proust.

Hugo — he says — wrote a number of admirable but entirely disconnected poems, and called the result *La Légende des Siècles*. The title has a beauty all its own, but the work as a whole, in spite of the excellence of its component pieces, does not really live up to it . . . Balzac, when he looked at his books with the eyes of a stranger who, in some odd way, was also endowed with the fondness of a parent, finding in one the sublimity of a Raphael, and in another the simplicity of the Gospel story, suddenly bethought him how much greater and more sublime the total effect would be if he could carry the same characters on from volume to volume, and so give to his *Comédie Humaine* a unity which, though it may be artificial, is, none the less, a final and superb triumph of the painter's brush.

All that I can discover of Proust's methods of work, in the *Memoranda* and the *Notebooks*, leads me to assert with complete conviction that, though he made full use of remarks, of gestures and of thoughts which he had come across in the different people he had met, in the creation of his characters, there is no 'key' with which we can open the door of the mysterious edifice, for the very good reason that each single person in the novel is a composite of many different persons whom he had actually known. The notes in the *Memoranda* in which, referring to some locution or other, he comments: '*For Bergotte or Bloch*', show how wide the margin of imprecision was, since two characters who to us seem so different as to be almost opposed, did, in his eyes, share a common zone, even though it might be a narrow one.

In this matter of 'keys', Proust himself must be called in evidence. His view of the subject is contained in a long dedicatory inscription which appears in a copy of *Côté de chez Swann* which he gave to Jacques de Lacretelle, who, very legitimately, had raised this very question. '. . . There are no keys to the characters in the novel, or, rather, there are eight or ten to each of them. . . When, for instance, I show Madame Swann walking near the Pigeon-Shooting Range, I had actually in mind a lovely *cocotte* of the period who rejoiced in the name of Closmesnil. I will let you see some photographs I have of her. Not that Madame

Swann, at the moment in question, looked particularly like her. No, the characters, I repeat, are all entirely fictional, and there is no key. . . .'

No key . . . In the literal sense, that is true enough: no single character in the book is a *copy* of any actual person. 'In some particular oddity the artist may see a general truth of great beauty: but because he sees the general truth incarnate in the individual case he happens to be studying, he will not necessarily assume that the *oddity* holds true of him, any more than a surgeon would make the mistake of concluding that he is suffering from a form of trouble in the circulatory system which happens to be very common at the moment. . .' Several persons in succession served as his models when he was brooding over the problem of love, but he himself would have found it impossible to say who the various individuals were from whom he had borrowed, here a phrase, there a look. 'A book is a vast cemetery, where, on most of the tombs, the names have become so wholly effaced that they can be no longer read . . .' We may think it sacrilege on his part to continue to paint, from a new model, an emotion which she who first posed for his study no longer rouses in him, but, from a purely literary point of view, and thanks to the similarity of human passions, it is not only legitimate but necessary that he should do so. It is the artist's privilege to 'make what use he pleases of some lovely memory, or to insert into the heart of his book some melancholy thought, livid yellow and darkly purple, like the evening remnant of a storm that has passed away, which for long he has treasured'. Sometimes he will turn a shepherdess into a queen; sometimes, the better to confuse his readers, he will set a duchess's drawing-room in a middle-class environment. Every form of disguise is grist to his mill. 'From all of which we see how vain is the attempt to guess at the actual person of whom an author may be speaking. For a literary work, even though it be one of deliberate confession, is, after all, a statement in which many different episodes in the writer's life are fitted together to make a whole; some, earlier in time, having inspired a passion which others afterwards have developed in the same general sense, so that the later love is, as it were, a tracing of something that belongs to a more distant past. . . .'

But though, in general terms, it may be true that there is no *one* model for any single character, it is no less true that several models served for the delineation of a given trait. Proust's letters make it clear that he never concealed from his friends the fact, when it was flattering, that he had made use of them. Much of the Duchesse de Guermantes's wit (though not all) he borrowed from Madame Straus, and he put into Oriane's mouth many phrases that Madame Straus was in the habit of using:

> *Marcel Proust to Madame Straus:* 'I couldn't think of the kind of phrase I wanted, so, naturally, I fell back on quotation: "*J'allais le dire*" — "*Cambron*" — "*Si nous pouvions changer d'innocent*" — "*J'ai beaucoup entendu parler de vous*" — "*Vous me mettez dans la situation de Chimène*" — "*Vous en avez donc?*" and a few more. But you must remind me of others — of the real gems. . . .'

The portrait of Madame de Chevigné in *Les Plaisirs et les Jours*, her birdlike profile and her husky voice, provides the solid, social outside of the Duchesse. The extremely beautiful Comtesse Greffulhe sat for the Princesse de Guermantes. Charlus is not Robert de Montesquiou, though his violent method of speaking and the picturesque arrogance of his pride are borrowed from Proust's imitations of the poet, while his physical appearance is modelled on that of a certain Baron Doazan, who was a cousin of Madame Aubernon and shared Charlus's tastes.

It has often been maintained that Swann was Charles Haas. Haas was the son of a stockbroker, a man 'much petted in the most exclusive circles, because of his elegance, his taste and his erudition', a member of the Jockey-Club, a favourite of the Greffulhes, a friend of the Prince of Wales and of the Comte de Paris and, like the Swann of the book, wearing his red hair clipped short in the fashion made popular by the actor, Bressant. Elisabeth de Grammont has pointed out the odd but undoubted fact that Haas, in German, means 'hare', and that by using the name Swann Proust employed a rather more stylish variant of the same kind of nomenclature. It can be said with certainty that Haas did supply the originals of some of Swann's characteristics, though his gifts or erudition, which never went deep, had to be strengthened by contributions levied on another child of Israel, Charles Ephrussi, the founder of the *Gazette des Beaux Arts*. It is far more important to realize that Swann was mainly a projection of Proust himself, as should be perfectly obvious from the passages in the *Notebooks* where Swann, as a young man, is presented as the hero of those self-same episodes which were afterwards fathered on the Narrator. Later (says Benjamin Crémieux), Proust, feeling the need of painting two different aspects of himself, and of exploiting both his Jewish and his Christian heredity, split himself into two separate characters — the Narrator, Marcel, and Charles Swann, the latter having Proust's own love of Society, his morbid jealousy, his aristocratic friends and his passion for the arts. Confirmation of this can be found in another unpublished fragment from the *Notebooks*:

> Monsieur Swann . . . as I knew him at first-hand, and, still more, as he seemed to me later, when I had supplemented my personal knowledge with the various odds and ends that I heard about him from others, was a man *to whom I felt myself to be peculiarly akin,* a man whom I could have loved very dearly. Monsieur Swann was a Jew. Though much younger than my grandfather he was his best friend, and that in spite of my grandfather's general dislike of Jews. This anti-semite feeling was one of those little weaknesses, one of those irrational prejudices, that one so often finds in upright and noble-minded persons — in fact, more often in them than in others. Examples of the kind of thing I mean would be Saint-Simon's attitude to the aristocracy, and the prejudice felt by certain doctors against dentists, and the dislike of certain middle-class persons for actors. . . .[1]

If it has been said once it has been said a hundred times that Bergotte was Anatole France. There are, undoubtedly, many passages in which Bergotte does approximate very closely to Anatole France. He shared his chin-tuft, his nose shaped like a snail's shell, and something, too, of his style: 'the rare, almost

---

[1] Unpublished fragment in the possession of Madame Mante-Proust.

archaic phrases which he liked to employ at certain points, where a hidden flow of harmony, a prelude contained and concealed in the work itself, would animate and elevate his style; and it was at such points as these, too, that he would begin to speak of the "vain dream of life", of the "inexhaustible torrent of fair forms", of the "sterile, splendid torture of understanding and loving", of the "moving effigies which ennoble for all time the charming and venerable fronts of our cathedrals"; that he would express a whole system of philosophy, new to me, by the use of marvellous imagery, to the inspiration of which I would naturally have ascribed that sound of harping which began to chime and echo in my ears, an accompaniment to which that imagery added something ethereal and sublime. . . .'[1]

All of that is France. But Bergotte is also Renan at such moments as when, having mentioned the name of some celebrated cathedral, he would interrupt the flow of his narrative and, 'in an invocation, an apostrophe, a lengthy prayer, would give a free outlet to that effluence which in the earlier volumes remained buried beneath the form of his prose . . .'[2] Bergotte, finally, is Proust himself, and the description of his death is based upon a fit of indigestion which one day attacked Marcel when, in the company of Jean-Louis Vaudoyer, he visited an Exhibition of the Dutch Painters in the Jeu de Paume.

Laure Hayman, then in her seventies, was much offended by the portrait of Odette de Crécy into which Proust had incorporated her trick of using English words. Moreover, he had given her a house in the Rue de la Pérouse which was where Laure Hayman lived. But Proust defended himself, and in seeming good faith, against the· charge:

> Not only is Odette de Crécy not you, she is the very opposite of you. That, it seems to me, is proved incontrovertibly, by every word she utters. I have placed in Odette's drawing-room all those highly individual flowers which a certain lady of the 'true Guermantes blood' (as you put it) habitually has

[1] *Swann's Way*, I. Translated by C. K. Scott Moncrieff (Chatto & Windus, 1922), vol. I.
[2] C. K. SCOTT MONCRIEFF, op. cit.

in hers. She has recognized these flowers, has written to thank me, yet never for a moment dreams that, because of them, *she* is Odette. You say that the interior in which you are 'cooped' (!), is just like Odette's. That, I must say, surprises me. The marks of your taste have always been sureness and daring. Whenever I have wanted to know the name of a piece of furniture or a fabric, it is to you rather than to an artist that I have invariably gone for my information. Now, very clumsily no doubt but to the best of my ability, I have tried to show that Odette was utterly lacking in taste, in her choice of interior decoration as in everything else, that she was always (except in the matter of clothes) a full generation behind the prevailing fashion. I could not now describe your apartment in the Avenue du Trocadéro, nor yet its successor in the Rue de la Pérouse, but I remember both of them as being in every way the opposite of Odette's. Even if certain details are common to all three, that no more proves that I was thinking of you when I drew Odette, than the fact that ten lines of a description which bears some resemblance to a certain Monsieur Doasan, inserted into a word-portrait of one of my 'persons' to whom several volumes are devoted, proves that I set out deliberately to depict Monsieur Doasan. I have drawn attention, in an article published in *Les Œuvres Libres*, to the stupidity of fashionable folk who think that that is how an author creates character. Alas! did I, perhaps, draw too much on you? You read my book and think that you find a resemblance between yourself and Odette. It really is enough to make one give up writing novels in despair! I have no very accurate recollection of all the details in mine, but this I can say, that when, in *Du Côté de Chez Swann*, I described Odette driving in the Rue des Acacias, I had in mind the clothes, the movements, etc of a woman who used to go by the name of Closmesnil, a handsome creature, who had just Odette's trailing skirts and slow saunter when she walked near the Pigeon-Shooting Range, and the very opposite of your particular species of elegance. But, except in that one passage (a bare half page) I never, in speaking of Odette, so much as thought of the Closmesnil.

In one of the volumes still to come, Odette marries a 'noble', and her daughter, with a grand title, becomes a close relation of the Guermantes. Women of the world, unless they are truly remarkable, have no idea what literary creation *is*. You have always lingered in my memory as indeed remarkable. Your letter was a great disappointment to me. . . .

That may have been just a piece of shrewd diplomacy. Still, to believe that a novelist can make a character come alive by using one actual person as a model betokens complete ignorance of the technique of fiction. Balzac was of the opinion that, though some of the greatest books, *Manon Lescaut, Corinne, Adolphe, René*, contain the elements of autobiography, 'the task of the historian of manners consists in fusing a number of analogous facts into a single composition. It is often necessary to put several real persons under contribution in the building of a single fictive character, just as there are plenty of people in real life who contain in themselves so many queer traits that, when separated out into their component elements, they furnish material for at least two individuals'. That is a sufficiently adequate description of Proust's method.

Thus it was that, somewhere about 1905, Marcel Proust, after twenty years spent in reading, in observation and in a close study of the styles of the masters, found himself in possession of an immense store of notes, fragments, portraits and metaphors. Slowly, born of his friendships and his antipathies, a number of characters took shape in his imagination, drew nourishment from his experiences, and became for him more living than the people whom he knew in the flesh. Through long periods of insomnia, he had formulated from his sufferings and from his weaknesses an entirely original philosophy which was to furnish him with a new and marvellous subject for his novel. On this vast stretch of sentimental landscape the distant light of his lost paradise cast an oblique and golden radiance, which touched every form to poetry. It remained for him to orchestrate this rich melodic material and, from a mass of fragments, to construct a work.

CHAPTER VI

LA RECHERCHE DU TEMPS PERDU (I)

'Do you believe in an eternal life in a world to come?'
'No, but I do believe in an eternal life in the here and now. There are
moments when time suddenly stands still, and gives place to eternity.'
DOSTOIEVSKY

1

THE SUBJECT AND ITS THEMES

How, precisely, did Proust conceive this work that was to be as long as the *Arabian Nights* or the *Mémoires* of Saint-Simon? What was it he had to say that could seem so important that everything else must be sacrificed to it? Even his friends had not understood much of what he had so far published. The general view was that he was occupied in describing certain mistresses of 'Salons', or in devoting microscopic study to infinitely minute sentiments. What, in fact, this disciple of Darlu and of Bergson was engaged upon was an attempt to express a whole philosophy in a work of fiction.

In a letter quoted by Princess Bibesco he says that his rôle is analogous to that of Einstein, and it is true that he did have many of the virtues of a scientist — accuracy in observation, honesty in dealing with facts, and a determination to discover the nature of certain general laws. For all his mysticism he was a positivist. Of all the many 'persons' who made up his individual self, the one that, in his opinion, clung most tenaciously to life was a certain philosopher 'who is never happy except when he has discovered the common qualities that bind together two works, two sensations' and two beings. What are these common qualities, these laws of existence and what are the leading themes in Proust's enormous Symphony?

The first, the one with which he began and ended his work, is the theme of Time. Proust was obsessed by the flight of the passing moment, by the perpetual state of flux of everything that makes

MARCEL PROUST IN 1921

Probably the last photograph of him

up our environment, by the changes wrought by time in our bodies and our minds. 'Just as there is a geometry in Space, so is there a psychology in Time.' All human beings, whether they accept the fact or not, are plunged into the dimension of Time, are carried away by the current of the moving days. Their whole life is a battle with Time. They seek to find an anchorage in friendship or in love, but these sentiments can remain above water only if they find expression in beings who, themselves, disintegrate and drown, whether because they die, whether because they pass out of our lives, or whether because it is we who change. Slowly forgetfulness mounts upwards from the great depths and sets a wall about our loveliest and dearest memories. The day will come when, meeting a fat lady and seeing her smile at us, we look at her and seek in vain the name that we shall never find until she tells it us, and only when that happens do we recognize the young girl who once held all our heart. Time destroys not only individuals, but societies, worlds and empires. A country may be torn by political passions, as was France at the time of the Dreyfus Affair, when friends quarrelled and families were broken up. Each actor in the drama holds that his own passions are absolute and eternal, but the implacable current carries all away, victors and vanquished alike, so that when they meet again as old men on the threshold of the grave it is to find that increasing feebleness has quenched old ardours, that passions have grown cold and been overlaid by the cooled and inoffensive lava of dead fires. 'Houses, avenues, roads are, alas, as fugitive as the years.' It is in vain that we return to the places that once we loved. We shall never see them again because they were situated not in Space but in Time, and because the man who tries to rediscover them is no longer the child or the youth who decked them with the fervour of his emotions.

The classic philosopher assumes that 'our personality is built about a hard and changeless core, is a sort of spiritual statue' which stands like a rock against the assaults of the external world. Such is man as viewed by Plutarch, by Molière and even by Balzac. But Proust shows us that the individual, plunged in Time, disintegrates. The day comes when nothing at all remains of the man who once loved, who once made a revolution. 'My life, as

I saw it,' wrote Marcel, 'presented me with the spectacle of a succession of periods so occurring that, but for a brief space of time, nothing of that which had been one's sustaining force continued to exist at all in that which followed it. I saw human life as a complex from which the support of an individual, identical, and permanent "self" was so conspicuously absent, was something so useless for the future, so far extended into the past, that death might just as well intervene at this point or that, because it could never mark a conclusion that was other than arbitrary, like those courses of French History, so prevalent in schools, in which the process may be held to have "ended", according to the whim of the syllabus or the fancy of the Professor, with the Revolution of 1830, the Revolution of 1848, or the end of the Second Empire. . . .'

The successive 'selves' are so different from one another that each ought, really, to have a different name. We see, as the novel develops, Swann, Odette, Gilberte, Bloch, Rachel, Saint-Loup, all coming into the beam of limelight focused upon them by different periods of life, and by different emotional states, so that each assumes a variety of changing colours like dancers who, although their dresses are, actually, white, seem to us to be wearing, in turn, yellow, green or blue. 'The time that is ours to use each day is elastic: the passions that we feel dilate it, those that we inspire contract it, and habit fills it . . .' Our *self* in love is incapable of imagining our *self* not in love; our young *self* laughs at those passions of the old *self* which will be ours when we have come into the beam of increasing age. The truth is that 'the disintegration of the self is a continuous death' and 'the natural stability which we assume to exist in others is as unreal as our own'.

This is Proust the realist, the man of science, who notes and scrupulously registers the destruction wrought by Time on human beings. But among the various philosophers who together make up his personality, there is also an 'Idealist', an unwilling metaphysician, who refuses to accept this notion of the total death of his successive 'selves', of the discontinuity of the individual, because, at certain privileged moments, he has had an intuition of himself as an absolute entity. There is an antinomy between his anguished sense that all vanishes, men no less than things, including himself, and the deep conviction that there is in his nature something permanent and even eternal. Proust knew this conviction in certain brief moments when, suddenly, an instant of the past became real to him, and he discovered that sights and feelings which he had thought of as gone for ever, must, obviously, have been preserved somewhere in him, since, otherwise, how could they reappear?

Our former 'selves', whether spiritual or physical, are *not* lost, because they can live again in our dreams, and sometimes even in our waking states. Each morning when we awake, there are a few confused moments during which we continue to float in a world of dreams. But from these we emerge and rediscover our identity. This can mean only one thing, that we have never wholly lost it. Towards the end of his life Proust could still hear the 'tinkle, urgent, metallic, interminable, shrill and clear, made by the little bell' — which in the days of his childhood used to bring him the news that Swann had taken his departure. It must, he decided, be the *same* bell, and it was now sounding again after the passage of so many years, because, in order to find once more the precise quality of its note, he had but to plunge into himself. So Time does not, as we think it does, die absolutely, but remains incorporated in us. Our bodies, our consciousness, act as reservoirs of Time.

From this arose the central, animating idea of the whole body of his work, the idea that we can set out to discover the Time that seems to have been lost, though really it is there still, ready to take on a new lease of life.

This voyage of discovery can be made only *within* ourselves. To revisit the places that we once have loved, to seek out memories in the external world, is an activity that must always end in disappointment. The real world has no independent existence. It is our own creation. It, too, moves in and out of the beams projected by our passions. A man in love will find heavenly beauty in a landscape which, to another, may seem hideous. A man in a state of emotional disturbance, whether as the result of love or of enthusiasm for a cause, is like someone who wears blue spectacles and insists, in perfect good faith, that the world is blue. Proust took little interest in 'realities' which cannot be compassed by knowledge, and devoted himself to describing 'impressions' — since only by recording impressions can the artist communicate to the spectator the world as it is seen by another. There is not one universe: there are a hundred universes, almost as many universes as there are human eyes and human intelligences, eyes that open after each night's sleep, minds that become once again conscious with the birth of each new day. It is we, with our desires, and with the heritage of that long past by which they have been formed, who give shape and value to other beings, other things. What mattered to Proust, after 1905, was not the world wrongly described as 'real', the world of the Boulevard Haussmann and the Ritz, but the world he could discover by searching his memory. Only in memory is the 'self' continuous. The recreation by memory of impressions which, later, must be plumbed, irradiated, transformed into intellectual equivalents, is the essence of every true work of art.

The first theme, then, is Time the Destroyer: the second, Memory the Preserver. But not just any kind of memory. One form of memory is deliberate, the child of reason. By applying it we can methodically climb up and down the infinite staircase of Time, seeking to set events and images in their precise and actual order. But to try to evoke the past in this manner is a waste of effort. The information about the past which deliberate memory can convey preserves nothing of its true essence. Is the past, then, dead for ever? Not necessarily.

'. . . I feel that there is much to be said for the Celtic belief that the souls of those whom we have lost are held captive in some inferior being, in an animal, in a plant, in some inanimate object, and effectively lost to us until the day (which to many never comes) when we happen to pass by the tree, or to obtain possession of the object, which forms their prison. Then they start and tremble, they call us by our name, and as soon as we have recognized their voice the spell is broken. We have delivered them: they have overcome death and return to share our life. . . .'[1]

So it is with our past, which continues to live on in an object,

[1] *Swann's Way*, I. Translated by C. K. Scott Moncrieff (Chatto & Windus, 1922).

a taste, a smell: and if, by chance, some day, we can give to our memories the support of a sensation in the present, it will come to life again, as the dead, in Homer, having drunk the sacrificial wine, find for themselves a habitation of flesh and blood.

'I must not forget', writes Proust in one of his *Memoranda*, 'that there is a recurrent motif in my life, more important than that of my love for Albertine, and analogous rather to that cockcrow in the Vinteuil Quartet which ushers in the eternal dawn — and that is the motif of recollection which is no less than the raw material of the artist's calling . . . the cup of tea, trees seen on a walk, belfries etc. . . .'

He dips a piece of bun into a cup of tea, and no sooner does the mouthful of liquid mixed with crumbs touch his palate than he gives a start, and is made aware of something taking place in his consciousness. 'An exquisite pleasure had invaded my senses, but individual, detached, with no suggestion of its origin. And at once the vicissitudes of life had become indifferent to me, its disasters innocuous, its brevity illusory — this new sensation having had on me the effect which love has of filling me with a precious essence; or rather this essence was not in me, it was myself. I had ceased now to feel mediocre, accidental, mortal. Whence could it have come to me, this all-powerful joy? . . .'[1]

Suddenly a memory comes back to him, a memory of the little piece of bun which, when he was a child, his Aunt Léonie had been in the habit of giving him on Sunday mornings, after first dipping it in tea or tisane, 'But when from a long-distant past nothing subsists, after the people are dead, after the things are broken and scattered, still, alone, more fragile, but with more vitality, more unsubstantial, more persistent, more faithful, the smell and taste of things remain poised a long time, like souls ready to remind us, waiting and hoping for their moment, amid the ruins of all the rest, and bear unfaltering, in the tiny and almost impalpable drop of their essence, the vast structure of recollection. . . .'[2]

As soon as he has tracked down the origin of the flavour, his whole childhood swims back into his consciousness, not in the

[1] *Swann's Way*, I. Translated by C. K. Scott Moncrieff (Chatto & Windus, 1922).
[2] C. K. SCOTT MONCRIEFF, op. cit.

form of a series of intellectual recollections emptied of all power, but solid, alive and still charged with the emotions which once had built about it such a world of happiness.

In that single moment Time is Regained and, in that same moment too, Time is conquered, because one whole section of the past has managed to become a section of the present. Moments like this give to the artist the feeling that he has gained eternity. He will never forget 'this new modulation of delight, this summons to a superterrestrial joy'. Other writers had had an inkling of it (Chateaubriand, Nerval, Musset), but no writer until Proust had thought of making the complex sensation-memory into the essential material of his work. The main subject of his novel would be, not the picture of a particular society to be found in France at the end of the nineteenth century, nor yet a new analysis of love (and that is why it is so foolish to maintain that Proust's work will not live because the society of which he wrote has vanished, or because the pattern of love has altered), but the struggle waged by the Spirit of Man with Time, the impossibility of finding in 'actual' life a fixed point to which the *self* can cling, the duty of finding that point within oneself, the possibility of finding it in a work of art. That is the essential, the profound, the novel theme of *A la Recherche du temps perdu*.

II

THE PLAN OF THE BOOK

As soon as he gave up the idea of writing an objective novel centred in the single character of Swann, Proust had to envisage, in a brief flash of intuition such as he describes at the end of *Le Temps retrouvé*, and in the same way as an architect must imagine the completed building before ever he begins to design it, a vast, semi-autobiographical book, constructed not like the ordinary work of fiction, in temporal, spatial or social terms, but in accordance with the laws of the world of spirit and of memory, a magic world 'in which space and time have been abolished'. One cannot but think that his thoughts must have been dwelling as much on Ruskin's *Praeterita*, on one of Thomas Hardy's novels (*The Well-*

Beloved), and on George Eliot (*The Mill on the Floss*), as on the art of Wagner to which so many passages are devoted in the *Notebooks*. Composition constructed round themes is no less rigorous than the linear method of the classic novelists. It cannot be too often repeated that Proust's great work has the simplicity and majesty of a cathedral. The carvings of the capitals, the figures in the stained-glass windows, the saints set about the doorways, the diffused light, the murmur of organ-music — all these things combine to make a world, but the great lines of the nave remain, for all that, simple and lucid.

> *Marcel Proust to Jean de Gaigneron:* 'When you speak to me of cathedrals, I cannot but feel touched at the evidence of an intuition which has led you to guess what I have never mentioned to anybody, and here set down in writing for the first time — that I once planned to give to each part of my book a succession of titles, such as, *Porch, Windows in the Apse*, etc. . . . so as to defend myself in advance against the sort of stupid criticism which has been made to the effect that my books lack construction, whereas I hope to prove to you that their sole merit lies in the solidity of their tiniest parts. I gave up the idea of using these architectural titles because I found them too pretentious, but I am touched at finding that you have dug them up by a sort of intelligent divination. . . .'[1]

This letter is dated 1919, but the reader who first opened *Du Côté de chez Swann* in 1913, could no more grasp the compositional plan of the whole work than a visitor entering Rouen Cathedral by the Library Door can understand the general scheme of the building. The reader, on the other hand, who, having worked through the whole novel, is struck by the secret symmetry of the composition, by the multiplicity of the details that balance one another from wing to wing of the structure, by the toothing stones set in position from the first moment that the work was begun, and designed to carry vaulting still to come, must be filled with wonder that Proust could envisage the whole gigantic edifice so completely. A character who, in the first volume, merely makes a momentary appearance on the stage, becomes, later on,

[1] From a letter in the possession of Comte Jean de Gaigneron.

like one of those musical themes which, sketched in a Prelude, is developed by degrees until it becomes the very centre of the Symphony and grows to dominate the whole medley of sounds with the savage timbre of its brass, one of the work's protagonists. The Narrator, when a child, sees one day in his uncle's house a lady in pink. He knows nothing about her. In the sequel she turns out to have been Miss Sacripant, Odette de Crécy, Madame Swann, Madame de Forcheville. In the little Verdurin 'group' there is a painter whom everyone calls 'Biche'. We are given no reason to suppose that he has any particular talent, but at a later stage he becomes the great Elstir of *Jeunes filles en fleurs*. The Narrator, visiting a bawdy-house, makes the acquaintance of a young woman of easy virtue who can be had for the asking. She develops into Saint-Loup's adored Rachel and, finally, into one of the most famous actresses of her day. Just as, when he wants to introduce one of his sinuous metaphors, Proust prepares the way for it by introducing into the paragraph that precedes it a few words that give us a foretaste of its tonal quality, so does he indicate in *Swann* the essential themes of the whole work, and these are afterwards amplified in *Le Temps retrouvé*.

The great arches that spring from their foundations in the first volume are brought to a graceful completion in the last. The theme of the bun in *Swann* is echoed, some thousands of pages further on, by the uneven paving-stone and the starched napkin. It is necessary to draw attention to these curves which form the structure of the work and carry its mass. The book begins with a prelude on the subject of sleeping and waking, because it is at such moments that the reversibility of Time, the dissociation of the *self* and its secret permanence, can be seen most clearly. Objects, country scenes, the moving years, play about the Narrator in the darkness. We are now equipped for wandering among his memories.

Then the curtain rises on the episode of the bun. This is the first statement of the theme of involuntary memory and its power to reconstitute Time in its pure state. The Narrator's childhood is evoked, and the whole country world of Combray emerges complete from the cup of tea in which the bun has been dipped. The essential characteristics of this magic world of childhood are:

(*a*) that it is peopled by good and powerful tutelary spirits who watch over the Narrator's life and make it happy (the grandmother, the mother); (*b*) that everything belonging to it seems to exist in a state of lovely enchantment — reading, walking, trees, church, the Méséglise Way, the Guermantes Way, the tinkling door-bell, metallic, interminable, shrill and clear, which announces Swann's arrival or departure, water-lilies in the Vivonne, hawthorns beside the steep hill path. All these things partake of the marvellous; (*c*) the child is surrounded by mysteries; words and *names* seem to him to designate persons who resemble those in legends and fairy-tales.

The name *Guermantes*, which is that of the local great family whose château gives its name to the Guermantes Way, evokes Geneviève de Brabant and all the paraphernalia of heraldic beauty. The name of Gilberte, who is Swann's daughter, stands for love, because the Narrator is not allowed to meet this particular little girl, for the good reason that Odette, Swann's wife, but formerly a 'kept' woman, is not received by the middle-class and puritanical families of Combray. Gilberte thus becomes invested with all the prestige of the inaccessible.

The Narrator's life is destined to become a long pursuit of all that lies behind these names. He wants to discover what is hidden in the word *Guermantes*, desires to penetrate into its closed world. He thus becomes, for a time, vulnerable to the attacks of snobbery. He sets out to discover love, and Gilberte, whom he sees again in Paris, in the Champs-Elysées, gives him his first, childish experience of it. He lives in the hope of getting to know certain places — Balbec, Venice — and to see certain theatrical performances — Berma, for instance, an actress of genius, in *Phèdre*. He begins, too, without knowing it, to seek something else, something more lovely, more durable, some state of grace which he glimpses in those very brief moments when he feels that it is his duty to give to special brief experiences the fixity of words (the three belfries, the three trees).

At this point comes an interlude which is almost a separate short novel. *Un Amour de Swann* is, undoubtedly, a left-over from an earlier construction which was planned when Swann was to be the hero of the whole work. It has survived much in the same way as a pagan temple or an early Romanesque church sometimes survives in the crypt of a Gothic cathedral. From it we learn the nature of Swann's love for Odette before the Narrator's birth. That love was unhappy (all love according to Proust is unhappy, and we are later to be told why). It was a passion which followed the curve that leads from enchantment to suffering, from suffering to forgetfulness, a curve which, further on, we are to study in greater detail. But Swann, like the Narrator, entertains at moments a fugitive hope that he may attain to a lovelier and more lasting reality. For him, too, it is art that opens the door into a species of eternity. But because Swann is not a creator, it is not by writing, but by hearing certain pieces of music, by looking at certain pictures, that he can pass beyond Time. The theme of the 'little phrase' in the Vinteuil Sonata — 'gentle, soothing and soft as a breath of perfume' now makes its appearance.

The interlude over, we return to the Narrator. It would be pointless to work through every detail of his novel. What matters is that we should understand the principles of its construction and design. The content of the work as a whole is the discovery by Marcel of what lies concealed behind the façade of names; his attempts to achieve a number of things that he has much desired; his inevitable and utter disenchantment. He longs passionately to be loved by Gilberte Swann, and dreams of sharing the delicious mystery of her existence. In course of time he becomes intimate with Swann, but by then Gilberte has ceased to love him. After a period of much suffering — for children can suffer from love just as surely as can adults — he forgets her so completely that when, years later, he meets her as a full-grown young woman he does not even recognize in her the girl who, in the Champs-Elysées days, had meant the world to him.

Second love: the 'little band' of young girls at Balbec. Here, too, curiosity and a sense of mystery breed in him a hope of hidden happiness. Once again, no sooner has he come to know the little band than he finds it mediocre and vulgar. It is not until long afterwards that he genuinely falls in love with his 'favourite' of those days, Albertine Simonet, whom, when that moment comes, a new sense of mystery and a new experience of suffering has once more made desirable.

Third love: the Duchesse de Guermantes. The woman who, at Combray, figured for him as a fairy-tale heroine turns out to be his neighbour in Paris, and the owner of the house in which both of them live. Gradually his desire to penetrate into her closed world is satisfied. Like Swann he becomes one of its familiars; but all he gets from his success is to be made aware of its vanity, its egotism and cruelty. The value of the Great World, and of love, lies only in desire — or memory.

Thus, little by little, Time devours all that has been the hope of a lifetime, all that has made for its greatness. Even filial love is in the end attacked by Time, and the Narrator, after his grandmother's death, notes in a mood of despair that the 'intermissions of the heart' (that is to say, the recurrent periods of forgetfulness) become increasingly longer. For weeks, for months, for years, he forgets his grandmother, as formerly he had forgotten Gilberte. The very places that he had loved are stripped of their poetry. Balbec itself becomes merely 'somewhere he had known', and 'place-names, once so thrilling that I had found as much emotional stimulus in turning to the "Manche" section of the *"Directory of Chateaux"* as in consulting the *Railway Time Table*, became, after a while, so familiar to me that I could consult that same *Time Table*, turning to the page that gave the trains — *Balbec-Douville* via *Doncières*, as calmly as I might have done a mere list of addresses. On this over-trodden thoroughfare, to the sides of which I felt that a numerous company of friends, whether visible or not, was clinging, the night's poetic call was no longer that of owl or frog, but only Monsieur de Criquetot's "How goes it?" or Brichot's "Hail!" Its atmosphere no longer bred in me dark agonies. Instead, charged with a content that was purely human, it had become an element that I could breathe without difficulty, an environment that was peaceful to excess.'

Venice, seen with the eyes of the flesh, ceased to be Ruskin's Venice, and even Combray, the Combray of the Vivonne and Méséglise, of Swann's lilacs and the belfry of Saint-Hilaire, lost the magic beauty with which the sentiments of childhood had clothed it. A day came when he walked there in the company of Gilberte — now a married woman, Madame de Saint-Loup: 'It distressed me to find how little I relived my early years. I found the Vivonne a meagre, ugly rivulet beneath its tow-path. Not that I noticed any important material discrepancies from what I remembered. But, separated by the whole expanse of a different life, from the places which I happened to be revisiting, there was not, between them and myself, that contiguity from which is born, before ever we can perceive it, the immediate, delicious and total deflagration of memory. Having no very clear conception, probably, of its nature, I was saddened by the thought that my faculty of feeling and imagining things must have diminished, since I no longer took any pleasure in these walks. Gilberte herself, who understood me even less than I understood myself, increased my melancholy by sharing my astonishment. "What", she would say, "you feel no excitement when you turn into this little footpath which you used to climb?" And she herself had so entirely altered that I no longer thought her beautiful, which, indeed, she had ceased to be.'[1]

Everything in which he had believed was now dissolved and smirched. And so we cross the threshold of that Hell which is named *Sodome et Gomorrhe*. His love for Albertine, as recounted in *La Prisonnière*, is nothing but a morbid curiosity. Marcel becomes increasingly convinced that love is no more than the association of the image of a young girl — who, met in any other circumstances would have been an intolerable bore — with the heart-beats inseparable from a long-drawn-out suspense, or from the agony caused him by her conduct and by the nature of her tastes. More painful still, and in the long run altogether monstrous, are the loves of Monsieur de Charlus, the thunder-wielding, fascinating and grotesque prince of Sodom.

As to fame, fashion and the verdicts of the world, none of these abstractions has any real existence. The song which for one brief season ravished Albertine, had become, a year later, nothing but a 'hackneyed tune of Massenet's'. Contrary to what the Narrator had believed when he was young, there is no such thing as a 'great position in the world'. Swann, who was once the friend of the Prince of Wales and the Comte de Paris, is reduced to currying favour with Monsieur Bontemps. A day comes when Bloch is

[1] *The Sweet Cheat Gone,* translated by C. K. Scott Moncrieff (Chatto & Windus, 1930).

more sought after in the great world than Monsieur de Charlus.
'Only too often, all that remains of a person — not after his
death, but during his lifetime — is a name. So vague, so fantastic
are our ideas about him, so little do they correspond to those we
used to have, that we forget entirely how close we once were to
fighting a duel with him. All we remember is that, as a child in
the Champs-Elysées (where, in spite of all we tell him, he has
entirely forgotten that we ever played together), he wore odd,
yellow leggings. . . .'

What is left of all these people? Odette is no longer beautiful,
nor the Duchesse de Guermantes witty. Bloch acquires good
manners and, in some sort, a handsome appearance. Monsieur
de Charlus, whose thunders once struck the presumptuous to the
earth, turns into an impotent, pitiful, humiliated old man who
seems to move through life seeking the support of all and sundry.
Saint-Loup, in spite of his heroic conduct during the war, is seen
to have shared his uncle's vices. The Narrator discovers in himself characteristics at which, when he noticed them in Aunt
Léonie, he used to laugh. Like her, though for other reasons and
as the result of other ailments, he becomes an invalid and a recluse,
hungry for the tittle-tattle of his visitors. We are reminded of
Hugo's lines:

> Toutes les choses de la terre,
> Gloire, fortune militaire,
> Couronne éclatante des rois,
> Victoire aux ailes embrasées,
> Ambitions réalisées,
> Ne sont jamais sur nous posées
> Que comme l'oiseau sur nos toits.[1]

Yes, 'Brightness falls from the air: Queens have died young and
fair.' The first part of *Le Temps retrouvé* resolves itself into a
picture of this tragic and autumnal corruption of all that is. The

[1] All the fame this world can yield,
Reputation, tented field,
Royalty of annointed kings,
Victory with flaming wings,
Splendours that ambition brings,
Do but for a moment light
Upon us, like a bird in flight.

persons whom the Narrator thought he loved have once again become the mere names they were at the beginning of *Swann*. But now those names conceal no mystery. The ends he sought to gain, once achieved, melt into thin air. Life in its ceaseless movement is but Time lost. At a party given by the Princesse de Guermantes, he sees again, disguised as dotards, those whom in his youth he had admired, and the sight of them reveals to him, in a flash, the emptiness of life.

But it is on this same occasion that, as the result of certain memory-sensations of the same general type as the bun (an uneven paving-stone transporting his mind to Venice, a 'stiff, starched napkin' bringing all Balbec into the library), and later his meeting with Mademoiselle de Saint-Loup, the daughter of Robert and Gilberte, 'a young girl of about sixteen, whose tallness was the measure of the very lapse of time I had wanted to forget', he makes his final discovery of Time Regained. 'Time, colourless and intangible, was — so that I could almost touch it, so that it seemed suddenly as hard and firm as a work of art — filled even now with hope. Smiling, compacted of the years that I had lost, it seemed the very echo of my youth.'

In the person of Mademoiselle de Saint-Loup, Swann's Way is made one with the Guermantes Way. The arch is completed, the cathedral finished. At last the Narrator understands the message of eternity, the same message that had been conveyed to him in the three trees, in the bun, in the 'little phrase'. The rôle he is destined to fill is the rôle of the artist who, by fixing such moments and all that they contain, can stop the flux of Time. Life as it passes is but Time lost: but all can be transfigured, found again, presented 'under the aspect of eternity, which is that of art'.

It is at this moment that salvation comes to the artist, and to all human beings. From the medley of relative worlds an absolute world emerges. In man's long struggle with Time, it is man, thanks to the talismans and charms of art, who remains the victor. Thus we see that the subject of *A la Recherche du temps perdu* is the drama of a marvellously intelligent and agonizingly sensitive being who, from the very threshold of childhood, sets forth to find happiness in the absolute. He tries to reach it in all its many forms, though refusing, with an implacable lucidity, to deceive himself as most people deceive themselves. For human beings, as a rule, accept glory and love and the triumphs of the world at their face value. Proust, declining to do so, is led on to seek an absolute that lies outside this world and outside Time itself. It is the absolute that religious mystics find in God. Proust, for his part, looks for it in art, thereby practising a form of mysticism that is closer to the other than might be supposed, because all art in its origins was religious, and because religion has often found in art the means of communicating to the human consciousness truths which the intelligence can discover only with difficulty.

Novel and life are, as we foresaw, made one. His hero's salvation becomes his own, and the work ends at the moment when the Narrator decides to start *his* book. Thus it is that the long serpent returns upon itself after describing its enormous circle. From the moment that he wrote the first page of *Swann*, he had made up his mind that the concluding passage of the novel should end with the word 'Time': and so it was: 'If, at least, time enough were allotted me to accomplish my work, I would not fail to mark it with the seal of Time, the idea of which imposed itself upon me with so much force today, and I would therein describe men, if need be, as monsters occupying a place in Time infinitely more important than the one reserved for them in space, a place, on the contrary, prolonged immeasurably since, simultaneously touching widely separated years and the distant periods they have lived through — between which so many days have ranged themselves — they stand like giants immersed in Time.'[1]

When in this sublime conclusion we hear the word 'Time' repeated on four separate occasions, we are reminded of Beethoven repeating, like an affirmation and a deliverance, at the close of a Symphony, the perfect chord.

And that is what Proust's novel really is — an affirmation and a deliverance. What the great artist can, and should, do is 'partially to lift for us the curtain of ugliness and insignificance which leaves us incurious before the spectacle of the Universe'. As Van Gogh from a straw-bottomed chair, as Degas and Monet from an ugly woman, conjured masterpieces, so did Proust, taking

[1] *Time Regained*, translated by Stephen Hudson (Chatto & Windus, 1931).

an old cook, a damp smell, a room in a country town, a hedge of blossoming hawthorn, say to us: 'Open your eyes and see how, beneath these simple forms, lie all the secrets of the world.'

Truly to travel is 'not to view fresh scenes, but to see the universe with the eyes of a hundred others'. It is such a journey that we take in Proust's company. In his immense Symphony two themes stand confronted, as in Vinteuil's Septet — Time the Destroyer, Memory the Saviour. 'At last', he says, describing the Septet, 'the motif of joy stood out triumphant: no longer was it a cry, almost of unease, from behind an empty Heaven, but joy ineffable seeming to have come straight from Paradise, a joy as different from that of the Sonata as a scarlet-robed archangel by Mantegna, blowing on a trumpet, is different from one of Bellini's sweet and grave-faced cherubs playing upon a lute. I realized then that I should never afterwards forget this new modulation of joy, this summons to delight that lies beyond the world of men....'

And we who love Proust, we who have found spiritual nourishment in his book which seems so melancholy, but which, to those who can read it aright, can so exalt the spirit, we know with certainty that we can never forget his enchanted world, his more than mortal intelligence, his brooding eye which, no matter where it rests, leaves traces of a masterpiece, his poetry that tells of God and of brotherhood.

III

THE TECHNICAL APPARATUS

I have said that time is regained by Proust (or by the Narrator) in rare moments of illumination, when the simultaneity of a sensation and of a memory brings into juxtaposition moments that normally exist at a great distance from one another, and awakens in us the consciousness of our own unity and duration. But such moments are infrequent and accidental. They can cast, for the artist, a revealing light upon the nature of his vocation, but they do not enable him to seek with certainty what lies behind all objects, and to bring into the light of day, in the pages of his book, the imprisoned beauty. What I now have to do is to describe the rites of this especial cult, in other words, to explain the technical means which the writer employs in order to give to the past the characteristic of 'immediacy'. Proust believed that the miracle was possible because the present is wholly filled by the past. Here is the key passage in which he works out his thought:

An image presented by life gives us, in fact, at the moment of its occurrence, a great number of different sensations. We look, for instance, at the cover of the book we have been reading, and are aware that the moonbeams of a distant summer's night are part and parcel of the printed title. The flavour of our morning coffee brings us the same vague expectation of a fine day to come which so often, of old, while we drank from a white china bowl the creased and creamy liquid which resembled petrified milk, used to smile at us from the ambiguous radiance of the early dawn. *An hour is not merely an hour; it is a vase filled with scents and sounds, with plans and climatic differences.* What we call reality is a certain relation subsisting between our sensations and our memories — a relation which any simple cinematographic vision destroys, because the nearer it seems to approximate to the truth the further does it diverge from it — a unique relation which the writer must recover, striving to imprison for ever in a single phrase the two separate terms of the experience. One can, in the process of pure description, set down, one after the other indefinitely, a number of statements about the objects to be seen in the place *described: but truth begins only at the moment when the writer takes two distinct objects, establishes between them that relation which, in the world of art is analogous to a causal relation in the world of science, and imprisons them within the necessary* constriction of a beautiful style, or, following in this the processes of life itself, isolates a quality which is common to both sensations, extracts their essence by merely bringing them into close association through the medium of a metaphor, and thus rescues them from the contingencies of time, and binds them together by that bond of verbal union which it is impossible to describe. Was it not Nature herself that set me, at this point, on the long road of art, Nature that so often made it impossible for me to realize the beauty of an object save through the medium of another object: noon at Combray long afterwards in the sound of bells, morning at Doncières in the hiccupping of our hot-water system? The relationship in question may not be particularly interesting, the objects may be mediocre, the style bad, but unless something of the sort is brought about the result is nothing. . . .'

Take two distinct objects . . . establish the relation between them: that, according to Proust, is one of the artist's secrets. We begin to see the beauty of something when we perceive behind it something else. Marcel, as a child, had often passed the palaces designed by Gabriel without noticing that they were more beautiful than the surrounding buildings. 'On a single occasion only did the sight of one of those palaces bring me to a prolonged halt, and that was when, darkness having fallen, its columns, etherealized by the moonlight, looked as though they had been cut from cardboard, and then, because they reminded me of the scenery of the Operetta, *Orphée aux Enfers*, impressed me for the first time with an idea of beauty . . .' Thus it is the memory of something less beautiful that, with reference to something else, awakes in us a sense of beauty. Why? — because there is a sharp intellectual pleasure in finding in an analogy the blue-print of a law.

This is especially true where the second term of the comparison, the something seen *through* the intervening transparency of the real, happens to be closely connected with the part of our nature that lives at a deep level and partakes of the elementary in ourselves. The sensations of taste, smell and touch, though we may think them less delicate than sight and hearing, and perhaps because, in truth, they are less intellectual, make a peculiarly sharp impact on the imagination. They establish a connection between the low and the high, between the body and the spirit. Jean Pommier has shown how predominant in Proust are images drawn from taste and eating. A tired face 'breaks up' like milk that has turned: a strip of red sky on the horizon at sunset has the solid consistency, the sharp edge, of a piece of brawn; the towers of the Trocadéro, flushed by the evening light, look like those pink sugar turrets which are to be seen in the shops of old-fashioned pastry-cooks.

Behind surface appearances the poet finds those images of growing things, of animals, of the great spectacles of nature, which form the basic elements in all art. The *Jeunes filles en fleurs* look to the Narrator like a thicket of roses. The porter of the hotel at Balbec when, at nightfall, he enters the great glazed hall, makes him think of some plant in a greenhouse, protected from the cold. The transformation of Monsieur de Charlus into a large bumble-bee, of Jupien into an orchid, of Monsieur de Palancy into a pike, of the Guermantes into birds, of footmen into greyhounds, brings to mind the metamorphoses hymned by the poets of antiquity. Flowers, by a reverse process, turn into women. The hawthorns are gay young girls, giddy, coquettish and pious: the eglantines wear bodices touched with red, and the apple trees of Normandy are decked out in ball-dresses of pink satin.

But, above all, the poet discovers behind material objects what Jung has called *archetypes*, that is to say the root fictions of the human mind, the source of all fairy-tale characters.[1] Behind the Duchesse de Guermantes stands the figure of Geneviève de Brabant: behind the three trees a vague memory of those legends in which a lovely body of flesh and blood (Daphne) is held prisoner within the covering bark, so that the waving branches seem like arms stretched in despairing supplication: behind the sleeping Albertine the murmur of the sea and all the mystery of the world. In this way it is that the myth of Proteus still helps our poets to sing more exquisitely still of ocean and its myriad forms.

To take two distinct objects, establish the relation between them . . . and imprison them within the necessary constriction of a beautiful style. It follows that, for Proust, the basic elements of a beautiful style are images. The only way of communicating to the reader the relationship existing between two objects is by the use of metaphor. The function of metaphor is to 'borrow from some object, not normally present in the situation described, a natural and perceptible image of the truth'. It assists both author and reader to evoke something till then unknown, or a feeling difficult to describe, by stressing the similarity of both to some familiar object.

[1] Cf. Jean Pommier, *La Mystique de Proust* (Paris, Librairie E. Droz, 1939), *passim*.

But if the image is to retain its full power of evocation it must not, in itself, be hackneyed or defaced by constant use. The term of comparison must be better known to us than the object it serves to evoke. The images employed by all great writers are original and *actual* — nor should they be shy of borrowing them from the most diverse fields of human activity. Proust draws many of his most striking images from physiology and pathology. 'Those who have never been in love think that a man of intelligence should be made unhappy only by a woman who is worthy of the agony she causes. To say that is very little different from expressing surprise that anyone should catch the cholera from something so trivial as a tiny bacillus . . .' There are passages in which he sheds a revealing light on one small corner of society by comparing it with another which, at first sight, has nothing to do with it. 'The man who was Prime Minister forty years ago is taken into a new Cabinet by a leader who offers him a portfolio much as theatrical producers give a part to some former colleague, now long retired, whom they think more capable than younger players of acting with subtle intelligence, whom, too, they know to be in straitened circumstances, and who, at nearly eighty, can come before the public with talents almost unimpaired, improved, indeed, by a length of days the extent of which one is amazed to discover only shortly before he dies. . . .'

Here are some images culled from a few pages of Proust taken at random. The Narrator's mother tells Françoise that Monsieur de Norpois has expressed the opinion that she is a 'chef of the very front rank, much as a Minister of War might transmit to a General, after a full-dress review, the congratulations of a visiting Crowned Head' . . . Marcel, in the days when he is in love with Gilberte, and regards everything to do with Swann as sacred, flushes with horror when he hears his father speak of Swann's apartment as he might have done had it belonged to some perfectly insignificant person: 'I felt instinctively that my mind must make any necessary sacrifice demanded by Swann's glory, and, by an act of will, in spite of what I had just heard, I put from me, as a religiously-minded person might put Renan's *Vie de Jésus*, the disturbing thought that his apartment might, just conceivably, be a perfectly ordinary apartment, such as we ourselves might have lived in . . .' The Narrator's mother compares Madame Swann's campaign for the extension of her social conquests to an episode in the history of colonial warfare: 'Now that the Tromberts have been subdued, it won't be long before the neighbouring tribes surrender . . .' When she meets Madame Swann in the street, she says, on returning home: 'I have just seen Madame Swann on the warpath. She must be setting out on some promising expedition against the Masséchutos, the Cingalees or the Tromberts . . .' Finally, Madame Swann asks to her house a boring but kindly woman who is for ever paying calls, because she knew 'the enormous number of middle-class flowers that this active bee, armed with a feathered hat and a card-case, can rifle in a single afternoon. . . .'

Another of Proust's favourite methods is to evoke the actual through reference to works of art. He was not, himself, either a painter or a musician, but both painting and music were for him sources of much happiness. He was on terms of intimacy with Jacques-Émile Blanche, with Jean-Louis Vaudoyer and with Berenson, all of whom acted as his guides when he was wandering among masterpieces. He had read Baudelaire, Fromentin, Whistler and, of course, Ruskin. Though he scarcely ever travelled, and went out hardly at all, he was quite capable of undertaking a journey to the Hague or to Padua, with the sole object of looking at a single picture. He never lacked terms of reference in this field.

He had begun by feeling affection for the painters whom he used to meet in the various drawing-rooms he frequented, or in Madeleine Lemaire's studio. They were not always the best. In the questionnaire which he filled up when still a child, he gave Meissonier as his favourite painter, and he always had a weakness (later kept to himself, but none the less persistent) for Helleu and La Gandara. But he had also known Degas at the Halévy's, and by combining the Impressionists and Helleu produced Elstir, the great painter of his novel. From his reading of Ruskin he had learned to love Giotto, Fra Angelico, Carpaccio, Bellini and Mantegna. At a very early stage in his career he had acquired the habit of seeking resemblances between persons whom he knew and figures in well-known pictures, primarily because he had a natural liking for such identifications, so that it pleased him to see a Paris crowd in Benozzo Gozzoli's processions, to recognize Monsieur de Palancy's nose in a Ghirlandaio, or Bellini's portrait of Mahomet II in Bloch's profile, but also because the evocation of a *known* atmosphere associated with the work of a great painter, conveys the author's meaning to his readers far better than pages of description could do.

Consequently, we find a fierce-faced footman compared to the executioner in some Renaissance picture, and the pregnant kitchen-maid at Combray to Giotto's *Charity*. Swann's dining-room is described as being as dark as the interior of one of Rembrandt's Asiatic temples, and a group of soldiers with faces reddened by the cold reminds him of Peter Breughel's cheerful, frost-bitten peasants. At Doncières, in a junk-shop, 'a half-consumed candle shining redly on an engraving turned the interior into a study *en sanguine*, while the radiance of the primitive light, giving colour to a scrap of leather, inlaying a dagger with glittering gems, laying a patina of seeming age or the varnish of a master on pictures which, actually, were only bad copies, turned the whole ramshackle establishment, with its medley of trashy curios and infamous daubs, into a priceless Rembrandt. . . .'

And just as scenes of squalor, or melancholy hotel corridors, can be transformed to enchantment by a light which brings to them the 'warm, golden, shimmering and mysterious quality of a Rembrandt, so, too, Odette's face, at first sight unremarkable, becomes for Swann uniquely beautiful as soon as it reminds him of a Botticelli. In order to make comprehensible certain moods of love, Proust has recourse to Watteau: 'At times . . . something of inestimable value seems to vanish into thin air, a whole lovely picture instinct with feeling, tenderness, sensual delight and blurred regrets, a whole *Embarquement pour Cythère* of the passions, whose subtle and delicious truth one would fain note for comfort in sleepless nights to come, disappears like a canvas that has faded too completely for restoration. . . .'

His favourite painter, whom he makes Bergotte praise unreservedly, about whom Swann planned to write a monograph, and of whom Proust himself in his letters to Vaudoyer speaks with fervent admiration, was Vermeer. Throughout *A la Recherche du temps perdu,* he is made to serve as a touchstone for the human heart. Marcel Proust the man, no less than the Narrator, held Vermeer to have been the 'greatest of all painters'. 'As soon as I first set eyes on the *View of Delft* in the Hague Museum, I knew that I had seen the loveliest picture in the world', he writes to Vaudoyer. 'In *Du Côté de chez Swann* I could not resist the temptation to make Swann plan a study of Vermeer . . . though at that time I knew very little about Vermeer . . . This artist who keeps his back to us, who set no store upon being seen by posterity, and who will never know what posterity thinks of him, moves me profoundly . . .' Very little thought will enable us to explain this preference. Like Proust, Vermeer never distorts reality. Instead, he transfigures it, and finds a way of expressing all the poetry of the world in a patch of yellow wall, a tiled roof, or a girl's yellow turban. He did for these things what Proust did for a room in a country house, for the hiccupping of a hot-water system, or for the leaves of a lime. Vermeer's colours have the velvety softness of Proust's adjectives. René Huyghe, who has studied the elective affinity of the two masters, says: 'Both Vermeer and Proust turn their backs on realism, and for the same reason. They share the conviction that sensibility can be substituted for imagination. Each has a *true* vision, that is to say a vision felt rather than imagined and wholly distinct from the ordinary, collective vision which is what lies at the base of realism.'

But Proust felt, too, that he was very close to the Impressionists who had achieved in painting much the same sort of revolution as he himself had brought to literature, and Debussy to music. The water-lilies of the Vivonne recall those of Giverny. 'Here and there the surface was flushed by a floating water-lily which lay upon it like a strawberry with a white-edged scarlet heart . . .' Already, in the *Bible of Amiens,* he had praised Monet for his series of paintings (mills and cathedrals), and had described the West Front of Amiens 'blue in the mist, dazzling in the morning light, drenched by the sun, heavily gilded by the radiance of the afternoon, pink, and already touched by the tender evening glow at sundown — all these times when the bells sound in the high heavens, times that Claude Monet has fixed in his sublime canvases displaying the life of that *thing* which men have created but which Nature has resumed and made part of herself — a cathedral whose existence, like that of the earth in her double revolution, has unwound through the long tale of the centuries, yet is every day renewed and achieved afresh. . . .'[1]

He makes use of Renoir and of Manet's *Olympia* to show how a great artist can change the way of looking at things among his contemporaries.

> People of taste tell us today that Renoir was a great *eighteenth-century* painter. But in saying that they omit the time-factor, and forget that, even in the middle of the nineteenth century, it took a long time for Renoir to be accepted as a great painter. If they are to succeed, they — the original painter and the original writer — have to proceed much in the manner of oculists. The treatment administered through their paintings or their literature is not always pleasant. When it is finished they say to us — '*Now* look!' — and suddenly the world, which, far from having been created once and for all, is created afresh each time that a new artist comes on the scene, is shown to us in perfect clarity — but looking very different from the one we knew before. The women walking in the street are different from those we saw formerly, because they are Renoir's, those women of Renoir whom once we refused to recognize as women at all. The carriages, too, are Renoir's, the water, the sky. We are seized with a longing to walk in the forest which is precisely like the forest that, when first we looked at it, seemed anything *but* a forest, seemed, for instance, like a tapestry, showing every shade of colour, every *nuance* of form, *except* the colours and the forms peculiar to forests. Such is the new and perishable universe freshly created. It will remain convincing until the next geological catastrophe precipitated by a new painter or a new writer of originality. . . .

The painter he himself created, Elstir, makes his first appearance at Madame Verdurin's, under the nickname of 'Biche'. He is,

[1] *Days of Pilgrimage: Ruskin at Notre-Dame d'Amiens, etc.* in *Marcel Proust: A Selection from His Miscellaneous Writings*, translated by Gerard Hopkins (Allan Wingate, 1948).

at that time, a rather vulgar creature given to making crude jokes, but he has already astonished the Verdurins because he 'sees purple shadows in a woman's hair'. When he reappears in *Jeunes filles en fleurs*, he has become a great Impressionist who tries to paint objects as they appear to us when first we see them, at the moment, that is, which is 'the only real moment, because, the intelligence not having yet intervened to explain to us *what* they are, we have not substituted our *notions* for the impression they produced upon us'.

Elstir (like Proust) composes his masterpieces from 'particles of reality, each one of which has been felt personally', thereby assuring the unity of his picture, since the humblest object is equal in value to the most precious if it is painted in the ambience of a Rembrandt or a Monet. 'The slightly vulgar woman, from whom the connoisseur of beauty would avert his eyes if he passed her in the street, would delete from the poetic picture composed by nature for his delectation, can also make her contribution of loveliness. The same light lies upon her dress and upon a boat's sail. It is not a question of any one object being more or less precious than any other: the common clothes and the sail — which is pretty in its own right — are merely two mirrors reflecting the same truth. The whole *value* is in the eye of the painter. . . .'

Elstir, with his model before him, makes a conscious effort to suppress his intelligence, and this, for him, is peculiarly difficult because that intelligence is richly cultivated. Proust worked in a precisely similar manner, forcing himself to study love, jealousy, forgetfulness, as though no one had ever before written about those subjects. Elstir's intention is to paint things, not as he knows (or believes) them to be, but strictly in accordance with those optical delusions of which human vision, in its simplest and most immediate form, is composed. He sets himself to create a feeling of 'ambiguity', so that the spectator can never be quite sure what, in the picture, is a record of objective fact, and what mirage: what is seen indirectly by reflection, and what is seen directly in space. In this, too, he resembles Proust who, in his finest metaphors, leaves us with a feeling of doubt whether the auditorium of the Opera is situated in Paris or at the bottom of the sea, whether Monsieur de Charlus is a man or a bumble-bee.

All art must observe the same rules — rules imposed by the laws of Nature and the exigencies of the human spirit. Though the novelist has much to learn from the painter, he should look for instruction to the musician as well. Did Proust have a genuine knowledge of music? Professionals, such as Reynaldo Hahn, said 'No', but it must be remembered that composers know music as scholars know history, in a way, that is, which is not necessary for the common run of mortals, though ordinary people are, nevertheless, perfectly capable of assimilating the spiritual nourishment which both music and history can provide. What is quite certain is that Proust had a great love of music, and was always eager to listen to it, whether at public concerts — Georges de Lauris once saw him seated in an obscure corner of the Salle Pleyel when Beethoven's Quartets were being performed — or in his own home, where he would get Reynaldo to sing old French songs, or to play over, twenty, a hundred, times some phrase from which he wanted to extract the full meaning, some phrase which was, so to speak, the musician's *senza rigore*.

In the *Memoranda* and the *Notebooks* we come on many attempts to find a literary equivalent for a musical phrase: 'The Wagnerian storm, which set all the strings in the orchestra moaning like a ship's rigging, while at intervals above them rose, oblique, powerful and calm as a gull, the strong stream of melody . . .' Again, on the subject of Wagner: 'Into the storm of this music, the little tune on a shepherd's pipe, a bird's song, the fanfare of hunting horns, were drawn like flecks of sea-foam or pebbles flung wide by the gale. They were sucked into the vortex of the music, atomized and distorted like those shapes of flowers or fruit, whose lines, separated one from another, simplified and stylized, merge into the general scheme of ornament and make the spectator forget their primal origin, so that all he can say is — "that's a hawthorn bud, that's an apple leaf'; or like the simple themes of a Symphony which one finds difficulty in recognizing when it is elaborated with semiquavers, enriched with accompanying modulations, reversed and broken up in subsequent variations; though Wagner, like those craftsmen who when set to execute a carving in wood are careful to let the lines of growth, the natural colour, the grain of the material, emerge, sees to it that something of the music's natural sonority and native origin remains distinctly audible amid the general torrent of sound' — all of which is an instance of fine and accurate analysis.

As he had had recourse to painting in order to make intelligible certain secret aspects of natural objects or of human faces, so, too, he drew analogies from music. The glances directed by Monsieur de Charlus at Jupien are compared to Beethoven's broken phrases. The Narrator recognizes the vague melancholy of the music of *Pelléas* in the cries of the snail-vendors: 'On les vend six sous la douzaine . . .' Françoise's conversation is likened to a Bach fugue. What, above all, he maintains is that the great musicians reveal us to ourselves, and force us into contact with a world for which we are not made. 'Is not music a unique example of what the communion of souls may be like?'

Just as he invented a painter, Elstir, so he created his own particular musician, Vinteuil, who is closely, if ambiguously, bound to himself. Vinteuil is a father who suffers from a daughter's vicious temperament (theme of the sensual-love/child-love conflict). At the same time he is the creative artist whose work reveals to Swann 'the presence of one of those invisible realities in which he had ceased to believe, but to which he now, once again, felt strong enough to devote the whole of his life'. Vinteuil is the artist Proust would have liked to be and indeed was; the artist who lays on, note by note and touch by touch, the mysterious colours of an infinitely valuable universe. The magic of the Septet, is, for the Narrator, proof that there exists something other than the emptiness which, so far, he has found in love and in the pleasures of Society.

Whether it be from Nature or from art that the second term of a metaphor is borrowed, Proust is always at great pains to prepare us for its entry. When we approach a stretch of flooded country we recognize it, long before the actual surface of the water becomes visible, by the sound our footsteps make upon the grass, by a vague *liquidity* in the feel of the ground, difficult though it is to describe. Similarly, even before the first phrase of the metaphor has been sounded, Proust has been careful to scatter, here and there, a number of adjectives designed to herald its approach. The classic example of what I mean is his account of that evening at the Opera, when he saw the theatre in terms of a submarine aquarium:

> . . . But in the other *baignoires* . . . the white deities who inhabited those sombre abodes had flown for shelter against their shadowy walls and remained invisible. Gradually, however, as the performance went on, their vaguely human forms detached themselves, one by one, from the shades of night which they patterned, and, raising themselves towards the light, allowed their semi-nude bodies to emerge, and rose, and stopped at the limit of their course, at the luminous, shaded *surface* on which their brilliant faces appeared behind the gaily *breaking foam* of the feather fans they unfurled and lightly waved, beneath their hyacinthine locks begemmed with pearls, which the *flow of the tide* seemed to have caught and drawn with it; this side of them began the orchestra stalls, abode of mortals for ever separated from the transparent, shadowy realm to which, at points here and there, served as boundaries on its *liquid*, brimming surface, the limpid and mirroring eyes of *water-nymphs*. For the folding seats on its *shore*, the forms of the monsters in the stalls, were painted upon the surface of those eyes in simple obedience to the laws of optics and according to their angle of incidence . . . Beyond this boundary, withdrawing from the limit of their domain, the radiant *daughters of the sea* kept turning at every moment to smile up at the bearded *tritons* who clung to the anfractuosities of the cliff, or towards some *aquatic* demi-god, whose head was a polished *pebble* to which the *tides* had born a smooth covering of *seaweed*, and his gaze a disc of rock crystal . . . Sometimes the *flood* parted to a fresh *Nereid* who, belated, smiling, apologetic, had just floated into blossom out of the shadowy depths; then, the act ended, having no further hope of hearing the melodious sounds of earth which had drawn them to the surface, *plunging* back all in a moment, the several sisters vanished into the night. But of all these retreats, to the threshold of which their mild desire to behold the works of man brought the curious god-

desses who let none approach them, the most famous was the cube of semi-darkness known to the world as the *baignoire* of the Princesse de Guermantes. . . .[1]

There is a hint of preciosity in this highly elaborated style and in the fine-spun periods. But everything in the passage is necessary for the poet's creation of a magic world. In this ceremony of a great work's gradual revelation, metaphors play the part accorded to sacred vessels in a religious service. The realities to which the soul of the believer clings are entirely spiritual, but because man is both soul and body he needs material symbols to serve as intermediaries between him and the inexpressible. Proust's magic art, as Arnaud Dandieu has already pointed out, owes much of its success to his use of the sensation-fetish as a means of stimulating a memory of the eternal. 'The spiritual intuition which is the source of his creativeness has to be expressed in the language of material things.'[2] Before it can make contact with human kind, the Idea, like God, must become incarnate.

That is what, in the days before his vocation became clear, had been vaguely present to the mind of the child who, as he walked by the banks of the Loir, or through the flat countryside of La Beauce, sought obscure and solemn verities behind certain trees, certain bushes, certain belfry-towers, all of which seemed to be in constant movement. He had, in those days, been obsessed by a feeling that these inanimate objects were imploring him to strike to the depth of the thought that they concealed, that they were mythical appearances, posturing Sorcerers or Norns. The artist, when he grew to the stature of a master, realized that the child had been right, that all valid thought has its roots in daily life, and that the 'rôle' of metaphor — a key-rôle in the whole performance — is to give strength to the Spirit by forcing it to renew its contacts with the Earth, its mother.

---

[1] *The Guermantes Way*, Part I, translated by C. K. Scott Moncrieff (Chatto & Windus, 1925). I have very slightly modified Mr. Scott Moncrieff's rendering so as to make clear the points stressed by Monsieur Maurois, who is, in every case, responsible for the *italics*. – Translator.

[2] NOEL MARTIN-DESLIAS, *Idéalisme de Marcel Proust* (F. Janny, Éditeur, Montpellier, 1945).

Art, as Proust conceived it, is guided on its way by the irresistible
demands of a metaphysic.   ALBERT BÉGUIN

PROUST'S PHILOSOPHY

'Is *that* all this immense voyage of discovery amounts to' —
some have asked: 'a bun dipped in tea, a starched napkin, two uneven paving-stones, and a few moments of aesthetic
ecstasy? Shall a man find his hope of happiness in things
like that after fixing it on love, ambition or the triumphs of the
mind? Have we got to admit that human life has no other purpose than to let down its nets and fish up from the ocean of pain
and sorrow, with infinite care, a few beautiful metaphors?' Such
objections are less serious than they may seem to be. They lose
much of their weight if the special coincidences (bun, napkin,
paving-stones) are seen merely as the means of achieving those
moments, miraculous and, therefore by definition rare, which
serve as the basis of a Faith. They collapse entirely as soon as we
realize that Proust constructed a whole philosophy on these
brief experiences of mystic ravishment.

Can it be said truly that Marcel Proust had a theory about the
human predicament? He would certainly have rejected the word
'theory' — holding it to be pedantic. 'A work of art which
contains theories', he said, 'is like an article on which the price-
ticket has been left.' In his youth, under the seductive influence
of Darlu, he thought of himself as marked out to be a student of
philosophy. But he very soon felt himself repelled by the abstract
vocabulary of the subject, finding that it set a barrier between
his mind and the world of actuality. He saw that he could better
express his ideas in symbolic form, using concrete objects for the
purpose. This, however, does not mean that we cannot recognize
in his work all the elements of a metaphysical theory in the grand
manner such as is to be found in the great classic systems. Per-
ception, dreams, memory, the problem of the *self*, the reality of
the external world, the puzzle of space and time — all the main
headings of Darlu's lectures, are to be found, brought to life and
given a poetical quality, in *A la Recherche du temps perdu.*

In his view of the reality of the external world he is, and quite rightly so, closer to Plato than to Berkeley. Man, imprisoned in his cave, sees only shadows, but they are the shadows of *something*. All art is built upon impressions. The duty of the artist is to rediscover 'sense-impressions uncorrected by intellectual judgments'. But there is no such thing as pure sensation. The act of seeing is always an interpretation of the shadows in the cave, an attempt to reconstruct, intellectually, the objects which must to all eternity remain invisible. Thought is an activity of continuous creation. Vision is nothing but 'an aggregate of mental processes' and, just as there are illusions of the senses brought about by false or incomplete mental processes (a stick that looks, in water, *as though* it is bent, the evidence of the stereoscope, etc.), so, too, there are illusions of feeling (Rachel as seen by Saint-Loup, Jupien by Charlus).

Now, the very use of the word 'illusion' presupposes the existence of a reality that is not illusory. Proust knew that behind our impressions there is an external world which we have got to understand, that the interplay — in his case, incessant — between sensibility and intelligence constitutes what Benjamin Crémieux has happily styled 'surimpressionism'. The Impressionist painter opens our eyes and says: 'Look at those ships at anchor *in* the town.' Similarly, Proust does not hesitate 'to make the rain murmur within the four walls of a room, or to set tisane pouring in torrents into the courtyard'. But he follows this up by using his prodigious intelligence to analyse the illusions of sense, sentiment and reasoning. The rôle of art is to demolish obstacles, those ready-made ideas which are interposed between man's spirit and the real. Philosophy follows hard on the heels of art and reflects upon its achievements. 'Thus, art treads the same road as metaphysics and constitutes a method of discovery.'[1]

To *understand* impressions or feelings means, first, to see them as they are, and then to analyse them: in other words, to separate them into their known elements so that they can be made to take their place within a system of general laws. Proust inherited from the medical environment in which he had been brought up an entirely scientific attitude. 'He mistrusted systems, and limited

---

[1] Cf. Noël Martin-Deslias, op. cit,

his efforts to establishing the relations linking a pair of facts.' He studied his characters with the passionate and detached curiosity of a naturalist observing insects or even vegetable phenomena. The *Jeunes filles en fleurs* are more than an image. They define a season in the brief life of the human plant. Even while he is gazing in wonder at their freshness, he is already noting the tiny signs which announce the successive stages of fruiting, maturity, seeding and desiccation. 'As in the case of a tree whose flowers blossom at different periods, I saw in the old ladies who thronged the beach at Balbec the hard, tough seeds, the soft tubers,' which those girls would, sooner or later, become . . .' Love, jealousy, vanity, are, to him, quite literally ailments. *Un Amour de Swann* is the clinical description of a specific case. Reading the painful precision of this pathology of the sentiments, we feel that the observer has himself experienced the sufferings he describes but, as certain courageous doctors have the power to separate completely the *self* that suffers from the *self* that thinks, and to note each day the progress of a cancer or the onset of paralysis, so, too, he can analyse his own symptoms with a technical integrity which is nothing short of heroic. He maintains that the world is governed by certain laws (since were it not, no science would be possible), and that there exists a definite connection between human intelligence and the universe. Can we say that he believed in a divine intelligence ordering both man and the movements of the universe? There is nothing in his work that leads one to think so. Henri Massis has collected every scrap of evidence, every statement however imperfect, which might be held to prove that Proust was ever worried by considerations of a religious nature. One of the characters in *Les Plaisirs et les Jours* says: 'I felt that I was causing the soul of my mother to weep, the soul of my Guardian Angel, the soul of God . . .' Marcel, when he meditates on the mechanics of waking, and on the surprising fact that, no matter how strange the dreams from which we emerge each morning we always manage to rediscover the personality that is ours, seems to be admitting that resurrection after death may be a phenomenon of memory. But, in the last analysis, the only form of eternity in which he believes unreservedly is that of art, and even the work of art is perishable.

We know only too well that a day will come when, on a planet at last grown cold, no human being will be left to read Homer, Bergotte or Proust. Nevertheless it remains true that, at the moment in which poets experience the intuitions and the ecstasies which are at the basis of all great works of art, they are free of Time's bondage, and thus to be free is the very definition of eternity. Art, therefore, does constitute a form of salvation, and the artists — painters, musicians, poets — play a part in this aesthetic religion comparable to that played by the saints of the Catholic Church. Between the mysticism of the artist and that of the believer there is no conflict. The men who built the cathedrals, the Italian Primitives, the inspired poets, have unified the 'two ways of seeking'. The saint and the artist, after many temptations and many struggles, are brought together in a life of self-discipline.

That, then, is Proust's metaphysic: the external world exists, but it is unknowable: the world of the spirit is knowable, but continually slips from our grasp because it is always changing. Only the world of art is absolute. Immortality is possible, but only during our lifetime. Nevertheless at the end of his description of Bergotte's death, in which, it seems, he saw the prefiguration of his own, he adds:

Permanently dead? who shall say? Certainly our experiments in spiritualism prove no more than the dogmas of religion that the soul survives death. All that we can say is that everything is arranged in this life as though we entered it carrying the burden of obligations contracted in a former life; there is no reason inherent in the conditions of life on this earth that can make us consider ourselves obliged to do good, to be fastidious, to be polite, even, nor make the talented artist consider himself obliged to begin over again a score of times a piece of work the admiration aroused by which will matter little to his body devoured by worms, like the patch of yellow wall painted with so much knowledge and skill by an artist who must forever remain unknown and is barely identified under the name of Vermeer. All these obligations which have not their sanction in our present life seem to belong to a different world, one founded upon kindness, scrupulosity, self-sacrifice, a world entirely different from this, which we leave in order to be born into this world, before, perhaps, returning to the other to live once again beneath the sway of those unknown laws which we have obeyed because we bore their precepts in our hearts, knowing not whose hand had traced them there — those laws to which every profound work of the intellect brings us nearer and which are invisible only — and still! — to fools. So that the idea that Bergotte was not wholly and permanently dead is by no means improbable.

They buried him, but all through the night of mourning, in the lighted windows, his books arranged three by three kept watch like angels with outspread wings and seemed, for him who was no more, the symbol of his resurrection. . . .[1]

'*So that the idea that Bergotte was not wholly and permanently dead is by no means improbable.*' By no means improbable? Yes, but also, in Proust's eyes, inconsistent. Each time that he tried to apprehend the idea of eternity, he found himself faced either with the mystic doctrine of creation or with the equally mystic fact of human feeling. 'God has no need of anything outside Himself: that everything is within Himself is one of the implications of His divine nature.'[2] It seems probable that he would have given whole-hearted assent to this passage from Gide: 'Of what interest would eternal life be to me if I were not, all the while, aware of its eternity? Eternal life may, at this very moment, be present in us. We live it as soon as we begin to die to ourselves, to force ourselves to make the renunciation as a result of which we can immediately rise again in eternity.' I have now to show how, as the result of a spiritual progress, similar to that of an anchorite, Proust actually attained to this condition of renunciation: how gradually, and without regrets, he freed himself from the tyranny of worldly goods, and how, at last, he could bring himself to think of the end of his painful and unhappy life as a Perpetual Adoration.

[1] *The Captive*, translated by C. K. Scott Moncrieff (Chatto & Windus, 1929).
[2] NOËL MARTIN-DESLIAS, *Idéalisme de Marcel Proust*, p. 140.

CHAPTER VII

LA RECHERCHE DU TEMPS PERDU (II)

LOVE AND ITS PASSIONS

Each time I wrote that Albertine was pretty I crossed the words out and
wrote instead that I had felt a desire to kiss Albertine. MARCEL PROUST

I T was always Proust's opinion that no literary representation
of love, whether in the classic or romantic authors, had ever
really plumbed the depths of the subject, and 'that nothing is
further removed from love than the ideas we entertain about it'.
Consequently, he set himself to define with greater exactness
those successive stages of love which may be defined as — first
meeting — selection — effects of presence and of absence — and
finally, forgetfulness, which, in its extreme form may become
complete indifference (an idea wholly at variance with the view
held by the romantics, as, for instance, in *Le Lac* and *La Tristesse
d'Olympio*, and with the mournful effects of regret as described in
La Princesse de Clèves). Thus, the picture that he paints for us of
love is both new and tragic.

I

THE BIRTH OF LOVE

In the temperament of every youthful human being there are
present two innate emotions — desire and anguish. These at
first exist in a void, being unattached to any specific object.
Desire is that natural propensity which draws us into the orbit
of any woman we may happen to meet — of the anonymous girl,
for instance, who sells milk to travellers at a mountain railway-
station. More commonly, it takes the form of a generalized sense
of mystery. When the Narrator, at Balbec, catches sight on the
sea wall of the *Jeunes filles en fleurs*, of those rose-buds in their

beauty whose chief charm it is that they stand out against the background of the sea like an antique frieze of maidens, he falls in love with all of them, not having personal knowledge of any separately, so that the 'processional goddesses' seem to him, in very truth, to be interchangeable. Anguish is the state of mind which certain persons experience when they are waiting for the onset of love: 'it floats, a vague, free presence as yet unattached, at the service now of this emotional uprush, now of that, taking shape at one time as the love of a child for its parents, at another as friendship for an adored companion. . . .'

Desire and anguish are, in each one of us, powers available for use, and seeking an object upon which they may be exercised. We find ourselves to be in love, but do not know with whom. On the inward stage of our being, a comedy of love is ready for production. The parts, already written, have been in our minds since the days of childhood's reading. We are looking round for an actress to whom we may confide the rôle of the beloved.

How are we to choose the 'star' who shall create, or succeed to, that rôle? Shall it go to her who is worthiest to fill it? That can scarcely be, for, at the moment when in search of such a woman our blind desire is eagerly exploring the environment in which she dwells — like some creature of the ocean deeps seeking its prey and spreading its tentacles through the darkened waters — it is unlikely that either the best or the most beautiful will be within our reach. We do not choose the object of our love 'after much deliberation' and because of any qualities or excellencies she may possess, but haphazardly, obeying the dictates of our impressions which, as we shall see, have often no relation to her real value, and primarily because the woman whom we choose merely happens to be available at the moment.

It is not, however, chance alone that determines the choice. 'There is', says Proust, 'a resemblance which changes as we change, between the women whom we love successively, a resemblance determined by our own fixed temperament, because it is our temperament that chooses, eliminating all who could be neither opposed nor complementary to ourselves. We pick out, that is, only those who are capable of satisfying our senses and agonizing our hearts . . .' Such women are the products of our own leanings, the image, the reversed projection, the 'negative' of our sensibilities. *Opposed and Complementary* . . . Schopenhauer had already said much the same thing, but he was speaking only of physical characteristics. Proust is concerned mainly with mental and emotional traits. 'The marriage of contrasting elements is the law of life, the principle of fecundation, and the cause of much unhappiness. As a rule we hate what is like ourselves, and our own faults, seen from without, exasperate us . . .' Quite often a man of culture will form an attachment for an uneducated woman because her simplicity attracts him: a sensitive man for a somewhat hard woman, because the sight of tears in another's eyes is painful to him; a jealous man for a coquette, because she can 'satisfy his senses and agonize his heart'. The Narrator could, and probably should, have loved Andrée rather than Albertine. 'But I could not genuinely love Andrée. She was too intellectual, too nervy, too ailing — in fact, too much like myself. If Albertine now seemed to me empty, Andrée was brimming over with something that I knew only too well.'

We seek the being who can bring to us 'that prolongation, that possible multiplication of ourselves which constitutes happiness'. If we believe that a woman leads a life unknown to us and to which her love will give us right of entry, that, of all the many things which love demands before it can be born, is what it values most, so that by comparison nothing else matters . . . The love which a woman is capable of arousing is all the greater if, in the eyes of one specific male, she is the expression of a double mystery — the mystery of a world, of a social group, to which she belongs, but which, for him, has all the charm of novelty, and the mystery of her unknown and secret thoughts. Marcel is attracted to the girls of the 'little band' because their movements, their appearances, their vanishings, their pleasures and their laughter, are incomprehensible to him. When, later, he is sated of Albertine as a result of keeping her prisoner, he is roused to curiosity by the mystery of young shop-girls whose beauty owes much, in his eyes, to the fact that they live lives of which he knows nothing. 'Are not the eyes at which one gazes filled with images of which one is wholly ignorant, with memories and expectations, with hints of a mysterious disdain? . . . Does not the unknown background of such of them as one meets quite casually in the street give definite value to brows drawn into a frown, to dilated nostrils? . . .' These charming creatures tempt Marcel, now that he is older, as Albertine tempted him in earlier years, and for the same reasons. They have become the cast from which love, the great producer, is to choose the new star.

And so, whenever we are in love with a woman, 'what we are really doing is to project on her a state of *ourselves*. What matters, therefore, is not the worth of the woman but the profundity of the state . . .' That is why the love-affairs of others are so difficult for us to understand. The man in love constructs the beloved object from a number of extremely small data. He does so, says Proust, with even greater success when the actual material on which he works is lacking in density. A neutral type of woman, a woman who says little and is scarcely more than a pleasing envelope of flesh, such as was Juliette Récamier, can strongly attract even men as exigent as Chateaubriand and Benjamin Constant. Where little is given, much is left to the imagination. A mutilated statue, without head or arms, becomes beautiful in our eyes because the imagination is a great artist and, from such fragments, models the perfect figure. Similarly, a silent woman can, without difficulty, give her lover the illusion of intelligence because he sees in her the reflection of his own brilliance. But how can another man, listening to her in cold blood, refrain from being critical at her expense, from viewing with amazement what he cannot but consider her lover's aberration? Those who see in others only what is actually present, are incapable of understanding the selective activities of love, for they are determined by something *that is not there at all* in the object selected, but only in the mind of the selector. Thus (according to Proust) the first phase of love is the pure product of our own imagination which, set in motion by desire and anguish, adorns with every possible charm some completely unknown woman, and prevails on us to give her the part of the beloved. For somebody has got to play it if the comedy of love is to get itself produced at all, and that it should be produced is the heartfelt desire of every human being.

THE PANGS OF LOVE

What is the second phase? It would seem, *a priori*, that for two
people to live together who have been united as the result of a
double misunderstanding (each seeing in the other things that
are not there at all) must end in a rude awakening and be productive of frustration. We become engaged to a woman whom
our imagination has substituted for the woman of flesh and blood,
but it is the woman of flesh and blood that we marry, or with
whom we form an attachment outside marriage. It looks as though
disappointment must be inevitable, and so, says Proust, it is. 'In
love we cannot but choose badly.' He points out ruthlessly and,
as he would have said himself, not without a degree of pleasurable
malice, that the realities of love are quite different from what we
had supposed they would be. The victory won, we find ourselves
in the presence of somebody we scarcely know at all: 'What did I
know of Albertine? a few glimpses of her face against the sea . . .
We fall in love with a smile, a glance, a shoulder. Nothing more
is necessary, and then, through long hours of hope or misery we
build up an individuality, we create a character . . .' Our feelings
may have become very strong, because we have fed them on
hypotheses and sufferings: but the foundations on which they are
built are too fragile to carry so heavy an edifice. Besides, the
woman (or the man) whom we love is, like all human beings,
unknowable, so that even if we did know her (or him) better, our
knowledge would amount actually to nothing at all. After a
lifetime spent together, what do we really know of our companion
or companions? A few phrases, a few gestures, a few habits. But
the secret thoughts that constitute their essence remain by definition inaccessible, while the thoughts that they express are distorted by language, by the desire to please, by the inability which
afflicts almost all human beings to express themselves. 'One is
always disappointed', says Proust, 'to find how little of a person's
real self gets into his letters.' Letters may be brilliant, tender,
moving. It is rarely that they express the whole nature of the
writer. The actress (or the actor) plays a part: the woman (or the
man) escapes us.

Our disappointment extends itself to physical attributes. The lover sees in imagination a creature of 'ivory and coral', a discarnate beauty like something in a bad novel, a bad film. But the actual beloved is a being of flesh and, as such, is subject to the vicissitudes and ailments of the flesh. Marcel, who had so eagerly awaited the moment when he would kiss Albertine, believes, when that moment comes and the happiness is at last within his reach, that he is about to know the flavour of the mysterious rose which has figured for him as the young girl's face. 'But, alas! — our noses and our eyes are as badly placed, in this matter of kissing, as our lips are formed. Suddenly my eyes could see her no longer; my nose, crushed against her cheek, ceased to be conscious of any odour, and, far though I was from savouring, as never before, the scent of the rose so long desired, I realized on the strength of all this detestable evidence that, at last, I was actually going through the motions of kissing Albertine. . . .'

If, in the course of a life lived in common, the veil of mystery is raised, it almost always reveals a landscape whether of society or of the heart which, contrary to our expectations, adds nothing to our experience. We embark upon a voyage of love in the hope of discovering unknown lands but, like the traveller who crosses seas and continents in pursuit of some African or Polynesian world, and finds that the scenes they have to offer are just like those that he has known before, we realize in the end that the 'little band' which, so long as it remained unknown, was rich in possibilities of wonder, turns out as soon as it has become familiar to be ordinary and even exasperating. The idea of the Verdurins' 'salon', simply because it provides the environment in which Odette moves, attracts the love-lorn Swann: but no sooner is he Odette's husband and master than he is plunged in misery at the thought that he has married a woman 'whom he does not like, and who is not at all his type' — a woman, in short, who brings him nothing.

It would seem, therefore, that the power of the feelings engendered by desire and anguish is not great enough to stand up against the fact of possession, and of the revelation that what we have prized so highly encloses utter emptiness. But at this point another Proustian law comes into play: *'Love can survive possession, can even grow, so long as it still contains an element of doubt.'* It is a terrible law, implying, as it does, that the most ardent passions are those inspired by beings who maintain about themselves a zone of mystery, whether consciously (the classic type of the coquette), or unconsciously (in which case we are confronted by the immoral triumph of lies and the passion for myth-making). 'Love is less frequently aroused by the personal attractions of another than by some such phrase as — "*I'm afraid I'm not free this evening.*" Faced by a long succession of hopes unsatisfied, the imagination, stimulated by the pin-pricks of anguish, works at such lightning speed, builds up with such mad rapidity all the details of a love-affair that has got barely beyond its initial stages, and, for months, has been nothing but a fond possibility for the future, that the intelligence, lagging behind the heart, is at times, astounded . . .' Proust discusses at length those whom he calls the 'fugitives', persons whose behaviour, whose attitude of indifference, whose still undetermined emotions, have the power to keep us in a constant condition of anxiety. Security spells the death of love. 'She has promised us a letter, we are calm, we are no longer in love. The letter has not come; no messenger appears with it; what can have happened? anxiety is born afresh, and love. It is such people more than any others who inspire love in us, for our destruction . . . Uncertainty adds to them a quality which surpasses even beauty; which is one of the reasons why we see men who are indifferent to the most beautiful women fall passionately in love with others who appear to us ugly. To these people, these fugitives, their own nature and our anxiety fasten wings. And even when they are in our company the look in their eyes seems to warn us that they are about to take flight. The proof of this beauty, surpassing beauty itself, which the addition of wings gives, is that very often the same person is, in our eyes, alternately wingless and winged. Afraid of losing her, we forget all the others. Sure of keeping her, we compare her with all those others whom at once we prefer to her. And as these emotions and these certainties may vary from week to week, a man may one week find himself sacrificing all that gives him pleasure, and the next week being himself sacrificed, and so for weeks and months on end. . . .'[1]

[1] *The Captive*, translated by C. K. Scott Moncrieff (Chatto & Windus, 1929).

Of this nature was the second phase of Swann's love for Odette. It was not difficult for him to be cured of his earlier passion, because he knew that Odette was devoted to him. But finding one day when he turns up at the Verdurins that Odette has left, he feels the old anguish of the heart return. 'He shook with the sense that he was being deprived of a pleasure whose intensity he began then for the first time to estimate, having always hitherto had that certainty of finding it whenever he would, which (as in the case of all our pleasures) reduced, if it did not altogether blind him to, its dimensions . . .'[1] He sets off immediately in pursuit of her, seeking her in every restaurant on the Boulevard, eagerly interrogating with his eyes the faces of all the mysterious strangers who pass him in the darkness, 'as though among the phantoms of the dead, in the realms of darkness, he had been searching for a lost Eurydice'.[2] The very fact of this pursuit gives to his love a new lease of life.

This particular form of anguish is as a rule, but not inevitably, linked with jealousy, with a brooding upon the loved one's lies. It can, so subjective an emotion is love, be altogether without relation to the particular woman in question. 'Sometimes, during those night-hours of waiting, our anguish may be due to our having taken some medicine. The sufferer makes a wrong diagnosis, and believes that his nervousness is due to the woman's failure to turn up. Love, on such occasions, is, like certain nervous ailments, the product of the inaccurate analysis of a painful illness . . . But that is an extreme case. More often love is but the by-product of illusion, and consists solely in the need we feel to have our sufferings allayed by the being who has caused them. . . .'

What Proust, in fact, maintains is that love is incapable of bringing happiness. The feeling of attachment which binds us to a woman or a man is an evil spell that has been laid upon us. 'Working always in the same manner, it tightens, with an alternating movement, the mechanism which makes it impossible for us either to give up loving or to be loved.' If such an attachment is to last, our anguish must be bound up with the idea

---

[1] *Swann's Way*, II, translated by C. K. Scott Moncrieff (Chatto & Windus, 1922).
[2] Ibid.

of another person; in other words, it must turn into jealousy. That is why Proust says that, in matters of love, our happy rival, in other words, our enemy, is really our benefactor, 'since if he were not there to act as a catalysing agent, desire and pleasure would never be transformed into love'. The pleasures of love are necessarily, inevitably, bound up with much terrible suffering.

III

INCURABLE JEALOUSY

The question arises, are these sufferings curable, and in what way does the sickness which we know as Proust's view of love develop? Faced by that problem, we must be careful to distinguish between several variants of the malady.

First variant. The lover finds himself, one morning, cured of doubt and completely reassured. The woman he loved, whom he did his best to win, has, at long last, become his, and he feels convinced that he will not lose her again, either because circumstances (perhaps their life together is to be set in some remote and isolated spot) makes jealousy absurd, or because, having already braved Society for his sake, she is not disposed to take further risks; or because her temperament, her faith, or her philosophy, makes of her a willing prisoner. 'Love in such a case', says Proust, 'cannot last.'

'In so far as relations with women whom we abduct are less permanent than others, the reason is that the fear of not succeeding in procuring them, or the dread of seeing them escape, is the whole of our love for them, and that once they have been carried off from their husbands, torn from their footlights, cured of the temptation to leave us, dissociated in short from our emotion whatever it may be, they are only themselves, that is to say almost nothing, and, so long desired, are soon forsaken by the very man who was so afraid of their forsaking him . . .'[1] Marie d'Agoult, who gave up everything for Liszt's sake, was soon abandoned by him.

Anna Karenina is a painful and classic example of this sort of

[1] *The Captive*, translated by C. K. Scott Moncrieff (Chatto & Windus, 1929).

situation. Vronsky passionately pursues Anna, but she cannot hold him, 'because, when love is born of desire, it can be maintained in the years to come only so long as the man remains in a painful state of anxiety . . . It may be that the beloved object must be capable of causing acute suffering so that, in the intervals, when the pain abates, she may be able to provide that calmness of mind which is more accurately to be described as a modification of suffering rather than as happiness. . . .'

Second variant. The woman may be cured of doubt, may win a complete victory, and get everything while giving nothing. This happens should the lover let her see too clearly his need of her presence.

> The relations one has with a woman one loves can remain platonic for other reasons than the chastity of the woman or the unsensual nature of the love she inspires. The reason may be that the lover is too impatient and by the very excess of his love is unable to await the moment when he will obtain his desires by sufficient pretence of indifference. Continually he returns to the charge, never ceases writing to her whom he loves, is always trying to see her. She refuses herself, he becomes desperate. From that time she knows that, if she grants him her company, this benefit will seem so considerable to one who believed he was going to be deprived of it, that she need grant nothing more and that she can take advantage of the moment when he can no longer bear being unable to see her and when, at all costs, he must put an end to the struggle by accepting a truce which will impose upon him a platonic relationship as its primary condition . . . Women divine all this, and know they can afford the luxury of never yielding to those who, from the first, have betrayed their inextinguishable desire. A woman is enchanted if, without giving anything, she can receive more than she generally gets when she does give herself. On that account highly-strung men believe in the chastity of their idol. And the halo with which they surround her is also a product, but, as we see, an indirect one, of their excessive love. . . .[1]

[1] *Time Regained*, translated by Stephen Hudson (Chatto & Windus, 1931).

Third variant. But the normal progress of the disease is as Proust describes it, first in connection with Swann and Odette; secondly, in connection with the Narrator and Gilberte; thirdly, in connection with the Narrator and Albertine. His clinical observations may be summed up as follows. Until the very end, jealousy remains inseparable from love, because the lover knows perfectly well that he is not himself faithful (at least in intention) and consequently that he is almost bound to find a similar instability in his partner, and also because the more he gets the more he wants. We begin by longing to catch the attention, even if it be only the fugitive attention, of some woman whom we find attractive. Having obtained this, we are hungry for a smile, for tender words, for a kiss. These preliminary stages of love once achieved, we yearn for complete possession and, no sooner have we got it, than we demand that it shall be exclusive. Nothing can appease the jealous man, because jealousy — which is exclusively an intellectual ailment — is born of our ignorance of the thoughts and actions of the person beloved. That is why, contrary to all logic, there are so many shameful shifts in love, so many cases of men putting up with deception provided the beloved is frank about it. Others there are who find it impossible to set their minds at rest unless they can maintain the woman they love in a condition of quite literal slavery. The Narrator in the long run makes Albertine a prisoner, but even when he has done so he still cannot reduce the margin of uncertainty to zero. There are love intrigues even within the four walls of a harem, and no amount of iron bars can make a man the master of another person's thoughts. 'One of the effects of jealousy is to make us realize that external facts and the movements of the human mind are, both of them, mysteries which give rise to a thousand suppositions.' Even imprisonment cannot bring us complete assurance. The Narrator is as jealous of Albertine's past as he is of her present and her future. To say 'her past' is of no avail, because jealousy knows neither past nor future. What it imagines is always its present.

From time to time suspicion vanishes:

The kindness that our mistress is showing us soothes us, but then a word that we had forgotten comes back to our mind;

221

someone has told us that she was ardent in moments of pleasure, whereas we have always found her calm; we try to
picture to ourselves what can have been these frenzies with
other people, we feel how very little we are to her, we observe
an air of boredom, longing, melancholy, while we are talking, we observe like a black sky the unpretentious clothes
which she puts on when she is with us, keeping for other
people the garments with which she used to flatter us at first.
If, on the contrary, she is affectionate, what joy for a moment
. . . Then the feeling that we are bored with each other
returns . . . Such are the revolving searchlights of jealousy. . . .[1]

Nothing is more profoundly symbolic than the wonderful
passage in which the Narrator looks at his mistress while she is
asleep. The unconsciousness of the being who brings him nothing
but anguish is productive of a kind of peace, and he finds it possible
to imagine happiness in love.

In solitude I could think of her, but she was absent, I did not
possess her. When she was present I was too far absent from
myself to be able to think. When she was asleep I no longer
needed to talk to her, I knew that she was no longer looking at
me, I had no longer any need to live upon my own outer surface. By shutting her eyes, by losing consciousness, Albertine
had stripped off, one after another, the different human characters with which she had deceived me ever since the day when I
had first made her acquaintance. She was animated now only
by the unconscious life of vegetation, or trees, a life more
different from my own, more alien, and yet one that belonged
more to me. Her personality did not escape at every moment,
as when we were talking, by the channels of her unacknow-
ledged thoughts and of her gaze. She had called back into
herself everything of her that lay outside, had taken refuge,
enclosed, reabsorbed into her body. In keeping her before
my eyes, in my hands, I had that impression of possessing her
altogether, which I never had when she was awake. Her life
was submitted to me, exhaled towards me her gentle breath.

[1] *The Captive*, I, translated by C. K. Scott Moncrieff (Chatto & Windus, 1929).

I listened to this murmuring, mysterious emanation, soft as a breeze from the sea, fairylike as that moonlight which was her sleep. So long as it lasted, I was free to think about her and at the same time to look at her, and, when her sleep grew deeper, to touch, to kiss her. What I felt then was love in the presence of something as pure, as immaterial in its feelings, as mysterious, as if I had been in the presence of those inanimate creatures which are the beauties of nature. . . .[1]

But, alas, the women whom we love cannot always be asleep, and, for a long time, the evil seems to be without a remedy. 'What I here call love,' says Proust, 'is reciprocal torture.' Even death cannot cure the jealous lover. He continues to brood upon the past, tries to reconstruct a past which, more and more, recedes into the darkness of the tomb. That is the theme of the whole first half of *Albertine disparue*.

I V

THE INTERMISSIONS OF THE HEART

Thus it is that not absence, not even death, can cure the lover. Fortunately, however, memory varies in strength, and forgetfulness, after a long absence, brings us that state of mental emptiness which is so necessary to the human spirit since only in it can the spirit find a renewal of its energies. 'Forgetfulness is a powerful means of enabling us to adapt ourselves to reality, because, little by little, it destroys in us that survival of the past which is forever at odds with it. . . .'

Marcel might have guessed that a day would come when he would cease to love Albertine. Because she whom he loved was not a real person at all, but an interior image, a fragment of his own thought, love might, for several months or, in the most recalcitrant of cases, for several years, survive her presence. But since it had nothing to support it outside his own consciousness, sooner or later, like every mental state, it must realize that it no longer had any useful part to play, that it had been replaced.

[1] *The Captive*, I, translated by C. K. Scott Moncrieff (Chatto & Windus, 1929).

When that moment came, what had bound him to Albertine's memory would exist no longer. The only inconsolable lovers are those who do not wish to be consoled, who turn their pain into a cult, perhaps into a means of escape. At the moment of a loved one's death, her room, her clothes, are precious fetishes to which we desperately cling. But inevitably a day will come when, with scarcely a thought, we shall give her room to another. 'For, with the lapses of memory are linked the intermissions of the heart.' Those whom we have loved die twice: first, in the death of the body which concerns only them, and leaves their memory still within our heart: a second time, when the tide of forgetfulness sweeps up and over memory itself.

It is not that we have become incapable of love, but that our desire, which has ever in its very nature been impersonal, concentrates upon new objects. Them, too, one after the other, we see as 'absolute ends, so that outside of them no happiness seems henceforth possible'.[1] Several times already the Narrator had believed that one only being filled his world — his grandmother, his mother, Gilberte Swann, the Duchesse de Guermantes, Albertine Simonet. Each time he had followed the same road of anguish, from enchantment to jealousy. But time had always done its work and ultimately forgetfulness had come. Because those whom we love are unreal persons, created or at least adorned, by the poetic invention of the lover, it is easy to strip them of the mental projection of glory, of the bright, theatrical colours in which they have been dressed. Time and indifference suddenly reveal them to us as they really were in their true nature. Marcel at last sees Gilberte's egotism, the Duchesse de Guermantes's hardness, Albertine's vulgarity. These women no longer fill the part adequately. It becomes once more 'vacant', available for some younger, newer actress, or for one, quite simply, who shall be more admirably favoured by circumstance. When the moment comes she will not fail to appear.

The cure proceeds gradually. At first, at the moment when the loved one vanishes from our life, we feel only in part the intensity of our loss. We apprehend it through the intelligence, but the intelligence functions only within limits. We do not *believe* in

[1] NoËL MARTIN-DESLIAS, op. cit.

our loss. It is only later that sensitive persons become actively aware of its full horror. Others never feel it at all. They are caught up again in the external world which denies and excludes the object of their memory. 'That is why so very few people are capable of a great grief.' But those for whom the life of the spirit counts for more than the external world live with their memories. Those memories, even when time seems to have erased them, live on sometimes in dreams, sometimes because a present image has the power to evoke the past. When that happens, those who think they have forgotten are sometimes invaded by the full force of their former passions. Memory rises to the surface ringed about by 'harmonics' and accompanied by 'the loveliness and magic of things lost'.[1] It is in this way that Marcel sees again in dreams the grandmother whom he has so greatly loved, and so too it is that, in the glare of a painful and poignant hallucination, we sometimes think we see the dear ghost of forgotten loves.

And so it is that men move on from desire to desire, from anguish to anguish, from ecstasy to ecstasy, from disappointment to disappointment, from regret to regret, from forgetfulness to forgetfulness, until at last the day comes when love becomes sublimated by the effects of age, and fails before the onset of emotions whether aesthetic or not.

V

OF INVERSION

Proust was one of the first among the great novelists who have dared to give to inversion the place that it occupies in modern societies, a place that the writers of the ancient world openly recognized. Before his time Balzac alone had set himself to study it seriously in the *Vautrin* cycle and in *La Fille aux yeux d'or*, where he had sketched one aspect of Gomorrah.

Proust, a passionate admirer of Balzac, had examined these precedents with his customary intelligence. In his unpublished *Notebooks* there occurs the following remarkable passage:

[1] NoËL MARTIN-DESLIAS.

A propos of what I wrote a page back, I should like to make the following comment on my use of the word 'invert'. Balzac, with a daring which I only wish I could imitate, employs the very term I need. 'Oh, I get you,' said Fil-de-Soie: 'he's up to something, wants to have another look at his *aunt*, what they're going to string up.' That I may give a vague idea of the kind of person whom the prisoners, the warders and the turn-keys call an *aunt*, I need only quote the superb remark made by the Governor of one of the large Penitentiaries to the late Lord Durham who made a point of visiting all the prisons of Paris during his stay in that city. Pointing towards one particular section of the building, he said, with a gesture of disgust, 'I won't take your Lordship there, it's where the *aunts* are kept.' 'Hao', said Lord Durham, 'and who may they be?' 'I may best describe them, my Lord, by saying that they are the third sex . . .' (Balzac: *Splendeurs et Misères des courtisanes*).

This word would be particularly appropriate to the purpose of my book in which the characters to whom it is applicable, being almost all old and worldly, appear for the most part, in social gatherings where they strut and chatter, magnificently dressed and widely ridiculed. The *aunts*! The mere word conveys to us a vision of their solemnity and their get-up. The mere word wears skirts and brings to the eye a picture of the *aunts* pluming themselves in that fashionable setting, and twittering like birds in all the strangeness of a different species. . . .[1]

Balzac never fully exploited the prodigiously romantic vein to be found in a form of love which, in so surprising a manner, can knit together men who, otherwise, in matters of social class, political belief and general temperament, may be widely separated from one another. It was Proust's view that he ought to push his researches in this field a great deal further, that he ought to describe the secret complexities of an International Free-Masonry which is more homogeneous than that of the Grand Orient:

[1] Unpublished fragment in the possession of Madame Mante-Proust.

. . . for it rests on an identity of tastes, needs, habits, dangers, training, knowledge, traffic and vocabulary, and its members, even those who are anxious not to meet one another, at once recognize the signs, whether natural or assumed, whether voluntary or involuntary, which reveal one of his kind to the beggar who shuts the carriage door of a great Lord, to the father who meets his daughter's betrothed for the first time, to the man who wishes to be cured, to make confession or to take legal advice, when he comes into the presence of doctor, priest or lawyer. All such persons, having of necessity to conceal their secret, but sharing part of the secret of others, a secret unsuspected by the rest of the world, are able to find truth in the most unlikely stories of adventure, since, in their strange, anachronistic world of romantic happenings, an ambassador may be a close friend of a convict, and a prince, with that freedom of behaviour which is the fruit of an aristocratic training beyond the reach of the middle-class citizen, may leave a duchess's party to hobnob with a hooligan. The whole business, condemned though it may be by the generality of mankind, is not without its importance. It is suspected where it does not exist, is insolently paraded and goes unpunished where it is not guessed, and draws its adherents from every walk of life, from the streets, the army, the church, the prison and the throne, its devotees living (at least a great number of them) in fond and dangerous intimacy with men of a different 'race', whetting their curiosity in the contact, taking pleasure in discussing with them their particular vice, as though they were not themselves addicted to it. This form of amusement is made easy for them by the blindness or the falsity of others, so that they can for years indulge it until the day comes when the scandal breaks which may plunge them into disaster, though before that day comes they have to conceal their way of life, to turn their eyes from what they would most like to look at and to look at what they would most like to ignore; to change the gender of many of the adjectives in their vocabulary, to submit to a social discipline which is mild indeed compared to the interior discipline which their vice, or what is improperly so called, imposes on them, not so much in their dealings with others as in the secrecy of their own hearts, so that they may convince themselves that it is not a vice at all. . . .[1]

The novelist who treats a subject which is generally held to be 'forbidden', the records of which are relegated to the locked cases of our public libraries, runs no little risk, and may even find himself in considerable danger. The fact that his work may have a high seriousness, his language be endowed with beauty, will not protect him except in the eyes of such readers as are worthy of him. Thousands of others, among them his fellow writers and the critics, will pass judgment and will leave him in the lurch merely on the strength of a book-title or the statement of a theme. Marcel Proust was perfectly well aware of all this. He fully expected to lose most of his friends as soon as it became apparent what Charlus really was. But he was strong in his belief that integrity is the artist's prime virtue. He had observed the very large part played in social life by the aberrations of love, and he felt an irresistible compulsion to express himself with sincerity on the subject. He was far, very far, from wishing to achieve a *succès de scandale*. The reader who turns to his work in the hope of finding scabrous descriptions or pornographic incidents will be disappointed. Proust's novel, in spite of the facts with which it deals, is infinitely more chaste than, for example, Rousseau's *Confessions* which obviously delights in describing the morbid forms of sensuality. Among the denizens of his Sodom is no Casanova, nor, in his Gomorrah, is there anything to remind us of the equivocal charm of *Les Chansons de Bilitis*. His book is neither more shocking nor more sensual than the volumes by Fabre or Jean Rostand which detail the love-habits of certain animals. Not that it is ever his intention to reduce life to the levels of bestiality. Far from it. We have seen that he indicates to others, and himself takes, the road to deliverance. But when he sets himself to observe the manifestations of desire, he does so with the eye of a naturalist. The man-woman preys upon a man as 'the convolvulus embraces with its tendrils a mattock or a rake'. Monsieur de Charlus makes straight for Jupien, the tailor,

[1] Unpublished fragment in the possession of Madame Mante-Proust.

'as the bumble-bee makes for the orchid which it alone can fecundate'. Observed by an objective inquirer, the invert is seen as someone whose course has been determined since childhood. There are in him, though he may not know it, elements which act as limitations on his temperament.

> When one is young one is no more aware that one is homo-sexual than one is aware that one is a poet, a snob, or a bad lot. The snob is not a man who loves snobs, but merely a man who cannot set eyes on a duchess without finding her charming. A homosexual is not a man who loves homosexuals, but a man who, seeing a soldier, immediately wants to have him for a friend. Every man, in his beginnings, is centrifugal, eager to escape from himself, turning his gaze outwards, contemplating his dreams, and believing that he receives his stimulus from outside himself . . . His eyes are fixed on some object far removed from himself, on the witty duchess, on the smart little soldier, and he prefers to believe that his artistic propensities are governed by their charms rather than by some absurd defect in his own nervous make-up, some twist in his own temperament. Only when the thought that eddies about his *self* has come full circle, only when his intelligence has come into the open so that he can see himself from the outside as he sees other people, do the words I am a snob, I am a homosexual take form in his mind, even if they do not always find a way to his lips, — for in the interval he has acquired sufficient hypocrisy to learn to speak a language which is more successful in deceiving the world about his true tastes than were the confidences which, at an earlier stage, when he did not know what they meant, he was led so imprudently to make. . . .

Some inverts, when first they begin to realize that they are different from the majority of their fellow men:

> . . . turn with feelings of contempt and disgust from the company of ordinary men whose wits they consider to have been dulled as a result of their traffic with women, interpret the great books of the past in the light of their fixed idea,

and, if they happen, in Montaigne, in Gérard de Nerval or
in Stendhal, on some phrase that seems to betoken a more
than normally ardent friendship, feel convinced that what
they find to love in these authors is a shared taste, though
the authors themselves had probably not been conscious of
it, and had needed someone like their latest reader to open
their eyes to the truth. And, should these men chance to
have an intelligent young friend, they make no effort to
protect him from exposure to the contagion of their vice, but
strive to convert him to a doctrine framed exclusively for the
unconventionally minded, and urge them to cultivate a love
for members of their own sex, as others might urge the claims
of anarchism, zionism, anti-patriotism or the duty of
desertion. . . .[1]

Another man, on the other hand, may adopt towards himself
and his instincts the general attitude of the 'normally minded'.
He feels overwhelmed by remorse, and hides the flames of his
desire in solitude.

. . . he lives on alone in his tower, like Grisélidis: his only
pleasure to make occasional trips to the local railway-station
in order to get into conversation with the new station-master,
or to take refuge in the kitchen where, having first, rather
nervously, sent the cook out on an errand, he waits in the
hope of being on the spot when the lad from the post-office
brings a telegram, or of telling the butcher-boy in person that
yesterday's joint was tough. The station-master gets moved
and is, the poor outcast discovers, to be sent to some remote
corner of France. No longer will he be able to ask him
the time of a train or the price of a first-class return-ticket.
Were it not that he fears to make a fool of himself, or dreads
to be thought a nuisance, he would gladly go and settle down
in the place where the man is now employed — instead of
which, he goes home thinking how badly matters in this
world are arranged, and how nice it would be if young men

[1] These passages are taken from Marcel Proust's unpublished *Notebooks* in the
possession of Madame Mante-Proust.

could become engaged to station-masters, if that was how they happened to feel. He lives on in a state of gloomy loneliness, sometimes, of an evening, when excessive desire has bred in him a sort of insane audacity, seeking relief in helping a drunkard to find his way home, or in brushing down the smock of a blind man.

Who has not seen beside the Ocean one or other of those miserable and lovely creatures, alone upon the shore, who might have brought a woman happiness, but instead, wonderful Andromedas chained to the rock of their peculiar vice, scan the horizon day after day, lest perchance some Argonaut, still sailing the blue waters, may come to snatch them from the land. Unguided and uncounselled they pursue their search, swallowing the insults of those about them, already, at sixteen, with red upon their lips and blackened eyes, staying all night upon some villa balcony, breathing the fragrance of a blossoming branch, and listening to the waves breaking one after another at their feet. Others, too, there are whom we have all of us encountered at least once in our lives, who haunt the waiting-rooms of stations, delicate creatures with sickly faces and strange, flamboyant clothes, scanning the crowd with eyes that seem indifferent though in reality they are searching the passing faces in the hope that now, at long last, they may light upon the addict, so hard to find, of that curious pleasure for which it is so hard to discover a market, the addict who will see in the expression of their glance, however well concealed from others it may be, the assumed look of lazy disdain, the sign sufficiently obvious which will set him in motion, darting from the booking-office to the waiting-room. But no, there are none amid the crowd who speak the same language, a language venerable and almost sacred by reason of its very strangeness, its antiquity and its grotesque oddity — none, save perhaps one shabby loiterer who will *pretend* to be a fellow-linguist in the hope of earning enough money for a night's lodging . . . just as another victim of poverty might pretend an interest in some other language, scarcely more current, so that thus he might enjoy an hour's warmth in a College Lecture-Room where the Professor on the dais has no other listener than the care-taker and his own eventual successor. In vain does the frail youth, his sickliness disguised by painted cheeks, search sadly in the crowd for someone who may share his taste, like certain flowers whose organ of love is so badly placed that they run the risk of fading on their stalks before ever they can achieve fecundation. Shared love, for them is so beset with special difficulties, in addition to those which hamper all mankind, that one may fairly describe the satisfying encounter, rare in the case of most human beings, as being for them almost an impossibility. But they have their consolation — because *should* such a meeting happily be brought about, or at least, should their temperament beguile them into the belief that it *has* been brought about by dressing up — like any Ma-dame to cater for the tastes of her customers — some wretched mercenary creature to *look* like a genuine soldier-boy, like the private who would have gone straight back to barracks, the working-lad who would have returned to the factory, had it not been for the dazzling chance of meeting a sister-spirit — their happiness is far greater than that of any normal lover could ever be. Knowing so well the hazards that beset their search for a partner, they feel that their form of love is not, like that of heterosexuals, born of the moment, is not a mere instant's fancy, but must be far more deeply rooted in the life of him who thus responds, in his temperament, maybe in his heredity: that the answer to their call has come from somewhere far beyond the passing minute, that the 'beloved' thus miraculously given has been his affianced love from days before his birth, has found his way to this moment of meeting from the depths of limbo, from those stars where all our souls inhabit before they are incarnate. Such love, they will be more than ever tempted to believe, is the only true love. For among the special, pre-established harmonies which it implies, there can be no room for mere caprice, but only for the working of destiny. . . .[1]

---

[1] Extracts from Marcel Proust's unpublished *Notebooks* in the possession of Madame Mante-Proust.

And just as inversion takes, in youth, two forms, the one aggressive, the other shamefaced, so, too, we can distinguish among men of mature age two secondary categories: the invert who has been almost cured and appears to have become normalized, and the ageing cynic who is content to buy what no young man will give him now 'for love'.

. . . In some, very rare, cases the disease is not congenital, and, being superficial only, can be cured. Sometimes its appearance may be due to the simple fact that a man has found the act of love difficult of performance with a woman, owing to some purely anatomical malformation. Some asthmatics can be cured by removing adhesions in the nose. Or, again, it may have been produced by a feeling of disgust for women, a repulsion caused by their smell or by the texture of their skin, and this repulsion may be dissipated, just as there are children who feel sick when they see oysters or cheese, but come, eventually, to have a great liking for both. But those who are born with a taste for men retain it, as a rule, to the end of their lives. To outward showing they may change, their lives become obscured in the welter of their daily habits. But nothing is ever lost; a concealed jewel always gets found. When a sick man's urine diminishes in quantity, he sweats the more: in some way or other the body has to excrete. A homosexual may, to all appearances, be cured. Contrary to the physical laws of the moral realm, the quantity of sensual vigour which *seems* to have been drained away, is merely transferred elsewhere. A day comes when such or such an invert happens to lose, say, his young nephew, and then, his refusal to be consoled makes it clear that his passionate desires had become sublimated into this quite other, and probably chaste, affection. But they are still *there*, whole and complete, as, in a balance-sheet, a sum of money may be carried over from one column to another. . . .

. . . In this case, however, a reservation must be made, since the phenomenon of *attention* is involved, love having acted as a powerful distraction, with the result that certain habits

have become less˙necessary, habits the need of which has
been in part imaginary, in part the result of mental laziness.
Similarly, strong political ambition, a religious vocation, the
need to complete some work of the imagination, will, over
considerable periods — often whole years — divert the mind
from those voluptuous images which formerly pricked the
homosexual to seek his quota of daily pleasure. . . .[1]

Such, in middle life, are the homosexuals who have been, or
appear to have been, cured. The others find yawning before them
that Hell into which Proust conducts the Baron de Charlus —
Jupien's 'establishment'. Charlus's ideal was to be loved by an
extremely virile man. But just because the object of his longing
was virile, reciprocal love was impossible, with the result that the
wretched Baron was reduced to the necessity of buying an illusion
of what reality could never give him. The youths who would
willingly prostitute themselves to a man like Charlus were
necessarily of a dangerous type, and that was why the Baron, and
later Saint-Loup, had that ever-watchful eye, that look of being
always on the alert lest irremediable scandal burst suddenly into
their lives, those dry, brittle movements which, though they had
the outward form of elegance were, in fact, nothing but the first
gestures of escape. Nor was their anxiety lessened by the fact that
inverts always recognize one another like the Gods in Homer, like
two compatriots meeting in a foreign land — 'as, in some small
provincial town a bond may grow up between the local lawyer and
the schoolmaster by reason of their shared liking for chamber-
music or medieval ivories' — though there is no real friendship to
unite them despite their casual familiarity.

Proust observed and analysed many other characteristics of the
inverted — their tendency to marry rather masculine women who,
because they love their husbands and divine their preferences, deliberately stress their own mannish traits (as in the case of Madame
Vaugoubert) — their charming qualities of taste and sensibility
which they derive from the feminine part of their natures — the
compulsion under which they feel themselves to win those to
whom they feel attracted by appealing to the woman in them:

[1] Extracts from Marcel Proust's unpublished *Notebooks* in the possession of
Madame Mante-Proust.

. . . ne would have been greatly astonished to note the furtive exchanges which passed between Monsieur de Charlus and several of the important male guests — for instance, two dukes, an eminent general, a great writer, a famous doctor, a distinguished lawyer. They took the form of scraps of dialogue on the following lines: 'Bye the bye, did you notice the footman, the young one, I mean, who got up on the box?' 'What do you know of that young chap we saw at cousin Guermantes?' — 'Nothing at all, actually.' 'There was a fair-haired boy, in a short jacket, at the hall-door, looking after the carriages. I thought him extremely attractive. He called up my carriage most charmingly: I should very much have liked to prolong our conversation.' 'I know the one you mean, but I had a feeling that, on the whole, he would not be very responsive. . . .'

He noted, too, the interest shown by the inhabitants of Sodom in those of Gomorrah:

> . . . Baudelaire . . . at first intended to call the volume, not *Les Fleures du Mal*, but *Les Lesbiennes* . . . how did he come to be so interested in lesbians that he actually proposed to use the word as the title of that whole superb work? When Vigny, raging against women, thought to find the secret of their sex in the fact that the female gives suck:
>
> *Il rêvera toujours à la chaleur du sein,*
>
> in the peculiar nature of their physiology: —
> *Enfant malade et douze fois impur*
>
> in their psychology: —
> *Toujours ce compagnon dont le cœur n'est pas sûr*
>
> it is easy to see why, in his frustrated and jealous passion, he could write: —
> *La femme aura Gomorrhe et l'Homme aura Sodome.*
>
> But he does, at least, see the two sexes at odds, facing one another as enemies across a great gulf: —
> *Et se jetant de loin un regard irrité*
> *Les deux sexes mourront chacun de son côté*

But this did not hold true of Baudelaire: —

Car Lesbos entre tous m'a choisi sur la terre
Pour chanter le secret de ses vierges en fleurs
Et je fus dès l'enfance admis au noir mystère

This connexion between Sodom and Gomorrha is what, in the final section of my novel (not in the first part of *Sodome*, which has just appeared) I have shown in the person of a brutish creature, Charles Morel (it is usually to brutish creatures that this part is allotted). But it would seem that Baudelaire cast himself for it, and looked on the rôle as a privilege. It would be intensely interesting to know why he chose to assume it, and how well he acquitted himself. What is comprehensible in a Charles Morel becomes profoundly mysterious in the author of *Les Fleurs du Mal*. . . .[1]

We can see in Gide's *Journal*[2] how Proust explained this mystery and how he asserted that he saw in Baudelaire an impenitent devotee of Uranian love, though the explanation has a much more direct bearing on Proust, with his intense interest in Lesbos, than on Baudelaire. The bitter jealousy inspired in the Narrator by Albertine's relations with other women must be interpreted as a transference of the jealousy felt by the invert towards other men, though he regards the beloved youth's brief *affaires* with women as regrettable episodes which, though they may repel and disgust him, are not emotionally important.

VI

EFFECTS OF INVERSION IN THE NOVEL

We have still to consider the effects of inversion on the artist, and, in particular, on the novelist. It may give him a deeper knowledge of Vautrin or of Charlus, but does it not impede his direct understanding of women? By transforming Albert into

[1] See 'About Baudelaire' in *Marcel Proust: A Selection from His Miscellaneous Writings* translated by Gerard Hopkins (Allan Wingate, 1948).
[2] ANDRE GIDE, *Journal* (Bibliothèque de la Pléiade, Gallimard, Paris, 1939), pp. 693-4.

Albertine, by retaining, as Proust told Gide he had done, only Albert's more charming traits, did he not run the risk of creating an Albertine who would have too little of the woman about her? This objection is only in part valid, for the following reasons:

(*a*) Proust, as we have seen, was on intimate terms with a great number of women. From his youth upwards he had more than once believed himself to be in love with young girls. His female friends had included a Marie Scheikevitch, a Louisa de Mornand, a Geneviève Straus, an Anna de Noailles and many others with whom he had maintained an uninterrupted correspondence. He liked the society of women, and they regarded him as a delightful and eminently desirable friend.

(*b*) What he was seeking to depict was the effect of love upon the temperament of the Narrator, or, more generally, of any man in love. It is, therefore, of very little importance to know the identity of the actual beloved since, according to Proust, the essence of love is that the beloved has no real existence outside the imagination of the lover.

Nevertheless, the transposition does involve several unlikely features:

(1) Albertine's stay in the house of a bachelor, and the fact that her imprisonment is accepted by her relations, are difficult to admit if Albertine is really a girl of middle-class origins. At the time of this supposed episode, that is to say, before the 1914 war, such a stay would have been absolutely inconceivable.

(2) In his presentation of this love affair, Proust shows no concern for the more peculiarly feminine instincts, for the quite different nature of a woman's sensuality, for the need that a woman feels for a close and durable bond. He would have been quite incapable of writing a *Lys dans la vallée* or *Les Mémoires de deux jeunes mariées*. It is, however, true that the very form of his book absolved him from the need to paint from the inside any character other than the Narrator (and Swann who is a projection of the Narrator).

(3) His representation of love is more productive of despair than it would have been had he been dealing with love in its more normal aspects, no matter how pessimistic his approach. Because he was by nature a worrier (here I follow his own diagnosis) he interpreted the unease of his characters in terms of jealousy. Even in Barbusse's *Enfer*, there are outbursts of happiness which are absent from Proust's Hell, a fact which is to be explained by the reasons which he himself gives: the secrecy of all love affairs which are held to be 'against nature', difficulty of choice, venality and the suspicion which all such relationships arouse in a hostile society.

If only to mark the contrast it is well to compare with *Sodome et Gomorrhe* Shakespeare's *Sonnets*, Gide's *Corydon* and certain passages in Wilde which paint the 'dionysiac aspects of Uranism'. But if Proust's picture is incomplete it is at least precise, and it does help to illuminate for the profane reader a phenomenon which is 'little understood and fruitlessly blamed'. Furthermore since it was Proust's object to show that love is essentially a product of the imagination, a study of inversion provided him with the most striking example of his theme possible. It is surprising enough, in cases of heterosexual passion, to find 'Beauty suddenly taking flight from the face of the woman we no longer love, in order to take up its lodging in features which, to others, are of an outstanding ugliness, but still more surprising to find it courted by some great noble under the peaked cap of an omnibus conductor whither it has migrated from the lovely princess whom he has abandoned so that he may pursue it in its fresh incarnation.'

There are those who have held that it would have been more courageous in Proust to have attributed the tastes of Charlus to the Narrator, instead of transforming Albert into Albertine. To this criticism he has himself made answer that, in order to make sure of being read and understood, it was necessary that he should take some account of the prejudices of his public. The eye-specialist says to the patient who consults him: 'You must decide for yourself whether you can see better with this lens or with that': similarly, the novelist, wishing his reader to grasp the important truth that what is normally called real is, actually, wholly unreal, must show him an image of the real which he is capable of accepting as such. The fact that different eyes need different 'glasses' in order to bring the object into focus does not in any way alter the optical principle involved. So, too, the fact that different individuals need different illusions to arouse in them the emotions of desire or jealousy does not, in any way, alter the laws of love.

The theory that love is always a form of frustration and a dark fatality, is not due, in Proust, merely to inversion. Ramon Fernandez has shown that it was widely accepted at that time in France, and appears both in the literature and the popular songs of the period. Many of the music-hall successes then in vogue recall, *mutatis mutandis*, the theme of *Swann*, as in an earlier generation, do those to be found in Murger. Fernandez has unearthed one of Musetta's songs which is curiously apt, and summarizes all Swann's mood of melancholy wisdom:

> *Ce n'est plus qu'en fouillant les cendres*
> *Des beaux jours qui sont révolus*
> *Qu'un souvenir pourra nous rendre*
> *La clef des paradis perdus. . . .*[1]

We have only to note, too, how Boylesve, Bourget and France harped, in their novels, as Racine had once done in his tragedies, on the 'strengthening of passion as a result of mutual misunderstanding', to realize that Proust's pessimism in this matter of love was no isolated phenomenon.

This is not to maintain that such pessimism is justified. Proust's fundamental error in dealing with the pleasures of love lay in his tendency to analyse the emotions concerned, and to reduce them to their component elements. It is as true of pleasure and of sentiment as it is of movement that atomization is bound to end in complete annihilation. Proust is the Zeno of love. Albertine's kiss, like the arrow's swiftness, is reduced to nothingness by the operation of reason. Love, it will be found, can no more succeed in overtaking jealousy than Achilles can succeed in overtaking

---

[1] Only in stirring the ember
Of a happiness that dies
Does the lover sadly remember
His long-lost paradise.

the tortoise. But both Proust and Zeno are in error. Achilles *does* overtake the tortoise, and there are some women who are to be accounted worthy of love. Present love may be as productive of happiness as is love past or love to come — and of even greater happiness.

V I I

THE GREATNESS OF LOVE

Though Proust describes with ruthless lucidity the ravages of love, it would be a mistake to conclude that he is blind to its greatness. He shows us that love is an illusion, but an illusion which can enrich our lives. This he does 'without malice or bitterness, without a trace of systematic pessimism, without denying the intoxicating magic of human feeling, without blinding himself to what the dream may contain, or refusing to admit that it may increase rather than impoverish the faculties of the human spirit' [1] It may be true that, more often than not, love is a form of lying by which we deceive ourselves, but its *intention* is the increase of our spiritual stature. It is 'the obscure desire to persevere in the fulfilment of ourselves that leads us to magnify the object of our passion'. Is it not a matter of common observation that men and women who become victims of a great love are worth infinitely more, in spite of all their faults, than those who have never loved at all?

It may well be that we lie to ourselves when we exaggerate the worth of the man (or the woman) whom we love, but the intention, and the effect, of that lie is to ennoble us. 'Average human beings are, as a rule, to such an extent objects of indifference to us, that when we confer on one or other of them the power to bring us joy or suffering he seems to belong to an altogether different world, to move in an atmosphere of poetry, to make of our own existence a moving panorama, whether we be close to him, or far away . . .' By re-awakening in Swann emotions which he had not known since the days of his youth, Odette stripped away from him the accumulation of the years. Moonlight and the beauties of

[1] JACQUES RIVIÈRE.

the world once more touched his heart as they had done in the dead years. 'For Swann was finding in things once more, since he had fallen in love, the charm that he had found when in his adolescence he had fancied himself an artist: with this difference, that what charm lay in them now was conferred by Odette alone. He could feel re-awakening in himself the inspirations of his boyhood, which had been dissipated among the frivolities of his later life, but they all bore, now, the reflection, the stamp of a particular being; and during the long hours which he now found a subtle pleasure in spending at home, alone with his convalescent spirit, he became gradually himself again. . . .'[1]

Love, too, is productive of much suffering, and 'it is only through suffering that we enter the Kingdom of Heaven'. The man who is too happy, too sure of himself, ceases to be human. How can he understand the lives of others, seeing that they, for the most part, are bruised with misery? How can he hope to penetrate beneath the appearances of beauty, power and eloquence, and see into the reality of an existence where pain holds sway? Only love and jealousy can open in us the door of true intelligence. For all the sufferings of the human heart are alike, and the agony which Marcel felt in the days when he used to wait in vain for his mother to kiss him good night is, in essentials, no different from that experienced by Swann when he was searching hopelessly for Odette. Love makes us brothers to a myriad of men, 'and bids us share with our friend the agonies of the past and the terrors of the future'. Love gives us the power to see and to distinguish. But for love we should never set ourselves the task of understanding our fellows. 'Love is space and time brought within the feeling competence of the heart . . . Happiness is good for the body, but it is pain that develops the power of the spirit . . .'

Love, by compelling us to come to grips with suspicion, to plumb another's character, brings us face to face with life. 'It tears up the poisonous weeds of habit and scepticism, of frivolity and indifference.' That is why the society of any young woman whom we love may be infinitely healthier for the spirit, and may awaken in it ideas far loftier than that of a mere man of genius. 'For what, then, are brought into the light of day are our own sentiments,

[1] *Swann's Way*, II, translated by C. K. Scott Moncrieff (Chatto & Windus, 1922).

our own passions . . . A woman of whose presence we feel the need
draws from us emotions that are vital and profound in a way quite
different from those aroused in us by some man of high talents in
whom we may happen to be interested . . . ' It was because
Albertine would probably have found it very difficult to understand what the Narrator wrote about her that her company was
for him far richer in power to stimulate than Andrée's would have
been. Not only did the pain she caused him water his spirit: she
forced him to think, if only because he had to imagine someone
who was different to himself. One of the special effects of love is
to make the lover more than ever susceptible to the influences of
art. Because Swann had listened to Vinteuil's 'little phrase' in
Odette's company, it became for him the 'National Anthem of
Love'. To what might have been a short-lived and disappointing
affection for Odette de Crécy, the little phrase added something
of itself, impregnating it with something of its own mysterious
nature. Swann, whose eyes bore the indelible traces of an arid
life, found a great peace, a mysterious renewal, 'in stripping his
existence of all the adventitious aids of reason, and letting it take
its way down the long corridor, through the filtered resonance,
of pure sound'.

> . . . He began to reckon up how much that was painful
> perhaps even how much secret and unappeased sorrow, under-
> lay the sweetness of the phrase; and yet to him it brought no
> suffering. What matter though the phrase repeated that
> love is frail and fleeting, when his love was so strong! He
> played with the melancholy which the phrase diffused.
> He felt it stealing over him, but like a caress which only
> deepened and sweetened his sense of his own happiness. . . . [1]

Thus can sensual love be transformed into love of art, into
poetry and into heroism. It can stimulate us not only to make
great sacrifices on behalf of the being whom we love, but even
to sacrifice the love we feel. It is the *master* of gods and men in
the double sense of being a tyrant and of having power to awaken
the powers of the spirit. Proust may have shown that it is a hard

[1] *Swann's Way*, II, translated by C. K. Scott Moncrieff (Chatto & Windus, 1922).

master, but he did not deny that it is man's only master and, all things considered, a benevolent one.

His weakness lay in never having known either marriage or the accepted adventures of the heart. It is nevertheless true that he did succeed, to a remarkable degree, in extending our knowledge of the passions: Those who fear the truth, who prefer to cling to the mirage of romantic love, who rest content with the limited horizons of writers they have always known, will find nothing in Proust. 'I can see all that my thought contains as far as its horizon,' he says, 'but the only things I really want to describe are those that lie beyond . . .' There are many who refuse to see what lies beyond that horizon. He did not write for them. But the courageous souls who are prepared to dare the adventures of the heart, those men and women who long to know themselves as they really are and not as they ought to be, those who value truth above happiness, and who believe that without truth there can be no happiness, will seek in the ordeals and miseries awaiting them in the new, harsh world of Proust, the difficult roads that lead to the goal of a far more beautiful love.

CHAPTER VIII

LA RECHERCHE DU TEMPS PERDU (III)

HUMOUR

STENDHAL said that the novelist, having constructed his novel, must add to it an element of the ridiculous. Proust uses an even stronger word. It was his opinion that there must, in every great work of art, be something of the grotesque. A short book, whether prose narrative or stage play, can be uniformly emotional and moving — though on this point Shakespeare would not have agreed with him. But in a long novel, as in life itself, there must be comic moments, the purpose of which is to restore the balance of the whole and to relieve the tension. Tolstoy, even, who as a rule was so serious, introduces into *Anna Karenina* a character whose besetting preoccupation is the hunting down of moths, and also much consideration of Oblonsky's frivolous love affairs. Balzac, too, has his comic moments (Bixiou's puns and Nucingen's accent) which, for all their occasional heaviness, are strictly necessary. Life is a tangle of the comic and the tragic. More precisely, it can be viewed in the light of the same events, now as comic, now as tragic. Proust, although, and perhaps because, he was one of the great analysts of misery, could note the oddities and futilities of mankind. The human comedy fascinated and amused him.

Before, however, I speak of the comic element in his work, I must, here following in the footsteps of others, make some attempt to define the nature and significance of the 'comic'.

I

THE NATURE OF THE 'COMIC' AND OF HUMOUR

What is the nature of the comic? Bergson says that it is a form of punishment inflicted by Society, a mass revolt against the rigidity of certain individuals, a rebellion staged by life at the

244

expense of men's thoughts and actions. That is partly true, but it does not explain all the effects of the comic. I should prefer to say that the comic aims at 'debunking' certain forms of seriousness that lie heavily upon the human spirit, and at reassuring us by stripping them of their importance. Only thus can we explain why it is that men like to laugh at what frightens them — death, sickness, doctors, women, love, marriages, government and the powers and principalities of this world. The American soldier, during the war, laughed at his sergeant, because he was afraid of him. The Englishman laughs at authority and tradition because he believes in both. Proust laughed at snobs and at Society in general because so much of his life had been overshadowed by dread of them. In this matter of 'debunking', of weakening the power of the serious, the comic spirit has a choice of many weapons: direct attack, or satire: irony, which consists in saying the opposite of what we mean, and thus reassuring the timid reader because the sacrilegious comment is not made openly: wit which focuses the attention on the form rather than on the content, and finally humour, which imitates the persons and the things at which it mocks, reproducing them, not exactly as they are, but slightly distorted. The humorist, says Meredith, walks behind his victim, imitating his gestures. The realism of his attitude, the accuracy of his imitations, their detailed exactness, deceive and enchant us. When Proust records the manner of speaking of Monsieur de Norpois, of Legrandin, of Monsieur de Charlus, he pretends that he is altering nothing, though, in fact, he gives to the clay that twist of the potter's finger which sets his mark upon it, and brings the ridiculous into the full light of day.

There is more of modesty in humour than in wit. By the mere fact of imitating his victim, the humorist admits his resemblance to him. Proust quite often laughs at himself and is willing to play a simple-minded and clumsy rôle in his story (the Narrator, for example, is inordinately slow in realizing the meaning of Charlus's advances). The laughter provoked by humour has its origin in the fact that we are frightened at seeing in the clarity of print any reference to what we most fear — death, madness, the arrogance of the great. If we had to endure Monsieur de

Norpois's solemnities in very fact, we should at first be intimidated, but the hollow emptiness of his measured periods is such that very soon our timidity would give place to amusement.

From his earliest years, Proust had a sense of humour and a feeling for the comic. In the first part of *Swann* we are introduced to a family the oddities of which, never absent for long from his account of it, are noted without malice but with a strong appreciation of their drollery. The scene in which the two aunts are convinced that the thanks they wish to express to Swann must be obvious in the many indirections to which alone they will commit themselves is obviously a reminiscence of some actual incident of childhood. His mother's failure ever to know where she is, and her pride in her husband when she realizes that he has led her by roundabout ways back to the garden gate, are all part of a kindly family joke. We see Proust, in his letters to Madame Straus, sharpening his gift of mockery at the expense of the Great World. His *Memoranda* are full of notes relating to the oddities he has observed — in especial, to oddities of language which he fits, even while he is listening to them, to this or that character of the work in gestation, or, sometimes, to more than one, leaving the final choice until later.

He rarely makes a note of 'sayings' in the Parisian sense of 'witticisms', except in the case of Madame Straus. Hers he keeps in reserve for the Duchesse de Guermantes. But it is worth remarking that, towards the end of the book, he finds himself wondering whether the intelligence of those in whom the Guermantes's brand of wit is prevalent (Swann has caught the infection) is not, all things considered, inferior to that of a man like Brichot. The characters of his novel (with the single exception of the Duchess) who utter witticisms, are all of them fools — Cottard, Forcheville, Bloch the elder — and one cannot help feeling that Proust regarded verbal wit as a sign of mediocrity, though he loved humour and is inferior to no French writer in the success with which he used that phlegmatic form of the comic.

THE COMIC THEMES

Proust's comic themes are of two kinds: those that are a permanent part of human nature, that have frightened and consequently amused mankind from the beginning of recorded history, and those that were peculiar to his period, his world and his temperament.

First and foremost among the permanent themes is what we may call 'La Danse Macabre'. From time immemorial the comic writer has always exploited the contrast between the panic engendered by the idea of death, and the mechanical routine of living which compels us, when faced by the most terrifying of all dramas, to continue acting and talking as we have always done. Tolstoy makes great play with this in the death of *Ivan Ilitch*, and again in *War and Peace* (the death of old Prince Bezoukhov). Proust shows us the stratagems which the egotism of the Duc de Guermantes employs in order to provide him with an alibi against someone else's death, and the effect which family mourning may have on his own life. One evening, when the Duke and the Duchess are planning to go to a fancy-dress ball which promises to be amusing, their cousin Amanien d'Osmond is lying at death's door. That he is 'at the point of death' does not matter, but if he actually dies they will have to give up all idea of going to the ball. The Duke arranges, therefore, to take a rapid survey of the situation beforeh is cousin's death shall be an established fact, before, that is, the family shall be plunged into mourning.

> Once covered by the official certainty that Amanien was still alive, he could go without a thought to his dinner, to the Prince's party, to the midnight revel at which he would appear as Louis XI and had made the most exciting assignation with a new mistress, and would make no more inquiries until the following day, when his pleasures would be at an end. Then one would put on mourning if the cousin had passed away in the night.

So the Duke inquires anxiously whether Jules, the footman, whom he has sent to his cousin's house, has yet returned.

. . . He's just come this instant, M. le Duc. They're waiting from one moment to the next for M. le Marquis to pass away. 'Ah! he's alive' exclaimed the Duc with a sigh of relief. 'That's all right, that's all right — sold again, Satan! While there's life there's hope', the Duke announced to us with a joyful air. 'They've been talking about him as though he were dead and buried. In a week from now he'll be fitter than I am.' 'It's the doctors who said he wouldn't last out the evening. One of them wanted to call again during the night. The head one said it was no use, M. le Marquis would be dead by then: they've only kept him alive by injecting him with camphorated oil.' 'Hold your tongue, you damned fool!' cried the Duke in a paroxysm of rage. 'Who the devil asked you to say all that! You haven't understood a word of what they told you." "It wasn't me they told, it was Jules.' 'Will you hold your tongue!' roared the Duke, and, turning to Swann, 'what a blessing he's still alive! He will regain his strength gradually, don't you know. Still alive after being in such a critical condition, that in itself is an excellent sign. One mustn't expect everything at once. It can't be at all unpleasant, a little injection of camphorated oil.' He rubbed his hands. 'He's alive; what more could anyone want? After going through all he's gone through. It's a great step forward. Upon my word, I envy him having such a temperament. Ah! these invalids, you know, people do all sorts of little things for them that they don't do for us. Now today there was the devil of a cook who sent me up a leg of mutton with *béarnaise* sauce — it was done to a turn, I must admit, but just for that reason I took so much of it that it's still lying on my stomach. However, that doesn't make people come to inquire for me as they do for dear Amanien. We do too much inquiring. It only tires him. We must let him have room to breathe. They're killing the poor fellow by sending round to him all the time. . . . '

In this way does the man of the world refuse to let Death have the better of his social duties. As for the doctor, he regards the whole business as a mere incident of professional routine. In one of the saddest passages of the whole book, the scene in which the grandmother dies, Proust, the humorist with the implacable eye, gives a subtle, balanced, but profoundly comic sketch of Professor Dieulafoy, the usher of Death and master of the funeral ceremonies.

At this point my father hurried from the room. I supposed that a change, for better or for worse, had occurred. It was simply that Dr. Dieulafoy had just arrived. My father went to receive him in the drawing-room, like the actor who is to come next on the stage. We had sent for him not to cure but to certify, in almost a legal capacity. Dr. Dieulafoy might indeed be a great physician, a marvellous professor; to these several parts, in which he excelled, he added a third, in which he remained for forty years without a rival, a part as original as that of the foil, the scaramouche or the noble father, which consisted in coming to certify an agony or a death. The mere sound of his name foreshadowed the dignity with which he would sustain the part, and when the servant announced: 'M. Dieulafoy', one imagined oneself at a play by Molière. To the dignity of his attitude was added, without being conspicuous, the suppleness of a perfect figure. A face in itself too good-looking was toned down by the convention due to distressing circumstances. In the sable majesty of his frock-coat the Professor entered the room, melancholy without affectation, uttered not the least word of condolence, which might have been thought insincere, nor was he guilty of the slightest infringement of the rules of tact. At the foot of a deathbed it was he and not the Duc de Guermantes who was the great gentleman. Having examined my grandmother, but not so as to tire her, and with an excess of reserve which was an act of courtesy to the doctor who was treating the case, he murmured a few words to my father, bowed respectfully to my mother to whom I felt that my father had positively to restrain himself from saying: 'Professor Dieulafoy.' But already our visitor had turned away, not wishing to seem to be soliciting an introduction, and left the room in the most polished manner conceivable, simply taking with him the sealed envelope that was slipped into his hand. He had not appeared to see it, and we ourselves were left wondering for a moment whether we had really given it to him, such a conjuror's nimbleness had he put into the act of making it vanish without thereby losing any of the gravity — which was increased rather — of the great consultant in his long frock-coat with its silken lapels, and his handsome head full of a noble commiseration. The slowness and vivacity of his movements showed that, even if he had a hundred other visits to pay, and patients waiting, he refused to appear hurried. For he was the embodiment of tact, intelligence and kindness. . . .[1]

The humour here is at once ferocious and caressing. From the days of Molière to those of Jules Romains, doctors have been among the favourite butts of comic writers because their power and their learning inspire all mankind with a secret terror. Proust, the son and the brother of doctors, is, at one moment, full of respect for medicine, at another, severe in his criticism of medical men. He created in Dr. Cottard a man who was almost half-witted, and yet at the same time a great practitioner. He wrote that — 'medicine knows nothing of the secret of curing, but has mastered the art of prolonging illness' — that — 'medicine is a compendium of the successive and contradictory mistakes of doctors'. But he could also give it as his opinion that 'to believe in medicine would be the greatest folly, were it not that refusal to believe in it would be a greater'.

The Comic Muse feels bound to mock not only at the doctor but also at the valetudinarian, because he brings to bear upon those who surround and care for him a species of blackmail and tyranny which inevitably produce a reaction. At the very opening of *Du Côté de chez Swann* we are introduced to Aunt Léonie who, since the death of her husband, Uncle Octave, has refused to leave

---

[1] All these passages are taken from *The Guermantes Way*, II, translated by C. K. Scott Moncrieff (Chatto & Windus, 1925).

first, Combray, second, her house, third, her room and finally her bed — 'next to which, on a table that fulfilled the double office of laboratory and altar . . . above a statuette of the Virgin and a bottle of Vichy-Celestins, were to be found both missal and prescriptions, everything, in fact, that made it possible for her to follow, from her bed, the offices of the Church and her medical routine, so that she need miss neither the moment for taking her pepsin nor the observation of Vespers. . . .'

Here the humour is indulgent, like that of Dickens, because the character mocked at is both inoffensive and diverting. Proust becomes harsher when he touches on his favourite theme of snobbery. That Proust himself, in the days of his youth, manifested certain symptoms of snobbery is of small importance. Not only is the perfect lucidity of the comic writer not incompatible with personal experience, it actually presupposes it. The sense of humour consists of mocking *in* oneself what deserves mockery. Molière knew the agonies of Alceste and doubtless too those of Arnolphe. For that reason he could the better interpret them. This double character in the comic writer is indispensable.

Snobbery is one of the key-themes of comedy because we all of us suffer from its effects. Human societies are divided into groups and classes arranged in multiple, complex and sometimes contradictory, hierarchies — all of which give full play to snobbery. Contempt and pride are to be found everywhere and at all times. An excuse for both can always be found. Among the French *émigrés* at Coblenz, the vintage of 1790 despised that of 1791, while those who had arrived in that year refused to be on terms of friendship with their fellow refugees of 1793. In the United States, Americans of the first generation were looked down upon by those of the second and third. From all these forms of snobbery spring insults and resentments. It is one of the functions of the Comic Muse to castigate these futile but harmful manifestations of self-conceit.

Snobbery, in Proust's novel, appears in many different forms. There is the snobbery of the man (or the woman) who, wishing to belong to a certain coterie, and having succeeded in getting a foot over the threshold, feels so little sure of himself that, rather than run the risk of compromising himself in the eyes of his new friends, he is prepared to deny his old ones. This is the case of Legrandin who, with his flowing spotted tie, his candid glance and his charming utterances, has the appearance of a poet though, in fact, he is obsessed by a violent and unsatisfied desire to be on terms of intimacy with the Duchesse de Guermantes and the local big-wigs. So long as no countess or marchioness is in sight he is extremely affable to the Narrator's grandfather, but when walking with one of the neighbouring great ladies he pretends not to know his Commoner friend. His manner of greeting a lady of the aristocracy is marked by a quite extraordinary eagerness and enthusiasm:

> Legrandin . . . made a profound bow, with a subsidiary backward movement which brought his spine sharply up into a position behind its starting-point . . . This rapid recovery caused a sort of tense muscular wave to ripple over Legrandin's hips, which I had not supposed to be so fleshy; I cannot say why, but this undulation of pure matter, this wholly carnal fluency, with not the least hint in it of spiritual significance, this wave lashed to a fury by the wind of an assiduity, an obsequiousness of the basest sort, awoke my mind suddenly to the possibility of a Legrandin altogether different from the one we knew . . . .[1]

When he is in conversation with a great lady, and Marcel passes him in the company of his father, Legrandin is torn by conflicting impulses. He does not like to refuse recognition to neighbours with whom he is on good terms, but hates the thought that the lady in question should discover that he knows them. Hence the following admirable passage:

> . . . He brushed past us, and did not interrupt what he was saying, but gave us, out of the corner of his blue eye, a little sign which began and ended, so to speak, inside his eyelids, and, as it did not involve the least movement of his facial muscles, managed to pass quite unperceived by the lady: but, striving to compensate by the intensity of his feelings

[1] *Swann's Way*, I, translated by C. K. Scott Moncrieff (Chatto & Windus, 1922).

for the somewhat restricted field in which they had to find expression, he made that blue chink, which was set apart for us, sparkle with all the animation of cordiality which went far beyond mere playfulness, and almost touched the borderline of roguery; he subtilised the refinements of good-fellowship into a wink of connivance, a hint, a hidden meaning, a secret understanding, all the mysteries of complicity in a plot, and finally exalted his assurances of friendship to the level of protestations of affection, even of a declaration of love, lighting up for us, and for us alone, with a secret and languid flame invisible to the great lady upon his other side, an enamoured pupil in a countenance of ice. . . .[1]

Second Specimen: the snobbery of genuine aristocrats belonging to a noble family, but to a junior branch of it, who, as the result of constant snubs, are like 'trees which, springing from a bad position on the edge of a precipice, are compelled to grow with a backward slant in order to maintain their equilibrium'. Of this type is Madame Gallardon:

> Since she was obliged, in order to console herself for not being quite on a level with the rest of the Guermantes, to repeat to herself incessantly that it was owing to the uncompromising rigidity of her principles and pride that she saw so little of them, constant iteration had remoulded her body and given her a sort of 'bearing' which was accepted by the plebeian as a sign of breeding, and even kindled, at times, a momentary spark in the jaded eyes of old gentlemen in clubs. Had anyone subjected Madame de Gallardon's conversation to the form of analysis which, by noting the relative frequency of its several terms, would furnish him with the key to a ciphered message, he would have at once remarked that no expression, not even the commonest forms of speech, occurred in it nearly so often as 'my cousins the Guermantes', — 'at my aunt Guermantes' ' — 'Elzéar de Guermantes' health' — 'my cousin Guermantes' box. . . .'[2]

---

[1] *Swann's Way*, I, translated by C. K. Scott Moncrieff (Chatto & Windus, 1922).
[2] *Swann's Way*, II, translated by C. K. Scott Moncrieff (Chatto & Windus, 1922).

Third Specimen: the snobbery of the Guermantes themselves, who are so sure of their own social superiority that they regard the whole of humanity with an undiscriminating goodwill born of an undiscriminating contempt. They attach very little import-ance to having aristocratic relations, because all their relations are aristocratic: they are severe in their judgment on those who want to move in high society, but, at the same time, find an odd sort of pleasure in entertaining a 'Highness', of speaking of their Royal connections, and also, or at least this was so in the case of the Duchess, of appraising intellectual achievements with an air of knowledgeable authority which had no real justification. The Guermantes, who had once been, for the Narrator, figures in a fairy-tale, quickly become a group of comic characters as a result of that artless self-assurance which led the Duke to quote and to provoke his Duchess's 'witticisms', and her to live up to the part for which she had thus been cast.

Finally, at the very top of the social ladder are perched those Royal Highnesses such as the Princesse de Parme and the Princesse de Luxembourg, who want to be kindly but behave in so remote and condescending a fashion that they give the impres-sion of being barely able to distinguish a human being from an animal, as when one of them offers a cake to the Narrator's grand-mother much in the same way as a visitor to the Zoo might feed one of the exhibits.

But the snobbery of the middle classes, no less than that of the aristocracy, is fair game for the Comic Muse. Madame Verdurin is an example of the snobbery of anti-snobbery. She has formed a social group, a 'salon' which, like that over which the Duchesse de Guermantes presides, has its 'familiars' and its 'bugbears':

> To admit you to the 'little nucleus', the 'little group', the 'little clan' at the Verdurins, one condition sufficed, but that one was indispensable; you must give tacit adherence to a Creed one of whose articles was that the young pianist whom Madame Verdurin had taken under her patronage that year, and of whom she said — 'Really, he oughtn't to be allowed to play Wagner as well as that!' — left both Plante and Rubinstein 'sitting'; while Dr. Cottard was a

more brilliant diagnostician than Potain. Each new recruit
whom the Verdurins failed to persuade that the evenings
spent by other people, in houses other than theirs, were as
dull as ditchwater, saw himself banished forthwith. Women
being in this respect more rebellious than men, more reluctant
to lay aside all worldly curiosity and the desire to find out
for themselves whether other drawing-rooms might not
sometimes be as entertaining, the Verdurins, feeling moreover that this critical spirit and this demon of frivolity might,
by their contagion, prove fatal to the orthodoxy of the little
church, had been obliged to expel, one after another, all
those of the 'faithful' who were of the female sex. . . .[1]

The culminating point of Proust's satirical treatment of snobbery is to be found in the 'Marquise' episode. 'Marquise' was the
nickname given by the Narrator's grandmother to the lessee of
the small, shabby pavilion, masked by a green trellis, which did
duty in the Champs-Elysées for a public lavatory. The 'Marquise'
was the possessor of an enormous face, smothered in a sort of
rough-cast of powder, and wore on her red wig a small black
lace bonnet. She was of a friendly disposition, but inclined to be
haughty, and was ruthless in the contempt with which she refused
admission to such visitors as she happened to dislike. 'I choose my
customers', she said, 'I don't let just anybody into what I call
my parlours. Don't they just look like parlours with all them
flowers? Some of my customers are very nice people, and not a
day passes but one or another of them brings me some lilac or
jasmine or roses — the which is my favourite blooms . . .' The
Narrator's grandmother who has overheard the conversation,
makes the following comment: 'No one could be more Guermantes
or more Verdurin-little-nucleus.'

That single short phrase pricks the bubble of snobbery more
effectively than any diatribe by a moralist could do, because it
shows that vanity and disdain are universal sentiments, and that
there exists no man or woman so completely disinherited but
can find someone to exclude from his or her own particular circle.

[1] *Swann's Vay*, I, translated by C. K. Scott Moncrieff (Chatto & Windus, 1922).

THE COMIC METHOD

The comic writer's favourite method is imitation. Dickens, when he wants to hold the barristers of his day up to ridicule, introduces into *Pickwick* a prosecuting Counsel's speech which is *almost* genuine, but sufficiently distorted to underline the point of the mockery. Proust was a perfect imitator. Imitation is a difficult art, because it demands not only that the imitator should be able to reproduce the very voice, the very gestures, of his victim, but also that he should have mastered his tricks of speech and ways of thinking. To be able to talk like Charlus or Norpois is nothing if one cannot think, and arrange one's thought, like Charlus or Norpois. Therein lay Proust's supreme gift. Not content with analysing a character in abstract phrases, he delighted in bringing him on to the stage and letting him speak for himself.

Take, for instance, the astonishing figure of the old diplomat. Proust never just says: 'This was what Monsieur de Norpois was thinking', but the long speeches which he puts into his mouth enable us to grasp the mechanism of his thought. The essence, the mainspring, of the Norpois style is this, that the diplomat will never allow himself to say anything that might possibly commit him irrevocably to any statement whatever. So precisely does he balance his sentences that they cancel one another out. At the end of any of his speeches we discover that he has said precisely nothing at all which could possibly be interpreted as a definite expression of opinion. Add to this his use of a number of professional formulae, his habit of referring to the Great Powers in terms of the buildings associated with the practice of diplomacy — the Quai d'Orsay, Downing Street, the Wilhelmstrasse, the Pont aux Chantres — or of revelling in subtleties and discovering in the use of an adjective the key to a national policy, and we are in a position to establish the true Norpois 'tone'. This particular character who, on his first appearance may deceive the reader just as he deceived the Narrator, is comic because, behind the imposing façade, there is nothing but utter emptiness, a sham subtlety and a few elementary emotions — an ambition that does not lessen with increasing age, and a rather touching desire to please Madame de Villeparisis.

Questioned, during the Dreyfus Affair, by Bloch who wants to find out whether or no the diplomat is a Dreyfusard, and puts a number of inquiries to him on the subject of Colonel Picquart, Monsieur de Norpois succeeds, by dint of committing himself to two contradictory statements, in reducing the sum total of his remarks to zero.

> Bloch tried to pin Monsieur de Norpois down on Colonel Picquart.
>
> 'There can be no two opinions' replied Monsieur de Norpois, 'his evidence had to be taken. I am well aware that by maintaining this attitude I have drawn screams of protest from more than one of my colleagues, but to my mind the Government were bound to let the Colonel speak. One can't dance lightly out of a blind alley like that, or, if one does, there is always the risk of falling into a ditch. As for the officer himself, his statement gave one, at the first hearing, a most excellent impression. When one saw him, looking so well in that smart Chasseur uniform, come into court and relate in a perfectly simple and frank tone what he had seen and what he had deduced, and say — "On my honour as a soldier" ... (here Monsieur de Norpois' voice shook with a faint patriotic throb) "... such is my conviction," — it is impossible to deny that the impression he made was profound.'
>
> 'There, he's a dreyfusard, there's not the least doubt of it,' thought Bloch.
>
> 'But where he entirely forfeited all the sympathy he had managed to attract was when he was confronted with the Registrar, Gribelin. When one heard that old public servant, a man who had only one answer to make' (here Monsieur de Norpois began to accentuate his words with the energy of his sincere convictions) 'when one listened to him and saw him look his superior officer in the face, not afraid to hold his head up to him, and say to him in a tone that admitted

of no response: "Colonel, sir, you know very well that I have never told a lie, you know that at this moment, as always, I am speaking the truth," the wind changed; Monsieur Picquart might move heaven and earth at the subsequent hearings; he made a complete fiasco.'
'No, evidently he is an anti-dreyfusard: it's quite obvious,' said Bloch to himself.[1]

It is a mistake to say that Proust delighted in giving a 'photographic reproduction of the little manias, the words, the slang phrases, the grammatical errors, of his characters'. There is in all art an element of selection and stylization. Monsieur de Norpois would never, in real life, have been at all times so completely Monsieur de Norpois. Legrandin is more wholly Legrandin than the real Legrandin would ever have been. From the interminable utterances of human beings the novelist chooses those that reveal character, just as the portrait-painter is always on the look-out for precisely that expression in his sitter which throws light on his deepest nature.

Like a geometrician who, in divesting things of their material qualities, sees only their linear substratum, I ignored what people said because I was interested not in what they wanted to say but the manner in which they said it in so far as it revealed their characters or their absurdities . . . No matter how stupid people may be, they give expression by their gestures, their words, the feelings which they involuntarily reveal, to laws of which they have not, themselves, the slightest idea, but which the artist, studying them, takes, as it were, by surprise.

The evolution, in time, of a character's vocabulary provides at once an element of the comic and a pointer to analysis. Albertine, when first the Narrator meets her, talks like a schoolgirl. With sparkling eyes she expresses her admiration of an essay written by her friend, Gisèle, who has been set the following

[1] *The Guermantes Way*, I, translated by C. K. Scott Moncrieff (Chatto & Windus, 1925).

problem in an examination paper: *Write a letter as from Sophocles in the other world to Racine, condoling with him on the failure of Athalie.* She has begun her letter as follows:

> Dear Friend: you must pardon me the liberty of addressing you when I have not the honour of your personal acquaintance, but your latest tragedy, *Athalie*, shows, does it not? that you have made the most thorough study of my own modest works. You have not only put poetry into the mouths of the protagonists, or principal persons of the drama, but you have written other and, let me tell you without flattery, charming, verses for the Chorus, a feature which was not too bad, according to what one hears, in Greek Tragedy, but is a complete novelty in France. Nay more, your talent, always so fluent, so finished, so winning, so fine, so delicate, has here acquired an energy on which I congratulate you . . . I have felt myself impelled to offer you all my congratulations, to which I would add, my dear brother poet, the expression of my very highest esteem. . . .[1]

That is Albertine the First. Later, when the Narrator meets her again, she uses words that come so strangely from her lips that he deduces from them a great change in her. She says *'Selection'* . . . *'To my mind'*. . . *'Lapse of time'*:

> 'To my mind that is the best thing that could possibly happen. I regard it as the best solution, the stylish way out.'
> This was so novel, so manifestly an alluvial deposit giving one to suspect such capricious wanderings over soil hitherto unknown to her, that, on hearing the words *'to my mind'*, I drew Albertine towards me, and at *'I regard'* made her sit down on the side of my bed.[2]

He wants to kiss her, but as yet dares not do so. One final philological discovery decides him. Speaking of one of the girls

[1] *Within a Budding Grove*, II, translated by C. K. Scott Moncrieff (Chatto & Windus, 1924).
[2] *The Guermantes Way*, II, translated by C. K. Scott Moncrieff (Chatto & Windus, 1925).

of the little band — 'Yes,' answers Albertine, 'she reminds me of a little *mousmé*.' *Mousmé* seems to the Narrator to be a revelation, if not of an outward initiation, at least of an inward evolution. Now, at last, he feels able to kiss her.

At times the Proustian form of imitation seems to go to the extreme of caricature, or exaggeration. This appears to be the case where Dr. Cottard's turns of phrase are in question. At the period of *Un Amour de Swann*, Cottard's vocabulary is so limited that he takes all metaphorical locutions quite literally, admires the manner in which Madame Verdurin employs them, finally takes the plunge in an access of timidity, and more often than not gets them wrong. Later, when he has become a famous professor, his language, though still vulgar, has taken on so adventitious a richness that it has become a mosaic of ready-made phrases:

> 'In any case, whether the Guermantes go to Madame Verdurin's or not, she entertains all the very best people, the d'Sherbatoffs, the d'Forchevilles, *e tutti quanti*, people of the highest flight, all the nobility of France and Navarre, with whom you would see me conversing as man to man. Of course, those sort of people are only too glad to meet the princes of science' — he added with a smile of fatuous conceit, brought to his lips by his proud satisfaction not so much that the expression formerly reserved for men like Potain and Charcot should now be applicable to himself, but that he knew at last how to employ all these expressions that were authorized by custom, and, after a long course of study, had learned them by heart. . . .[1]

But that is not caricature. The man's superb vulgarity is under-lined with cruel, but scrupulous, truth. Is the word 'caricature' applicable to the language used by Bloch the younger, all heavily charged with Homeric images which he uses in reference to the most ordinary happenings? No, for what Proust is doing is merely to give a slight distortion to the absurd sort of phrase-

[1] *Cities of the Plain*, II, translated by C. K. Scott Moncrieff (Chatto & Windus, 1929).

making which is the stock-in-trade of thousands of educated adolescents. His own letters are proof that he himself passed through just such a phase: and when Bloch, in order to make people think that he knows English, pronounces (wrongly) *lift* as *laïft*, and says *Venaice* instead of *Venice*, that, too, may be an amused but somewhat rueful recollection of his own past misdoings.

The only caricatures that are carried too far, and are over-elaborated, are those of Françoise's daughter, and of the manager of the Balbec Hotel whose malapropisms, at first amusing, become in the long run wearisome:

> . . . The manager had come in person to meet me at Pont-à-Côuleuvre, reiterating how greatly he valued his titled patrons, which made me afraid that he had ennobled me, until I realised that in the obscurity of his grammatical memory *titré* meant simply *attitré*, or accredited. In fact the more new languages he learned the worse he spoke the others. He informed me that he had placed me at the very top of the hotel. 'I hope,' he said, 'that you will not interpolate this as a want of discourtesy, I was sorry to give you a room of which you are unworthy, but I did it in connexion with the noise, because in that room you will not have anyone above your head to disturb your trepanum' (tympanum). 'Don't be alarmed, I shall have the windows closed so that they shan't bang. Upon that point I am intolerable' (the last word expressing not his own thought, which was that he would always be found inexorable in that respect, but, quite possibly, the thoughts of his underlings) . . . He informed me with great sorrow of the death of the leader of the Cherbourg bar: 'He was an old retainer' he said (meaning probably 'campaigner'), and gave me to understand that his end had been hastened by the quickness, otherwise, the fastness, of his life. 'For some time past I noticed that after dinner he would take a doss in the reading-room' (take a doze, presumably). 'The last times he was so changed that if you hadn't known who it was, to look at him, he was barely recognisant' (presumably, recognisable).

A happy compensation: the chief magistrate of Caen had just received his 'bags' (badge) as Commander of the Legion of Honour. . . .[1]

The passage may seem surprising until one remembers, in the first place,. how much cruder both Balzac and Dickens were (Baron Nucingen's accent and Gaudissart's jokes), and secondly, that the changes in the meanings of words, their lack of precision and stability, their differing fortunes in the minds of different people, are all connected with that philosophy of relativity and of the nothingness of reality, which was so markedly Proust's own.

Another method common to Proust and Dickens, which partially confirms Bergson's theory of the significance of the comic, is that by which amusing effects are produced from the mechanical aspects of the human creature, or from his occasional resemblance to members of the animal, vegetable or mineral worlds. The passage in which Proust describes the auditorium of the Opera as being an immense aquarium, a sort of marine cave, where Nereids float in the recesses of their boxes, is followed by this:

> The Marquis de Palancy, his face bent downwards at the end of his long neck, his round, bulging eye glued to the glass of his monocle, was moving with a leisurely displacement through the transparent shade, and appeared no more to see the public in the stalls than a fish that drifts past, unconscious of the press of curious gazers behind the glass walls of an aquarium. Now and again he paused, a venerable wheezing monument, and the audience could not have told whether he was in pain, asleep, swimming, about to spawn, or merely taking breath. . . .[2]

This transformation of man into fish is as productive of laughter as might be the successful completion of a conjuring trick.

For a third method he was indebted to France, rather than to

---

[1] *Cities of the Plain*, I, translated by C. K. Scott Moncrieff (Chatto & Windus, 1929).
[2] *The Guermantes Way*, I, translated by C. K. Scott Moncrieff (Chatto & Windus, 1925).

Dickens — for the method, that is, which consists in achieving a comic contrast between the nature of the thing described and the solemn tone of a description conceived in terms of Homer or of Bossuet. To write with gravity about frivolous subjects, or with magnificence about trivial objects or mediocre people, produces just that sense of shocked surprise which is the very essence of the comic. Proust (like Aristophanes) loves to spin out a long lyric line, and then end it by a sudden drop into bathos.

An early example of what I mean, rather too precious, and of which his grandmother's taste would not, I think, have approved, is a passage in which he describes a telephone conversation:

> To renew this miracle, we have but to put our lips to the magic disk and call up — and I admit that, at times, the answer is slow in coming — the vigilant Virgins whose voices we hear every day, though we never know what they look like — who are our Guardian Angels in that dark and dizzy world over whose gates they maintain a jealous watch: the All-Powerful Fates who conjure up for us the faces of our absent friends, though we are never granted a sight of their own. We have but to summon these Danaides of the Invisible who ceaselessly empty, refill, and pass to one another, the dark urns of sound; the jealous Furies who, while we murmur sweet nothings to the lady of our choice, exclaim ironically — 'I can hear you!' just at the precise moment when we are hoping that no one else at all can hear us; the touchy Servants of the Mysteries; the Implacable Divinities; the Ladies of the Telephone Exchange. . . .[1]

And here is another example, where the effect is the same but is obtained in rather a different manner, since the triviality of the street-cries of Paris and the poetry of liturgical music mingle in every paragraph and the passage ends on a religious and not a popular theme.

> It was true that the fantasy, the spirit, of each vendor or vendress frequently introduced variations into the words of

[1] *Days of Reading*, II, *Marcel Proust: A Selection from His Miscellaneous Writings*, translated by Gerard Hopkins (Allan Wingate, 1948).

all these chants that I used to hear from my bed. And yet a ritual suspension interposing a silence in the middle of a word, especially when it was repeated a second time, constantly reminded me of some old church. In his little cart drawn by a she-ass which he stopped in front of each house before entering the courtyard, the old-clothes man, brandishing a whip, intoned: 'Habits, marchand d'habits, ha . . .bits', with the same pause between the final syllables as if he had been intoning in plain chant, 'Per omnia saeculo . . . rum' or 'requiescat in pa . . . ce', albeit he had no reason to believe in the immortality of his clothes, nor did he offer them as cerements for the supreme repose in peace. And similarly, as the motives were beginning, even at this early hour to become confused, a vegetable woman, pushing her little hand-cart, was using for her litany the Gregorian division:

> A la tendresse, à la verduresse,
> Artichauts tendres et beaux
> Arti . . . chauts.

although she had probably never heard of the antiphonal, or of the seven tones that symbolize, four the sciences of the quadrivium, and three, those of the trivium. . . .[1]

Like Anatole France, too, Proust turns to account the traditional, instinctive and pious respect which all Frenchmen feel for the classics of their language, when he applies lines from Racine to incongruous situations. Thus when Françoise, after the departure of Eulalie whom she detests, says 'Lickspittle folk who are clever at getting their hands on the dough: but her time'll come — the Good God will punish 'em all one of these days' — she is described as giving the same sidelong glance, and making the same sort of insinuation as Joas, when, thinking only of *Athalie*, he says:

> *Le bonheur des méchants comme un torrent s'écoule.*

Another example, in which the classical-trivial discord is accentuated by a still further discord produced by linking lines written in honour of women with the emotions of homosexuality:

[1] *The Captive*, I, translated by C. K. Scott Moncrieff (Chatto & Windus, 1929).

At sight of the youthful staff of this Embassy advancing in a body to shake hands with Monsieur de Charlus, M. de Vaugoubert assumed the astonished air of Élise exclaiming in *Esther*: 'Great Heavens! What a swarm of innocent beauties issuing from all sides presents itself to my gaze! How charming a modesty is depicted on their faces. . . .'[1]

And, again, in the hotel at Balbec:

> . . . For in the doorway of the hall, what in the seventeenth century was called the portico, 'a flourishing race' of young pages clustered, especially at tea-time, like the young Israelites of Racine's choruses. But I do not believe that one of them could have given even the vague answer that Joas finds to satisfy Athalie when she inquires of the infant Prince — 'What is your office, then?', for they had none. At the most, if one had asked of any of them, like the new Queen: 'But all this race, what do they then, imprisoned in this place?' he might have said: 'I watch the solemn pomp and bear my part.' Now and then one of the young supers would approach some more important personage, then this young beauty would rejoin the chorus, and, unless it were the moment for a spell of contemplative relaxation, they would proceed with their useless, reverent, decorative, daily evolutions. For, except on their day off, 'reared in seclusion from the world' and never crossing the threshold, they led the same ecclesiastical existence as the Levites in *Athalie*, and as I gazed at that 'young and faithful troop' playing at the foot of the steps draped with sumptuous carpets I felt inclined to ask myself whether I were entering the Grand Hotel at Balbec or the temple of Solomon. . . .[2]

[1] *Cities of the Plain*, I, translated by C. K. Scott Moncrieff (Chatto & Windus, 1929).
[2] Ibid

If we are fully to explore this whole great subject, it is important to note how ill-defined is the dividing-line between the comic and the monstrous. I have already pointed out that men laugh whenever the shock of surprise, provoked by extraordinary actions or words, is followed by a feeling of safety, born of the fact either that the oddities to which their attention has been drawn are harmless, or that they decide, as a result of their amused scrutiny, that such things are only a part of that same human nature which can be seen at work in ourselves. This feeling of safety ceases to exist when the actions (or the words) in question overstep the normal limits of human fatuity, and we find ourselves in the presence of a strange and anti-social phenomenon which, by its very nature, produces a sense of terror. This overstepping is what happens in the case of Monsieur de Charlus who, when he first appears upon the scene, merely provokes us to laugh at his inordinate pride but who later in the book turns into a monster.

It is a fact of importance that in all the greatest works of fiction there is almost always a monster, and sometimes more than one. The characters thus designated are at once superhuman and inhuman, and they dominate the works in which they appear, giving them unity in a way that nothing else could do. This is true of Balzac's Vautrin, and it is true of Proust's Charlus. The monster opens windows on to mysterious depths just because it is beyond our power to understand him completely. He passes beyond our range of vision, if only by the horror he inspires: but he does, nevertheless, contain elements of a kind that are in us as well. Had the circumstances been different we might have become what he is, and this thought at once terrifies and fascinates us. Monsters provide the novel with unexplored and secret deeps which reveal the sublime.

Before Proust, Shakespeare alone had succeeded in orchestrating the magic dissonances amidst which these monsters move. The humour which expresses itself in lovely lines, the earth-bound bodies which can loose spirits on the world, the allegories and the ravishing images which end in horseplay, the flicker of fairy lights, all these things bring the world of Shakespeare to our minds. Proust, like Shakespeare, had plumbed the extremes of human misery but, like Shakespeare, found in humour a saving grace, and, again like Shakespeare, serenity in Time Regained. The end of *A la Recherche du temps perdu* is not unlike the end of Shakespeare's *Tempest*. The play is ended: the Enchanter has surrendered his secret. Back into their box he has put the marionettes whom he has shown us for the last time, touched with hoar-frost, at the Prince de Guermantes's great reception. Now he says, like Prospero: 'We are such stuff as dreams are made on, and our little life is rounded with a sleep' . . . The Guermantes and the Verdurins vanish in smoke: Swann's bell tinkles for the last time at the garden gate and, while the final cadences on the nature of Time are drawing to a close, we seem to hear, in the moon-drenched trees, far away and barely audible, Marcel's laughter, the laughter of a schoolboy spluttering behind his hand, but softened now, and become the laughter of a very old child to whom life has taught the lesson not only of pain but of pity.

CHAPTER IX

IN WHICH THE DILETTANTE BECOMES A MASTER

Beautiful books are written in a kind of foreign language. Beneath the words each one of us has written in what we think they mean, and often what we think is wrong. But so long as a book is beautiful, the wrong meanings are all of them beautiful, too.   MARCEL PROUST

I

'SWANN' IS BORN

ROUND about 1911, believing himself to be within sight of the end of his great book, Marcel Proust must have been ruefully wondering whether any publisher would ever be willing to undertake it. His relations with a number of journals and reviews had been uniformly unhappy. Because of his reputation as a rich amateur, both the professional writers and the devotees of 'pure literature' looked at him askance. It was only through the friendly offices of Calmette that he had succeeded in forcing an entry into the *Figaro*. Twice he had submitted articles to the *Temps*, and twice he had been turned down. Ganderax, editor of the *Revue de Paris*, had sat on his Ruskin essay for a long while. 'He is', said Proust in a letter to Jean-Louis Vaudoyer, 'a friendly little man, but he is torn between friendship for me in the flesh and the horror that I inspire in him by my writings.' Finally he refused it *'on grounds of conscience'*. Ruskin, however, having died in the interval, the manuscript which he had decided was 'detestable as literature' became of possible value for its 'topicality'. No other critic was available to write on Ruskin, and Ganderax, caught on the horns of a dilemma, and having to decide whether to go to press without an obituary notice, or 'to publish', wrote Proust, 'what afterwards became my Preface to the *Bible of Amiens*, preferred the first of these two great tragedies. The reason he gave me, with unfailing regularity and

268

in tones of melancholy affection, for declining my works, was that
he had not "enough time to *reconstruct* and rewrite them". . . .'

> *Proust to Madame Straus:* 'I am not blaming Monsieur
> Ganderax, who has many good qualities, and is a type that
> one doesn't often meet nowadays, a type that is becoming
> less and less common, and that I, for my part, much prefer
> to the current variety. But why, oh why, does he write as
> he does? Why, when I put "1871", must he add "that year
> to be abominated above all years"? Why must Paris always
> be 'the great city,' Delaunay "the master painter"? Why
> must an emotion inevitably be "discreet", good-nature
> "smiling", mourning "cruel", and so on and so on, through a
> thousand fine phrases which I have now forgotten? It would
> never have occurred to me, unaided, that when Ganderax
> sets himself to correct others he really believes he is doing
> a service to the French language. But that's what he says
> in that article you sent me — "the little marginal notes which
> I have added for the purpose of illustrating and defending
> the French language . . ." "Illustrating?" — no, and "defend-
> ing"? no, too. The only persons who really "defend" the
> French language (or who defended the French Army during
> the Dreyfus Affair) are those who attack it. . . .'[1]

If Marcel Proust had found it so difficult to get a few essays
and articles published, how much more difficult would it be for
him to find a publisher willing to undertake a long work which,
in its first version, looked like running to twelve or fifteen hundred
pages, according to the format adopted? He wanted to issue it in
a single volume so as to produce an effect of massive solidity,
and because, too, the concluding section (which even then was
called *Le Temps retrouvé*) would alone make it possible for readers
to grasp the rigorous design of the whole composition. But the
fashion at that time was for short novels, and what publisher
would be prepared to take so great a risk?

He at first hoped that Calmette, who was a friend of Fasquelle's,
might prevail upon the latter to bring out *La Rercherche du temps*

---

[1] Unpublished extract from a letter in the possession of Madame René Sibilat.

perdu. Negotiations were begun and seemed to promise success. Fasquelle talked of three volumes to be issued at three-monthly intervals. Proust accepted the proposal, though with considerable regret, because 'he couldn't be certain that when I go to bed each night, I shall be alive in the morning'. He suggested as the three titles: *Du Côté de chez Swann* (or, perhaps, *Le Temps perdu*); *Le Côté de Guermantes* and *Le Temps retrouvé*. To Louis de Robert, a novelist whose work he held in high esteem, and who had been one of the few people to see something more than talent in *Les Plaisirs et les Jours*, he wrote:

> I have been working, as you may know, ever since I began to be ill, at a long book which I call a novel because it lacks that quality of the casual which is the mark of a volume of Memoirs (it is casual only in so far as it presents the casual nature of life), the design of which is strongly marked though not easy to grasp because of its complexity. I am quite incapable of telling you what *kind* of novel it is. Some sections of it have a country setting, others varying social backgrounds: some parts are quite family affairs, many are terribly indecent. I have dedicated the whole thing to Calmette, who has promised to get Fasquelle to publish it, and there the matter rests. The whole thing is settled (settled, I mean, between Calmette and me, because I have no idea whether he has had any preliminary discussions with Fasquelle). The position at the moment is this. The novel is so long (though, to my mind, very concise) that it will run to three volumes of four hundred pages each, or, what would be much better, two, one of seven hundred, the other of five. I have been told (not by Calmette whom I have not seen since) that it would be quite useless to ask Fasquelle to bring out a single work in two or three volumes, and that he would *insist* on different titles for each volume and an interval between their dates of publication. I hate the idea, but am told that I should get the same answer no matter what publisher I tried. On the other hand, I am ill, very ill — and consequently in a great hurry to get into print, so that there is this advantage of going to Fasquelle, that he will issue the book (I hope) at once. But I am told,

too, that he goes through all the manuscripts he publishes with a very critical eye, demands modifications, and won't hear of anything that may have the effect of slowing down the action. You, I know, have a wide experience of this sort of thing (whereas I have published nothing but an illustrated volume for Calmann-Lévy for whom the present volume would be far too indecent, and a few translations in the *Mercure*), and I should be very grateful for your advice. Is it your view that, since the book goes to Fasquelle via Calmette, he will be willing to publish it as it stands, with all its lyrical interpolations, and without making changes? (I am prepared to split it into two parts, though, since the development of the subject is very slow, it would be an immense advantage if the first volume could have seven, or six, hundred pages, printed very small, like those of *l'Education*. . . .

Then comes this pathetic postscript:

Don't judge by your own experience as author of an admirable book which is *not* a novel. When you published it you were already well known, I, on the other hand, am known only to a handful of writers. To most men of letters I am *completely unknown*. On the rare occasions when, as the result of some article of mine, readers address letters to me at the *Figaro* office, they are usually forwarded to *Marcel Prévost* — of whose name mine is taken to be a mistaken rendering.

But Calmette (and Proust, always so prompt to suspect a misunderstanding or a quarrel, analysed every word and every thought in order to get at the reasons for this coolness), showed but a small amount of zeal, and Fasquelle little enthusiasm. What lay behind all these delays? Was Fasquelle annoyed with Calmette, and was Marcel Proust being offered up as a sacrifice on the altar of their friendship? That, certainly, was what he feared. Jean Cocteau wrote to Edmond Rostand — one of Fasquelle's 'best sellers' who had considerable influence with the publisher. Rostand, always generous in his attitude to fellow authors, took a hand in the discussions. Fasquelle did not actually refuse the book but, as Proust had feared he would, demanded extensive alterations. Such a condition was enough to terrify and outrage an author who had been making 'alterations' in his novel for the past ten years.

Meanwhile Proust had been venturing on a few timid approaches to the *Nouvelle Revue Française*, which he regarded as being his true spiritual home. He had known Gaston Gallimard for some time. He now sent him several specimen sections of his manuscripts, and these Gallimard showed to the next meeting of his editorial board. But the dedication to Calmette caused offence and, what was even more damning, the members of this exacting group, all obsessed by the idea of literary integrity, looked on Proust as a smart dilettante, whose manuscript, when they glanced through it, gave off a distinctly 'aristocratic smell'.

Proust to the N.R.F.: 'I think I should give you some idea of the shocking nature of the second volume, so that you may be spared the trouble, should it seem to you impossible to publish it, of reading the first. At the end of the first volume (part III), you will make the acquaintance of a certain Monsieur de Fleurus (or de Guray, for I have changed his name more than once) who has been vaguely referred to in the earlier portions of the book as Madame Swann's supposed lover. Now, as in life, where reputations are often groundless and where it often takes us a long time to realize what people really are like, it becomes apparent, but only in the second volume, that this elderly gentleman, so far from being Madame Swann's lover, is a paederast. The character I have painted is, I think, something quite new, that of a virile paederast, attracted by virility in others, hating effeminate young men, hating, indeed, all young men, just as men who have suffered at the hands of women often become misogynists. This character makes only occasional appearances in the volume, which contains so much else that there is no danger of its being taken for a specialized monograph like, for instance, Binet-Valmer's *Lucien* . . . Nor is my treatment of the subject in any way coarse, and it should be fairly clear that the work as a whole reflects a metaphysical and moral outlook. Still, the fact remains that this elderly personage does carry off a porter, and does 'keep' a pianist. It seems to me better to warn you in advance of what might discourage you from publishing the book. . . .'

André Gide, opening the manuscript at random, happened on a passage in which the Narrator described his Aunt Léonie as: 'holding out for me to kiss her sad brow, pale and lifeless . . . through which the vertebrae showed like the points of a crown of thorns or the beads of a rosary'.[1]

What! vertebrae in a forehead! . . . Gide sent in an unfavourable report.

No sooner were negotiations in this direction broken off than something 'detestable' occurred.

Proust to Madame Straus: 'By the mere fact of breaking off these other negotiations, I made it plain that I was willing to accept with resignation the changes on which Fasquelle was insisting. And now, lo and behold, two days ago I get a letter from him which, without any further beating about the bush, says that he can't undertake the book (the whole thing plentifully larded with compliments, but so definite that it is impossible to re-open negotiations — besides, he has had the MS. returned to me) . . . I am afraid that I was only too well justified in my belief that Calmette had never had a promise from Fasquelle, and that that was why he was avoiding me. Whatever the reason, it no longer matters, and I shall have to begin all over again somewhere else, which is a fearful bore. Dismiss the whole thing from your mind. We won't mention it again until I send you a copy of the novel — for I'm going to get it printed even if I have to pay for it . . . I want to give a little token of my gratitude to Calmette (who really has been *very kind*, though he did not understand that it would have been better to do nothing at all than to do things by halves). Can you suggest anything he might find

---

[1] *Swann's Way*, I, translated by C. K. Scott Moncrieff (Chatto & Windus, 1922) – slightly modified.

acceptable, something he could use, for instance, when he is playing cards (a purse? — a cigarette-case — but is he a smoker? — a Bridge-set?). Since I no longer need his help I can make him a little present now without the risk of seeming indelicate. In my present ruined state I don't want to go to more than a thousand or fifteen-hundred francs, though if by spending twice that amount I could be sure of giving him *great* pleasure, I would gladly do so. . . .'

Madame Straus approved the suggestion of a cigarette-case, and Marcel got Tiffany's to make him one — in black watered silk, with an initial in brilliants: 'really very simple and extremely pretty, and its going to cost rather less than four hundred francs . . .' But everything to do with this episode seemed fated to go wrong. The very day after he took his little gift to the *Figaro* office for Calmette, the Congress was due to elect a new President of the French Republic, and Calmette could think of nothing else.

Proust to Madame Straus: '*He has never even thanked me*, which seems so very odd that I am beginning to wonder whether he's ever seen it. I took it to him done up in a parcel: he made an evasive sort of a gesture, and I just left it on his desk. I said to him that it was such a trifle, I hardly dared, etc. — this because, knowing he would realize when he opened the parcel that, on the contrary, it really was rather a precious little thing, I thought I should add nobility to magnificence by appearing to make little of it. He said: "I hope it'll be Poincaré", to which I replied, "well, we can't do anything about it", and kept my eyes fastened on the parcel. His gaze followed mine, but no sooner did it encounter the parcel than, as though in obedience to some centrifugal force, it shied away and focused itself on something else. There was a moment's silence: then he said: "Still, there's just a chance it may be Deschanel." Then we talked about Pams, and, seeing that there was to be no mention of Fasquelle or of the cigarette-case, I got up and left, quite convinced that I should receive a letter next morning, something like: "My dear fellow: a trifle indeed! why, it's an exquisite little example of the jeweller's art!" — but not a line have I had — neither next morning, nor any other morning. . . .'

Fasquelle and the *N.R.F.* being out of the question, Proust, by now thoroughly discouraged, resigned himself to having the book published at his own expense. 'Not only am I prepared to pay all the costs of production, but I am ready to give the publisher an interest in the sales, not from any motive of generosity, but because I want him to have a motive for making a success of it . . .' There is something touching about all his correspondence at this time, partly because it offers us the spectacle of a great writer fighting against incredible difficulties in his struggle to get a masterpiece into print, partly by reason of his obstinate determination to reach, not the handful of friends who had read *Les Plaisirs et les Jours*, but 'the kind of people who take a book with them on a railway journey'.

On the advice of Louis de Robert, who was afraid that if Proust published at his own expense he would be regarded as a dilettante, the manuscript was submitted to yet another firm, Ollendorff, to the manager of which Louis de Robert wrote explaining that this was not a question of an amateur, but of a writer of first-rate ability. A fortnight later, Louis de Robert received an answer from Monsieur Humblot, the managing director of Messrs. Ollendorff. It ran as follows: 'Dear friend: I may be thicker skinned than most, but I just can't understand why anyone should take thirty pages to describe how he tosses about in bed because he can't get to sleep. I clutched my head. . . .'

This time, Proust was deeply and legitimately wounded:

I find Monsieur Humblot's letter (which I return herewith) completely idiotic. What I have tried to do is to create about my first chapter (and I suppose it is the first chapter he means, because, frankly, I entirely fail to *recognize myself* in what he writes) an atmosphere of semi-wakefulness, the point of which does not emerge until later, but which I have elaborated as far as my very mediocre gifts of penetration permit. The significance, as should be obvious, is not that I want to describe how I twist and turn in bed — which I could certainly do in much fewer pages — but that the twisting and turning provides me with a means of analysis. Fasquelle, I know, doesn't agree with him, because, in the letter — whose destruction I shall never cease to regret — he said: 'What a pity that you didn't make a whole volume out of that one chapter which you devote to describing a sickly childhood, and which is so infinitely curious and remarkable!' The part, of course, which contains the indecencies moves, I know, much more rapidly, but doubtless Monsieur Humblot never got as far as that. I am afraid that a great many readers may agree with him. But have people like that never bothered to read — well, Barrès, for instance? I very much doubt it: or Maeterlinck? If one sent Monsieur Humblot to *La Colline Inspirée* of the one, or to *La Mort* of the other, being careful to suppress the author's name in each case, I feel that he would 'whittle them down' to such an extent that very little would remain, and that he really *would* have to clutch his head. . . .

But, in a very short while, Proust recovered the serenity of an author who knows that his work is good. 'What does all this amount to? All of us, more or less, suffer from the same sort of thing. I have known France, even after he became famous, France whose limpid genius seems to embrace all readers in a warm smile, to have articles refused by the *Temps* on the ground that nobody could make head or tail of them, and the space given to heaven knows whom. I have been told that the *Revue des Deux Mondes* found his novel *Thaïs* so badly written that, after asking his permission to discontinue serialization, they said that in any case they couldn't find room for the usual instalment. Those same organs today would fight like tiger-cats over a scrap of France's prose in no way different from the things they once refused, and you can take my word for it that it's not because he is more talented now than he was then. . . .'

After this new failure to place the book, Proust hesitated no longer about proceeding with his plan of publishing at his own expense. His friend, René Blum, a brother of Léon, a man with a smiling face and a fair, drooping moustache, who was gifted with taste and much natural kindliness, and whom Marcel had met round about 1900 at the house of Antoine and Emmanuel Bibesco, knew Bernard Grasset, a recent recruit to publishing. Grasset was young, without very much capital, but intelligent, full of a noble passion for his craft, and he had recently discovered Giraudoux. Proust asked Blum to act as go-between, and not to waste a moment. 'I have been working for a long time at this book: I have put the best of myself into it, and what it needs now is that a monumental tomb should be completed for its reception before my own is filled . . . Don't say to me: "My dear chap — Grasset will be enchanted at the opportunity to take you on at his own expense..." — I am very ill, and I must have certainty and peace of mind...' René Blum at once took a hand, and the manuscript was sent to Bernard Grasset. Free to make his own decisions, since he was paying for everything, Proust wanted to publish a first volume of seven hundred pages, printed *solid*, without breaks even to indicate passages of dialogue, 'because that', he said, 'will make for textual continuity...' Louis de Robert managed to persuade him to limit the first volume to five hundred pages, and to agree to a small number of paragraph divisions.

The title of a literary masterpiece seems, to its enthusiastic readers, to be so inevitable a part of the whole, so much bound in with the universe the book creates, that they find great difficulty in realizing that it was chosen only after long deliberation.

Proust to Louis de Robert: 'What I want is some very simple, very colourless, title. The *general* title is, as you know, to be *A la recherche du temps perdu*. Would you have any objection to *Charles Swann* for the first volume, in two parts (if Grasset agrees to produce two volumes, boxed)? If, however, I have got to have a single volume of five hundred pages, then I am against it, because it will not contain the conclusion of *Swann*, and will therefore be deceptive. How would you like *Avant que le jour se lève?* (I don't). I have had to give up the idea of *Les Intermittences du cœur* (the original title), *Les Colombes poignardées, Le Passé intermittent, L'Adoration perpétuelle, Le Septième Ciel* and *A l'Ombre des jeunes filles en fleurs*, all of which, actually, will be chapter-headings in the third volume. I think I've explained to you already that *Du Côté*

de chez Swann refers to the two "Ways" at Combray. You
know how one says in the country — "Are you going Monsieur
Rostand's way?". . . .
'P.S. What do you think of *Jardins dans une tasse de thé*, or
L'Age des Noms? Then, for the second, *L'Age des Mots*, and,
for the third, *L'Age des Choses*? My own choice is *Charles
Swann*, but with something additional to show that it does not
cover the whole of *Swann: Premiers crayons de Charles Swann*.'

At last, on November 12th, 1913, the *Temps* carried a long
article by Élie-Joseph Bois, in which it was stated that *La Recherche du temps perdu* would be published the next day over the
imprint of Bernard Grasset. The rare favour of this piece of
publicity had been won by Marie Scheikevitch, a friend of
Proust's who was on intimate terms with Adrien Hébrard, the
editor of the *Temps*. Bois had found the author in bed in a room,
'the shutters of which are never opened'. Proust told him how
much he regretted having to break up his book. 'Publishers no
longer issue literary work in several volumes. I am like somebody
who owns a piece of tapestry which is too large for the rooms he
lives in, and has to have it cut up. . .' The Boulevard Haussmann
had furnished this very Proustian image! After this opening, he
explained that his book was an essay on the subject of psychology
in Time, and that the characters, by the way in which they
changed, would give the feeling of the passage of time. 'You
might, perhaps, call my work an attempt to achieve a number of
novels of the unconscious: I shouldn't in the least mind saying
Bergsonian novels, if I thought that was accurate, but it isn't.'

Although, in this interview, he expressed his gratitude to Calmette, to whom *Swann* was dedicated, Marcel, who had watched
over the birth of his novel with a father's solicitude, expressed
himself as feeling rather sad that the *Figaro*, a friendly journal,
was showing no very great anxiety to be of service to the book.
Marcel Proust to Robert Dreyfus: 'I am far from wanting to be talked
about, but this is a really important book . . . If you write anything
about it, I do hope you won't indulge in such epithets as "subtle"
and "delicate", and that you won't draw attention to *Les Plaisirs
et les Jours*. This is a powerful work — at least that is what it sets

out to be . . .' A powerful work . . . nothing could be more true, but the readers who realized that fact, even among those who loved it in the early days, were very few. There was much praise of its minute detail. But the only thing in which he took pride was his discovery and exposition of certain general laws. 'My book is not microscopic but telescopic', he said.

The *Figaro* made generous atonement for its sin of omission. It published not only a paragraph by Robert Dreyfus and a review by Francis Chevassu, but a long front-page article by Lucien Daudet, who was 'wonderfully kind' and wrote precisely what Proust would have liked to write himself. But with the knowledge of flowers and country life which all members of the Daudet family possessed, he pointed out to the author, in a long private letter, that (1) one doesn't eat a chicken on the same day as it is killed: (2) that verbena and heliotrope are not in flower at the same time as the hawthorn. Marcel attempted to justify himself by describing his conscientious researches into Gaston Bonnier's *Flore* which, said he, had already informed him that he must not dress the Combray hedgerows with hawthorn and wild roses in the same month.

Marcel Proust to Lucien Daudet: 'Dear old man: I awoke in an almost dying condition to hear myself summoned by you from the columns of the *Figaro*, like one of the departed whom you long ago described, to the Last Judgment, and rose in my bed as though in response to the Archangel in the Porch of Notre Dame . . .' Meanwhile, Jacques-Émile Blanche, another arch-angel, sounded a blast in the *Écho de Paris*, Maurice Rostand wrote in *Comoedia* and Souday in the *Temps*. 'Souday', says Léon-Pierre Quint, 'was the first to set the seal on what, a few years later, was being regarded as a species of revelation.' The article, as a matter of fact, had been commissioned from Souday by Hébrard, the editor, once more at the instigation of Marie Scheikevitch. This kind of luck does sometimes come a critic's way.

But the public responded scarcely at all to these archangelic trumpets. Friends repeated, in and out of season and quite rightly, the word 'genius', but readers in general remained rebellious. 'It is only', they said, 'what a few men of the world think about one of their number.' Those who knew the author by sight, and read these resounding praises, said: 'What, Marcel Proust? Little Proust of the Ritz?', and shrugged their shoulders. Anatole France, who had received a copy of *Swann* with this inscription: 'To the first of all masters, the greatest and the best beloved', confessed that he could not read it, and remarked later to Madame Alphonse Daudet who loved the book and spoke to him about its author, 'I used to know him. I rather think I wrote a Preface for one of his early books. He's the son of a Medical Officer of Health. I gather that he has become, most unfortunately, a terrible neurasthenic. He never leaves his bed, and keeps his shutters closed all day long with the electric light burning. I don't begin to understand the book. He used to be a charming and witty fellow, with a keen gift of observation. But I long ago lost sight of him. . . .'[1]

'As to Robert de Montesquiou,' wrote Madame de Clermont-Tonnerre, 'nothing will make him abandon the transcendental and patronising *rôle* which he has adopted, once and for all, towards Marcel . . . "I have no idea", said he, "whether this irreparable young man will one day give the measure of his powers — to use a much abused locution — in a published work. I have, I confess, my doubts, because his powers consist precisely in his having none to show. He is the author of a laborious and inextricable book for which, at first, he found a charming title, *A la recherche du temps perdu*, though for this he afterwards substituted another which is both extravagant and bad . . . He once made a phrase about me which is a good deal more apt than any of those coined by my contemporaries: he said: 'You rise above hostility like a gull above the storm. Were you deprived of that sustaining pressure, you would miss it' . . ." ' In Montesquiou's eyes Proust existed merely by reason of the praise that he had given to Montesquiou.

The author himself, once *Swann* had been launched, suffered from a feeling of failure. 'The words *triumphant success* make me smile rather bitterly (*grâce à Dieu, mon malheur passe mon esperance*). Could you see me now you would find nothing triumphant in my appearance.' Some of the compliments that he received from

---

[1] Quoted by MARCEL LE GOFF in *Anatole France à La Béchellerie* (Alban Michel' Paris, 1947), pp. 331-2.

friends to whom he had sent *Swann* proved, unfortunately, that they had not read it. *Marcel Proust to Madame Gaston de Caillavet:* 'Thank you for what you say about my book. I have had so many vexations since I wrote it, and have thought about it so little, that I may have forgotten a good deal. It may, therefore, be I who am at fault in believing that I nowhere wrote of a 'fervent and dis-illusioned First Communion', or anywhere mentioned a First Communion at all. But I am inclined to think that it is you who have got things mixed. However that may be, *felix culpa*, as Renan once said, because the mistake has brought me your memories of your own First Communion, and I find them full of poetry. Thank you again for your kind reply, the promptness of which adds much to its kindness. Don't think me too much of a pedant if I quote the Romans and say: *Qui cito dat, bis dat* — who gives quickly, gives twice over. . . .'[1]

But the game wasn't, he thought, yet won. Writing in June to Madame Straus, who had been 'so very sweet' as to say that she wanted to see more of his characters — in whom she had a very special interest, Marcel having told her that she was to play a part in the volumes still to come — he announced the imminent publication of the next, the proofs of which he had already re-turned to Grasset: 'Don't let yourself be put off: there are passages on love, and the pains of love, which I think you will consider to be not without merit. You will find a lovers' quarrel, and a scene in which a woman is described as she appears to two different men, one of whom is in love with her, while the other isn't. I think I have managed to get some genuine humanity and sense of suffering into the episode. But I am ashamed of talking about myself like this. . . .'

Every since the appearance of the first volume, Grasset, with the support of Louis de Robert, had been trying to get the Prix Goncourt for *Swann*. Léon Daudet's friendship made the idea less wildly fantastic than it might otherwise have seemed. All of a sudden, Proust began to centre his hopes upon the award, so eager was he for a wide circle of readers. Should this be held against him as vanity? Can one seriously call vain a man who for so long had faced isolation and obscurity? It is fairer to say that

[1] From an unpublished letter.

it was no more than the natural ambition of a writer who knows the value of the seed he has sown, and does everything in his power to protect the still fragile shoot. Afraid lest his reputation as a rich, or at least as a comfortably-off, man might lose him the prize, he wrote round to all and sundry saying that he was ruined. 'You will say that my personal poverty is irrelevant, seeing that in any case I belong to a rich family, that I cut a figure in the great world, and that even if I *have* got no money I give the appearance of wealth . . .' As matters turned out, he was scarcely even considered at the first meeting of the Jury, and the Prix Goncourt for 1913 went elsewhere.

But support from quite another quarter, which meant much more to him, was forthcoming — from no less an organization than the *N.R.F.* The 'big guns' of the board, whose good opinion he had desired with as much eagerness as that with which he had once courted the young girls of Balbec, had, from motives of literary self-righteousness, met his overtures with snubs. A novel bearing such obvious marks of the Right Bank set the hackles of this publishing house of the Left Bank rising — as Fernandez has pointed out. When, however, the book appeared, Gallimard and Rivière sent a copy to Henri Ghéon with a request that he should write something on it for the *Nouvelle Revue Française*. Ghéon was quite 'carried away' and spoke of it with enthusiasm to Rivière. He, in his turn, passed the word to Gide who, so far, had only skimmed the manuscript, and got him to read the whole volume. Gide, completely won over, wrote with characteristic sincerity to Proust: 'For the last few days I haven't been able to lay your book down. I am deep in the waters of delight, I wallow. I only wish that my passion for it didn't cause me so much pain . . . The *N.R.F.'s* refusal of it is the worst blunder they ever made, and (for I — to my eternal shame — was largely responsible for their decision) sorrow and remorse will torment me until the end of my life . . . It is not enough to say that I have come to love it. What I feel for it and for you is a sort of burning affection, a feeling of admiration, an adoration of no usual kind . . .'[1] To this letter Proust replied:

[1] From a letter published by Léon Pierre-Quint in *Comment parut 'Du Côté de chez Swann'* (Kra), p. 140.

'My dear Gide: I have long known that certain varieties of pleasure come one's way only when one has been deprived of others less important . . . But for the *N.R.F.*'s refusal — its repeated refusals — I should never have heard from you . . . My joy at reading what you say goes far beyond the pleasure I might have derived from being published by the *N.R.F.* . . .' But even this satisfaction was now, at last, to be offered him. The editorial board of the *N.R.F.* expressed itself, 'unanimously and with enthusiasm' in favour of publishing the two remaining volumes. *Proust to Gide:* 'For this honour I have always, as you know, been ambitious . . . but even if my [contract] allowed me full liberty, I don't think I could take advantage of it for fear of making so ill a requital to Grasset for all his friendliness. . . .'

In its June and July numbers for 1914, the *Nouvelle Revue Française* printed long extracts from *Le Côté de Guermantes* (which, in their final form, were actually to form part of *A l'Ombre des jeunes filles en fleurs*). Gallimard renewed, even more earnestly, his offer to publish the next volume and any successors that it might have. Fasquelle showed a change of heart. Grasset, to whom Proust, overcoming his scruples of friendship, expressed the wish that his work should be transferred to Gallimard, was loud in his disappointment. And so it came about that the author who had been refused by so many publishing houses, became the one author for whom every publisher in Paris was ready to give his eyes. In August 1914 came the war, and one of its results was the temporary closing down of Grasset's business. Proust used this as an excuse to resume full liberty of action. Was it not his duty, he said to Grasset, to do his best for his book? *Marcel Proust to Bernard Grasset:* 'In your firmament my book is but as a grain of sand. For me it is everything. I have no idea whether I shall live long enough to see it all published, and it is only natural that, with the instinct of an insect whose days are numbered, I should be in a hurry to find some sure refuge for this child born of my entrails who is destined to be my sole representative on earth . . .' Grasset, very generously, gave way, and *Du Côté de chez Swann* 'migrated to Gallimard'. The war delayed, for five years, the appearance of the remaining volumes of *La Recherche du temps perdu*. This enforced interval gave it time to proliferate.

THE EFFECT OF THE WAR ON PROUST'S NOVEL

Proust's undeviating attitude to the war was that of the French-men of Saint-André des Champs. *Marcel Proust to Paul Morand:* 'I am not going to talk to you about the war. It has, alas, become so much a part of myself that I can't stand back and look at it as something apart. I can no more discuss the hopes and fears with which it fills me than I could discuss those feelings that lie so deep as to be indistinguishable from myself. For me it is not so much an object, in the philosophical meaning of the word, as a substance interposed between me and all objects. As men once lived in God, so do I live in this war . . .' Marcel Proust, the man, never spoke of the front or of the armies, save in the terms consecrated by custom, partly because he had always accepted the ritual and the conventions of his world, partly because he was 'more than usually sensitive to feelings of honour, even to specific points of honour'. But, if the citizen in him, and the man of the world, behaved with deliberate conformity, the novelist observed, ruth-lessly and without self-deception, those collective passions which are so like the passions of individuals, and noted the way in which the high temperature generated by war was distorting classes and nations. In the characters of his book the war produced a number of highly dramatic changes. Saint-Loup became the hero he had always been without knowing it: Brichot passed from the criticism of literature to that of strategy: Monsieur de Charlus remembered his Bavarian ancestors: Madame Verdurin made use of an ex-cessive chauvinism to land her at last within the portals of High Society.

To Lucien Daudet Proust pointed out the hypocritical 'squin-neries' of the back-area folk, the women's 'so very warlike tunics', and the high leggings which they were adopting in imitation of those worn by 'our dear lads at the front'. He was irritated by the idiocy of journalists who talked about nothing but 'Boches' and 'Kultur', who refused to listen to *Tristan* or *The Ring*, and waxed violent over the thought of anybody learning German. 'With one or two honourable exceptions, the men of letters who think that they can best "do their bit" by writing, are behaving very badly . . . As to the big-wigs they are as ignorant as babes. I don't know whether you read an article by General O. . . . on the origin of the word "Boche", which, according to him, goes no further back than last September, when our men, etc. . . . I can only assume that he has lived exclusively in the "best circles", otherwise he would know, as I do, that domestic servants, and the "People" generally, have always said "Une tête de Boche" and "C'est un sale Boche". In their mouths it just sounds rather comic (for instance, in that excellent account given by Paulhan's mechanic). But when Academicians start saying "Boche" in tones of false heartiness, with the intention of talking down to the "People", like grown-ups who use baby-talk in their dealings with children . . . it really is rather more than I can stomach.'

The war was striking hard at all around him. His brother Robert, serving as an M.O. at Verdun, was wounded very early on and got a mention in dispatches. Reynaldo was at the front, behaving with a reckless daring that worried his friends. Bertrand de Fénelon (the *Nonelef* of the *Ocsebibs*), the 'best, the bravest, the most intelligent of men', had been killed on December 17th, 1914. Gaston de Caillavet died on January 13th, 1915.

Marcel Proust to Madame Gaston de Caillavet: 'In the midst of all the griefs by which I am truly being overwhelmed . . . the thought of Gaston has never left me for a single day, and I cannot get used to the idea that life, which he was so well fitted to enjoy, has been taken from him in the high season of his youth. I have so clear a picture of the time when you were engaged, of your marriage; and the knowledge that you are a widow, you who have always remained for me the young girl whom once I knew, tears at my heart. I have no idea whether I shall be able to see you, sweet though I should find such a meeting. I have a medical board next week. In my present state of health I shall find it so exhausting that I shall have to prepare for it by resting completely, and, when it's over (assuming that they don't "take" me, which I can't be sure about) I shall quite certainly be ill. But if I do feel strong enough one of these days, and especially if my

current daily crises finish sufficiently early, I will telephone
you at once. It is so bitter a grief to me to have to weep in
solitude for Gaston, that it would do me good to have you
here. I have thought so constantly of his daughter, in whom
he took such pride, dear young Mademoiselle Simone, that
I simply don't know whether I have written to her or not,
so often have I sent her a letter in imagination. If I haven't
(but I am sure I have, though the letter is probably lying
somewhere in the muddle next my bed) tell her that she
might put all the letters she has received end to end and still
not find as much constant thought about her as there is in
my heart. . . .'

He tried to see his women friends:

. . . Having managed to get up yesterday (Friday) evening,
I telephoned. There was no answer. I came round on
chance, but by the time I had dressed it was too late, and I
didn't reach your triple-arched doorway until twenty to
eleven (or a quarter to). The whole place was in darkness;
not a light on any of the floors. I kept the car standing there
for a full hour with its engine running, just in case a curtain
might be drawn aside, but, since nothing happened, didn't
dare ring the bell in case you had gone to bed . . . The last
time I came to No. 12 [Avenue Hoche] was one evening when
I walked back, very late, with Gaston. I was deeply moved
on that occasion by the sight of a house which brought back
so many memories, but that emotion was as nothing compared
to the flood of feeling that overwhelmed me the other evening.
Now, it is not merely a matter of sentimental memories, but
of irreparable loss. I have no idea when I shall be able to
leave my bed, and when that time does come, you will
almost certainly have gone away. But perhaps it is better so.
For me *the dead still live.* That is certainly so where I have
loved, and also where I have lost a friend. I can't explain
what I mean in a letter. When the whole of *Swann* has
appeared, if you ever manage to read it, you will understand.
I wrote to you the other day; I hope that you got my letter;
I have no idea what happens when I am left alone here in

bed. I think with the utmost tenderness of you, of your
daughter, of Gaston. . . .[1]

Though Marcel had for some time, owing to his chronic ill-
health, been removed from the Army List, he still had to attend
medical boards. His condition could not for a moment be in
doubt, but: 'the examinations are often hasty and slap-dash.
Reynaldo told me that he was present at one interview at which
the following little scene was played: "What's the matter with you?"
— "I have heart-disease" — "Nonsense — passed for service" —
whereupon the sick man fell down dead. It is more than possible
that something of the sort will happen in my case. But if so, it
will certainly not be sorrow at leaving that will kill me. The sort
of existence I have been living for close on twelve years is too
gloomy for me to mind the idea of changing it . . .' What he really
dreaded were those visits to the medical authorities which deprived him of the few hours he might have had for sleep. As the
result of a curious mistake, he was told to report to the Invalides
at half-past three in the morning. It was a clerical error, but
Proust regarded it as the most natural and admirable thing in the
world.

Beneath the threat of Taubes and Zeppelins he continued to
live his night-bird existence. He would go off to Ciro's, of an
evening, to an accompaniment of sirens, with some friend,
Jacques Truelle, for instance, a young diplomat who had talked
intelligently about *Swann*. The conversation would be good,
Proust mingling historical characters higgledy-piggledy with
those of fiction. 'He would combine the Maréchal de Villars with
Colonel Chabert or General Mangin, Dr. Cottard with the
Médecin de Campagne, Madame de Guermantes with Madame de
Maufrigneuse. Feeling that he might be tired after meeting so
many people, I would suggest going home. His reply would be:
"as a matter of fact I *am* feeling *quite* dead. What a bore it is!
We've said nothing about Cardinal Fleury and the d'Espards.
We must come here again soon and discuss them — or Albertine,
since she seems to interest you". . . .'

He would be taken back to his front door, and there he would

[1] From an unpublished letter.

stand for a while talking of his characters in the detached manner of a Balzac. 'No,' he would say, 'you're entirely wrong if you think that the Duchesse de Guermantes was a good-natured woman. She was capable of being absent-mindedly kind, but . . .' On another later occasion, he said to Guiche: 'The Duchesse de Guermantes was rather like a tough old hen that I once mistook for a bird of paradise . . . By making her a powerful vulture I do at least keep people from taking her for a magpie.' — 'Why are you so hard on Monsieur de Charlus? When you know him better, I think you'll find him rather fun to talk to. Still, there is, I admit, something rather nasty about his charlism. But most of the time he's kindly enough, and frequently eloquent. . . .'

Once he went to fetch Marie Scheikevitch. 'This evening', he said, 'I'm going to drag you away. We'll go to Ciro's if you like . . . but *please* don't catch cold. Whatever you do, don't look at my collar. If you see some cotton wool sticking out, that's Céleste's fault. She *would* stuff it in, despite my protests. . . No need for you to call a taxi, mine's waiting in the street. And don't be afraid your feet will be cold. I told them to put a hot-water bottle in for you. How nice of you to wear that lovely white fox . . . Sure you're not ashamed of being seen out with somebody so badly dressed?' Then, to the head waiter, 'Have you some fillets of sole done in white wine? some beef *à la môde*? a nice salad? After that I recommend a lovely creamy chocolate soufflé.' (Marcel's guests almost always had the same things to eat — dishes that he would have liked himself, had his state of health allowed him to indulge in them.) 'Oh don't bother about me, I eat hardly any-thing — just bring me a glass of water. I have some tablets with me which I mustn't forget to take . . . and some coffee, good, strong coffee. I'll drink several cups, if you don't object. . . .'

Often, too, driving through the darkened streets of war-time Paris, he would join the Princesse Soutzo at the Ritz, where, when Paul Morand (her future husband) was in town he would dine with the two of them. Edmond Jaloux has given us a delight-ful picture of Proust in 1917:

There was, in his very physical appearance, in the atmosphere that he created about himself, something so remarkable that, seeing him, one had a feeling akin to amazement. He did not belong to the common run of mankind, but always produced the impression that he was a figure of nightmare, or of a different age, almost of a different world — but of what world? He could never bring himself to abandon the fashions of his youth. His collar was very high and stiff, his shirt-front starched, the opening of his waistcoat generous, and he habitually wore a very narrow tie. He would come forward with an air of embarrassment, of shy astonishment: or, rather, it would be more accurate to say that he did not come forward at all — but just materialized. It was impossible to keep one's eyes from him, impossible not to be struck by his extraordinary countenance which seemed, quite naturally, to be more than life-size.

He was rather sturdily built and had a full face. The first thing one noticed about him was the quality of his eyes. They were remarkable eyes, feminine eyes, oriental eyes, with a tender, ardent, caressing yet passive expression that reminded one of a hind or an antelope. The upper lids were slightly hooded (like Jean Lorrain's) and their shadowed orbits were so dark, so excessively large, that they gave to the whole face a look of passion and ill-health. He had thick black hair which was always too long and seemed to fit his head like a skull-cap of some heavy material. One could not but help noticing, too, the exaggerated curvature of his chest which Léon Daudet likened to the breast-bone of a chicken — pointing out that he had this feature, too, in common with Jean Lorrain.

But this description leaves me unsatisfied. That curious something, I don't quite know what, which set him apart from other men, is missing from it — a mixture of physical solidity, winged words and airy thoughts, of ceremonious manners and casualness, of apparent strength and femininity — with a hint of reticence, of vagueness, of absent-mindedness. It was as though he were making an alibi of politeness, a screen behind which he could legitimately hide, withdrawing into the secret intimacies of himself, into the anguished mystery of his temperament. One felt that one was in the presence of somebody who was both a child and a very old mandarin.

All through this particular dinner he was, as always when he had finished complaining, extremely gay, talkative and charming. He had a most attractive laugh. It seemed to burst from him, but he at once concealed it behind his hand like a small boy overcome by mirth in class, who is afraid that the master will catch him. Was it that he thought his gaiety so extravagant that he ought to hide it, or had that gesture of his a more immediate significance?

The Duc de Guiche left very soon after dinner, and I was left alone with Marcel Proust in the large vestibule of the Ritz. It was at the time when the Gothas were carrying out raids over Paris. . . .

Proust made notes for use in his novel of 'the Paris sky at night, during a raid' as, formerly, he had jotted down descriptions of 'stormy days at Balbec'. He recorded how the planes — to which he always gave their full appellation of *aeroplanes*, 'climbed like rockets, how the searchlights wandered about the sectioned sky like a powdering of pale stars or moving milky ways, like bright jets of towering water, seeming like a reflection on the clouds of the fountains in the Place de la Concorde or the Tuileries Gardens'.

When he was not well enough to go out, Henri Bardac and a few other friends used to dine at his bedside off roast chicken and mashed potatoes. One evening Reynaldo, on one of his rare periods of leave, suddenly turned up about midnight and sat playing Schubert, Mozart and scraps from the *Meistersinger*. About four o'clock in the morning, Proust asked for the 'little phrase'. Some time later, Bardac asked Reynaldo where the little phrase actually came from. 'Most of it', said Reynaldo, 'is a passage from Saint-Saens' Sonata in D Minor, but Marcel has embroidered it with things he has remembered from Franck, Fauré and even Wagner.'

The effect of the war on the novel was profound and surprising. When the life of the world is proceeding normally, a book breaks free of its author as soon as it is published: the umbilical cord is cut, and new stimulus produces new works. But because *La*

Recherche du temps perdu could not appear, it went on developing in a pathological manner. All the cells of that magnificent and monstrous body proliferated at will. As in one of Piranesi's engravings, growing things and creepers burst through the walls of the original construction.

Professor Feuillerat has studied the extent and nature of these developments by comparing the proofs of the second volume as printed by Grasset in 1914 with the final version as published by the *N.R.F.* The conclusions which he drew from his researches are as follows. Contrary to what has been said by most critics, Proust, whose mind was lucid, logical and trained in the classics of French literature, had constructed his novel on very simple lines: the *Côté de chez Swann* (or, the middle classes): the *Côté de Guermantes* (or, the aristocracy): the *Temps retrouvé* (or, the reconciliation of the two 'Ways' by *l'Adoration pérpetuelle* (in other words, by aesthetic contemplation).

But he had begun his book when he was thirty-four and, not only because of the war, but because the work took so long, did not publish the second volume until he was forty-eight. In the course of this long interval he had changed a good deal. The war (and life) had revealed to him a whole world of evil instincts which, formerly, he had not suspected. 'The man who re-read the pages he had written when the bloom almost of childhood was still upon him, was someone whose mind had been enriched by an abnormally rapid rush of experience, someone who was infinitely older than his age.'[1] All the characters, especially those connected with the Guermantes Way, took on much darker colours. The Duchesse de Guermantes turned completely rotten. Madame de Marsantes revealed, beneath a deceptive kindliness of manner, the incurable pride of the aristocrat. Robert de Saint-Loup, formerly so charming, became one of Jupien's clients. What had been a fairy-story of youth was turned into a mature and misanthropic novel. Many of the additions took the form of psychological and philosophical dissertations, in which the author commented upon the actions of his characters. One could extract from the finished book a whole series of essays in the

[1] ALBERT FEUILLERAT, *Comment Marcel Proust a composé son roman* (Yale University Press, New Haven, U.S.A., 1934; London, Oxford University Press), *passim.*

manner of Montaigne: on the function of music — on novelty
in the arts — on the beauty of style — on the restricted number
of human types — on instinct in medicine, etc. Proust the First
(says Feuillerat) had worked on the assumption that the intelligence should have nothing to do with the construction of a work
of art. Instinct, intuition, involuntary memory should reign
supreme. Proust the Second articulated his thoughts with such
words as 'so' and 'consequently': he made use of a number of
formulae familiar to us from Balzac — *'To cut a long story short'* . . .
'This reply of my father's demands a few words of explanation . . .'
even Balzac's famous *'this is why . . .'* the reappearance of
which in Proust has been studied by Pierre Abraham. What it
all amounts to, says Feuillerat, is that Proust proceeded in
precisely the same manner as those ordinary novelists whose too .
humble submission to the laws of logical thinking he had criticized
so harshly.

Simultaneously with a change of thought came a change of
style. It lost 'its pristine bloom and mystery, its once musical
character. The vocabulary became abstract'. Proust himself
wrote: 'Very often authors in whom the working of mysterious
truths has ceased to operate, write, after they have reached a
certain age, only with the intelligence, and the older they grow
the more powerful do the claims of the intelligence become. For
that reason, the books of their maturity may have greater
power, but they have it at the expense of a certain density of
texture. . . .'

Just as a geologist, when confronted with a stretch of ground
which has suffered a convulsion, tries to determine from the
study of fossils and the examination of rock structure the quality
of the primary, secondary and tertiary deposits, so does Professor
Feuillerat, on the evidence of his observations and on the strength
of certain general laws, recover from beneath the immense weight
of the ten volumes with which the original work had been overlaid,
the probable form of the Third Volume as it had been originally
conceived by Proust at the time when Grasset printed the plan
of the first three instalments.

DILETTANTE BECOMES A MASTER

For Publication in 1914
A la recherche du temps perdu
Le Côté des Guermantes

(Chez Madame Swann: Noms de pays: le pays: — Premiers crayons de Monsieur de Charlus et de Robert de Saint-Loup: — Noms de personnes: La Duchesse de Guermantes: — Le salon de Madame de Villeparisis.)

Un vol. in-18 jésus .... 3 fr. 50

A la recherche du temps perdu
Le Temps Retrouvé

(A l'ombre des jeunes filles en fleurs: — La Princesse de Guermantes: — Monsieur de Charlus et les Verdurins: — Mort de ma grandmère: — Les intermittences du cœur: — Les 'Vices' et les 'Vertus' de Padoue et de Combray: — Madame de Cambremer: — Mariage de Saint-Loup: — l'Adoration perpétuelle.)

Un vol. in-18 jésus .... 3 fr. 50

Albert Feuillerat's study is extremely ingenious. He proceeds rather in the manner of a literary Sherlock Holmes. He bases his investigation on: (*a*) The Narrator's age (whenever he shows himself to be a man of experience and reveals an extensive knowledge of matters concerned with love, the passages in question must belong to the second version). (*b*) The state of health of the Narrator who, in the first version, was not addicted to narcotics, did not lose his memory, and was not obsessed by thoughts of death. (*c*) A note of disillusionment, and a hostile attitude towards his characters. (*d*) All allusions, needless to say, to events occurring later than 1912. (*e*) The author's intensified interest in class differences and social evolution. (*f*) Finally, the style and the Table of Contents itself. By employing this method, Monsieur Feuillerat has managed to extract from the two thousand five hundred pages which he has examined the five hundred which he describes as comprising the original version. He has accomplished, very skilfully, an enormous labour of erudition, though his conclusions must, by definition, remain conjectural.

It is quite clear that Marcel Proust's 'Summa' shared its author's life and grew older as he grew older. That must happen in the case of any extended work. True, this process of slow maturing somewhat blurred the outlines, though at the same time it gave to the novel that especial beauty which belongs to all buildings the construction of which has covered a long period and shows a mixture of styles. We may, for instance, see in our examination of some château how the medieval towers enhanced the beauty of the main block which dates, perhaps, from the reign of Louis XIII. No one would dream of denying that conscious intelligence plays a far larger part in the novel than Proust had at first intended. He was perfectly well aware of that: 'I realized, however, that such truths as the intelligence deduces from a direct study of reality are not to be entirely disdained, for they can provide a setting, less pure maybe, but nevertheless coloured by feeling, for those impressions which are brought to us from outside Time, by an essential unity of sensations belonging simultaneously to the past and the present. More valuable though these may be, their occurrence is so occasional, so rare, that no work of art can be constructed from them alone. I felt within myself the pressure of a vast number of truths concerned with human passions, human character and social manners, which could be used in just that way. . . .'

When one reads Feuillerat, three objections at once spring to mind. The first is this: that the evolution of the characters and the Narrator's increasing misanthropy formed part of the original plan, and that the passage of time could, in Proust's opinion, be made perceptible only through the medium of such changes. 'I share your pain', he wrote to a friend, 'in seeing Swann becoming less sympathetic and even somewhat ridiculous . . . but art means a perpetual sacrifice of feelings to truth.'

The second is that the *Notebooks* show clearly how Proust's earlier style could be just as dry, just as 'intelligent', as some of the pages that he wrote at the end of his life. Proust's first sketches were often flat. It was by re-writing the same passages again and again that he imparted to them, by applying successive 'washes', a translucent softness of texture.

Finally, wherever Proust has had time to revise, his style shows the same sort of finish as we find in the first *Swann*. The *Côté de Guermantes*, which he worked over *in toto* is just as fine in quality as *Swann*. In the final volumes, which death did not allow him to re-read and re-touch, the only passages which resemble the 'long-drawn-out, sinuous and inordinately extended phrases of Chopin' are those belonging to the first version — for instance, the whole of the final section of *Le Temps retrouvé*. In just such a way may we see, emerging from the surface of a sea that has covered a drowned continent, islands shining in the soft light of the moon and crowned by palm groves, islands which are the summits of submerged mountain-ranges.

We know that the first drafts which Barrès used to dictate contained the facts which he wished to communicate, but lacked his style. 'And now,' he said to Tharaud, 'I've got to start on the music . . .' whereupon, he would set himself to weave about a banal theme those grave and lovely harmonies which turned the final version into genuine Barrès. The same sort of thing occurred with Proust. There is no reason whatever for thinking that towards the end of his life he had lost his magic touch, but death came to him before he could take up his draft and 'start on the music'. Had it not been for the war, his book, published in the form given to it at the moment of initial inspiration, would have been shorter and considerably closer to the classical ideal, but it would have lacked that monstrous quality of excess which is what makes it unique.

III

PEACE AND THE PRIZE

On November 11th, 1918, Proust wrote to Madame Straus: 'We have shared too many thoughts about this war to make it possible for us not to exchange a tender word on the evening of Victory — rejoicing because of it, but saddened, too, because of those we loved who are not here to see it. What a wonderful *allegro presto* in the finale after the infinite slowness of the first movement and of its subsequent developments! What a superb dramatist Destiny is, or Man, who has been made its instrument! . . .'

The crowds which had filled the streets that day had enormously interested him, because, seeing them, he had found it easier to envisage those of the Revolution. 'But however great may be the joy of this immense, this unexpected, victory, we mourn so many dead that certain forms of gaiety are unsuited for such a celebration. In spite of myself I find the lines of Victor Hugo echoing in my mind:

> Le bonheur, douce amie, est une chose grave,
> Et la joie est moins près du rire que des pleurs.

(I am not sure about 'douce amie'. The passage I mean comes in the last scene of *Hernani*. . . .'[1]

He was far too intelligent not to realize how imprudent all this joy might turn out to have been. 'The only kind of peace I want is the peace that leaves no bitterness anywhere. But since *this* peace is not of that sort, it might be wiser, now that a desire for vengeance has taken root, if we saw to it that it should never be allowed to find expression in action. Something of the kind *may* be in course of preparation, but I rather think that President Wilson is a soft man. There is no question, because of Germany's guilt, there *can* be no question, of a peace of conciliation, and, that being so, I should have preferred to see more rigorous conditions. My fear is that German Austria may be called in to swell Germany proper as some kind of compensation for the loss of Alsace-Lorraine. But this is all mere guess-work, and I may be wrong. Perhaps everything is all right as it is. General de Gallifet said of General Roget, "He speaks well, but he speaks too much." President Wilson does not speak very well, but certainly he speaks a great deal too much. . . .'

His personal life was, as always, in a state of complete confusion.

---

[1] The quotation from *Hernani* (Act V, Scene 3) runs, actually, as follows:

Tu dis vrai. Le bonheur, amie, est chose grave.
Il veut des cœurs de bronze et lentement s'y grave.
Le plaisir l'effarouche en lui jetant des fleurs.
Son sourire est moins près du rire que des pleurs.

(Well, said: there is, my dear, solemnity in joy.
It would set its mark deep in hearts of bronze, without alloy,
Loud pleasure, strewing flowers, that leaps apace
Affrights it. There is far more of tears than laughter in its face.)

'I have embarked on affairs of the heart which will lead nowhere, will bring me no happiness, and are a constant source of weariness and pain besides leading me into absurd expense. . .' To meet this expense, he wanted to sell the dusty litter of carpets, sideboards, chairs and lustres that lay piled in his dining-room. 'The quantity, I hope, will make up for the quality which is no more than so-so. With the enormously increased cost of certain materials, such as leather and glass, I ought to get a good price. I have no idea whether bronzes fetch anything at auction these days. If they do, I have no objection whatever to stripping the drawing-room of the ones I don't like. I have a vast amount of table-silver which I never use, because either I eat at the Ritz, or lie in bed drinking coffee . . .' Then (for masochists never go short of miseries, since they themselves create them), he received a fatal item of news. His aunt, during November 1918, sold the house in the Boulevard Haussmann. Where could he find anywhere to live in post-war Paris? There was a housing shortage, and his health was bad. In order to get any sleep at all he had to take as much as a gramme and a half of veronal a day, which left him dazed and almost speechless when he woke and, though caffeine would dissipate this condition, it reduced him to such an extent that he was almost at death's door. Sick as he was, must he again be exposed to the hammering of upholsterers?

Meanwhile he had delivered the second volume of his book, *A l'Ombre des jeunes filles en fleurs*, to Gaston Gallimard, who planned to publish it simultaneously with *Pastiches et Mélanges*, a volume of odds and ends which had already appeared in various magazines and newspapers. The second volume (later to be split up into three) was so long that it produced the odd impression of a serried mass of print, which attracted by its very strangeness, though it terrified by the denseness of its texture.

Marcel Proust to an unidentified typist: Almost a month ago I asked Gaston Gallimard whether he agreed that I should intersperse the text with chapter headings giving the same information as that in the printed summary. He replied that he didn't much like the idea, and, after thinking the matter over, I am inclined to agree with him. We are of the opinion that the * * which I have introduced throughout wherever

a fresh piece of narrative begins, will be enough, and that the reader, thanks to the summary, and to the page numbers to be inserted in it (but which we can't fill in until page-proof stage) will be in a position to affix to each section of the whole the appropriate title.

'P.S. I notice that the * * have, as a matter of fact, not

been retained in the last lot of proofs. At least two of them must be restored: — below the third line on page 177 (that is to say, after the words, "un berceau de glycines" we must have * * — and similarly, on page 298, under the twenty-

ninth line, i.e. after the words "je 'm'endormais dans les larmes" another * * ....'[1]

Over the birth of this volume Proust brooded with an even greater tenderness than over that of its predecessor. Calmette had been murdered, but a preliminary warning was sent to Robert de Flers, a lifelong friend, who was now editing the *Figaro*. Could Marcel be *sure* of getting a front-page article? Robert de Flers replied that, with so much of importance going on in the world, it would be difficult to devote a Leader to a novel. Proust remarked, bitterly, that he realized that 'men of letters, even those whose books, like mine, are closely concerned with the war and the peace, must learn to efface themselves and behave with becoming reserve. *Cedant armis libelli!*' Well then, would they at least give him a 'snapshot'? Robert Dreyfus was invited to contribute one, which he entitled *A Literary Re-appearance*, and signed *Bartholo*; Marcel sent his thanks but, as Robert de Flers said at the time, 'Whenever poor Marcel happens to write me a letter in which he doesn't call me his "dear old Robert", and doesn't mention his "affection", I know that he is thoroughly put out! . . .' He *was* put out. Why had Robert Dreyfus mentioned

[1] From an unpublished letter in the possession of Alfred Dupont.

his ill-health? Why had the article been printed in such small type? . . . smaller than the type announcing a Poland Day at the Hôtel Doudeauville?' — and why the signature *Bartholo* 'which turned this magnificent compliment into a joke'? And all this at a time when the 'noise of my death-rattle is drowning the sound of my pen, and the row made by the bath that someone is drawing on the floor above'?

Fortunately, there was no lack of enthusiastic articles. Léon Daudet started an agitation to get Proust awarded the Prix Goncourt. Proust, though he pretended to be entirely detached, was careful to take a hand in the fray, and showed himself not wholly unskilful in the organization of publicity. He set himself to enlist the support of Louis de Robert, Reynaldo Hahn, Robert de Flers, and met with considerable success. At last, on November 10th, 1919, he was successful on a vote of six to four, the runner-up being *Croix de Bois* by Roland Dorgelès. Gallimard, Tronche and Rivière rushed round with the news, and found him in bed. The Selection Committee had hesitated for a long time. Dorgelès had fought in the war and was deservedly popular in the world of letters. Would it not be foolish to pass him over in favour of a difficult book by a rich amateur? A great many journalists were certainly of that opinion, and the award had a bad reception.

To justify it, Proust wrote an article with his own hand, which he got Léon Daudet to send to Georges Bonnamour, the editor-in-chief of *l'Éclair*:

> As we prophesied in our yesterday's issue, the Académie Goncourt has awarded to Marcel Proust the Prize which has been the subject of so much curiosity and competition, and for which there were no less than thirty candidates, all writers of merit. By choosing Marcel Proust, the Académie has to some extent, and quite deliberately, violated the provisions of the Goncourts' will, which, in establishing the Prize, laid it down that its intention was to encourage young writers. Monsieur Marcel Proust is forty-seven. But the superiority of his talent was so outstanding that the judges agreed to waive the question of age. . . .
> We should like to add that the author of *Recherche du temps*

perdu (a work which is by no means an autobiography as
has sometimes been erroneously stated, and which authors
of the standing of Henry James and Francis Jammes
have ranked with the productions of Cervantes and Balzac)
is not a newcomer. Shortly after leaving College, he published
a book entitled *Les Plaisirs et les Jours*, which Anatole France
described as being the production of a depraved Bernardin
de Saint-Pierre and an innocent Petroneus. But it is another
aspect of this writer's art, marked by a totally different kind
of vitality, that is responsible for *A la recherche du temps perdu*,
and also for a volume of *Pastiches*, recently published, which,
by an amusing coincidence, contains a slightly irreverent
parody of the brothers Goncourt. . . .'[1]

The most hostile of his critics (though expressing himself
privately) was Montesquiou. It was not without a certain amount
of uneasiness that he had witnessed the arrival of Charlus on the
beach at Balbec. In the secret recesses of his *Mémoires*, which were
to be made public only after his death, he poked much bitter fun
at the 'theatricality' of the Prix Goncourt affair, which, he said,
was a 'put up job'. Not that he denied all merit to the author,
for he had too much taste. But he took delight in denouncing,
behind the mask of Marcel's seeming humility, a 'careerism'
which found its support in Reynaldo — an only too willing
tool — in Robert de Flers who, in his conduct of the *Figaro*,
behaved like 'a ferryman on a lake of holy water', and in Léon
Daudet, who had swung the voting by a violently aggressive
article. Montesquiou was indignant at the acclamation accorded
to a novel which he regarded as frivolous, and gave it as his
opinion that in the Proust-Dorgelès battle, 'l'ombre des jeunes
filles en fleurs' had won the day over 'l'ombre des héros en sang'.
Was it possible that 'little Marcel' was about to force his way into
the Temple of Fame ahead of his master?

Bourget, who had encouraged Laure Hayman's young friend,
when speaking about Proust to Mauriac pretended to laugh at
'this lunatic with a mania for dissecting flies' feet', but he was too

[1] The manuscript of this unpublished fragment belongs to Monsieur Theodore
Tausky.

sensitive not to see that *A la Recherche du temps perdu* cast a dangerous shadow over his own novels. Bernard Grasset, though heart-broken at the thought that he had so nearly captured the Prix Goncourt for his own firm, cordially congratulated his former author. 'The charming feeling of melancholy to which you refer,' replied Proust, 'touched me the more nearly because I, too, felt something of the sort as soon as I learned that I had been awarded the Prix Goncourt (actually I did not know when the verdict would be given, and it was Léon Daudet who came to me with the news). Our two minds had but a single thought — and that is truer than you think. . . .'

Revived by his new happiness, Proust made a brief return to the world of fashion and gave a series of dinners at the Ritz for his new friends and for the critics. Jacques Boulenger and Paul Souday were even invited to a meal in his bedroom. *Marcel Proust to Paul Souday:* 'I don't mind in the least losing a certain amount of reputation because of winning a prize provided it gets me readers. And I value it more highly than any other honour that could have come my way. To be perfectly candid, I never, as P. S. guessed, dreamed of getting it. But when I knew that Léon Daudet, Monsieur Rosny the elder, and others were going to vote for me whatever happened, I was careful to send copies of my book to the rest of the Academy. It was, as Monsieur de Goncourt used to say, "a shot in the dark". I had no idea when the award was going to be made, and was genuinely astonished when friends came and woke me with the news. Since my state of health made it impossible for me to grant interviews to the journalists who came along with the offer of their "front pages", they had a sudden change of heart, and filled the space with a lot of rather dis-agreeable chatter. . . .'

But what did a few detractors matter? Proust had wanted readers. Now he had them: they were springing up all over the world. He received eight hundred letters of congratulation. He wrote with naive satisfaction to his old concierge at the Boulevard Haussmann: 'So far I have answered only Madame Paul Deschanel and Madame Lucie Félix-Faure . . .' In England, Arnold Bennett and John Galsworthy recognized in him the lineal descendant of Dickens and George Eliot. No praise could have

gone more straight to his heart. Middleton Murry, in an enthusiastic article, showed that artistic creation was, for Marcel Proust,
the only medium through which he could achieve the complete
flowering of his personality, and spoke of the *ascetic* and educational
value of his book. In Germany, Curtius wrote: 'a new era in
the history of great novel-writing has opened with Proust . . . he
imposes himself on our intelligence no less than on our admiration
as a master who ranks among the greatest . . .' The Americans
relished his humour which, they found, was at once poetic and
profound. They were soon to turn Proust into a classic.

How are we to explain this universal success of a difficult work?
Is it possible that a vast and varied public could be genuinely
interested in the people of Combray, in Madame Verdurin's
'salon', in the beach at Balbec? Many French critics, even in
the teeth of the evidence, remained for long doubtful. 'How',
they said, 'can we regard as representative of our age an author
who takes no stock of our social struggles, who paints the picture
of a dead world, who, when faced by a choice between the worldly
and the human, chooses the worldly? . . .' Nevertheless, as time
passed, 'the massive figure of Proust came more and more, in
foreign eyes, to dominate the first half of the twentieth century,
as the massive figure of Balzac dominated the nineteenth. What
was it, exactly, that made Proust's novel so important?

IV

PROUST AS A SOCIAL HISTORIAN

'Balzac painted *a* world; Proust paints The World.' There, in
a nutshell, is the gist of the charge made against him. 'In his
novel', says the anti-Proustian, 'we find a picture of certain
drawing-rooms of the aristocratic and upper-middle-class world
observed on those rare occasions when rank and fashion are
gathered together, and a study of the kind of passions that thrive
in an atmosphere of over-fed leisure: love reduced to the status
of a disease, jealousy, snobbery. Not there do we find, and less
and less *shall* we find, the true representation of a society. The
world of leisure is rapidly disappearing, and, with the passing

of its denizens will vanish their artificial emotions, their thin-blooded anxieties. Business-men, workers, peasants, soldiers, scientists, conservative statesmen, revolutionaries — those are the types of which our society is composed. Balzac foresaw the change: Proust is unaware of it.'

Pierre Abraham points out that if, like Proust, Saint-Simon concerns himself with a world of limited extent, the world of the Court, he does at least show it in action, and at a time, too, when that world was the scene of great happenings. Saint-Simon's courtiers are men with a career, men who have set out to achieve power, and from whose ranks Ministers and military commanders are recruited. But Proust's heroes waste their lives in pursuing a social round 'as destitute of interest as it is sterile'. 'Here and there we may find a lawyer, a doctor, a diplomat, but we never see them in the exercise of their profession. We are never shown the inside of a lawyer's chambers or a Minister's room. What we are offered is Society as seen from a sick-room whose cork-lined walls deaden the sounds of life. It is a Fair-ground observed through the eyes of Lucien Lévy-Cœur'.[1] It is true that work, other than the work of the artist, is absent from Proust's world. Nevertheless we know, by the way in which his novel keeps its hold on our affections, and because of its universal appeal, that there must be some answer to these brilliant speeches for the prosecution.

It should be realized, in the first place, that no novelist, however large his canvas, can paint everything. A man is no more than a man, and life is short. A novel can have but a limited number of characters. Even Balzac falls short of describing the whole of society as it existed in his day. An occasional workman crops up in his pages, an odd peasant or so, but the rôles that they play are subordinate. Balzac may have known a great deal about the inside of politics, but what he knew he did not reveal. As to the life of the soldier — Jules Romains, in *Verdun*, tells us a hundred times more on that subject than ever Balzac did. It is with no wish to diminish Balzac's stature that I draw attention to these blanks in his canvas, but only in order to show how impossible it is even for a writer of genius to give us the whole of any society.

[1] PIERRE ABRAHAM, *Proust, Recherches sur la création intellectuelle* (Rieder, Paris, 1930).

Nor is it true to say that, in Proust, we are presented only with men and women of the world and their servants. Let me make a rough census of his universe. The aristocracy plays a part in it, and it would be a mistake to reproach Proust for that. Our old families still occupy a place in the life of the nation. The heyday of the Republic of Dukes may have come to an end on May 16th, but it is still capable of action. It took a part in the Boulanger adventure, it was involved in the Dreyfus Affair. Even now it has its share in the various public services and has thrown out advance-guards even as far as the Communist Party. Proust understood the historic importance of this particular class. It is inexact to say that his book describes the decadence of the nobility and the triumph of the bourgeoisie. When Madame Verdurin or Gilberte Swann intermarries with the Guermantes, it is the Guermantes who assimilate these foreign elements.

Proust was never blind to the deficiences of the Guermantes. Though he delighted in the courtesies and the surface charm of the great world, attributes, both of them, which he possessed himself and of which his painfully acute sensibility stood in need, he saw clearly enough what underlay the exquisite manners of the world of fashion, and had no doubt that it was, essentially, pride, indifference and a sense of effortless superiority. He realized, too, why it was that the nobility continued to attach such fantastic importance to details of precedence. Since ceremony is its sole support, it cannot but respect it. The Guermantes hold it to be a duty 'more important than chastity or pity to address the Princesse de Parme in the third person'. Proust has clearly defined, within the confines of aristocratic circles, the superimposed layers of disregard: Royal Highnesses, the great families (Guermantes), withered branches of the same tree (Gallardon), provincial nobility (Cambremer) and the shifting fringe of doubtful titles (Forcheville).[1] The Parisian middle class lives on this fringe, and is susceptible to the attraction exercised by the nobility. Hence the coats-of-arms furbished up with the new gold of intermarriages; hence the transformation of Madame Verdurin into Duchesse de Duras, and later into Princesse de

---

[1] HENRI BONNET, *Le progrès spirituel dans l'œuvre de Marcel Proust: Le monde, l'amour et l'amitié* (Librairie philosophique J. Vrin, Paris, 1946).

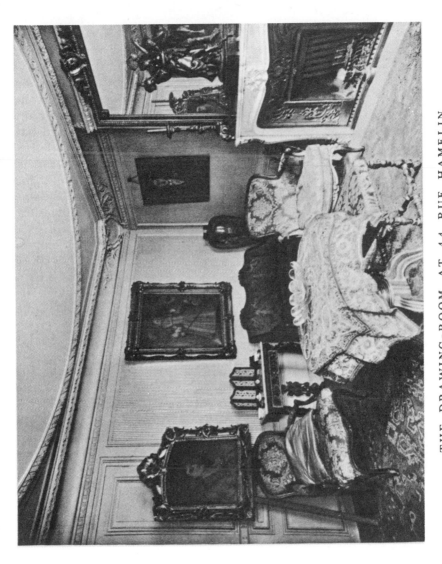

THE DRAWING-ROOM AT 44 RUE HAMELIN

Guermantes. But the 'solid bourgeoisie', especially outside Paris, has no wish to achieve a change of class. It is shocked at the spectacle of Swann, a stockbroker's son, 'having it all his own way' in the Faubourg Saint-Germain, and dining at the Elysée. It holds the view that a stockbroker's son should consort with stockbrokers. 'To lose caste does not mean merely to hob-nob with one's inferiors, but also to push one's way into an upper class where one does not belong: the rule is absolute.'[1] It never occurs to this middle class that it can 'better itself', because it refuses to recognize anything better than itself. The middle-class circles of Combray profess, even if they do not practise, an austere morality. There is a quite definite Combray 'code' before which all bow — Françoise, the Narrator's family, and Dr. Percepied.

The 'People' are inadequately represented. The only full-length portrait in this genre is that of Françoise, a countrywoman who has transplanted to Paris the native idiom of her world, a modernized version of the traditions associated with the 'folk' of Saint-André des Champs. But those French types carved in the porch of the church standing not far from Combray have an eternal quality. 'How typically French that church was! Over its door the saints, the kings of chivalry with lilies in their hands, the wedding scenes and funerals, were carved as they might have been in the mind of Françoise. The sculptor had also recorded certain anecdotes of Aristotle and Virgil, precisely as Françoise in her kitchen would break into speech about Saint Louis as though she herself had known him, generally in order to depreciate, by contrast with him, my grandparents, whom she considered less "righteous . . ."'[2] In the porch of Saint-André des Champs Marcel recognizes Théodore, Camus's errand-boy. The historic character of the 'People' interests Proust no less than does that of the Nobility. Françoise regards mourning in terms of the *Chanson de Roland*. Albertine Simonet is an incarnation of the little French peasant girl carved in stone at Saint-André des Champs. Saint-Loup, during the war, proves himself a Frenchman of Saint-André des Champs . . . even Marcel himself. . . .

[1] HENRI BONNET, *Le progrès spirituel dans l'œuvre de Marcel Proust: Le monde, l'amour et l'amitié* (Librairie philosophique J. Vrin, Paris, 1946).
[2] *Swann's Way*, I, translated by C. K. Scott Moncrieff (Chatto & Windus, 1922).

For it is false to say that Proust was indifferent to the public and national life of his day. He set himself to demonstrate the effects on French society of such upheavals as the Dreyfus Affair, and the war. Far from having no views on politics, he was for ever developing the theme — an important theme, and the father of all civil peace — that society is essentially fluid, that its values are relative and in a constant state of flux; that the emotional life of peoples is no less mad than that of individuals. But human beings, blinded by their passions, refuse to see that emotions are transitory and vain. 'We may know that revolutions always end in tyrannies, that parties dissolve, that quarrels grow old, and that the adversaries of today will become, because of overriding necessities, the allies of tomorrow. But that does not prevent us from playing out with fury or enthusiasm the parts for which we have been cast by the chance of birth or the influences of friendship.' Proust, merely because he was human, participated in the collective past. His attitude to the war was that of a Frenchman, to the Dreyfus Affair that of a partisan. But his intelligence held his feelings in check sufficiently at least to save him from the hysteria of hatred. Such an attitude has a political complexion, and is very definite.

To the anti-Proustian who protests: 'All this only goes to prove what I have been saying: he observes all these political changes, but only within the limits of a tiny world', we can reply without difficulty. Proust is not so much interested in this or that social 'milieu', as anxious to discover and to formulate the general laws that control human nature. There is, in all human beings, a fundamental identity, so that a rigorous analysis of any one of them provides the most precious documentation we can have on all. From a *single* skeleton, a *single* diagrammatic figure, we can be taught anatomy. We require to study only a *single* temperament, a *single* heart, to learn all that there is to know about love, about vanity, about man's heights and depths. Experience teaches that jealousy as Swann knew it, that the Verdurins' snobbery, or Legrandin's, that the Narrator's agonizing affection for his mother, are to be found, if not in identical at least in analogous forms, at all times and in every land.

Proust's observations of snobbery were carried out in the world that happened to be his, the world of the Guermantes and the Verdurins, but the *laws* of snobbery are roughly the same in all classes and in all countries. As soon as any human group is formed there are those who belong to it and those who do not.

The outcasts long to be accepted; the accepted protect their privileges and look with disdain on the outcasts. That is true of the Great World to which birth or achievement is the 'open sesame', but it is no less true of an American College where membership of a particular Fraternity is the snob's ambition, of a Trade Union where vital decisions are taken by a small inner circle of initiates to which the other members would dearly like to belong. It matters little within what social group Proust carried out his researches. The conclusions at which he arrived, given the correct coefficients and indices, take on a universal validity. Fernandez has shown that, in Proust, the relationship established between an individual of superior gifts and any given group always obeys the same laws, no matter what that group may be. The 'little band' undervalues the Narrator just as the fashionable world 'falls out of love' with Monsieur de Charlus, because *all* groups have a horror of the superior individual.

It is a mistake to think that a book is great only because the events it describes are important 'A second-rate writer, though he may live in a period of epic deeds, will still be a second-rate writer.' There is, for the scientific observer, a difference of scale, but not of importance. The study of one order of phenomena throws light on another. 'Every social condition has its interest, and it may be as rewarding for an artist to depict the manner of life of a Queen as the daily habits of a seamstress.' During the war, Marcel discovered that his quarrels with Françoise or with Albertine, by training him to suspect them of keeping their thoughts to themselves, increased his ability to foresee the machinations of a William II or a Ferdinand of Bulgaria. The life of a nation 'merely repeats, on a larger scale, the lives of its component cells: and he who is incapable of understanding the mystery, the reactions, the laws that determine the movements of the individual, can never hope to say anything worth listening to about the struggles of Peoples. . . .'

It comes to this: that Proust, who never prided himself on

writing about social problems, does so much oftener and much better than many solemn and futile thinkers who deal only in abstractions. 'I came to the conclusion that there was no need for me to concern myself with all the different literary theories which, for a brief moment, had been worrying me — those, in particular, which had been formulated at the time of the Dreyfus Affair with the avowed intention of "forcing the artist from his Ivory Tower", of persuading him to abandon such frivolous matters as the study of emotional reactions, and concern himself, instead, with the great movements of organized labour, or, if he did not feel himself competent to deal with humanity in the mass, to depict, at least not leisured nit-wits' ('I confess', said Bloch, 'that all this portraiture of useless persons leaves me cold') 'but intellectual aristocrats or heroes. True art can ignore manifestoes of that kind: for true art is pursued in secret. . . .'

The reader curious about French Society can find, in this great book, a picture of that society as it existed between the years 1880 and 1919 when it was still living in a past that gave it meaning and beauty. Those who are looking for a statement of the general laws that govern human activity cannot fail to find it in the writings of the most profound moralist who has appeared in France since the seventeenth century. Those who want, as most novel-readers do, to find in their author an understanding temperament with which they can share their troubles and their sufferings, will find what they seek in Proust, and are grateful for the chance of making contact with one of those great 'intercessors' which is what true artists are. No doubt the reality that he paints, a reality peculiar to himself, is particular and private. But if it be true that the evils with which men struggle are never the same for all of them, and that what is good for one is never equally good for others, it is no less true that we are all partakers in the same humanity, and that none of us can remain indifferent to the evidence marshalled by the man of good will 'who travels with an observant eye along the road which leads to the discovery of himself, bumping against every obstacle, tripping over every rut, losing his way at every cross-road'.[1] Not less than *Wilhelm Meister*, and more completely than the novels

[1] PIERRE ABRAHAM, op. cit.

of Stendhal, *La Recherche du temps perdu* is quite obviously an experimental work, though at the same time, like the *Essays* of Montaigne or the *Confessions* of Rousseau, it sums up the human predicament, and offers for our consideration a metaphysic of aesthetics. The Englishmen, the Americans, the Germans, who have seen fit to rank this vast piece of autobiographical fiction higher than the productions of Anatole France, of Paul Bourget, of Maurice Barrès and all the French writers of their day, are not wrong.

CHAPTER X

LE TEMPS RETROUVÉ

Who knows but what from our marriage with Death may be born
conscious immortality?   MARCEL PROUST

I

THE LAST MOORINGS

P R O U S T ' S affection for Madame Catusse was 'filial'
though intermittent. Sometimes a whole year would go by
without his writing to her, but anything in the nature of
a domestic difficulty was enough to waken his dormant feelings.
Some such problem had only to take shape for Madame Catusse
to find a deluge of letters pouring in upon her. Whenever Proust
wanted to sell those of his chairs that belonged to the Malesherbes-
Courcelles period, or some of the family carpets, he set Madame
Straus and Madame Catusse competing with one another, and
the two ladies at once became eager rivals in their efforts to serve
him.

Proust to Madame Catusse: 'I have just had a letter from Madame
Straus telling me that the brother of the English dealer is
prepared to offer ten thousand francs for the sofa and the
armchairs . . . but that he doesn't seem to want the hangings,
and quite definitely takes no interest in the green settee. She
is going to get somebody who knows his business to put the
hangings up to auction for me, and the said somebody is of
the opinion that the reserve price should not be more than
four or five thousand francs . . . because the best of them is
made up of two separate pieces — which detracts from its
value. I shall tell him to throw in the green settee as well. . . .'

Proust to Madame Catusse [December 22nd, 1917]: '. . . The
results achieved, so far as concerns the hangings, seem to
me to be quite detestable . . . but brilliant in the matter of
the furniture, *your* furniture (because the extra profit should,

by rights, be yours). They [the Strauses] sold two sets of
hangings to the same purchaser for a total of four thousand
francs! — though I seem to remember that the lady experts
put a much higher value on them — though considerably
lower than Berry's and yours. They sold the sofa and the four
armchairs for ten thousand (making, in all, for the hangings
and the furniture together, fourteen thousand). They are
"hoping" to get five or six hundred francs for the little green
settee. . . .'

Proust to Madame Catusse [May 1919]: 'I was *terribly* disappointed to learn that Papa's huge, handsome sofa from the
Rue de Courcelles went, though almost new, for forty francs!
The dining-room lustre, (which I don't so much mind about,
because I don't associate it with you as I do the sofa) fetched
thirty-eight! . . . But in view of the much increased commis-
sion demanded by the auctioneer, wouldn't it have been
better to arrange things privately? The panels of flowered
tapestry, the wall-brackets, the easy chair, and the old sofa
which you found under all that rubbish, and even the little
green settee (doubtless inferior to the easy chair, but rather
charming, all the same) ought to have a more or less stable
value. . . .'

In 1919 he had had to move out of his flat in the Boulevard
Haussmann which had formed his last fragile link with the family
past. His aunt without 'saying a word' to him beforehand, had
sold the whole house, and the new owner, a banker, had decided
to give the tenants notice. Any form of move from familiar
surroundings was, for Marcel, a quite appalling drama. Bad
enough in itself, this one was made worse by the fact that for
several weeks he had lived in dread of having to pay back-rent
amounting to many years — for which his aunt had never asked
him — 'at least twenty thousand francs at one fell swoop'. He was
still announcing to all and sundry, and perhaps believing, that he
was ruined. But there is always this advantage for the helpless of
this world, that their friends take compassion on them. *Proust to
Madame de Noailles:* 'Guiche, who has been quite superb all through
this frightful move, went to see the directors in an effort to get

some money for me (to which I believe I am entitled), and has put his own engineer on to finding some firm capable of tackling the cork lining. . . .'

The house in the Boulevard Haussmann became, in due course, the Varin-Vernier Bank, and Marcel had to move out. 'I can't, alas! give you any address at present, because so far I have found nowhere to go. I am reduced to repeating to myself the verse of the Scriptures which says: — "the foxes have holes and the birds of the air have nests; but the Son of Man hath not where to lay his head". . . .'

Réjane, having by chance got wind of his complaints, offered him a 'wretched lodging' in a house which she owned in the Rue Laurent-Pichard, but he stayed there only a few months. Finally, he settled down in a 'hideous furnished flat' on the fifth floor of No. 44 Rue Hamelin. This, 'the exiguous proportions and discomfort of which were equalled only by its exorbitant rent', was so close to the Bois that his hay-fever got worse. He regarded it as no more than a temporary solution of his problems, though, as things turned out, he stayed there until he died. All his own 'things', his hangings, his lustres, his sideboards and even his books, were sent to store. 'Nothing', says Edmond Jaloux, 'could well have been more arid, more poverty-stricken, than this room, the only ornament in which was the pile of notebooks, which formed the manuscript of his novel, stacked on the mantel-piece . . .' Torn strips of papers covered the walls. The whole place looked like the ascetic cell of some mystic of the arts. 'Whenever you feel rather lonely', he wrote to Robert Dreyfus, 'comfort yourself with the thought that, far away, a Benedictine (I was about to say a Carmelite) of friendship is thinking of, and praying for, you.'

Ever since 1913 his domestic affairs had been run by Céleste Albaret. She was a personable young woman with a good figure who spoke French pleasingly and exercised a quiet authority which he found very restful. She had come into his life when she married Odilon Albaret, the taxi-driver whose cab was entirely devoted to Proust's needs. He used it sometimes when he wanted to go out, sometimes when he wanted letters delivered by hand, sometimes when, at all hours of the night, he would send it to fetch those of his friends whom he suddenly felt a desire to see.

It was a matter of surprise to many that Marcel could endure the presence of a young woman in his room but gradually he grew accustomed to letting her look after him, and even, on occasion, dictated parts of his book to her.

Marcel Proust to Madame Gaston de Caillavet: 'The charming and perfect maid who, for some months now, has combined the functions of valet and nurse — I won't say of cook, except for herself, since I eat nothing these days — entered my room today in tears. The poor dear had just heard that her mother has died. She set off at once for Lozère, leaving her sister-in-law in charge, a woman whom I don't know, and, what is far worse, who doesn't know the flat, can hardly find her way to my room if I ring, and is quite incapable of making my bed if I get up. I hope I shall manage to get to you. The alternative (your coming to me) would be much more difficult. My room is almost always filled with dense smoke in which you would find it as hard to breathe as I should without it. Had my maid been here and had there been a day when the atmosphere happened to be breathable, I would have sent her to you (because I haven't got a telephone now, and so can't get into touch with you that way). With her substitute everything has become far more complicated. Still, *if* in the course of the next day or two I can manage to do without my fumigations . . . But what time would be best for you? Would six o'clock be convenient? But then again, by what time ought I to get a message to you? (either by sending my taxi, or by getting somebody to telephone you — probably a rather more tiresome business) — from a café where there is an instrument? — You must promise not to notice the disorder either of my room or myself. I would very much rather go to you: but that, until my maid gets back, will be exceedingly difficult. . . .'[1]

Céleste had orders never to go into his room unless he rang, which he usually did about two or three in the afternoon. He insisted that his coffee — a brew as strong as Balzac's — should

[1] Unpublished letter.

be ready for him. If he was late in waking, Céleste had instructions to make it fresh, and to serve it up in several relays, 'because', he said, 'the aroma loses its strength'. Almost his only food was coffee and milk. Occasionally (though very rarely) he felt a longing for fried sole or roast chicken, and these dishes he had sent round from Larue's or Lucas-Carton's (towards the end of his life, from the Ritz Hotel). Any cooking in the flat was forbidden, because the faintest smell would have precipitated an attack of asthma. Meals for his staff were sent in from the Restaurant Édouard VII in the Rue d'Anjou, at enormous cost, which accounts for the comparative poverty of so rich a man. Nor would he permit the use of gas whether for lighting or heating, and had it removed from the flat altogether, for fear of the smell. He was always complaining in his letters of a radiator which gave too much heat and brought on his breathlessness.

At his bedside stood a small bamboo table — his 'pinnace' of the old days — on which there was always a silver salver with a bottle of Évian water, a supply of lime-tisane and a candle which was kept burning night and day, in case he might have to ignite some of his fumigation powders. Céleste used to buy candles by the five-kilo box. At the other side of the bed, on a second table, were his *Notebooks*, several odd volumes, a bottle of ink and a supply of fountain-pens. 'He was', said Céleste, 'a gentleman who could do nothing for himself. If his fountain-pen fell on the floor he never picked it up. When *all* his fountain-pens were on the carpet, he rang for me . . . His bed had to be completely re-made every day, and the sheets changed because he said that the moisture of his body made them damp. When he washed, he used sometimes as many as twenty or two-and-twenty towels, because as soon as one got wet, or even damp, he wouldn't touch it.'

When he was working or sleeping, he must not be disturbed on any pretext whatsoever. Every day he read his mail aloud to Céleste, with a running comment, from which she was left to guess by intuition whether or no he was willing to see his correspondents, whether he wanted to arrange a meeting, or whether he would accept an invitation to dinner or to supper at some restaurant. It was she who kept open his communications with the outside world by going round to a neighbouring café — kept by 'people from the Puy-de-Dôme' — and telephoning from there. Céleste had caught many of his habits, his peculiar tricks of phraseology and even the tone of his voice. Like him, she imitated his friends. 'The other evening,' said Gide, 'when Céleste opened the door to me, after expressing Proust's regrets that he could not see me, she added — "Monsieur begs Monsieur Gide to believe that there is no moment when he is not thinking of him" (I made a note of the phrase at once). . . .'[1]

After a while she imported her sister, Marie Gineste, and her niece, Yvonne Alberet (who could type) to help her with her work. Often, of an evening, Proust would summon these young women to his room, together with Odilon, the taxi-driver, and give them a little lecture on French history. What a wonderful experience it would have been to hear a lesson on Saint-André des Champs from the lips of the man who had created that imaginary church down to every detail of the sculptured figures in its porch! Céleste's vocabulary and that of her relations, enchanted him:

> With a familiarity which I have in no way enhanced, in spite of the praise (which I include here, not because I am its object, but because it redounds to the credit of Céleste's curious genius) and the criticism — no less baseless but no less sincere — which the following remarks seem to express on the subject of myself — Céleste said, while I dipped my *croissants* in the milk: 'Oh! you little demon with your jay's feathers, Oh! you deep little piece of mischief! I'm sure I don't know what your mother was about when she made you, seeing as you're altogether a bird! Look at him, Marie, isn't it just as though he were a-smoothing of his plumage, twisting and turning his cute little neck, he looks so light one'd almost swear he was a-learning to fly! Lucky for you that those who had a hand in your making saw to it that you were born with a silver spoon in your mouth! What would have become of you otherwise, you wasteful creature! —

---

[1] ANDRE GIDE, *Journal, 1889-1939* (Bibliothèque de la Pléiade, Gallimard, 1939), p. 693.

There, if he hasn't gone and thrown away his roll just because it happened to touch the bed! And now, bless my soul, if he isn't spilling his milk! Wait till I arrange a napkin for you, because you certainly can't manage it yourself! I've never set eyes on anyone so stupid and awkward as you!' Then followed the more measured sound of the outpourings of Marie Gineste, who turned on her sister in a fury of reproof. 'You just hold that tongue of yours, Céleste! You must be mad to speak to Monsieur like that!' Céleste merely smiled and then, because I hate having a napkin tied round my neck — 'Look at him Marie! — *bing*! rearing of his head like a snake — *just* like a snake!'

What is remarkable is that he found genuine happiness in living with the Albaret family. As in the old days at Illiers, the days of Félicie and of Madame Amiot's garden, he needed no wider field of observation in the Rue Hamelin than that provided by the little group of human beings among whom his life was spent. Here, it seems, one touches 'Proust's ultimate *self*',[1] that goodness of heart in which there was nothing of morality but only an essential simplicity, an intellectual integrity, and also the power to enrich the persons, the objects and the events of every day which made it possible for him to impart to them a vivid and enduring interest. Céleste Albaret and Marie Gineste seemed to him to be as 'gifted as poets, with a good deal more modesty than poets usually have'.

Céleste never went to bed before seven o'clock in the morning, because Proust, who worked all night, expected her to answer his bell promptly whenever he should happen to ring. At dawn he took his veronal, and then slept from seven a.m. until three p.m. Sometimes he would increase the dose and sleep for two or three days on end. When he awoke, it took him some time to recover, with the help of strong coffee, his clearness of mind, but by evening he was once more in brilliant form. Occasionally Vaudoyer, Morand or Cocteau would come to see him. Mauriac, who had written an excellent article about him, was, on one occasion, invited to dine in the Rue Hamelin. On the previous

[1] STEPHEN HUDSON.

evening he was rung up on the telephone: 'Monsieur Marcel Proust would like to know whether Monsieur François Mauriac would like to hear the Capet Quartet during dinner, or whether he would prefer to meet the Comte and Comtesse de X. . . .?' Proust's attitude of humility was a hang-over from the days of his obscurity: he could never believe that his own, unaided company was, in itself, an incomparable attraction.

Mauriac has described the sinister room, 'the black grate, the bed on which a spread overcoat did duty for a coverlet, the waxen mask through which our host seemed to watch us as we ate, the hair that seemed to be the only living thing about him. For a long time now he had ceased to be concerned with earthly food'.[1]

One by one, he was cutting the 'last mooring ropes'. He knew now that the writer has one duty only, to live for his work: that friendship, because it wastes time, can involve a breach of that duty, an abdication of the self: that conversation is a 'superficial vagary which brings us nothing'. Inspiration, profound thought, the inner thrill — these things are possible only in solitude. Even love is less dangerous than friendship, because, being subjective, it does not turn us from ourselves.

On the occasion of this dinner, Mauriac caught a glimpse of the last of the 'Prisoners', the man whom Proust called 'my only H. . . .', a young Swiss, or so it was generally believed. But H. . . . was already under notice, and Proust was busy trying to find him an opening in the United States. Was this parting due to weariness, to a final ascesis, or to the determination that now, when he was about to publish *Sodome et Gomorrhe*, there should be nothing in his life but crystal clarity? Was he behaving 'like one of those unfrocked priests who observe the rule of complete chastity, so that no one shall be tempted to think their abandonment of the soutane to be due to anything but loss of faith'? In the main it was a complete and natural stripping of the self to the bare bones, willed by a man who was living no longer in the world of men, but only in the universe of his own creation. Within measurable distance of his end, 'he lived, a solitary, in his furnished room, concerned only with the proofs of his book, and with the inter-

[1] FRANÇOIS MAURIAC, *Du Côté de chez Proust* (La Table Ronde, Paris, 1947), pp. 41-3.

polations which he was busy adding in the margins between bouts of breathlessness'. Not on his own account was he worried by the knowledge that only a short span of life remained (the intermissions of the heart had taught him that all men die more than once), but only because of his work, since, when he came to die, the miner and the seam would both disappear together.

I I

MAGNUM OPUS FACIO

Between 1920 and 1922 this desperately sick man produced a prodigious amount of work. He had long ceased to be an amateur, that is to say, one for whom 'the quest of beauty is not a profession' — a dangerous state of mind — and had become what every writer ought to be — a craftsman. In 1920 he published *Le Côté de Guermantes* (11) and *Sodome et Gomorrhe* (I), to be followed in 1922 by *Sodome et Gomorrhe* (II), or, rather, the first part of it because, so swollen had it become as the result of additions, that he was seeking new titles for the later sections: *La Prisonnière — La Fugitive* (which afterwards became *Albertine disparue*). And all the time that he was further embellishing the volumes still to come he was correcting the proofs of those already printed — and with him correcting meant doubling, trebling, the extent of the text, adding so much that the publisher, in an access of terror, had finally to give the 'O.K. for press' himself, because something must be done to contain the torrent of waters that otherwise would break their banks. But Proust was convinced that this mass of new matter was what constituted the style of his work.

> *Marcel Proust to Gaston Gallimard:* 'Since you are so good as to find in my books a certain richness which gives you pleasure, you must realize that the richness is due entirely to the extra nourishment which I re-infuse into them as a result of living, and that this extra nourishment takes the material form of additions. . . .'

318

Again, in September 1921:

> To sum up: in this matter of *Sodome et Gomorrhe* II, I did say
> to someone in the office (I think it was you, though as to that
> I am not prepared to swear) that, in view of the enormous
> amount of revision that would have to be done, and which
> has vastly improved the literary (and living) value of the
> book, I couldn't expect to have everything ready until May.
> Actually I think that I shall be able to deliver a good deal
> earlier, but the original revision took a very long time, and
> I have added some new sections. All that I can assure you
> is that I spend my whole time working, and doing nothing
> else at all. . . .

Nothing else at all . . . those words expressed the strict truth. He
looked on his work as a race with death. 'I know what will happen;
you will end by sending me my proofs when I am no longer able
to correct them . . .' He wanted Gallimard to entrust his books
to four different printers, so that he might, at least, be able to re-
read the whole novel before he died. Can we be sure that the
state of his health had really deteriorated? There were those who
had their doubts. So used had his friends become to hearing
about his grievances and his wretchedness, that they had come to
regard him as one of those valetudinarians who finally live to be
a hundred. But not for nothing was he the son of a doctor. The
changes that he noticed in himself made him anxious. There
were periods when he was afflicted, as his mother had been on her
deathbed, with aphasia, so that he sought for words without being
able to find them. He could no longer leave his bed because, as
soon as he got up, he was overcome by dizziness.

One day in 1921 he wrote to Jean-Louis Vaudoyer:

> I refrained from going to bed at all, so as to be able to pay a
> visit to the Vermeers and Ingres this morning. Can you
> bring yourself to act as companion to a living corpse, and let
> me lean on your arm?

While at this exhibition of Dutch Masters in the Jeu de Paume, he had a seizure which he attributed to some potatoes which he had not properly digested, and the incident gave him the idea for that lovely passage in which he describes the death of Bergotte. The umbilical cord between his work and his life remained uncut. A word, an expression, a gesture seen at the side of the road along which, so painfully, so breathlessly, with so dragging a step, he was moving towards the end of his earthly pilgrimage, still served to nourish the monster. *Proust to Gaston Gallimard:* 'I want to add a short paragraph to the pages of ruled paper — if you have them handy — in which I describe two messenger-girls talking to me in the manner of Chateaubriand's Indian maidens (about page 245, I think) . . .' No doubt, Céleste had let fall some locution that evening, which had taken his fancy.

Sometimes he deliberately induced the impressions of which he stood in need. One evening he got the Capet Quartet to visit the Rue Hamelin, and there they played, during the night, to an audience consisting of himself alone. He wanted to hear a Debussy Quartet which would help him, indirectly, to complete his observations on the Septet of Vinteuil. He had thought at first of asking a few friends as well, but had finally said to Céleste: 'On the whole, no! If there are other people listening, I shall have to be polite and shan't be able to give my whole attention to the music . . . The impressions I need for my book must be clear-cut and unadulterated . . .' All the time the musicians were playing he lay on a sofa, his eyes shut, trying to enter into mystical communication with the music, as once he had done with Reynaldo's roses.

He had long been dreading the day when he should publish *Sodome.* That terrible book would, he believed, lead to ruptures with old friends. The inverts would be furious at what they would take for denunciation, the non-inverts would be disgusted and would blame him for having written it. Little by little, however, his increasing fame in every country had reassured him. From now on he felt himself invulnerable. No doubt Montesquiou would recognize himself in Charlus, but what did Montesquiou matter? He never saw him nowadays and, if he had met him, would have felt pity rather than fear. Around the old gentleman-poet there was now a tragic emptiness. Anatole France had left

MARCEL PROUST ON HIS DEATHBED, NOVEMBER 1922

a room when he came into it, murmuring: 'I can't stand this fellow who's for ever talking to me about his ancestors!' Perhaps it was because Proust had been moved by feelings of compassion for this fall from greatness — borne with such adamantine pride, that he described the insulting behaviour of Madame Verdurin to Monsieur de Charlus.

Proust's success was still a cause of offence to Montesquiou. Writing to Madame de Clermont-Tonnerre, he said: 'I, too, should like to have a little fame. To get it, I have only to call myself Montesproust!' When *Guermantes* II appeared in 1921, together with the terrible opening section of *Sodome et Gomorrhe*, Proust did not at once send him a copy, explaining this failure to do so by the difficulty of laying his hand on a first edition:

Proust to Montesquiou: 'It has been an *idée fixe* with me, an obsession such as one sometimes gets for one particular flower on a piece of wall-paper, to find at least two copies of the first edition — if more were not obtainable — one for a poor old friend of Mamma's who has really been a second mother to me, the other, for you. . . .'

Montesquiou to Proust: 'I am filled with admiration for the strategy of your art (which is probably a combination of natural instinct and deliberate planning, because, no matter how much one may scheme, one can never be quite sure of producing the effect at which one aims) — with its succession of lightning blows, book following book so quickly that those who read them merely because it is "the thing to do", are given no breathing-space, no time in which to realize that, in point of fact, they really like something else much better though it may not be nearly so good. . . .'

Proust to Montesquiou: 'If you still have a vague recollection of *A l'Ombre des jeunes filles en fleurs* (forgive me for referring to my own forgotten works, it is you who lure me on to do so), you may recall a scene in which Monsieur de Charlus looks fixedly but absent-mindedly at me one day when we are both near the Casino. When I wrote that, I had in mind, for a

moment, the late Baron Doasan, who was a familiar figure
in the Aubernon "salon", and shared the tastes of Monsieur
de Charlus. But I soon forgot all about him, and set myself to
construct a Charlus conceived on much larger lines and
entirely invented . . . *My* Charlus has a terrible fall in the
last volume, but does (to my mind) take on a certain ampli-
tude. There are plenty of people who are convinced that
Saint-Loup is Albuféra, though I never even remotely
intended anything of the sort. I have an idea that he must
think so himself: I can't otherwise understand why he should
have quarrelled with me: but he has, and I feel deeply hurt
in consequence. . . .'

Montesquiou to Proust: 'To revert for a moment to the subject
of "keys". Whether they be true or false, the work of Louis
XVI or of Gamain, concerns only the author. For us the
interest is merely secondary . . . Why should we care? Does
it really matter to us whether the cook has put vinegar or
savoury herbs into his sauce? I live retired from the world,
but I was familiar with the men of the generations you are
concerned to portray, though I never knew Albuféra. His
mother was my sister's daughter-in-law, but we lost touch
with the family after Élise's death. As you describe him he
seems a pleasant enough creature, especially in the picture
you give of him, sitting alone in the restaurant with his back
to the wall, and fidgeting about for all the world like a
dancer of the Russian Ballet. There is a shade of the obsequious, perhaps, in his friendship for you, but he is not without a certain elegance in the high-kicking episode which you
describe. But everything you say of him might apply equally
well to Guiche, who, so it always seems to me, must have
been the model for Saint-Loup . . . For the first time, someone has ventured, you have ventured, to deal openly and
on a big scale with the vice associated with the names of
Tiberius and the Shepherd Corydon. You have made it the
subject of a novel, as Longus or Benjamin Constant made the
emotion of love . . . What the consequences may be we shall
see, and I have little doubt that you are already feeling some

of the effects . . . You have made for yourself a name in the world; you are an influence among those who control decorations and literary prizes (though you are worth something better than such baubles), and it may be, therefore, that you will succeed in your tilting at hypocrisy, or, if you prefer it, at assumed decency of behaviour. But will you? I wonder . . . the enemy is very powerful. . . .'

From this point on a bitter note creeps into the correspondence, and the two writers keep up a cross-fire of references to their respective ailments, not excluding their death-rattles:

Proust to Montesquiou: 'For many long weeks now I have been at death's door, not as the result of a *cancer* — as you so kindly assume . . . but literally succumbing to fatigue. I must ask you to permit me, after so much bowing and scraping, to make, with due respect, my final adieu. In a note which might have been written by a man of twenty-five you convey sad news to your obedient, your more than centenarian friend . . . Do you really believe that my feelings of admiration and gratitude have cooled? . . . Your charge is completely unfounded. It was *I* who wrote last, and you who never deigned to reply to my letter. . . .'

It was Montesquiou who died first, at Mentone, on December 11th, 1921, quite alone except for a secretary. *Proust to the Duchesse de Clermont-Tonnerre:* 'Madame: I gather that you were almost the only one of poor Montesquiou's old friends to be present at his funeral. I say "poor Montesquiou", though I feel convinced that he is not really dead, and that at the obsequies, conducted in a manner befitting Charles-Quint, the coffin, fortunately, was empty. So certain am I that this was so, that I have delayed writing the Essay I have in mind on his work . . . I was too ill myself to tell him by letter how fond I was of him, and if, contrary to what I believe, he really *is* dead, I shall never forgive myself for having failed to send him that message while there was still time. . . .'

With Madame Straus, who had recently undergone an operation, and was lying in a condition of 'chronic death', his relations were much like those of Chateaubriand in old age with Madame Récamier:

> *Madame Straus to Marcel Proust* [1920]: 'I should like to write to you of many contradictory matters. First, of my sadness at knowing you to be ill: then, of my own irritation at being dead — which makes it so difficult for me to go on living: also, of the pleasure with which I look forward to renewing acquaintance with my old friends of chez Swann. That pleasure will be as keen as that of any living woman, nor is my tender affection for you that of one who is no more . . . I feel very "Aunt Léonie". You will, therefore, understand my state of mind and forgive my many erasures. . . .'

> *Madame Straus to Marcel Proust* [1921]: 'I am heartbroken to think that I have come to the end of my lovely book, and do so want to know what happens next. You have left me alone with your grandmother in the Champs-Elysées at the moment of her seizure . . . and I have no clue to what follows. Because of this "Act of Separation" which keeps us physically apart since you never go out in the daytime, do send that lovely Céleste of yours to see me. She will let me know how you are, and that will save you the trouble of writing. . . .'

Dead Madame Straus might be, but when *Sodome et Gomorrhe* reached her, she swore that she was not in the least shocked by the subject. Here is her last letter, dated May 13th, 1922:

> Marcel, my dear: how very much I should like to see you! I feel that we have so much to tell one another. But a meeting would be too delightful and too sad, and I am afraid it will never come off. *Never* — how cruel that word is! I can't get used to the idea of not seeing you again. . . .

Of his oldest and fondest friends, many, though still devoted, silently effaced themselves. Such was the case of Reynaldo Hahn, of Lucien Daudet, of Robert Dreyfus. They felt hurt to think that newcomers, drawn to him by his fame, bound to him by professional links, seemed to find a warmer welcome than the companions of a lifetime. It was, said Lucien Daudet, the

Parable of the Vineyard over again: 'These last have wrought but one hour, and thou hast made them equal unto us.' If only *their* Marcel could have remained an amateur of genius, caring nothing about what people said of him, indifferent to honours, large editions and advertisement!

But he *was* interested, curiously interested, in 'these wretched details', and brought to their consideration the same exhaustive and suspicious intelligence with which he approached everything. He sent Céleste's niece and sister on a round of the bookshops to see whether *Côté de Guermantes* was adequately displayed in the windows. He wrote daily letters to Gallimard, complaining of the insufficient size of his editions. In announcing the number of times that *Swann* had been reprinted, they had omitted to add Grasset's figures to those of the *N.R.F.*

> *Proust to Gaston Gallimard:* 'It would look as though I were copying my own parody of the Goncourts if I told you that *Les ieunes filles en fleurs* is on every table in China and Japan. But, to some extent that is true. So far as France is concerned, and the neighbouring countries, not to some extent, but wholly. I don't know a Banker who hasn't found it on his cashier's desk, nor a friend on her travels who hasn't seen them in the houses she has visited, in the Pyrenees and in Le Nord, in Normandy and in the Auvergne. I am in daily contact with my readers as I never was in the case of *Swann*. The requests for newspaper articles never cease. All this doesn't make me vain, because I know that reputation is often achieved by bad books. No, it doesn't make me vain, but I very much hope that it will make me — some money . . . The number of copies printed is not the only test of reputation, but it is *one*, like a Stock-Exchange quotation or a sick man's temperature. But the more the *jeunes filles* sell, the fewer copies do you print. . . .'

He draws comparisons, he complains:

> On taking the wrapper from my *Nouvelle Revue Française* today, I see on the cover — PÉROCHON: *Nène* 75th thousand. Now, *Nène* came out more than a year after *Les jeunes filles*. What's

more, though I have very warm feelings for Monsieur Péro-
chon, I would point out that *Nène* is not the kind of book that
wins the Prix Goncourt, the Selection Board of which,
rightly or wrongly, dismissed it as a 'sincere' work though
without much brilliance. That being so, the disproportion
between the numbers printed of *it* and of *Jeunes Filles* strikes
me as enormous. . . .

He applied himself with passion to the task of getting people to
write articles on his book, and, if put to it, wrote them himself,
quoting with pride something that Lemaître had once said to the
effect that 'When Proust is bad, he is still as good as Dickens, and
when he is good he is much better.' He was prepared, he said,
to pay for the reprinting, in other papers, of the more dithyrambic
of the praises accorded to him. He wanted a noisier publicity
campaign, and regretted that his book should not have been
announced, like Paul Morand's, with a showcard bearing the
words, *Not for Young Girls!* Far from being content with the Prix
Goncourt, he tried to discover his chances of winning the great
literary prize awarded annually by the Académie Française. He
loved the daily mail-bag that was stuffed with praises of the kind
that Alphonse Daudet had once called 'bouquets of poppies', because of their highly-coloured appearance and lack of staying-
power. It pleased him to think that the *Notebooks* piled on the
'pinnace' were, because of their manuscript value, now worth
their weight in gold.

Should we blame him? When a writer has had to wait too long
for the recognition he deserves: when, after so many years of
doubt and despair, he finds happiness in seeing his work loved
and praised, it is only natural. 'After all,' he wrote, 'it is no more
absurd for a man to regret that a woman died without ever knowing that she had failed to deceive him than to want one's name to
be known in two hundred years . . .' Lucien Daudet, though at
first he regretted the friend who had been modest to excess — 'the
indefinable and charming Marcel Proust' — admitted later that
he had been wrong to do so, because 'during his very short period
of success, Marcel Proust, knowing that he was soon to die, and
quite resigned to his fate (I don't think he wanted to live longer),

was consumed with the desire that his work should survive him, and therefore had to play to the end the game that makes or mars a book . . .' The truth of the matter is that Marcel developed like one of his own characters and, as a sort of epilogue to *Temps retrouvé*, stood caught in the beams of Fame's spotlight, revealed in its glaring colours.

He went out less and less, but his seclusion was never absolute, except during his bad attacks. He was to be seen still, supping alone at the Ritz, with almost all the lights out, surrounded by waiters whom he had trained to manipulate the switches, the positions of which he knew by heart. Boylesve, who met him at a meeting of the jury which awarded the Blumenthal Bursaries, felt as though he were seeing a ghost, a human version of Edgar Poe's *Raven*:

Rather tall, almost stout, high-shouldered, and huddled in a long overcoat. This he kept on, like an invalid who goes in deadly fear of a draught. But the most extraordinary thing about him was his face: it had a bluish tinge, the sort of colour one sees in game that has gone 'high', and his eyes, like those of a dancing-girl, were deeply sunk, and seemed as though supported on half circles of shadow. His hair was thick, straight and black and badly cut, or, rather, not cut at all for at least two months. His moustache, too, was black and ill-tended. He had the appearance and the smile of a fortune-teller. When I shook his hand, I could not keep my eyes off his collar which fitted his neck loosely, was badly frayed, and I can say without exaggeration had not been changed for a week. He was shabbily dressed, and his tiny, womanish feet were encased in dress shoes. He wore a dilapidated tie, and his wide trousers must certainly have been ten years old. I thought of all that 'dated' in his recently published books. He was seated next to me. I looked at him. He had, in spite of his moustache, the appearance of a Jewess of sixty who might once have been beautiful. His eyes, seen from the side, had an oriental cast. I tried to see his hands, but they were hidden in a pair of white, and remarkably dirty, gloves. I did, however, get a glimpse of his wrist which was delicate, white and plump. His face seemed to have been deflated and then imperfectly reinflated in such a comic manner that the fleshy parts seemed distributed at random and not at all where one would have expected to find them. Young, old, sick, and feminine — an odd creature. . . .[1]

In the late spring of 1922 he once more made his appearance in the Great World, at an evening party given by the Comtesse Marguerite de Mun, whom he loved for her wit and for her natural goodness of heart. There he met for the last time the friend of his childhood and youth, Jeanne Pouquet (the widow of Gaston de Caillavet, who had married again and was now the wife of her own cousin). After greeting a number of people, and scattering a few protestations of affection and admiration ('He was a marvellous source of compliments and sly touches of humour', said Barrès), he sat down beside her and, there being no further need for pretence of flattery, let himself go in a series of comic remarks on the company at large, acute observations, profound judgments and high philosophical reflections.

That evening he was very gay, and seemed in better health. Nevertheless, when all the guests had gone he begged Madame Pouquet to stay with him for a while, and not to go away at once. But it was late, and she refused, saying that she was tired. Marcel's face took on an expression of indefinable sweetness, irony and melancholy.
'So be it, Madame: good-bye.'
'Not good-bye, Marcel dear, au-revoir.'
'No, Madame, good-bye: I shall never see you again. You think I am looking better, don't you? In point of fact, I am dying, Madame, dying. Looking better, am I? — that really *is* comic . . .' (his laugh sounded false and made her feel uncomfortable). 'Never again shall I go to a party. This evening has been a great strain, Madame: good-bye.'
'But, *dear* Marcel, I could so easily come to see you one day soon: even if you insisted on it's being the evening.'

[1] RENE BOYLESVE, *Feuilles tombées* (Editions Dumas, Paris, 1947), pp. 266-7.

'No, no, Madame, don't come! You mustn't take my refusal of your offer in bad part. You are very kind. I am touched, but I can no longer receive my friends. I have an urgent piece of work that must be finished . . . very . . . *very* . . . *urgent*. . . .'

So urgent was it, that he felt he owed every minute to his book. When Jacques Rivière asked him to write an article on Dostoievsky for the *Nouvelle Revue Française* he refused: 'I have an enormous admiration for the great Russian, but I know him only very imperfectly. I should have to do a lot of reading and re-reading, and that would mean that my own work would be interrupted for several months. I can only answer like the prophet Nehemiah (I think) who was summoned, for some reason I have forgotten, when he was up his ladder: *Non possum descendere: magnum opus facio*. . . .'

'I can't come down . . . I am engaged on a great work . . .' He was a prey to constant anxiety. For nearly twenty years he had been struggling with images and with words in order to express certain ideas which would, he hoped, liberate his spirit, and the spirits of those who were in sympathy with him. He had almost reached the end, but it was essential that everything should be said before he died. 'I decided to dedicate all my remaining strength to the task. But that strength was slipping away, as though reluctantly, as though anxious to leave me just enough time, the circle completed, to close the door of the tomb. . . .'

III

THE FINAL STRUGGLE WITH TIME

In June 1922, Lucien Daudet went to say goodbye before leaving Paris. He found him looking paler than usual, his eyes ringed in dark shadows. Daudet felt embarrassed. He knew that he was in the presence of a very great man, but was too shy to tell him so. Marcel tried hard to speak with the tender humility of former days. They talked of one of his new friends, and of the profound antipathy that existed between him and the old familiars. 'Neither sympathy nor antipathy can be transmitted,' said Proust sadly; 'that is the great tragedy of friendships and family bonds . . .' Long ago he had written that friendship is more delusive even than love. 'I felt a lump in my throat when we parted,' wrote Daudet: 'I wanted to give him a kiss, but he drew back in his bed. "No," he said, "don't kiss me, I haven't shaved . . ." On a sudden impulse I took his hand and pressed it to my lips. I can still see his gaze, framed in the doorway, fixed upon me. . . .'

Throughout the summer his health grew worse. *Proust to Gaston Gallimard:* 'I don't know whether I have written to you since I discovered that I fall down whenever I try to walk, and that I can no longer speak properly. It is frightful . . .' A martyr to his craft, he was literally killing himself by working all night at the proofs of *La Prisonnière* and dictating 'additional matter' to Céleste's niece. *To Gaston Gallimard:* 'No sooner do I get out of bed than I feel giddy and fall down. I have at last decided, though perhaps wrongly, that the reason for this is a crack in the chimney which has developed since it last caught fire. Since I always keep a fire burning, I am, to some extent, suffering from asphyxia. I ought, really, to get out, but before I can do that I must manage to reach the lift. Living's not always an easy business. . . .'

He continued to harass his publisher and fiercely to defend his work:

> Others, and I am glad of it, can enjoy the world about them. I can make no movements, form no words, think no thoughts. I am deprived even of the happiness of not suffering. Thus expelled, so to speak, from myself, I take refuge in my books which I handle rather than read, and, on their behalf, take the precautions of those digging-wasps about which Fabre wrote that admirable passage, quoted by Metchnikoff and, I doubt not, familiar to you. Curled up like one of them, and deprived of everything, I am concerned only to see that my books shall achieve, in the world of men's minds, the further expansion which is now denied to me. . . .'

Someone having been so foolish as to tell him that the brain functions best on an empty stomach, he refused all food in order that *La Prisonnière* should be worthy of the earlier volume. There is something sublime in this sacrifice of a mortal body to an immortal book, in this act of transfusion in which the donor deliberately chooses to shorten his life that the characters who are dependent on his gift of blood may live.

To a few of his friends he wrote that he was definitely on the eve of departure. 'That', he added, 'will really be, so far as I am concerned, *le Temps retrouvé*.'

> His thoughts had already leaped ahead of the days that still remained to him. He was worried about the forthcoming publication of Montesquiou's *Mémoires*. He had been vaguely told that the gentleman-author had said a number of very unpleasant things about several people, including himself. 'I am dying,' he said, 'and it would be much better that my name should not appear, since I shall not be able to reply. . . .'[1]

One evening in October 1922 he went out to pay a visit to Étienne de Beaumont. It was foggy, and he caught a chill which turned to bronchitis. At first there seemed to be no great danger, but he refused to have himself looked after properly, refused even to let the room be kept warm because the central heating brought on his asthma. Céleste could do nothing because he forbade her to call in a doctor. It was soon obvious to her that his condition was far worse than usual. Nevertheless, with stoic disregard, he insisted on spending every night working on his revision of *Albertine disparue*. At last, round about October 15th, feeling that his feverish condition was impeding his work, he consented to see his usual medical man, Dr. Bize. The verdict was that there was no cause for alarm, but that he must consent to rest, and must take nourishment. Marcel remembered his mother, who had always prescribed better for him than any doctor, and had had a strong belief in the virtue of dieting. He argued that food would send his temperature up, would make it impossible for him to go

[1] LEON PIERRE-QUINT, *Marcel Proust, sa vie, son œuvre* (Editions du Sagittaire, 1935).

on with his work. 'Death is close behind me, Céleste,' he said: 'Gallimard is waiting for the proofs, but I shan't have time to get them back to him. . . .'

'He was very weak,' records Céleste, 'and persisted in his refusal to take any food. The only thing he could fancy was iced beer which Odilon was told to get in from the Ritz. He was very breathless, and kept calling for me. "Céleste," he said, "this time I really am going to die. I only hope I shall have enough time to get through with what I'm at . . . Promise me, Céleste, that if, when I'm too weak to put up a fight, the doctors want to give me one of those injections that only prolong one's sufferings, you won't let them . . ." He made me swear I wouldn't. He was just as sweet and gentle with me as ever, but was so obstinate with the doctor that Monsieur Bize called in Monsieur Robert. The Professor came and begged his brother to let himself be taken care of, if necessary, in a nursing-home. Monsieur Marcel got proper angry at that. He refused to leave his room or to have any nurse but me. When the two doctors had gone, he rang his bell. "Céleste," he said, "I don't want to see that Dr. Bize again, nor my brother, nor my friends, nor anybody at all. They shan't stop me from working. Stay in the room next door, keep awake, and don't forget for a single moment what I told you about injections!" As he said this he gave me a terrible look, and said that if I disobeyed he would come back and haunt me. But he told me to send a basket of flowers to Dr. Bize. That had always been his way of saying he was sorry when he had had to hurt anybody's feelings. "Good!" he said when I told him the basket had been sent off: "that's one more thing settled if I die." . . .'

This final offering, floral and funereal, to the God of medicine brings to mind Socrates' last words as he lay dying: 'Do not forget that we owe a cock to Aesculapius.' And, as Socrates in his prison summoned a lute-player, that he might still learn something before he died, so Marcel Proust, well aware that he had been condemned by a judge no less pitiless than the Eleven, surrounded himself on his deathbed with books and notes and proofs, busying himself with giving the final touches to the text that would survive him.

On November 17th he believed himself to be much better. He agreed to see his brother, and Robert stayed with him for quite a long while. To Céleste he said: 'It remains to be seen whether I shall get through the next five days . . .' He was smiling, and went on: 'If, like the doctors, you're bent on my eating something, fry me a sole. I know it won't do me the slightest good, but I should like to please you.' Professor Proust thought it best to forbid this particular pleasure, and Marcel realized that the decision was wise. After a further talk with his brother, he told him that he was going to spend the whole night working, and that he would keep Céleste in the room to help him. The sick man's courage was sublime. He settled down to the correcting of his proofs, and made some additions to the text. At about three o'clock in the morning, exhausted and fighting for breath, he made Céleste sit by him, and dictated to her for a considerable while. . . .

It has been said that what he dictated on this occasion were the notes he had made for the death of Bergotte, making use, for the purpose, of his own sensations as a dying man, but nobody, so far, has ever been able to produce any proof that this was so. 'Céleste,' he said, 'I think that what I've just made you take down is very good. I shall stop now. I can't go on any longer . . .' Later, he murmured: 'This night will show which of us was right, I or the doctors.'

Next morning, about ten o'clock, Marcel asked for some of the cold beer which he used to have sent in from the Ritz. Albaret went for it at once, and Marcel whispered to Céleste, that it would be with the beer as with everything else — it would come too late. He was finding it very difficult to breathe. Céleste could not take her eyes from the bloodless face, the pallor of which was accentuated by the stubble of his unshaved beard. He was appallingly thin. So intense was his gaze that he seemed to be looking into the invisible. Standing beside his bed, and scarcely able to keep herself from collapsing (she had not been to bed for the last seven weeks) Céleste watched his every movement, trying to guess and anticipate his least wish. Suddenly he flung his arms free from the sheets. He seemed to see a fat and hideous woman in the room with him. 'Céleste! Céleste! she's very fat and quite black — she's dressed entirely in black: — I'm frightened . . .' Word was sent to Professor Proust at the hospital, and he came round as quickly as he could.[1] Dr. Bize came too. Céleste, in despair at the thought that she was disobeying Marcel's orders, watched the arrival of all sorts of medical appliances, oxygen balloons, syringes . . . A look of irritation came into the dying man's eyes when Dr. Bize entered the room. Marcel, who as a rule was so punctiliously polite, gave him no word of welcome, and showed his annoyance by turning to Albaret who had just got back with the beer. 'Thank you, my dear Odilon, for fetching the beer'. . . Dr. Bize leaned over the bed in order to give the patient an injection. Céleste helped him to turn down the sheet. She heard the words: 'Oh, Céleste, why?' and felt Marcel's hand, which was resting on her arm, give it a pinch as though he were making a final protest.

They were crowding round him now. Everything that could be tried was tried, but it was too late. The cupping-glasses could no longer get a hold. With infinite precautions, Professor Proust lifted his brother on to the pillows. 'I'm afraid I'm moving you a lot: am I hurting you, old boy?' Marcel's last words came in a whisper: 'Yes, Robert dear, you are.' The end came very quietly at about four o'clock. He made no movement, and his eyes were wide open. . . .[2]

That evening, his friends rang one another up on the telephone, and spoke with sadness, almost with incredulity, of the terrible news. 'Marcel is dead.' Some of them went to see him when the body had been laid out for burial. The wonderful face, bloodless and emaciated like that of a figure in a painting by El Greco, gave an air of indescribable dignity to the furnished, featureless room. 'The sunken, fleshless mask, with the black smudge of a

[1] As a matter of fact, Dr. Robert Proust had not been out of the sick-room for the last three days, and nursed his brother with tireless care and devotion.

[2] MARIE SCHEIKEVITCH, *Souvenirs d'un temps disparu* (Plon, 1935).

sick man's beard, lay bathed in those greenish shadows which certain Spanish painters gave to the faces of their dead.'[1] A large bunch of Parma violets had been laid on his breast. 'We saw,' says Mauriac, 'on a soiled envelope which had contained tisane, the last illegible words that he had written. The only one that we could make out was the name *Forcheville*. To the very end his creatures had been feeding on his substance, had drained him dry of what remained of life. . . .'

Faced by the poverty-stricken appearance of the room in which this man, crowned with every gift, had just died, those present suddenly realized the meaning, the solemnity, of that asceticism which, in the last months of his life, he had imposed upon himself. 'The impression was there and then borne in upon us,' wrote Jaloux, 'that he was very far from us, not simply because he was dead, but because his whole existence had been profoundly different from our own; because the world of investigation, imagination and sensibility, in which he had lived, was not our world; because he had suffered in strange ways; because, that his spirit might find nourishment, he had needed excessive miseries, and been rapt up into meditations such as most men know nothing of. . . .'

'No one, seeing him lying there on his deathbed, would have believed that he was fifty. He looked barely thirty. It was as though Time had not dared to lay its hand upon the man who had grappled with, and overcome, it . . .' He had the appearance of eternal youth. After the funeral service, Barrès, bowler-hatted and with an umbrella on his arm, met Mauriac as they were both leaving the church of Saint-Pierre de Chaillot. 'Ah well,' he said, 'so that's the last of our young man.' But he was much more than that, as Barrès was later to realize, he was our *great* man. 'Ah! Proust, dearest of companions, what a phenomenon you were, and what levity I showed in daring to pass judgment on you!'

Now that we have reached the moment when Marcel Proust's earthly and tormented life ended, and his true life, his life of glory, began, it is impossible not to quote the final sentence of the passage in which he described the death of Bergotte:

[1] EDMOND JALOUX.

They buried him, but all through the night of mourning, in the lighted windows, his books, arranged three by three, kept watch, like angels with outspread wings, and seemed, for him who was no more, the symbol of his resurrection.

I remember how, when I once gave a public reading of that passage a few months ago, I was struck by the silence, heavily charged with emotion, that surrounds the works of genius. It is such as Proust himself described when Swann heard the Vinteuil Sonata, and the little phrase had died away into silence:

> Swann dared not move, and would have liked to compel all the other people in the room to remain still also, as if the slightest movement might embarrass the magic presence, supernatural, delicious, frail, that would so easily vanish. But no one, as it happened, dreamed of speaking. The ineffable utterance of one solitary man, absent, perhaps dead (Swann did not know whether Vinteuil were still alive), breathed out above the rites of those two hierophants, sufficed to arrest the attention of three hundred minds, and made of that stage on which a soul was thus called into being one of the noblest altars on which a supernatural ceremony could be performed. . . .[1]

Our quest is ended. I have attempted to recapture the story of a man who, with heroic courage, sought, through ecstasy, for truth; who dashed himself against the apathy of men, the mystery of things and, above all, the obduracy of his own weaknesses; who, having chosen to renounce all else that he might give freedom to the images that dwelt within him, saw, between four bare walls, in solitude and fasting, in sorrow and in labour, that last door at length fly open at which, before him, no writer had ever knocked; of a man who revealed to us, in our own hearts and in the humblest of objects, a world so beautiful that one may say of him as he once said of Ruskin: 'Though dead, he still shines for us like one of those extinguished stars whose light yet reaches us': and, again: 'it is through those eyes, now closed for ever in the grave, that generations yet unborn will look on nature'.

[1] *Swann's Way*, II, translated by C. K. Scott Moncrieff (Chatto & Windus, 1922).

In the beginning was Illiers, a small town on the borders of La Beauce and Perche, where a few French folk lived huddled about an old church which wore its belfry like a hood, where a nervous and sensitive child would sit on fine Sunday afternoons, beneath the chestnuts in the garden, reading *François le Champi* or *The Mill on the Floss.* Whence he saw, through the hawthorn hedge, paths bordered with jasmine, with pansies, with verbena, and sat on, motionless, gazing at the scene before him, breathing in its scents, striving to let his thoughts range beyond the thing seen, his senses catching the fragrance of a more than earthly sweetness. 'Thus raptly contemplated by this humble passer-by, this dreaming boy, that corner of a country world, that scrap of garden, could never guess how it would be that, thanks to him, they would know a new life of survival in every passing, ephemeral detail.' Yet it is his exaltation that has brought us the perfume of the hawthorn trees that died long years ago — that has made it possible for men and women who have never seen, nor will ever see, the land of France, to breathe with ecstasy through the curtain of the falling rain the scent of invisible yet enduring lilacs. In the beginning was Illiers, a market-town of two thousand inhabitants, but in the end was Combray, the spiritual home of many million readers scattered today over all the continents. Tomorrow they will stretch in long processions across the centuries — in Time.

BIBLIOGRAPHY

Correspondance Générale de Marcel Proust, 6 volumes (Plon, Paris, 1930-36). The first five volumes were edited by Robert Proust and Paul Brach (1930-35): volume VI by Suzy Proust-Mante and Paul Brach (1936)

MARCEL PROUST: *Lettres à la N.R.F.* (Gallimard, Paris, 1932), being volume VI of *Les Cahiers Marcel Proust*

MARCEL PROUST: *Lettres à une amie* (Calame, Manchester, 1942). Forty-one unpublished letters addressed to Marie Nordlinger (1899-1908)

MARCEL PROUST: 'Lettres à Maurice Duplay' (*Revue Nouvelle*, XLVIII, 1929), pp. 1-13

MARCEL PROUST: *Lettres à Madame Catusse* (J.-B. Janin, Paris, 1946).

Quatre Lettres de Marcel Proust à ses concierges (Albert Skira, Geneva, 1945)

BARNEY (NATALIE CLIFFORD): *Aventures de l'esprit* (Émile-Paul, Paris, 1929), pp. 59-74

DAUDET (LUCIEN): *Autour de soixante lettres de Marcel Proust* (Gallimard, Paris, 1929), being volume V of *Les Cahiers Marcel Proust*

Hommage a Marcel Proust (Gallimard, Paris, 1927), being volume I of *Les Cahiers Marcel Proust.* A reprint of the special number of the *Nouvelle Revue Française* devoted to Marcel Proust (January 1st, 1923), with the addition of one unpublished section

LAURIS (GEORGES DE): *A un ami. Correspondance inédite de Marcel Proust, 1903-1922* (Amiot-Dumont, Paris, 1948)

PIERRE-QUINT (LÉON): 'Lettres inédites de Marcel Proust à Paul Brach' (*Revue Universelle*, XXXIII, April 1st, 1928)

PIERRE-QUINT (LÉON): *Comment parut 'Du Côté de Chez Swann', Lettres de Marcel Proust à René Blum, Bernard Grasset et Louis Brun* (Kra, Paris, 1930)

POUQUET (JEANNE-MAURICE): *Quelques lettres de Marcel Proust à Jeanne, Simone et Gaston de Caillavet, Robert de Flers et Bertrand de Fénelon* (Hachette, Paris, 1928)

ROBERT (LOUIS DE): *'Comment débuta Proust. (Revue de France*, January 1st and 15th, 1925)

ROBERT (LOUIS DE): *De Loti à Proust* (Flammarion, Paris, 1928)

Unpublished Letters and Manuscripts belonging to Madame Gérard Mante-Proust, Professor Henri Mondor, La Marquise Robert de Flers, Madame Laurent du Buit, Monsieur Alfred Dupont, Comte

BIBLIOGRAPHY

Jean de Gaigneron, Madame Maurice Pouquet, Madame René Sibilat, Madame Jacques Brissaut, Mr. Edward Waterman and Monsieur Théodore Tausky.

ABATANGEL (LOUIS): *Marcel Proust et la musique* (Imprimerie des Orphelins Apprentis d'Auteuil, Paris, 1939)

ABRAHAM (PIERRE): *Proust. Recherches sur la création intellectuelle* (Rieder, Paris, 1930)

AMES (VAN METER): *Proust and Santayana. The Aesthetic Way of Life* (Willet, Clark & Co., Chicago, 1937)

BÉDÉ (JEAN-ALBERT): *Marcel Proust, problèmes recents* (*Le Flambeau*, XIX, 1936), pp. 311-24 and 439-52

BÉGUIN (ALBERT): *L'Ame romantique et le rêve* (Librairie José Corti, Paris, 1939)

BIBESCO (PRINCESSE): *Au Bal avec Marcel Proust* (Gallimard, Paris, 1928): volume IV of *Les Cahiers Marcel Proust*

BIBESCO (PRINCESSE): *Le Voyageur voilé* (La Palatine, Geneva, 1947)

BILLY (ROBERT DE): *Marcel Proust. Lettres et conversations* (Éditions des Portiques, Paris, 1930)

BLANCHE (JAQUES-EMILE): *'Du côte de chez Swann'* (*L'Écho de Paris*, December 16th, 1913)

BLANCHE (JACQUES-EMILE): *Souvenirs sur Marcel Proust* (*Revue Hebdomadaire*, July 21st, 1928)

BLANCHE (JACQUES-EMILE): *Mes Modèles* (Stock, Paris, 1928)

BLANCHE (JACQUES-EMILE): *Propos de peintre*, 3 volumes (Émile-Paul, Paris, 1919-28). Volume I, *De David à Degas* (1919): volume II, *Dates* (1921): volume III, *De Gauguin à la Revue Nègre* (1928)

BLONDEL (CHARLES-A.): *La Psychographie de Marcel Proust* (Vrin, Paris, 1932)

BONNET (HENRI): *Le Progrès spirituel dans l'œuvre de Marcel Proust: le monde, l'amour et l'amitié* (Librairie philosophique J. Vrin, Paris, 1946)

BOYLESVE (RENÉ): *Feuilles tombées* (Éditions Dumas, Paris, 1947)

BRASILLACH (ROBERT): *Portraits* (Plon, Paris, 1935)

BURNET (ÉTIENNE): *Essences* (Éditions Seheur, Paris, 1929)

CATTAUÏ (GEORGES): *L'Amitié de Proust* (Gallimard, Paris, 1935): volume VIII of *Les Cahiers Marcel Proust*

CELLY (RAOUL): *Répertoires des thèmes de Marcel Proust* (Gallimard, Paris, 1935), volume VII of *Les Cahiers Marcel Proust*

CHERNOWITZ (MAURICE-E.): *Proust and Painting* (International University Press, New York, 1945)

CHERNOWITZ (MAURICE-E.): *'Bergson's Influence on Marcel Proust'* (*Romantic Review*, XXVII, 1936), pp. 45-50

CLERMONT-TONNERRE (ELISABETH DE GRAMMONT, DUCHESSE DE): *Robert de Montesquiou et Marcel Proust* (Flammarion, Paris, 1925)

COCHET (MARIE-ANNE): *L'Ame proustienne* (Imprimerie des Établissements Collignon, Brussels, 1929)

CŒUROY (ANDRÉ): *Musique et Littérature, études comparées* (Bloud et Gay, Paris, 1923)

CRÉMIEUX (BENJAMIN): *XXᵉ Siècle* (Gallimard, Paris, 1924)

CRÉMIEUX (BENJAMIN); *Du côté de Marcel Proust* (Lemarget, Paris, 1929)

CURTIUS (ERNST-ROBERT): *Marcel Proust*: translated from German into French by Armand Pierhal (Éditions de *La Revue Nouvelle*, Paris, 1928)

DANDIEU (ARNAUD): *Marcel Proust, sa révélation psychologique* (Firmin-Didot, Paris, 1930)

DAUDET (CHARLES): *Répertoire des personnages de 'A la recherche du temps perdu'* (Gallimard, Paris, 1928): volume II of *Les Cahiers Marcel Proust*

DAUDET (LÉON): *Salons et Journaux* (Grasset, Paris, 1932)

DAUDET (LUCIEN): *Autour de soixante lettres de Marcel Proust* (Gallimard, Paris, 1925): volume V of *Les Cahiers Marcel Proust*

DELATTRE (FLORIS): *Bergson et Proust* (Albin Michel, 1948): volume I of *Les Études bergsoniennes*

DREYFUS (ROBERT): *Souvenirs sur Marcel Proust* (Bernard Grasset, Paris, 1926)

DREYFUS (ROBERT): *De Monsieur Thiers à Marcel Proust* (Plon, Paris, 1939)

DU BOS (CHARLES): *Approximations* (Plon, Paris, 1922): volume I, pp. 58-116

FERNANDEZ (RAMON): *Messages* (Gallimard, Paris, 1926)

FERNANDEZ (RAMON): *Notes on L'Esthétique de Proust* (*Nouvelle Revue Française*, XXXI, 1928), pp. 272-80

FERNANDEZ (RAMON): *Proust* (Éditions de *La Nouvelle Revue Critique*, Paris, 1943)

FERRÉ (ANDRÉ): *Géographie de Marcel Proust* (Éditions du Sagittaire, Paris, 1939)

FEUILLERAT (ALBERT): *Comment Marcel Proust a composé son roman* (Yale University Press, New Haven, U.S.A., 1934; London, Oxford University Press)

FISER (EMERIC): *L'Esthétique de Marcel Proust* (Rieder, Paris, 1933): with a Preface by Valéry Larbaud

BIBLIOGRAPHY

GABORY (GEORGES): *Essai sur Marcel Proust* (Emile Chamontin, Le Livre, Paris, 1926)

GERMAIN (ANDRÉ): *De Proust à Dada* (Kra, Paris, 1924)

GRAMONT (ÉLISABETH DE): *Marcel Proust* (Flammarion, Paris, 1948)

GREGH (FERNAND): *L'Age d'or* (Bernard Grasset, Paris, 1948)

HAHN (REYNALDO): *Notes* (Plon, Paris, 1933)

HIER (FLORENCE): *La Musique dans l'œuvre de Marcel Proust* (Publications of the Institute of French Studies, New York, 1932)

Hommage à Marcel Proust (Gallimard, Paris, 1927): volume I of *Les Cahiers Marcel Proust*

HUDSON (STEPHEN): *Céleste, and Other Sketches* (The Blackmore Press, London, 1930)

HUYGHE (RENÉ): '*Affinités électives: Vermeer et Proust*' (*Amour de l'Art*, XVII, 1936), pp. 7-15

IRONSIDE (R.): '*The Artistic Vision of Proust*' (*Horizon*, IV, No. 19, 1941), pp. 28-42

JÄCKEL (KURT): *Bergson und Proust* (Priebatsch, Breslau, 1934)

JÄCKEL (KURT): *Richard Wagner in der französischen Literatur* (Priebatsch, Breslau, 1932)

KINDS (EDMOND): *Marcel Proust* (Collection Triptyque: Richard Masse, éditeur, Paris, 1947)

KOLB (PHILIP): *Inadvertent repetitions of Material in 'A la recherche du temps perdu*' (P.M.L.A.LI., 1936), pp. 249-62

KRUTCH (JOSEPH WOOD), *Five Masters, a Study in the Mutations of the Novel* (Cape & Smith, New York, 1930)

LARCHER (P.-L.): *Le Parfum de Combray* (Mercure de France, Paris, 1945).

LAURIS (GEORGES DE): '*Marcel Proust d'après une correspondance et des souvenirs.* (*Revue de Paris*, XLV, 1938), pp. 734-76

LAURIS (GEORGES DE): *A un Ami. Correspondance inédite de Marcel Proust, 1903-22* (Amiot-Dumont, Paris, 1948)

LAURIS (GEORGES DE): *Souvenirs d'une belle époque* (Amiot-Dumont, Paris, 1948)

LAURENT (HENRI): '*Marcel Proust et la musique*' (*Le Flambeau*, I, 1927, pp. 241-56; also, *Le Flambeau*, II, 1927, pp. 49-64

LE BIDOIS (ROBERT): '*Le Langage parlé des personnages de Proust*' (*Le Français moderne*, Paris, 1939), pp. 197-218

LE GOFF (MARCEL): *Anatole France à la Béchellerie* (Albin Michel, Paris, 1947)

LEMAÎTRE (GEORGES): *Four French Novelists* (Oxford University Press, London, 1938)

BIBLIOGRAPHY

LINDNER (GLADYS DUDLEY): *Marcel Proust, Reviews and Estimates in English* (Stanford University Press, Stanford, California, 1942)

MARTIN-DESLIAS (NOËL): *Idéalisme de Marcel Proust* (F. Janny, Montpellier, undated)

MASSIS (HENRI): *Le Drame de Marcel Proust* (Bernard Grasset, Paris, 1937)

MAURIAC (FRANÇOIS): *Proust* (Marcelle Lesage, Paris, 1926)

MAURIAC (FRANÇOIS): *Du Côté de chez Proust* (La Table Ronde, Paris, 1947)

MONTESQUIOU (ROBERT DE): *Les Pas effacés, Mémoires* (edited by Paul-Louis Couchoud, 3 volumes (Emile-Paul, Paris, 1923)

MOUREY (GABRIEL): '*Proust, Ruskin and Walter Pater*' (*Le Monde Nouveau*, August-September 1926, pp. 702-14, and *Le Monde Nouveau*, October 1926, pp. 896-908)

MOUTON (JEAN): *Le Style de Marcel Proust* (Éditions Corrêa, Paris, 1948)

MURRAY (J.): '*Marcel Proust et John Ruskin*' (*Mercure de France*, CLXXXIX, 1926), pp. 100-12

MURRY (JOHN MIDDLETON): '*Marcel Proust: a new sensibility*' (*Quarterly Review*, New York, 1922), pp. 86-100

O'BRIEN (JUSTIN M.): *La Mémoire involontaire avant Proust* (*Revue de Littérature comparée*, XIX, 1939), pp. 19-36

PIERHAL (ARMAND): *Sur la composition wagnérienne de l'œuvre de Proust* (Bibliothèque Universelle and *Revue de Genève*, June 1929), pp. 710-19

PIERRE-QUINT (LÉON): *Comment travaillait Proust* (Editions des Cahiers Libres, Paris, 1928)

PIERRE-QUINT (LÉON): *Comment parut 'Du Coté de chez Swann'* (Kra, Paris, 1930)

PIERRE-QUINT (LÉON): *Marcel Proust, sa vie, son œuvre* (Kra, Paris, 1925). A new edition of this book, with additional matter, was published by Les Editions du Sagittaire, Paris, in 1935)

PIERRE-QUINT (LÉON): *Une nouvelle lecture dix ans plus tard* (*Europe*, issue for October 1935, pp. 185-98, and the issue for November 15th, 1935, pp. 382-99)

POMMIER (JEAN): *La Mystique de Proust* (Librairie E. Droz, Paris, 1939)

POUQUET (JEANNE-MAURICE): *Le Salon de Madame Arman de Caillavet* (Hachette, Paris, 1926)

RAPHAEL (PIERRE): *Introduction à la Correspondance de Marcel Proust. Répertoire de la Correspondance de Proust* (Editions de la Sagittaire, Paris, 1938)

ROBERT (LOUIS DE): *De Loti à Proust* (Flammarion, Paris, 1938)

343

BIBLIOGRAPHY

SACHS (MAURICE): *L'Air du mois* (*Nouvelle Revue Française*, issue for July 1st, 1938, p. 863)

SACHS (MAURICE): *Le Sabbat* (Éditions Corrêa, Paris, 1946)

SAURAT (DENIS): *Tendances* (Éditions du Monde Moderne, Paris, 1928)

SCHEIKEVITCH (MARIE): *Souvenirs d'un temps disparu* (Plon, Paris, 1935)

SCOTT MONCRIEFF (CHARLES KENNETH): *An English Tribute* (T. Seltzer, New York, 1923)

SEILLIÈRE (BARON ERNEST): *Marcel Proust* (Éditions de *La Nouvelle Revue Critique*, Paris, 1931)

SOUDAY (PAUL): *Marcel Proust* (Kra, Paris, 1927)

SOUZA (SYBIL DE): *L'Influence de Ruskin sur Proust* (Montpellier, 1932)

SPIRE (ANDRÉ): *Quelques Juifs et demi-Juifs*, volume II, pp. 47-61 (Bernard Grasset, 1928)

SPITZER (LÉO): *Zum Stil Marcel Prousts, Stilstudien*, II, pp. 365-497 (M. Hueber, Munich, 1928)

TIEDKE (IRMA): *Symbole und Bilder im Werke Marcel Prousts* (Evert, Hamburg, 1936)

VETTARD (CAMILLE): *Proust et Einstein* (*Nouvelle Revue Française*, issue for August 1st, 1922)

VIGNERON (ROBERT): *Genèse de Swann* (*Revue d'Histoire de la Philosophie et d'Histoire générale de la Civilisation*, issue for January 15th, 1937, pp. 67-115)

VIGNERON (ROBERT): *Marcel Proust and Robert de Montesquiou* (*Modern Philology*, XXXIX, pp. 159-95, 1941)

WEGENER (ALFONS): *Impressionismus und Klassizismus im Werke Marcel Prousts* (Carolus Druckerei, Frankfurt, 1930)

ZAESKE (KÄTHE): *Der Stil Marcel Prousts* (Emsdetten, Lechte, 1937)

INDEX

[This is an index to the actual people mentioned in the text of the book, and contains no references to the characters of Proust's novel.]

INDEX

Daudet, Léon, 110, 111, 281, 289, 299, 300, 301
Daudet, Lucien, 23, 69, 82-3, 84, 133, 138, 158, 279, 284, 324, 326, 329
Delattre, Floris, 64
Deschanel, Paul, 274
Deschanel, Madame Paul, 301
Desjardins, Paul, 18, 140
Dickens, Charles, 28, 36, 251, 256, 262, 263, 301
Dierx, Leon, 35
Doazan, Baron, 171, 174, 322
Dorgelès, Roland, 299
Dreyfus, the 'Affair', 100-7, 257-8, 304, 306, 308
Dreyfus, Robert, 35, 37, 43, 74, 75, 92, 94, 278, 298, 312, 324
Dubois-Amiot, Marthe, marries Robert Proust, 124
Durham, Lord, 226

Eliot, George, 28, 36, 154, 183, 301
Ephrussi, Charles, 172

Fasquelle, Eugéne, 269, 270, 271, 273, 275
Fauré, Gabriel, 143
Félicie (Madame Proust's maid, and the model for 'Françoise'), 141, 143, 144, 156, 159
Félix-Faure, Madame Lucie, 301
Fénelon, Bertrand de, 95, 109, 285
Fernandez, Ramon, 137, 239, 282, 307
Feuillerat, Albert, 291-3, 294
Finlay, Hugo, 79, 111
Flers, Robert de, 35, 74, 84, 298, 299, 300
Fleury, Cardinal de, 287
France, Anatole de, 35, 45, 59, 73: writes a Preface for Les Plaisirs et les Jours, 88-9, 97, 102, 103-4, 110, 123, 141, 172-3, 239, 262, 264, 280, 300, 309

Gagey, Dr., 137
Gaigneron, Jean de, 183
Gallifet, General, 296
Gallimard, Gaston, 111, 272, 282, 283, 297, 299, 318-19, 320, 325, 330
Galsworthy, John, 301
Ganderax, Louis, 76, 268
Gaucher, Maxime, 39
Ghéon, Henri, 282
Gide, André, 18, 19, 52, 151-2, 210, 237, 238: advises Gallimard to refuse Swann's Way, 273, 282, 283, 315
Gineste, Marie, 315

Giraudoux, Jean, 277
Gramont, Élisabeth de (Duchesse de Clermont-Tonnerre), 18, 140, 280, 321, 323
Grasset, Bernard, 277, 278, 281, 283, 292, 301
Greffulhe, Comtesse, 65, 68, 96, 139, 156
Greffulhe, Elaine, 124
Gregh, Fernand, 35, 64, 73, 74-5
Guiche, Duc de, 83, 95: marriage, 124, 290, 311, 322

Haas, Charles, 171
Hahn, Reynaldo, 65-6, 71, 82, 84, 88, 96, 107-8, 115, 127, 138, 150, 285, 287, 290, 299, 300, 324
Halévy, Daniel, 35, 37, 44, 74
Halévy, Fromenthal, 47
Halévy, Ludovic, 48
Hardy, Thomas, 36, 154, 182
Haussonville, Comte d', 102
Hayman, Laure, 29, 38, 48, 85-7, 173, 300
Heath, Willie, 71, 147
Hébrard, Adrien, 278, 279
Hermant, Abel, 73
Hervieu, Paul, 73, 97
Homer, 263
Hugo, Victor, 28, 169, 189, 296
Humblot, 275
Humières, Robert d', 115
Huyghe, René, 199
Huysmans, Joris Karl, 66

Illiers, Marquis de, 16

Jaloux, Edmond, 288, 312
James, Henry, 300
Jammes, Francis, 300
Jung, Carl, 195
Katz, 136
Katz, Madame, 136

La Bruyere, 36
Lacretelle, Jacques, 169
Larbaud, Valéry, 93
Lauris, George de, 94, 109, 115, 117, 123, 134, 135, 153, 154
Leconte de Lisle, 35, 47
Le Cuziat, Albert, 147-8
Lemaire, Madeleine, 47, 48, 65, 66, 88, 96, 197
Lemaître, Jules, 35, 102, 107
Léon, Princesse de, 68
Leroy-Beaulieu, Anatole, 61
Liszt, Franz, 219
Longus, 322

INDEX